Fada'i Guerrilla Praxis in Iran
(1970–1979)

Fada'i Guerrilla Praxis in Iran (1970–1979)

Narratives and Reflections on Everyday Life

Edited by
Touraj Atabaki
Nasser Mohajer
Siavush Randjbar-Daemi

I.B. TAURIS
LONDON • NEW YORK • OXFORD • NEW DELHI • SYDNEY

I.B. TAURIS
Bloomsbury Publishing Plc
50 Bedford Square, London, WC1B 3DP, UK
1385 Broadway, New York, NY 10018, USA
29 Earlsfort Terrace, Dublin 2, Ireland

BLOOMSBURY, I.B. TAURIS and the I.B. Tauris logo are trademarks of
Bloomsbury Publishing Plc

First published in Great Britain 2023
This paperback version published 2025

Copyright © Touraj Atabaki, Nasser Mohajer and Siavush Randjbar-Daemi

Touraj Atabaki, Nasser Mohajer and Siavush Randjbar-Daemi have asserted their right under the Copyright, Designs and Patents Act, 1988, to be identified as Editors of this work.

Series design by Adriana Brioso
Cover image: Red Rebellion, copyright Khavar, 2023

All rights reserved. No part of this publication may be reproduced or transmitted in any form or by any means, electronic or mechanical, including photocopying, recording, or any information storage or retrieval system, without prior permission in writing from the publishers.

Bloomsbury Publishing Plc does not have any control over, or responsibility for, any third-party websites referred to or in this book. All internet addresses given in this book were correct at the time of going to press. The author and publisher regret any inconvenience caused if addresses have changed or sites have ceased to exist, but can accept no responsibility for any such changes.

A catalogue record for this book is available from the British Library.

A catalog record for this book is available from the Library of Congress.

ISBN: HB: 978-1-7883-1468-8
PB: 978-0-7556-5127-6
ePDF: 978-0-7556-3886-4
eBook: 978-0-7556-3887-1

Typeset by Newgen KnowledgeWorks Pvt. Ltd., Chennai, India

To find out more about our authors and books visit www.bloomsbury.com and sign up for our newsletters.

Contents

List of contributors		vii
Note on transliteration		xi
Preface		xii

1 Formation of thoughts and foundation of the Iranian People's Fada'i
   Guerrillas   1
   Nasser Mohajer and Mehrdad Vahabi

2 The labour movement in the words and deeds of the Iranian People's
   Fada'i Guerrillas   35
   Touraj Atabaki

3 The foreign relations of the Organization of Iranian People's Fada'i
   Guerrillas: From formation to the Revolution of 1979   57
   Heydar Tabrizi

4 A glance at the Organization of Iranian People's Fada'i Guerrillas (1976–9)   69
   Qorbanali ʿAbdolrahimpour

5 Military actions in the Organization of Iranian People's Fada'i Guerrillas:
   Scales and modalities   83
   Hamid Nowzari

6 From school to safehouse: A woman Fada'i's account   101
   Marziyeh Tohidast Shafiʿ

7 My beloved Organization   121
   Nahid Qajar

8 Female prison   151
   Roqiyeh Daneshgari

9 The Organization of Iranian Peoples Fada'i Guerrillas' prison organization   167
   Nasser Rahimkhani and Nasser Mohajer

10 The Organization of Iranian People's Fada'i Guerrillas and the University
   of Tabriz: A personal memoir   189
   Sorour ʿAli Mohammadi

11	The Confederation of Iranian Students (National Union) and the Fada'i Guerrillas 'Ali Nadimi	203
12	From Mehrabad-e Jonoubi to the technical faculty Siavush Randjbar-Daemi	217
13	Poetry praising passion Saeed Yousef	237
14	Reflections of the guerrilla struggle and the Siyahkal incident in literary prose and fiction Nasim Khaksar	259
15	Looking back Esfandiar Monfaredzadeh	275
16	The impact of the guerrilla movement on contemporary Iranian theatre Houman Azarkolah	291

Notes 297
Select Bibliography 329
Index of Names 331

Contributors

Sorour Alimohamadi was born in Tehran. She studied sociology at the University of Tabriz where she became involved in the students' radical movement supporting the Organization of Iranian People's Fada'i Guerrillas (OIPFG). She joined the OIPFG after the 1979 Revolution and joined the Majority Faction after the split of June 1980.

Qorbanali ʿAbdolrahimpour was born in Sarab, in north-west Iran. From late 1960s he became involved with communist circles in the Azerbaijan province in the north-west of Iran. He was arrested in 1971 and sentenced to one year in prison while he was a student at the Agricultural Applied University in Rezaiyeh (present-day Urumiyeh). A few months following his release from jail, he was arrested again and sentenced to one and half year of imprisonment. In 1974 he opted for clandestine life and joined the OIPFG. He became a member of the Leadership Committee of the Iranian People's Fada'i Guerrillas in 1976, upon the killing of Hamid Ashraf and the rest of the leadership. He joined the upper ranks of the Majority Faction after the split of June 1980.

Touraj Atabaki is Senior Research Fellow at the International Institute of Social History and Professor Emeritus of Social History of the Middle East and Central Asia at Leiden University. Atabaki studied theoretical physics and later history at the University of London and Utrecht University. Following positions at Utrecht University and the University of Amsterdam, he joined Leiden University where he held the Chair of Social History of the Middle East and Central Asia. Atabaki's research encompasses historiography, social history of labour and subaltern studies in Twentieth century Iran, the Ottoman Empire and Turkey as well as the Caucasus and Central Asia. His forthcoming publications are: *Social History of the Iranian Oil Industry* (Cambridge University Press) and *Fallen in the Whirlwind: Life and Time of Iranian Migrant Labour and Political Activists during the Soviet Great Purge* (Cambridge University Press). Atabaki's major publications and research projects can be found on: https://socialhistory.org/en/staff/touraj-atabaki.

Houman Azarkolah was born in 1949 and graduated in theatre and acting from the Faculty of Dramatic Arts of the University of Tehran. In 1977 he was amongst the founders of the 5 Azar Theatre Group which was headed by Rokneddin Khosravi. He produced works inspired by Bertolt Brecht, Jean Paul Sartre and Nicolo Machiavelli during and after his university years in Iran. As a well-known leftist actor he decided to leave Iran clandestinely in January 1982 and settled in Paris. He has produced works with the late Gholam-Hossein Saʿedi, Mohsen Yalfani, Reza ʿAllamehzadeh and Iraj Jannati-Ataei whilst in exile.

Roqiyeh Daneshgari was born in Bijar, a city in north-west Iran in a non-political family with nationalist tendency. She studied pharmacology at the University of Tabriz and achieved a doctorate in this field from the same university. She was a member of the leftist intellectual circle which formed around Samad Behrangi and joined the OIPFG in the first half of 1971. She was imprisoned later in that year and was released from jail in October 1978. She was an OIPFG candidate in the Constituent Assembly elections of Islamic Republic in July 1979 and the first Islamic parliamentary elections of March 1980. She became a member of the Majority Faction after the split of June 1980 and served in the Central Committee of this formation from June 1982.

Nasim Khaksar was born in Abadan, a city in the south-west Iran. He graduated from Teacher Training Institutes in Isfahan and Hamedan. He was a teacher in the villages of Abadan and Boyer-Ahmad in south-west of Iran. He was arrested in 1967 due to his literary anti-establishment activities and sentenced to two years of imprisonment in Ahvaz prison. He was arrested for a second time in 1973 due to his support and association with the Organization of Iranian People's Fada'i Guerrillas and was sentenced to six years in Qasr prison in Tehran and Ahvaz prison. Nasim Khaksar is a novelist who started his literary endeavours in 1965. Thirty-five volumes of his books have been published in various genres: short stories, novels, plays, poems, translations, travelogues and literary criticism.

Nasser Mohajer is an independent scholar of modern Iranian history. He studied Sociology in the United States and History and Economics in France. He currently resides in Paris, is on the editorial board of Nogteh Books and works with Nogteh Resources on Iran (http://www.noghteh.org). He is the former editor in chief of two periodicals on Iranian politics and culture: *Aghazi Now* (1985–1994) and *Noghteh* (1995–1999). He served on the editorial board of the periodicals, *Noghteh Review* (1995–1997) and *Iran Bulletin* (1992–2000), which covered Iranian history and culture. He has authored and edited *Voices of a Massacre : Untold Stories of Life and Death in Iran, 1988* (OneWorld, 2020) and *The Uprising of Iranian Women, March 1979*, 2 Vols., co-authored with Mahnaz Matin, (Noghteh Books, 2013). His articles have been published in numerous journals, including *Annals of the Iranian Women's Studies Foundation, Arash, Azadi, Baha'i Studies Review, Bukhara, Baran, Ceshmandaz, Comparative Studies of South Asia, Africa and the Middle East, Daftarha-ye Kanun, Iran Namag*, and *Iran Nameh*. He has taught courses and given lectures on aspects of modern Iranian history.

Esfandiar Monfaredzadeh was born in Tehran and is recognized for his contribution to Iranian film and pop music. He started playing instruments in 1953 and started his career as musician by working in the Iran Radio Youth Orchestra from 1956, which lasted for eight years. He went to the Faculty of Fine Arts of Tehran University to study music, but left this study halfway. He would later leave his studies at the University of Music in Vienna unfinished. Monfaredzadeh has been composing music since 1968 and is considered one of the early and leading Iranian film composers. He left Iran in

1983 and has since lived a life of self-exile in Sweden. He has continued his avant-garde music composition in exile alongside his relentless opposition intellectual activity.

'**Ali Nadimi** was born in Ahvaz, a city in the south-west Iran. After finishing high school, he joined a literary circle where most of its members were political activists. In 1965 he was arrested and spent a few months in prison. He left Iran in 1968 and studied political law in Austria. With communist leanings, he joined the network of the supporters of the National Front of Iran outside the country and within some communist tendencies. He then became supporter of radical armed movement and cooperated with the Iranian People's Fada'i Guerrillas. He became a member of the Confederation of Iranian Students abroad and the national and international secretary of that organization for many years. He also joined the Setareh group and was later involved in the Organization of Communist Unity in 1980.

Hamid Nowzari was born in Abadan, a city in the south-west Iran. He studied at the Technical University of Berlin. As a communist activist, he supported the Organization of Iranian People's Fada'i Guerrillas and was of one the leading activists in its student supporters' branch in West Berlin. At present he is the professional director of the Iranian Refugee Association in Berlin.

Nahid Qajar was born in Gorgan, a city in the north-east Iran. She graduated from high school and got her diploma in industrial chemistry. Upon finishing high school, she joined the clandestine activities supporting the radical political movement in the northern cities of the country. In 1974 she became a member of the OIPFG. She lived in the Fada'i safehouses and was in charge of various team activities until the Revolution of 1979. She joined the Majority Faction after the great split of June 1980.

Nasser Rahimkhani was born in Dezful, a city in the south-west Iran. During his study of law and political science at the Tehran University he joined the communist students' circles. In 1969 he was arrested for his association with a group committed to armed struggle against the regime of Shah Mohammad Reza Pahlavi and sentenced to seven years in prison. Released from prison in 1977, he became a supporter of the OIFPG. Rahimkhani's interests lie in the study of social and political movements in contemporary Iran, and he has published several articles and longer-length research studies in this field.

Siavush Randjbar-Daemi is Lecturer (Assistant Professor) in Modern Middle Eastern History at the University of St Andrews, Scotland. He was previously Lecturer in Iranian History at the University of Manchester. He specializes in the political history of Iran since 1941, with a current emphasis on the Left and periods of political diversity, particularly 1941–1953 and 1977–1981. He is the author of the *The Quest for Authority in Iran: A History of the Presidency from Revolution to Rouhani* (I.B. Tauris, 2018).

Heydar Tabrizi was born in Tabriz in north-west Iran. He studied mechanical engineering at the Aryamehr Technical University (presently Sharif Technical

University). He joined the Iranian People's Fada'i Guerrillas in summer of 1971. He was imprisoned four times during the reign of Mohammad Reza Shah Pahlavi. He was one of the cadres of Fada'is in charge of activities outside Iran. Following the 1979 Revolution, he joined the Central Committee of the OIPFG and became a member of the organization's political bureau and was in charge of the OIPFG's official newspaper *Kar*.

Marziyeh Tohidast Shafi' was born in Tehran. During her high school studies, she was acquainted with the political activists who supported armed struggle against the regime of the Shah. Following the formation of Iranian People's Fada'i Guerrillas she joined the OIPFG. Since 1973, she opted for clandestine life, living in safehouses and was in charge of three operational teams in Tehran, Isfahan and Mashhad and the production of the organization's publications during six years living there. She joined the Majority Faction of the OIPFG after the great split of June 1980.

Mehrdad Vahabi was born in Tehran. He is Professor of Economics at the Université Sorbonne Paris Nord. His interests include political economy, economics of development, economics of conflict, institutional economics and comparative economics. He has published many books in English, French and Persian, both within the theoretical context as well as in the empirical framework. He is also interested in global contentious politics and has contributed to developing an economic viewpoint in this field.

Saeed Yousef was born in Torbat Heydarieh, a city in the north-east Iran and began writing and publishing poems in mid-1960s. He was a political prisoner in 1971–4, because, among others, of translating into Persian a book by Che Guevara. Yousef had to leave Iran after the all-out repression that swept the country in 1982. After living in Paris for a while, he went to Germany as a refugee. He has a PhD in comparative literature from the University of Toronto and has published about ten books of poems, several translations and books of literary criticism, as well as three books of Persian grammar. He taught Persian language and literature at the University of Chicago from 2002 until 2020.

Note on transliteration

This book follows the simplified *Iranian Studies* journal transliteration system. The partial exception to this rule is Saeed Yousef's chapter (Chapter 13).

Preface

The idea of collecting the narratives of women and men who had a role in the guerrilla movement of the late 1960s and 1970s Iran, or those with profound knowledge of this struggle, goes back to more than a decade ago. During the 2005–10 period, the International Institute of Social History in Amsterdam organized a series of conferences and seminars with the purpose of documenting the daily experiences of guerrilla warfare in the Global South. With reference to Iran, while the institute approached some of the former guerrillas to narrate their daily life experiences in the late 1960s and 1970s, scholars were also called to join the eyewitnesses and give their scholarly assessment of that era, the consequences of guerrilla warfare within Iranian political landscape and the society in large, as well as placing the Iranian communist guerrilla movement in its proper historical context. These scholars had either witnessed the events or developed their accounts by revisiting relevant documents and reflecting on them during their individual research.

What makes the gathering of narratives regarding the guerrilla struggle in Iran and other parts of the Global South pressing for historians is the hitherto marginal nature of independent historical research into this widespread transnational phenomenon of the 1960s and 1970s. This occurrence had cast its shadow over social and political life in Asia, Africa, South and Central America, and even Europe and the United States. It is important to note that the guerrilla movement in Iran had a notable influence on political processes which were conducive to the Revolution of 1979. A critical analysis of this event would not be possible without developing a clearer understanding of the armed political opposition of the 1970s.

What inspired us to take on this research project was that the guerrilla movement took place in the recent past, hence a considerable number of survivors were able to share their narratives. Indeed, for them and many others, the life and times of organizations such as the People's Fada'i Guerrillas is very much part of the living history of Iran.[1] Our ability to rely on their accounts is a blessing for better documenting that unique event.

The minimal scholarly work on Iranian guerrilla movement cannot be only attributed to political autocracy, which has prevailed over Iranian society during most of the twentieth century. It is true that those in power have often prevented affiliated and unaffiliated historians from gaining access to state archives, and often sought instead to fulfil the role of sole narrator of the history of their perennial opponents. It is also true that some foreign archives, particularly the Soviet ones, have not granted access to material relevant for this book which has been collected by their security and diplomatic agents under the pretext of Cold War dynamics and out of consideration for their own current international relations dynamics.

We are also conscious that the persistent climate of political repression makes organizations and parties engaged in guerrilla warfare less capable or willing to preserve documents or maintain detailed profiles of their fallen comrades, but none of these challenges adequately justifies the less-than-optimal state in the documentation of the history of guerrilla movement in Iran.

Despite such shortcomings in the documentation of Iranian social and political historiography, the historian can avail from a scattered number of narratives as well as political memoirs by leftist activists, particularly since the 1940s. These memoirs and narratives elucidate certain aspects in the lives, experiences or praxis of activists within the broader contours of the Left. In this tradition, usually the narrator has a top-down approach, and in his/her narrative, he or she talks more about political and intellectual change and is less concerned with the lives and actions of the experiences of the activists.

It was against this backdrop that we came to the realization that it is necessary to document the history of the Iranian communist guerrilla movement by utilizing the accounts of those who were directly involved and had first-hand knowledge of everyday life in safehouses or political wards of Iranian prisons. These narratives are the outcome of both oral as well as written accounts of the contributors.

This collection is composed of both personal and scholarly narratives. The personal narratives consist of eyewitness accounts from veteran guerrillas on themes such as everyday life in safehouses, the activities of the small but active guerrillas' representation abroad, the experience of guerrilla men and women who were subject to long imprisonment in the 1970s or perspectives on military and logistics organization. It should be emphasized that the sole criteria for choosing the contributions of these narratives consisted of their authors' specific role within the guerrilla movement up to the Revolution of 1979. Their political trajectory since then falls outside the purview of this study.

The scholarly narratives present a set of accounts of various aspects in the history of the communist guerrilla process in Iran, which cover elements such as the ideological foundations and political orientation, the importance of the Iranian labour movement in guerrillas' thought and praxis or the impact of the guerrilla movement in literature, music and visual arts.

The chapters in this collection cover the period which began with the inception of armed assault at the Siyahkal gendarmerie post in the northern province of Gilan in February 1971 and the demise of the monarchy on 11 February 1979. We asked the contributors to distance themselves as much as possible from their present disposition and worldview and cast themselves in the role of independent narrators in order to capture their experiences of the past in their entirety. We have striven to impart a factual basis befitting the scholarly nature of this project to all contributions. Like many other militant organizations of that period, the OIPFG's history includes instances of internal score settling and retribution. Some lost their lives as a consequence of an internal decision to exert capital punishment. As an example, the editors have not been able, despite their best efforts, to shed full light on the circumstances concerning Panjehshahi's fate, which is mentioned in the narratives provided for this volume by Qorbanali 'Abdolrahimpour and Nahid Qajar.

We do not believe that this collection presents an all-encompassing balance sheet of the lives and praxis of the Iranian communist militants in the guerrilla warfare. Some aspects, such as the impact of guerrilla struggle on the broader Iranian society or on the country's ethnic minorities have been given less attention. To the extent possible, we sought gender balance by inviting both male and female narrators to contribute to this collection.

Following the publication of the Persian edition of this book, we received constructive feedback mainly from veteran political activists who cross-checked the narratives in that volume with their own experience and testimonies. All these comments were carefully scrutinized and discussed with the contributors and changes were applied accordingly.

In preparing the English version of this book, we benefitted from the collegial support of the following friends, who translated some of the narratives in this volume: Morteza Abdolalian (Chapter 6), Koroush Bahar (Chapter 15), Eskandar Sadeghi-Boroujerdi (Chapter 3), Arash Davari (Chapter 11), Amin Dorougar (Chapter 5), Ladbon Kia (Chapter 8), Sina Navaie (Chapter 16), Hossein Pourbagheri (Chapter 2), Shervin Shahbaz (Chapter 10). Banafsheh Massoudi also kindly assisted us with the preparation of the index. We would like to extend our sincere gratitude to all of them.

September 2022
Touraj Atabaki
Nasser Mohajer
Siavush Randjbar-Daemi

1

Formation of thoughts and foundation of the Iranian People's Fada'i Guerrillas

Nasser Mohajer and Mehrdad Vahabi

Introduction

The Organization of Iranian People's Fada'i Guerrillas (OIPFG) started its first armed confrontation with the Shah's military forces on 8 February 1971 and was at the forefront of the struggle against Shah Mohammad Reza Pahlavi's dictatorship until the February Revolution of 1979. Fada'is were the founders of a New Left in Iran.

Who were the two formative groups of the People's Fada'i Guerrillas (PFG) that broke the deadly political silence which had dominated the Iranian society and challenged the political autocracy in Iran? What were the main elements of their discourse? How did they manage their differences and how did they work together? How did they join together after the Siyahkal event and found a new communist movement in Iran?

The first period: 1967–71

The People's Fada'i Guerrillas (PFG) unveiled their struggle against the Shah's dictatorship and on 7 April 1971 – a few weeks after the raid on a gendarmerie outpost in the village of Siyahkal on 8 February 1971 – through the 'revolutionary execution' of General Zeinolabedin Farsiu. Farsiu was the head of the military tribunal who had issued the death sentences of the Siyahkal militants. The very fact that the gendarmerie post was situated in the jungles of Gilan province demonstrated the importance of 'the mountain' terrain in guerrilla warfare which had to be carried on and accelerated in the cities.

Thus, the long process of discussions and negotiations of the two founding groups, which had been going on since September 1970, bore fruit. Despite their differences, the Jazani-Zarifi and the Pouyan-Ahmadzadeh-Meftahi groups relied on their common political and ideological grounds, especially their firm belief in the necessity of urban guerrilla struggle, to join ranks and initiate a new communist movement in Iran.

The raid carried out by what became known as the Forest Team caused a strong reverberation in the entire country and brought about the merging of the two groups, which then formed the People's Fada'i Guerrillas. In a short span of time, this movement attracted dozens of Marxist-Leninist circles and hundreds of leftist intellectuals to its ranks and posed itself as a strong opponent to the Shah's dictatorship, which enjoyed the support of the United States, Western European governments and their allies.

The Jazani-Zarifi group

The Jazani-Zarifi group was formed in March 1963 under the leadership of Bijan Jazani with Hassan Zia-Zarifi as the second in command. The formation of the group occurred almost two months after the arrest of the leaders of the second National Front, and a few weeks after the six-point referendum of what the Pahlavi regime termed the 'Revolution of the Shah and the People' on 26 January 1963. In effect the group emerged at the beginning of a transient political opening which was propitiated by the most severe economic and political crisis the Shah's regime had faced since the CIA-MI6 organized coup of August 1953. This crisis brought about an array of social forces to the fore, including students, both white- and blue-collar workers and the intellectual strata of society.

Almost all the founding members of the Jazani-Zarifi group were activists during the 1960–3 period and a few of them were quite well known within the opposition milieu of the time. Some, such as Bijan Jazani and Hassan Zia-Zarifi, were former members of the Tudeh Party's youth organization. A number of them had taken part in clandestine activities from 1956 to 1960 and had experienced organized and semi-organized cooperation with the National Resistance Movement which was to resist the Coup between 1953 and 1959.

The members of the group were white-collar as well as blue-collar workers, teachers, students and self-employed individuals. They all considered themselves to be Marxist-Leninist. All had rejected the Tudeh Party and considered it a follower of the Communist Party of the Soviet Union. They all believed in the authoritarian nature of the Shah's regime and sought its overthrow by the masses through an armed struggle. They all considered themselves freedom fighters and advocates of a National Liberation Movement. Genuine belief in democratic and anti-imperialist struggle was the modus operandi of the group and the precondition of cooperation with other formations.

From the outset the members of Jazani-Zarifi group were divided into three subgroups: those who were engaged in overt activity, those who were engaged in semi-covert activities and finally those who were engaged in clandestine work. The clandestine section consisted of provisional and operational teams whose members were 'carefully selected from a large number of revolutionaries'. Some were 'professional and others were semi-professional cadres'.[1] Members engaged in overt and semi-covert work were in charge of contacting other opposition circles and networks whose numbers had increased, especially after the suppression of the 5 June 1963 uprising led by Ayatollah Khomeini's followers. The 5 June uprising left no doubt for the members of the group that society had entered a new era and the movement had transitioned into a new phase. The critical evaluation of the paths and processes taken became the group's order of the day and was reflected in a series of writings for some four years. Most of these writings were never published as 'the group did not believe in the open publication of matters related to its political strategy before the inception of armed struggle against the enemy'.[2] The title chosen for each of these critical studies and evaluations manifests the importance the group attached to the study of contemporary history of Iran and the national democratic struggle of the Iranian people:

1. *Tajrobeh-ye Gozashteh ra Tusheh-ye Rah Ayandeh Sazim* (Let the Experience of the Past Serve as Provision for the Future) is about the activities in the years 1960 to 1963 and 'the role played by the opportunistic leadership of the Tudeh Party and the conservative leadership of the Second National Front'. This writing was circulated amongst the students supporting the National Front.[3]
2. *Hezb Tudeh va Kudeta-ye 28 Mordad 32* (The Tudeh Party and the 28 Mordad 32 [19 August 1953] Coup) is most probably the pamphlet Hassan Zia-Zarifi penned on the Tudeh Party and the 1953 coup in Iran.[4]
3. *Masaleh-ye Hezb* (The Question of the [Political] Party).
4. *Masaleh-ye Vahdat* (The Question of Unity).
5. *Masa'el Jonbesh-e Zed-e Emperialisti va Azadibakhsh Khalqha-ye Iran va Vazayef-e Asasi-ye Komunistha dar Sharayet-e Kununi* (The Question of the Anti-Colonial and National Liberation Movement of the Iranian People and the Main Tasks of the Communists at Present), is 'a summation of the group's viewpoints by the end of 1967',[5] a brief exposé of the socio-economic undercurrents of Iranian society, global politics and the extent of repression and violence which had become an inseparable part of the system since the coup of 1953. The historical background and consequential necessity of armed struggle against the Shah's regime is discussed in this article.

The question of constructing a communist party, which was one of the main topics of debate among and within the Marxist-Leninist groups of the time, was not a priority for the Jazani-Zarifi group. Even though the group had a clear-cut position against the central committee of the Tudeh Party, the demarcation line was mainly in the realm of politics and tactics rather than the ideological foundations of the party:

> During its years of activity, the Tudeh Party was never immune from fundamental shortcomings and deviations ... opportunism became a dominant trend in the party. It was so pervasive that it hindered the growth, evolution, and renovation of the party ... Here's a summary of the most important deviations and defects:
>
> 1. Erroneous understanding of a principled international relationship and establishing an unsound bond with the Communist Party of the Soviet Union from day one.
> 2. Not having a comprehensive understanding of Iran's socio-historical conditions and a disastrous disregard of the anti-imperialist struggle culminated in losing ground to the National Liberation Movement and relegating the leadership of the movement to the national bourgeoisie.

3. The incorrect and detrimental position they took against Mossadeq and the National Front who had taken over the leadership of the anti-imperialist movement ...
4. Irresoluteness, a form of conservatism and fatal hesitation in the face of the 19 August 1953 coup, culminating in the strategic defeat of the Tudeh Party and the labour movement.
5. The incompetence of the leadership in confronting the enemy manifested itself as frailty, surrender to the enemy and betrayal of the working class and the masses ...
6. The perpetuation of these deviations and shortcomings by the remnants of the Tudeh Party (inside and outside the country) is one of the impediments on the road to unity of the working class and the labour movement.[6]

The Jazani-Zarifi group believed that the antidote for 'the fundamental shortcomings and deviations' of the Tudeh Party consisted of waging a decisive struggle against the Shah's dictatorship, a solid ideological education of militants and an effort to acquire a comprehensive understanding of Iran's society in the direction of acquiring

> The most needed revolutionary political goal ... which can be summed up in the slogan of the 'establishment of a democratic republic'. This slogan was also the by-product of a careful examination of different phases of land reform which drastically changed the socio-economic structure of Iranian society, ..., caused the migration of peasants to the cities, multiplied the number of daily paid workers and developed and expanded capitalist relations.[7]

It was after the six-point referendum and the Shah's White Revolution that the representatives of the comprador bourgeoisie replaced the aristocrats and feudal lords in the state apparatus, and repression and violence took new forms and dimensions, which turned the Pahlavi state into an authoritarian and autocratic one.

For this reason, during the years 1963 to 1967, the group decided to undertake two different yet at the same time related projects: on the one hand, research and field study on domestic land reform, its three different stages and the 'agricultural corporations', on the other hand, the translation of books on the Cuban Revolution, guerrilla movements in South America and partisan warfare, such as *Aya Enqelab-e Cuba Yek Estesna' Bud?* (Was the Cuban Revolution an Exception?)[8] and Guerrilla Warfare by Che Guevara (which was published at the beginning of the group's activities). Later, *Revolution in the Revolution* by Régis Debray, *Reminiscences of the Cuban Revolutionary War* and *Bolivian Diaries* by Che Guevara, *Military Art of People's War* by General Giap and the article 'For the Liberation of Brazil' by Carlos Marighela were published and distributed.[9]

The group's attraction to the Cuban Revolution by no means meant copying that revolution or 'following this political epicentre. Cuba could not act as a political hub in our region. Yet, the group was one of the first political fronts who tried to understand the experience of the Cuban Revolution and systematically employed its lessons.'[10]

The influence of Cuba's Revolution and the implementation of some of its victorious experiences are manifested in the group's early interpretations of the armed struggle:

> In order to launch an armed movement, we believe that a small mobile group with consciousness and necessary political courage could succeed in its mission by combining the work inside and outside the cities and by connecting the political, military and propaganda work inside and outside the country. Cuban revolutionaries achieved their goal with seventy people and Che Guevara suggested twenty people. It goes without saying that we should not be misled by historical analogies. The bare minimum needed to set off the movement is determined by an understanding of the specific characteristics of our society and the underlying subjective and objective conditions of our struggle.[11]

Avoiding analogy and imitation and emphasizing on the 'concrete analysis of the concrete situation', was proof that the Jazani-Zarifi group was not inclined to emulate the Cuban Revolution. The group was quite conscious that the 'objective conditions of revolution' has not yet developed in Iran and clearly stated that 'the goal of the armed struggle was to open 'a military front against the Shah which meant the beginning of a protracted, persistent, tenacious struggle accompanied by extreme difficulties, sufferings and distress'. It stipulated that the 'active intervention of the armed vanguard of the working class and the liberation movement would lead to acceleration, crystallization and manifestation of class and political contradictions of our society'.[12] In other words, it was the recognition of a revolutionary process which the group characterized as a 'National Democratic Revolution' with the following general strategy:

> To bring down the imperialist dependent regime, to establish a national and democratic state capable of improving the living conditions of the toiling masses of cities and villages and to lay the necessary foundation for the healthy growth of Iran's national economy, sever the penetration of the political and economic influence of imperialists and their agents, democratize the political life of the Iranian society and drive it towards progress and improvement through fundament changes. In terms of foreign policy, Iran will be set free from serving the reactionary and imperialistic forces and will be capable of mobilizing its forces in the anti-imperialist struggle .... Thus, the first step in fulfilling the general strategy of the Iranian revolution is to overthrow the Shah's autocracy. Considering the contradictions between the masses and the regime and the international state of affairs, our most urgent political objective could be summed up in the following slogan: 'Republic and Democracy.' ... The movement will strive to intensify class struggle in cities and villages, coordinate these struggles and take advantage of the situation to enhance its strategic political slogans. The class bases of the movement must take the interests of the peasants and the working class as its raison d'etre.[13]

In preparation of armed struggle

Drawing up the general strategy for the 'National Democratic Revolution' in 1967 was part of a well-planned preparation for the armed struggle which the Jazani-Zarifi group was hoping to launch in the spring of 1968. According to one of the survivors of the group,

> On day one, the urban team was to attack a power station, expropriate the money of a government bank south of Tehran and then join the Forest group who would simultaneously launch their operation in the jungles north of Iran. The semi-clandestine cells would connect with other political circles and groups and organize a demonstration. At the same time the workers of Abyek Cement factory would go on strike. We were hoping that by the end of this phase, a few military personnel and some other groups who were in touch with us, would join the movement. Our assessment was that the propaganda effect of the operation would be powerful enough to reveal the regime's vulnerability. We had also planned to disseminate for the first time our – as of then – unpublished viewpoints, so that other like-minded groups could join us. Our hope was that the struggle in the jungle would sustain for at least six months.[14]

However, three days prior to the day of expropriating the savings of Taʿavoni and Toziʿ Bank, on the eve of the planned attack (6 January 1968) the group was raided by SAVAK and many of the members of Jazani-Zarifi group were arrested. Despite horrendous torture, the arrested members not only avoided uttering a word and revealing none of the secrets of the group to SAVAK but also managed to transmit SAVAK's atrocities to the outside world. Consequently, the Confederation of Iranian Students abroad organized a major campaign in defence of the fourteen arrested members of the group: Bijan Jazani, Hassan Zia-Zarifi, ʿAbbas Souraki, Aziz Sarmadi, Zarar Zahedian, Mashʾouf Kalantari, Heshmatollah Shahrzad, Mohammad Choupanzadeh, Ahmad Jalil-Afshar, Mohammad-Majid Kianzad, Kiumars Izadi, Farrokh Negahdar, Qasem Rashidi and Majid Ahsan. This campaign resulted in the military tribunal commuting their death sentences to ten to fifteen years of imprisonment and reduce other sentences to three to five years.[15]

Despite the devastating blow of 6 January 1968, the group was not dismantled. Those who were not arrested, especially the members of the clandestine nucleus, continued vigilantly and rebuilt the group:

> The few months of continuous preparedness, safeguarding the cadres the police was looking for, and the resistance of the arrested comrades significantly boosted the group's revolutionary morale and devotion. In reviving the group, section one and section two were eliminated. The group was reconstructed around a central cell which took charge of organizing the teams and sympathizers.[16]

The quantitative growth and expansion of the number of members at the end of 1970 allowed the group to start the process for preparedness for guerrilla struggle once again. The return of ʿAli Akbar Safaʾi Farahani and Mohammad Saffari Ashtiyani, who were sent to Palestinian camps for military training and to procure weapons after the 6 January 1968 incident, gave impetus to the group. Both rejoined the group in the spring of 1971 and from the very start 'assumed a leading role along with Hamid Ashraf,

Eskandar Sadeqinezhad, Hadi Fazeli, Esmaʻil Moʻini-ʻAraqi and Ghafour Hassanpour in organizing and running the group.'[17] In autumn 1970 the group managed to contact Bijan Jazani, then detained in Qom prison.[18] It appears that the revised version for the preparation of armed struggle was ratified upon consultation and coordination with Bijan Jazani and the rest.[19] Thus, the writing of *Ancheh Yek Enqelabi Bayad Bedanad* (What a Revolutionary Must Know) became the order of the day. This pamphlet 'which is in fact ... the summation of the group's political and ideological viewpoints and their protracted experience',[20] could be considered as the 'manifesto' of the Jazani-Zarifi group.

Similar to the two other pamphlets of the group, *Masa'el Jonbesh-e Zed-e Emperialisti va Azadibakhsh Khalqha-ye Iran va Vazayef-e Asasi-ye Komunistha dar Sharayet-e Kununi* is also drafted in two parts. The most important point in the first of these is the characterization of the Iranian revolution and the replacement of the slogan 'People's Revolution' with 'National Democratic Revolution'. It is noteworthy to reiterate that the essence of the 'People's Revolution', like 'National Democratic Revolution', is to democratize society and to lay the foundation for a 'democratic Iran' in five spheres: economic, agricultural production, political affairs, foreign policy and international relations as well as national/cultural issues. Here is a brief summary of the major points of the 'manifesto':

- The big landowners have been expropriated, but a progressive order has not replaced the ancient [mode of production] in rural Iran to end the enslavement and deprivation of the Iranian peasantry. Neither does the bourgeoisie have the power and essential social characteristics to establish a capitalist order in the domain of agriculture.[21]
- The Iranian bourgeoisie, in all three domains of its activity (commerce, finance and industry) is dependent on multinationals and is anti-democratic and non-patriotic to its core. Thus, there is no need to add the adjective 'comprador' or 'dependent' each time we refer to it.
- Economic developments without appropriate social and political developments are in effect as defective as political developments without corresponding economic undertakings.
- It is a mistake to think that the ruling establishment of Iran is solely a lackey servant of imperialism and completely obedient to its orders. The existing political-administrative ensemble, while having its own class attachments has certain concerns and interests which has made it dependent on [world] imperialism. It is known that Iran's ruling establishment is not dependent on one imperialist [power]. American and British imperialists, along with other imperialist, have influence over the ruling apparatus and have interests in Iran in their turn. The ruling administration assures its stability and survival by cleverly walking a tightrope between the imperialist powers ... It employs an array of means to preserve its position.
- The most definite and appropriate name we can bequeath to the present regime is a 'despotic monarchy'. All the institutions that are apparently 'representative' of the people, such as the two houses of congress, the councils, and assemblies

and all the administrative organizations such as the cabinet and the judicial committees, are ostentatious and no more than a showcase.
- We are not hostile to the culture of the West. Neither do we perceive the technology of the West as the enemy of our people or culture. We object to the colonial relations of the West, and everything which has kept our people poor and backward. We oppose colonialism. We are looking to all peoples who have overthrown capitalism and colonialism, whether they are of the West or the East. We intend to recuperate our national identity along with Western technology by positioning ourselves in the front row of progress and advancement ... We do not intend to go back to ancient times and bygone periods of our history. Such regression is neither accessible nor desirable for us ...

...

- Adequate economic resources, geographical location and international relations will enable us to go through this phase in a short time. Within the same period, foundations for a democratic society will be laid out and the people will be able to determine their destiny democratically ... Taking into consideration such a level of political and class consciousness, there is no need for the previously privileged minority, and for those who subscribe to bourgeois thinking, to lose their social and political rights. There is no fear from free and open competition between different political parties.
- Our country is home to several peoples and various languages are spoken in different parts of the country. Facing this question realistically, consciously, courageously and answering it in a decisive and determined manner is the only way for strengthening national unity and overcoming some fundamental problems permanently. At present, there are many countries in the world who are comprised of various peoples, States, federal or autonomous republics while enjoying maximum national unity ... The mother tongue of millions in our country is Turkish; and they learn Persian in schools .... The Turkish speaking people of Iran ruled the entire country for almost ten centuries, but for historical and cultural reasons did not make Turkish the official language of the country ..., Turkish speaking people inhabit all parts of our country in addition to Azerbaijan. They are in the army and in government organizations occupying important political, scientific positions. In economic, financial and industrial sections they too enjoy the same opportunities as the rest of the nation. The only discrimination they suffer from is in the realm of language and the fact they are condemned to speak a foreign language ... In the Democratic Iran, Turkish speaking people can teach their language in schools without no fear, and Persian can maintain its position as a language of literature and science. Turkish books and newspapers can be published, and local Turkish radio stations can be established. Depending upon the will of the people of Azerbaijan, this province can be autonomous or, as with other parts of the country, beneficiary of a provincial parliament and economic administrative powers.

Kurdistan is a special case. At the first opportunity, Kurds can obtain autonomy in a referendum. Should racial and lingual linkages make autonomy in Kurdistan unnecessary, it will be the Kurds themselves who will determine their need to obtain Provincial Parliaments or otherwise. And the people of Iran's Baluchistan province will have the same right and the same choice ... Thus, the various peoples of Iran who share the same history and have their own unique culture and destiny, will be able to preserve the national unity of the Iranian nation in the future. A unity beneficial to all.[22]

The second part of *Ancheh Yek Enqelabi Bayad Bedanad* is concerned with the immediate problems and challenges the new movement had to deal with. Above all, the mobilization of the working class, as the Jazani-Zarifi group did not consider the peasantry 'a major force with a decisive role in the "people's revolution"':[23]

Workers and other strata of the toiling and deprived masses in cities form a multi-million human force. ... [However] the workers, that is the most receptive force of the masses to call for a revolutionary struggle, suffer from weariness and lack of organization. Workers and other toilers of the urban proletariat must be confident that the aim of the intellectuals is merely their emancipation.[24]

In the eyes of Jazani-Zarifi group, the youth, university students and intellectuals had the greatest potential to join the revolutionary movement:

Political awareness and the effect of the world's developments on this dynamic section of the urban petit bourgeoisie enables them to appreciate the cause and join the movement in a short period of time .... This force does not carry the burden of the political blunders and erroneous indoctrination of the past .... They readily recognize the need for self-sacrifice and heroism. The major short coming of this force is the lack of leadership and coherent revolutionary thinking. The enlightened youth are not fully aware of the important role of the toiling forces in realizing the revolution and forget that they themselves can only spark the revolution rather than provide the whole of the explosive force.[25]

... The organization of revolutionary networks will begin in towns and cities. The urban proletariat and the militant intellectuals will stand at the vanguard of this movement. Having organized themselves, the revolutionary cells cannot embark on rural guerrilla warfare as the Iranian peasantry with its rustic environment is not conducive to revolutionary preparedness.[26]

Ancheh Yek Enqelabi Bayad Bedanad was prepared for publication in the summer of 1970, simultaneous with the negotiations between the Jazani-Zarifi and Pouyan-Ahmadzadeh-Meftahi group and immediately after a group of six vanguard guerrillas were dispatched to the 'highland forests of Gilan and Mazandaran provinces' to 'survey the region and plan the start of military operations'.[27] The six were under the command of 'Ali Akbar Safa'i Farahani who had just returned from Palestine.

Pouyan-Meftahi-Ahmadzadeh group

Safa'i Farahani was friends with 'Abbas Meftahi since 1963, when Farahani left Tehran for Sari and started teaching at the Sari Technical School.[28] 'Abbas was not only the top student in his high school, but also one of the brightest youths in town. He was one of the few students there who had read Marx, Engels, and Lenin.'[29]

'Abbas Meftahi had cofounded a Marxist-Leninist group with Amir-Parviz Pouyan and Masoud Ahmadzadeh. Both Pouyan and Ahmadzadeh were born in 1947 in Mashhad and two years younger than Meftahi. Both were honours students of that province and very close friends. They converted to a modern version of political Islam at a young age and actively participated in the 5 June 1963 uprising in Mashhad. After the uprising was suppressed, they distanced themselves from the National Front, the Liberation Movement of Iran under Mehdi Bazargan and the Shi'ite clergy who had a strong hand in the uprising. However, they did not abandon Mossadeq's ideas and religious viewpoints.[30] Both left for Tehran after graduating from high school, passed the university entrance exam (concours) and were accepted at Tehran University; Pouyan in social science and Ahmadzadeh in mathematics. Through the study of philosophical and revolutionary writings, especially Mao Tse Tung's, they turned to Marxism and undertook the task of re-examining the past.[31] This was on the threshold of the reshaping of the students' movement after the 5 June 1963 uprising, when the third National Front was in decline and the leadership of the second National Front was investing in the policy of wait and see.

The group had no interest in student movements that came to life to ameliorate campus life. They did not participate in sporadic economic and political eruptions, such as ceremonies commemorating the seventh and fortieth days since the passing of the famed wrestler Gholam-Reza Takhti (27 December 1967), or the demonstrations against the increase in bus fares (February 1970).[32] This was one of the characteristics of a number of communist circles and tendencies of the 'path finding period'. It is noteworthy to remember what Ahmadzadeh wrote about the first phase of the group's evolution:

> Our group was also formed with the immediate goal of studying Marxism-Leninism and analysing the socio-economic conditions of our country.[33]

Jazani's criticism of the methods of the newly founded groups of that period is plausible:

> Thus, the first characteristic of the group was its tendency towards studying Marxism-Leninism and comprehending Iranian society. Many intellectual Marxist-Leninist groups of our country started out as such. By setting this goal for the group, the experiences of a decade of the working-class movement were ignored. Past movements have repeatedly proven the failure of such a program ... Consequently, the movement started back at zero. The comrades relying on their theoretical knowledge made a wholehearted attempt to start a positive move in accordance with general Marxist theories. The end result was that the group took on the characteristics of a political underground group.

The second characteristic of the group was its pro-China tendencies. The allure of the Chinese Communist Party's theories as well as valid reasons to object to the Soviet Union's policies towards Iran – not only regarding world affairs but also vis-à-vis their program and praxis – affected the group considerably. The analysis of the prevailing socio-economic conditions was considered a part of the educational program for the future cadres of the party.

The third characteristic of the group was the total absence of party structure. Intellectual ability and theoretical knowledge of individuals played an important role in recruitment and assigning responsibilities. There was no objective understanding of the secret police and no proper apprehension of the repressive police state for an underground political organization.[34]

Notwithstanding these factors, in a short time, the group grew considerably among students and young intellectuals and expanded in Mashhad, Tabriz, Sari and Tehran. This had a lot to do with intellectual activism: finding and laying the foundation of solid relations with young thinkers and writers in order to strengthen the network of old friendships. Amir-Parviz Pouyan played a unique role in the advancement of the group during this period, which lasted until March 1970. He wrote incessantly and without fear, translated texts from English into Persian and published both in authorized journals and in semi-clandestine and underground publications.[35] He wrote *Konoun Rah-e Ou bar Kodamin Bi-neshan Qolheh ast, dar Kodamin Sou?* (On Which Unknown Peak and Direction Now Lies his Path) in honour of his friend and companion Samad Behrangi. He penned *Khashmgin az Emperialism, Tarsan az Enqelab* (Angry at Imperialism, Afraid of Revolution) as a critique of Jalal Al-e Ahmad's reactionary viewpoints. His *Bazgasht be Nakoja-abad* (Return to No One's Land) and *Bazgasht be Khish* (Return to Self) were a blaming of conventional, pretentious and wishy-washy intellectuals and other writings which resonated amongst the curious, progressive and nonconforming youth. The joining of these cultivated intellectual youth, fighting against existing inequalities, brought about qualitative and quantitative changes in the group. A few are listed below:

1. The attempt to understand the socio-economic structure of Iran after the Shah's land reform in Sari, Rezaiyeh, Kurdistan, Kerman with the aid of those members and supporters who were serving in the Literacy and Health Corps. As an example, Naqi Hamidian's memoirs of 1967–8 are worth mentioning. After finishing his service in the Literacy Corps, and newly employed in the Ministry of Finance in Sari, he recollects:

From the beginning of our organizational activities, 'Abbas (Meftahi) urged us to start studying the socio-political and cultural conditions of the villages in Sari … We found out that two of the Shah's brothers, Abdolreza and Mahmoud Reza, had each appropriated thousands of hectares of the best farmlands around Sari near the shores of Farah Abad and also in another region called Shah Abad from the villagers by force or with money. The production on these lands was completely mechanized. The fearful and regretful eyes of the neighbouring villagers witnessed how the Shah's brothers profited from the automation and facilities provided by the road department and the office of agriculture which were all served their personal profit.

> ... Our covert chronicling turned into a lengthy analysis of the socio-economic conditions of the villages around Sari. In those years, we were trying to understand the reasons behind the growth and expansion of capitalism in the villages near Sari. Our research was aimed at understanding the characteristics and particulars of capitalist development. We also wanted to learn more about class contradictions and their main and fundamental axis, the limits and peculiarities of class mobility taking place in society and to find out their depth, intensity, and irreconcilability. During our research, we were constantly confronted with repressive government agents. In our opinion, capitalism in Iran was bureaucratic and dependent on the West. Its distinctive characteristic was repression through harsh dictatorship ... Despite the heavy shadow of our political stance, our research and analysis of the socio-economic conditions of the regions around Sari was, to a large extent, realistic, extensive, and objective.[36]

As a result of our research projects, the group saw the reality of the growth of capitalism throughout society, rejected the Chinese model of revolution in Iran and, to some extent, distanced itself from the political line of the Chinese Communist Party. Masoud Ahmadzadeh believed that the goal of land reform was the 'expansion and ever-more influence of imperialism in the city and the countryside'. Here is a brief synopsis of his conclusion:

> Usually, in a bourgeois revolution, it took decades for the newly liberated masses to experience the new conditions, gain an understanding of their nature and feel the new bonds and new forms of repression over them; here, the urban masses understood all this beforehand ... If, afterwards, the waves of struggle ebbed, it was not due to an acceptance of the regime's lies but to the violent suppression of the struggle. How was it possible to believe in the so-called 'White Revolution' in the face of increasing poverty, continuous insolvency, the intensification of exploitation by the violent domination of foreign capital and the fattening of a handful of comprador capitalists and big-shot bureaucrats at the expense of the bankruptcy of the commercial and industrial bourgeoisie and the brutal exploitation of workers? Thus, while two generations sufficed until 'the interests of the peasants were no longer (as under Napoleon) in accord with, but, in opposition to the interests of the bourgeoisie and capital,' and 'hence, the peasants found their natural ally and leader in the urban proletariat whose task was the overthrow of the bourgeois order'. Here in Iran, from a historical standpoint, the peasants, like the past semi-serfs in a semi-feudal, semi-colonized country, find their natural ally and leader in the urban proletariat ... This process has developed through the confinement of any capitalist mode of production to that of comprador capitalism through the ruination and gradual elimination of the national bourgeoisie by the imperialist monopolies.[37]

We shall soon see the consequences of such an understanding in the political and military praxis of OIPFG.

The Tabriz branch

Acknowledging the 'national question' in Iran and trying to find a progressive solution to eliminate national oppression in Azerbaijan were the main concerns of the members of the Tabriz circle who had considerable influence among the revolutionary avant-garde youth of Tabriz. First and foremost of these revolutionary intellectuals were Samad Behrangi, Behrouz Dehqani, ʿAlireza Nabdel, Kazem Saʿadati, Asghar Arab Herisi and Abdollah Afsari. They were familiar with the political developments of the Azerbaijani autonomous government during the years 1945–6. Most of them were graduates of Teachers' Training College and later became teachers in Azerbaijan village schools.

Their efforts and enthusiasm in the education of village kids and their close relationships with the peasants had made them popular among the villagers. One of their routine projects consisted of visiting the neighbouring villages and getting acquainted with village life. Some of the reports about the villages written by the other members of the group were published in a joint collection co-authored by Samad Behrangi and Behrouz Dehqani.[38]

Behrouz Dehqani and his friends continued their 'research' methodically and extensively. In time, their work took various forms and scopes. They read European and American plays and novels, studied Iran's history (especially the Constitutional Revolution), wrote short stories, recorded certain historical and sociological events of our country, translated Azeri poetry and expressions to Persian, and wrote about the life and work of great authors such as Sean O'Casey and William Faulkner.[39]

The amount of research and scope of the fieldwork and significant historical research conducted by the members of the Tabriz circle was not constricted. Some of their noteworthy and prevalent writings such as *Investigations into the Educational Problems of Iran* (Samad Behrangi), *Afsaneh-ha-ye Azerbaijan* (Tales of Azerbaijan; Samad Behrangi and Behrouz Dehqani) and *Azerbaijan va Masaleh-ye Melli* (Azerbaijan and the National Question; Alireza Nabdel) attracted many Azeri young intellectuals to the new communist movement.

In his essay *Azerbaijan va Masaleh-ye Melli*, Nabdel with rare boldness names 'Fars-Aryan chauvinism' as the other face of provincial nationalism and wrote:

> Reza Shah's dictatorship, which was based upon a chauvinist-fascist way of thinking, inflicted abominable cultural and national pressure on Iranian peoples. The present regime also consistently intensifies this pressure; the weight of which is mainly on the shoulders of the people of Azerbaijan, Kurdistan, and Khuzestan. Provincial nationalism, as a divisive and regressive tendency, is at the most, a reaction to such chauvinism.[40]

It was in this spirit that the prominent members of the Tabriz branch followed the same program as Amir-Parviz Pouyan: intellectual activity, seeking and connecting with young authors and strengthening networks of old friendships. Samad Behrangi and his *Mahi-ye Siyah-e Kouchulou* (Little Black Fish) played a crucial role here.

The political dead-end that all the activists had reached in the 1960s did not make them passive, rather the way out of this impasse was discussed in Behrangi's book. This work addressed vanguard armed struggle and the importance of devotion and sacrifice: 'What does matter is the influence that my life or death may have on the lives of others.' In *24 Saat dar Khab va Bidari* (24 Restless Hours) he talks about the desire to hold a machine gun in his hands: 'I only wished the machine gun in the store window belonged to me.'[41]

Opting for Urban Guerrilla Struggle

In 1970, the Pouyan-Ahmadzadeh-Meftahi group entered another stage of life. The Cuban Revolution was studied along with the experiences of South America's guerrilla movements through works such as Régis Debray's *Revolution in the Revolution*, the Tupamaros of Uruguay, Carlos Marighella's *Mini-Manual of the Urban Guerrillas* and the writings of Brazilian Jose Gomes da Silva 'which helped to balance Debray's views concerning guerrilla focus theory and the question of the party'.[42] After a period of intense discussion, the group finally adopted the course of urban guerrilla struggle and brought changes to its structure and political discourse:

1. The Chinese Communist Party view lost its relevance in determining the political line of the group. But the group kept its pro-Chinese tendencies in terms of world polarization in this stage too.
2. In this phase, centralism was enhanced in the group. Vestiges of pre-party formation came to an end and those who didn't have the necessary qualifications to realize the new goals were either purged or became passive. In the new stage, characteristics such as militancy, discipline and devotion were valued, and those who had joined the group in the intellectual atmosphere of the past had to adapt to the new situation and step up to a new level ... Membership rules changed as well. Three stages were set for membership; sympathizer, advanced sympathizer and then membership ... Candidates for membership participated in a series of preparatory activities.
3. The training and teaching methods of the members were also modified. Physical fitness, identification and pursuit, acquaintance with arms and incendiaries and construction of improvised explosive devices became part of the training program.

Theoretical education of the members consisted of a general overview of Marxist-Leninist theories, analysis of the revolutionary movements in the world and their adaptation to the Iranian situation, the study of Latin American revolutionary literature and the essays the group had compiled concerning their research of social and economic conditions of different regions of the country. Members were asked to express their opinion about various matters, which were usually transmitted to the central organ in writing.

4. All the members and even sympathizers were given pseudonyms. Inspired by revolutionary literature, the pseudonyms were chosen in honour of

various world revolutionaries – especially from Latin America …. The financial needs of the group were provided by voluntary contributions of the members. Later, the robbing of the Vanak Bank improved their financial situation.[43]

It was through this process that Amir-Parviz Pouyan formulated the group's new line of thought and presented a solid and coherent manuscript to his fellow combatants in the spring of 1970. This pamphlet, which defines the quintessential position of the 'revolutionary vanguard' on guerrilla movement and its rationale for taking up arms against the Shah's dictatorship, was based on two pillars: 'absolute power of the ruling power and the absolute inability presumed by the masses to emancipate themselves'.

Towards unification

As mentioned earlier, 'Abbas Meftahi and 'Ali Akbar Safa'i Farahani group started their formal negotiations in spring 1970. By the autumn of that year, the process entered its final phase. Meftahi, representing Pouyan and Ahmadzadeh, was of the opinion that armed operation should be first launched in a major city. According to Hamid Ashraf, one of the cadres of the Jazani group, the future leader of PFG and the then secretary for external relations of the Jazani-Zarifi group:

> Based on experiences of the Brazilian revolutionary movement, [Meftahi] recommended organizing guerrilla warfare in urban areas. The group favoured the idea that the movement should first flourish in cities and then shift to the countryside. On the other hand, the Jungle Group suggested the simultaneous beginning of the struggle in urban and rural areas. We thought the task should be carried out in both town and countryside. We gave priority to urban struggle – this priority was tactical because we thought operations in cities would prepare public opinion to pay attention to the operations in the mountains and would render greater influence. But, to comrades in Ahmadzadeh group the time preference had a strategic character. At any rate, connections between the two groups focused on theoretical issues throughout the fall of 1970.[44]

Hamid Ashraf continues:

> After a few rounds of discussion, comrade Masoud's [Ahmadzadeh] group accepted the theory of the Group in January 1970 and both groups agreed to prepare an action plan together.[45]

When Ahmad Farhoudi from the Pouyan-Ahmadzadeh-Meftahi group joined the Jungle Group in January, their number increased to nine.[46] The Jungle Group attacked the gendarmerie post in Siyahkal on the eve of 8 February 1971. The assault failed, two members were killed and five others were arrested. They were immediately sent to Tehran and executed amongst a large number of the urban team members of the Jazani-Zarifi group on 17 March 1971.

The news of the Siyahkal assault and the arrest and killing of the guerrillas echoed extensively throughout society. However, this tactical failure was the beginning of a new strategy in the anti-Shah movement which put an end to the past fifteen years of passivity by the progressive movement and promised the beginning of a new communist movement. In this spirit, Jazani says: 'Siyahkal deserves to be called resurrection.'[47] The alliance of the Jazani-Zarifi and Pouyan-Ahmadzadeh-Meftahi groups, 'between 6–11 April 1971, led to their unification.'[48] The militant members of the Pouyan-Ahmadzadeh-Meftahi group's attack on a police station in Qolhak on 3 April 1971, the execution of General Farsiu, chief military prosecutor, by Hamid Ashraf and Eskandar Sadeqinezhad on 7 April 1971 and the subsequent reaction to the previous execution of thirteen Fada'i members on 17 March 1971 strengthened the aspirations of both groups for unity more than ever.[49]

In a short span of time after the revolutionary execution of Lieutenant General Farsiu, thirteen flyers were distributed in Tehran and abroad by the supporters and sympathizers of urban guerilla movement in Iran. The flyers were concerned with the *raison d'être* of the incipient PFG, whose very name was revealed as such for the first time in one of these flyers, their intentions and objectives, as well as their political aspirations. Each of the flyers shed light on a specific subject, such as introducing the guerrillas, the participation of Safai-Farahani in the struggle of Palestinian people, the reason why Farsiu, the executioner of the thirteen revolutionaries of Siyahkal became the subject of the wrath of people, the principle of political and financial independence of the Fada'is and the need to finance their operation by the 'expropriation' of state funds from major banks. One of the most important points raised through this collection is the comparison between the failed attack on the Siyahkal gendarmerie station and the defeated offensive on the Moncada military base which paved the way for the success of the Cuban Revolution:

> In the same way in which the defeat of Fidel Castro at Moncada fostered the Cuban Revolution, Siyahkal should be considered as Iran's Moncada with this difference that armed struggle here [in Iran] will proceed relentlessly, with more experience and more forces.[50]

Second period, 1971–4

The People's Fada'i Guerrillas[51] wrote two forewords for Masoud Ahmadzadeh's treatise *Mobarezeh Mosallahaneh, Ham Estrateji, Ham Taktik* (Armed Struggle, both a Strategy and a Tactic) (Summer 1970). The first foreword was written four months after the Siyahkal incident in June 1971.[52] The second foreword was dated July 1972.[53] Most of the Jazani-Zarifi Group's members were either killed in the Siyahkal episode or captured and incarcerated in the Shah's prisons. A great number of Fada'i Guerrillas in Tehran, Mashhad and Tabriz were under the influence of Pouyan-Ahmadzadeh-Meftahi group ideas. The second preface clearly confirms this fact by informing 'the malevolent' that they 'were mistaken by claiming the lack of objective conditions of revolution'.[54] Whereas Ahmadzadeh had written that the objective conditions of the revolution were indeed present, and the military operation of the vanguard should be considered as the start of the insurrection of the masses:

> Why is insurrection the work of the masses? Didn't the Cuban experience show that a small armed motor can initiate and gradually lead the masses to insurrection?[55] If the guerrilla struggle is the beginning of the insurrection, then it is wrong to consider armed struggle as 'armed self-defence' or 'armed propaganda'. Armed struggle is necessary to give military, economic and political blows to the ruling apparatus. For some comrades armed operations means armed self-defence (armed self-defence means military support of political action. That is, arms play a defensive – not an offensive – role to resist the probable aggression of the enemy and thus to protect the self.) Some members understand armed action as armed propaganda (to expect only the propaganda effect of the armed struggle on the masses). Such understanding limits the extent of armed action. With armed operations, we inflict military, economic and political blows upon our enemy.[56]

As such, the period from 1971 to 1974 cannot be portrayed as the years of absolute prevalence of Ahmadzadeh's line in the OIPFG. In those years, the Organization was not the only medium for theoretical work and formulation of ideas. Prison was, if not the first, at least the second most important location for theoretical reflections and political considerations for the revolutionary activists and militants. It was in prison where new ideas were shaped, new cadres were trained and contacts with the outside world took place. Bijan Jazani, the most prominent theorist of the Fada'i Guerrillas, had his most productive years in prison. Many of his theoretical writings were formulated during one-on-one conversations with other inmates or in group discussions with his fellow inmates and then written on scrap paper and later smuggled out of prison. A considerable number of these writings were published in London by Manouchehr Kalantari and the 19 Bahman group in a series entitled *19 Bahman Teorik* without mentioning the name of the original author.

The period 1971–4 also witnessed some of Jazani's open debates with proponents of the dominant line of thought in the organization. He insisted upon transparency of ideological differences and the importance of ideological struggle within the ranks of Fada'i Guerrillas.

The appearance of ideological disagreements amongst the supporters of Ahmadzadeh with Jazani's line of thinking between 1971 and 1974 was the primary factor in the ideological orientation of the organization in the years to come. However, the significance of 1971–4 was not only because the group's differences became apparent, but also because in this period, notably during 1972–4, two important polemics took place between the OIPFG and two other theoretical tendencies. The first debate was with Mostafa Sho'aiyan. The second was with the Setareh Group which was going through a process of 'homogeneousness' with the OIPFG (this group later called itself the Communist Unity). In both debates, Hamid Momeni's role, as the theoretician of the organization, was of great importance. The ideological debates with those 'outside' the organization helped bring about political coherence and 'unity of thought' within the organization. As shall be seen below, the characteristic of this cohesion was more 'ideological' and leaned towards a kind of Stalinism as the only 'correct interpretation of Lenin's thought.'

First, we will look at the internal differences in the OIPFG and then, to the external skirmishes.

Major topics of discussion and disagreement within the OIPFG

Jazani's thoughts challenged the dominant political line of the Fada'i Guerrillas in various aspects.[57] He was of the opinion that even though the 'objective conditions of Revolution' did not exist at that point in time, the vanguard armed struggle that has begun should not be understood as the beginning of the revolution.

> The onset of armed struggle does not mean that the objective conditions of the revolution are present and that with the beginning of the struggle, the revolution has started.[58]

Earlier, in proving that the objective conditions of revolution existed, Ahmadzadeh wrote:

> Should we deduce that the lack of broad and spontaneous movements indicates a lack of objective conditions of the revolution and that the revolutionary phase has not yet arrived? In my opinion, no ... The causes of the absence of mass movements are on the one hand, the violent repression, constant and lengthy terror imposed by the imperialist dictatorship as the principle in the survival of imperialist domination; and on the other hand, the crucial weakness of the revolutionary forces should be kept in mind. But what enables us to say that the objective conditions of evolution exist? ... Is not this enthusiasm and ardour of the revolutionaries, these tireless quests of the intellectual forces of the revolutionary and progressive classes in search for the path to revolution, these recurring police raids, these lockups, these tortures, and these assassinations, manifestations of the subjective reflection of the readiness of the objective conditions of revolution?[59]

However, Jazani, in accordance with Lenin's definition of the 'objective conditions of the revolution' argued that political and economic crisis, intensification of the internal contradictions of the governing classes, the regime's weakness in governing and controlling the system and the immense dissatisfaction of the people who cannot bear the existing conditions of cruelty perpetuated by the regime and the ruling class anymore will lead the masses to take exceptional and historical action which would not happen otherwise or under normal circumstances. According to Jazani, the absence of widespread mass movements was not only because of political oppression. In his opinion the land reform and the establishment of dependent capitalism as the dominant mode of production have brought with itself economic growth. This system, which is condemned to permanent dependence on imperialistic monopolies has, despite its historical shortcomings, lead to a period of prosperity since it is a more advanced system compared to the previous one ... The new order, quite apart from failing to tackle the contradictions between feudalism and the bourgeoisie, has utterly failed to solve the fundamental contradictions that beset our society. Its economic prosperity will be brief and the contradiction within the system, together with the main contradiction between the people on the one hand and imperialism and comprador bourgeousie on the other, will be accentuated.[60]

This economic growth paralleled the increasing authority of the Shah himself and the royal family, who held all the power in their hands and forced the foreign-dependent capital and imperialist monopolies to operate through him and his cronies. Such a situation was far from an economic and political crisis that does not permit the ruling class to rule like previously, and the people to live like before. As the Shah's dictatorship was the main stumbling block for the movement of the masses, as well as the political and economic growth of the society in general, fighting the Shah's dictatorship became the main target for the National Liberation Movement. In Jazani's view the entire political and economic order could only be challenged when the revolutionary conditions materialized itself and the ground was prepared for the working class and communist movements to exert their hegemony:

At present, the conflict between the masses, the comprador bourgeoisie and imperialism is not the main one, rather, the regime's dictatorship (which is an aspect of this conflict) plays the main role.[61]

Based on his assessment that the 'objective conditions of revolution' do not exist, Jazani concluded that the adoption of armed struggle by vanguard intellectuals does not lead to an immediate acceptance of armed struggle by the masses. Only by engaging in political and economic struggle would the masses gradually become prepared for the final fight. Jazani called this process 'masses joining the armed struggle', the precondition of which was the creation of a political organization who could work parallel to a political-military organization and as the second leg of the armed movement.

There are three stages to the strategy of the Iranian revolutionary movement. The first is aimed at establishing the armed struggle. In the second the masses will begin a struggle against the enemy and provide material and moral support for the movement. In the third, the masses will themselves take part in the armed struggle, transforming the movement into a mass one, which will in turn establish the people's leadership.[62]

One of the fundamental contradictions of the Fada'i Guerrillas was that in theory they admitted the existence of 'objective conditions of revolution' but, in practice, they adopted and emphasized the propaganda aspect of armed struggle. This discrepancy not only existed during 1971–4 but also continued until armed struggle was negated by the majority of the Fada'i Guerrillas. Jazani, who was sensitive towards this contradiction, warned that it was possible that those who insisted on the existence of 'the objective conditions of revolution' would reject the armed struggle of the vanguard. The indisputable proof of this foresight can be seen in the refutation of armed struggle by a large number of Ahmadzadeh's sympathizers, especially in 1974, and in the Shah's prisons.[63]

The disagreements and disputes amongst the Fada'i Guerrillas which were made public

The theoretical debates of the OIPFG with Mostafa Sho'aiyan and the Setareh Group in 1973–4 had no serious impact on the political and military practice of the organization. Even though such polemics could undermine some of the fundamental pillars of the organization, they did not intensify the internal disagreements but rather consolidated its unity by sharpening the ideological character of the group. Our evaluation of these two polemics does not mean in any way that Sho'aiyan's points of view were the same as the Setareh Group's. Not only are the fundamental differences between the two political currents undeniable, but the history of their relationship with the OIPFG and the way in which each of them came into contact and cooperation with the latter are also quite different.

In analysing the relationship of the above-mentioned currents, we will only allude to the points that solidified the ideological and political features of the organization.

The polemic between Mostafa Sho'aiyan and the OIPFG

In his critique of Ahmadzadeh's theoretical delineations, Sho'aiyan's criticism could be summarized as such: because 'communism is a path other than Leninism,'[64] the communist project under the influence of Leninism has failed all over the world, capitalism has been revived in countries such as the Soviet Union, China, Vietnam and Cuba and the role of the national bourgeoisie as an independent political movement in the emergence of anti-colonial and freedom fighting movements has to be emphasized.

> Will capitalism in Russia rise again like Dracula from his coffin and bite the neck of the working class? Or has it putrefied forever in the grave dug by the October Revolution? No! Capitalism has been revived once again in the Soviet Union and has cast its poison in the October blood![65]

With such introduction, Sho'aiyan refutes Ahmadzadeh's points of view and asks:

> How is it that capitalism ... is so powerful that, on the one hand, can transform a victorious socialist revolution to revert to capitalism, and on the other hand, you and many others claim that 'an independent political power' for the bourgeoisie is absurd? Is this not confounding? .... It is incredible to believe that the bourgeoisie

... cannot form an independent political power throughout the anti-colonial world and amongst it, in Iran, while on the other side of the border North of Iran, the foundation and values of the October Revolution are falling apart and the victory of capitalism is becoming crystal clear.[66]

To prove the ever-historic role of the national bourgeoisie as an independent political power, Sho'aiyan points to revolutions of National Liberation. Hamid Momeni, the leading theoretician of the Fada'i Guerrillas at the time and one in charge of carrying out the polemics, wrongly attributes Sho'aiyan's interpretations to Trotsky's *Permanent Revolution* and other viewpoints concerning 'the impossibility of constructing socialism in one country'.

The crux of what Sho'aiyan advocated is the necessity to take distance from Leninism, and to initiate an anti-colonial revolution based on the potential of Iran's national bourgeoisie as an independent political force. However, in March 1964, he suggested the necessity of adopting a 'new tactic for the national liberation movement of the Iranian nation' to the former prime minister Mohammad Mossadeq, the Freedom Movement of Iran and three leading Grand Ayatollahs. Yet, in response to Sho'aiyan's criticism, the OIPFG did not delve on the aforementioned points. Instead, Momeni called Sho'aiyan an advocate of Trotsky's 'permanent revolution', and praised Stalin instead. By reiterating Stalin's accusations and the slanders, he fabricated against Trotsky; he scrutinized Trotsky's record and made a case against him. Moreover, in his Stalinist historiography, Momeni did not fail to denigrate those Marxist historians who were critical of the Soviet's official version on Trotsky and those who had proven Stalin's claims to be false.

The Fada'i Guerrillas' polemic with the Setareh Group

The OIPFG polemic with the Setareh Group occurred when the two formations started the 'homogenization process' around the following points: (1) The significance and purpose of the armed struggle of the vanguard, the propaganda aspect of armed and unarmed praxis, (2) The stage of revolution in Iran, (3) Revisionism and the construction of socialism in the USSR.

The Setareh Group were mostly members of the youth wing of the National Front in Europe and the United States. Not only they did not believe in the existence of the 'national bourgeoisie', but due to the rapid growth of capitalist relations of production in Iran, they concluded that the main characteristic of Iran's social revolution is socialistic. This ideological difference was overshadowed for a while by both groups' evaluation of Stalin. Again, Hamid Momeni came to the defence of Stalinism. As was common with communists in the former Soviet Union, he defamed his ideological opponents. Trotsky, Kamenev, Zinoviev and Bukharin were called representatives of the defeated bourgeoisie and their purge from the party along with their 'rainbow of sympathizers' was considered a necessary step towards socialism. Even Khrushchev's proposal in the Twentieth Congress of the Soviet Communist Party against the 'cult of personality', exposing Stalin's authoritarian behaviour, was ridiculed:

The cult of personality is indeed not favourable and should be opposed as much as possible. However, we should not forget that it is inevitable in socialist revolution and society and can be fought only to a certain degree ... for example, in China, during the cultural revolution and the uprising against the majority of the Central Committee, worshipping Mao reached its height, but has now waned.[67]

In line with Stalin's understanding of 'historical and dialectical materialism', a very linear and schematic outline of the five stages of societal development (from collective primitive society to communism) was provided. Even Marx's explicit allusion to the Asiatic mode of production was portrayed as an 'oversight'. Moreover, anyone who analysed the system in the East as anything other than feudalism, such as Wittfogel, would be called a pseudo-Marxist bourgeois scientist.

The presence of such views among the OIPFG militants demonstrated that the break with the Tudeh Party's mindset was not thorough and that the organization was still far away from a radical refutation of the Stalinist foundations of the Tudeh Party. A number of OIPFG leaders and theoreticians, such as Amir-Parviz Pouyan in *Tarsan az Emperialism va Harasan az Enghelab* and Masoud Ahmadzadeh in *Mobarezeh Mosallahaneh* praised Stalin as the 'great leader of the proletariat'. Yet their emphasis on Régis Debray and interest in Jesús Silva Herzog had no affinity with Stalinism. The decrees ratified in the 20th to 22nd Congress of the USSR's Communist Party with regard to 'peaceful transition', 'peaceful coexistence' and 'peaceful political competition', were rejected by Pouyan-Ahmadzadeh-Meftahi group as Khrushchev's revisionism and Ahmadzadeh was open about his inclination to Mao Tse Tung's thoughts. In his essay on the Azerbaijan National Question, Nabdel writes about 'Khrushchev's revisionism' and 'Stalin's and Mao's valuable guidelines' for solving the 'national question'.[68] However, such opinions and occasional references by the Pouyan-Ahmadzadeh-Meftahi group calling Stalin the 'great leader of the proletariat' manifested the poverty of theory and paucity of knowledge about the history of the Third International more than anything else. Unlike the Pouyan-Ahmadzadeh-Meftahi group, the Jazani-Zarifi group distanced itself from both Stalinism and Maoism. For example, in *Ancheh Yek Enqelabi Bayad Bedanad*, we read:

> Faced with the erroneous policy of Soviet Russia and the Stalinist deviation of the Russian Communist Party from Marxism-Leninism, the leadership of the Tudeh Party became utterly subservient to the Russian policies with regard to our country and thereby lost all credibility amongst the masses and especially amongst the petit bourgeoisie.[69]

In *Tarh-e Jamehshenasi va Mabani-ye Estratejik-e Jonbesh-e Enqelabi-ye Iran*, Jazani writes in more detail about 'Stalin's line':

> The dominance of Stalin's line of thought in the international movement was demonstrated by the unconditional compliance of the Soviet Communist Party by 'brother parties' ... In Iran, Stalin's line of thought was two-fold: the existence of the Tudeh Party and the overthrow of Reza Khan's dictatorship- not by the masses

... but due to mechanical blows caused by the Second World War (that is, Iran's military occupation).[70]

Jazani, however, had reached a different conclusion by witnessing the actual policies the Soviets had pursued vis-à-vis Iranian political affairs. Critical of the Soviets, Jazani openly depicted the Soviet Union's political conduct during the Azerbaijan crisis and the nationalization of the Iranian oil industry. Furthermore, he not only agreed with the decrees of the Twentieth Congress of the CPSU concerning Stalin's cult of personality, but also welcomed more profound criticism of Stalinism.[71] He explicitly distanced himself from 'Mao's thoughts' and 'Maoism' and criticized the 'social-imperialist' thesis that had become attractive in some communist circles.[72]

Yet, despite basic differences between the Pouyan-Ahmadzadeh-Meftahi and Jazani-Zarifi groups, both ardently believed in OIPFG autonomy and independence from outside powers. No doubt, the two formative Fada'i groups differed in their approach to Soviet Union and Stalinism. But even Ahmadzadeh or Pouyan would not consider themselves and their group Stalinists. It was only in the years 1973–4 and during Hamid Momeni's ideological polemics with Sho'aiyan and the Setareh Group, that Stalinism surfaced and gained ideological hegemony within the OIPFG. This new mindset and its internal hegemony were exposed in the articles published in the second issue of *Nabard-e Khalq*, which was the first public organ of the OIPFG. On the one hand, in an article titled 'Mao Tse-Tung's Thoughts and Our Revolution', Mao's thoughts were commemorated as a 'creative interpretation of the Marxism Leninism of our time', and Stalin was called 'the great leader of the proletariat'.[73] On the other hand, in the editorial of the same issue, the righteousness of propaganda and the agitational aspect of armed struggle is discussed as conceived by Jazani.[74] Thus, despite the organization's ideological tendency towards Ahmadzadeh's views,[75] in practice the agitational character of armed operations advanced by Jazani was adopted as the core of OIPFG militancy, while the ideological hegemony of Stalinism gained more currency and was incorporated into the overall formal views of OIPFG eclipsing Jazani's critiques of the Soviets and Stalin.

Third Period, 1974–6

The years from 1974 to 1976 were a period of growth and considerable expansion of the OIPFG throughout the country. This development was reflected in the revised organization's name and emblem: now a nationwide formation, they could call themselves the Organization of Iranian People's Fada'i Guerrillas.

In this period, the OIPFG raised the slogan of unity for all Marxist-Leninists who supported armed struggle and spoke of its strategic, or rather its hegemonic role in bringing about this unity. However, the former contradictions, foremost, the belief in the presence of the objective conditions of the revolution in theory, and the emphasis on 'armed propaganda-agitation' in real practice, not only persisted but also expanded. As workers' strikes and acts of popular protests increased, so did the organization's armed operations. Yet there was no indication that masses were intending to take up arms, a fact which was disregarded by the Organization.

The callous murder of Bijan Jazani and the imprisoned members of his group, along with two members of the Mojahedin-e Khalq in the Evin hills by SAVAK in April 1975 was followed by other fatal blows that year and extended throughout 1976 to the leadership of the organization itself, which led to the death of the majority of senior cadres such as Hamid Ashraf, Hamid Momeni and Behrouz Armaghani, was a severe blow to the process of growth and expansion of the organization.

Between 1974 and 1978, two important events took place as well: first, an ideological shift in a number of Mojahedin cadres and members, the split in that organization and the bloody elimination of some its religious members by the faction which labelled itself as Marxist-Leninist, and second, the split of Touraj Heydari Bigvand and his supporters from the OIPFG, who had rejected the principle of urban guerrilla struggle with most of them later joining the Tudeh Party of Iran. We will examine these events in relation with three different domains: (1) The continuation and intensification of internal contradictions within the OIPFG, (2) the question of unity and the strategic role of the OIPFG and (3) the split of Touraj Heydari Bigvand and like-minded cadres from the organization and their rejection of armed struggle.

The continuation and intensification of the internal contradictions of the OIPFG

Nabard-e Khalq no.6 (May 1975) was published with the motto 'armed propaganda is the pivotal form of the struggle of our people'. In *Nabard-e Khalq* no. 7 (6 June 1976), an article titled 'The Propaganda Aspect of Armed Operations and what it meant in the Past', distinguished two phases in the conceptualization of armed propaganda:

In the first phase, which occurred during the early years of the armed struggle, the objectives of armed operations were as follows: (1) The propagation of the movement's political goals, (2) the preparation and support of the movement financially and militarily. In the second phase, activities related to armed propaganda characterized by 'popular type' armed operations in the years 1974–5. In this period OIPFG resorted to specific exemplary operations.[76]

The OIPFG refrained from Jazani's plan to form 'the second leg of armed movement',[77] that is, forming a political wing parallel to the military organization. Nevertheless, the organization promulgated the importance and necessity of 'armed propaganda' more than ever and launched a new stage in the propagandistic aspect of armed struggle, namely *'amaliyat-e nemune khalqi or* symbolic popular operations. This incongruity becomes even more apparent when in the foreword of *'Edam Enqelabi-ye 'Abbas Shahriari* (The Revolutionary Execution of 'Abbas Shahriari), a booklet published in 1975, the OIPFG emphasized once again the presence of the objective conditions of the revolution and the regime's liquidation of all bourgeoisie parties and the establishment of one party state, Rastakhiz (Resurrection) Party with its obligatory membership of all citizens, and the promise of free education and free healthcare which were interpreted as signs of the existence of revolutionary conditions.[78]

The publication of *Nabard-e Khalq,* no.6 one month after the execution of the Jazani-Zarifi group in the Evin hills provided an opportunity for the re-evaluation of the role and position of Jazani's thoughts on the path of no return that the OIPFG had chosen. In the same edition, in an article titled 'The Shah's Great Crime against Iran's New Revolutionary Movement', it is noted that

> Comrade Jazani has left us unique and invaluable works about the conditions for Iran's revolution. He sent his work regularly from prison to the organization, which we published in limited edition and put at the disposal of the members and supporters of the organization … These writings were the best guides for the theoretical education of our comrades. In these writings Iran's socio-economic and political conditions are depicted realistically and with profound knowledge of Marxism-Leninism and provide valuable guidance as to how to conduct the struggle. As of now, these studies are the best examples for adopting general principles of Marxism-Leninism to the specific condition of Iran.[79]

It is furthermore pinpointed that Comrade Jazani, because of the conditions of his imprisonment and limited contact with the organization, in a few instances makes generalizations based on the few objective facts he had at his disposal. These cases were mostly about internal matters of the movement. In such cases, the organization would send its point of view to comrade Jazani and he would consider them in his future writings. We admit that such cases were very few and many revisions were done by himself, unless when communication and exchange of opinion with the organization was not possible for him.[80]

A year after, the first signs of a new approach manifested itself in the organization. For the first time, in the foreword of *Nabard-e Khalq* no.7 (28 May 1976), Jazani's 'What a Revolutionary Should Know' was hailed as one of the theoretical pillars of the guerrilla movement. Notably, between 1974 and 1976, the organization did not follow Jazani's practical scheme for struggle based on forming two parallel organizations, one military and the other political, and instead the emphasis was placed on the agitational aspect of armed operations. If this contradiction was tolerable in the years 1971 to 1974, it could not be pursued in the years 1974 and 1975. It was within such a contradictory situation that the blows upon the leadership and the organization itself made it possible for some militants to renounce urban guerrilla struggle.

The question of unity and the strategic role of the OIPFG. The split in the People's Mojahedin Organization of Iran

Giving priority to the formation of the working-class party versus the construction of the united, anti-imperialist front was one of the points of contention from day one. Masoud Ahmadzadeh believed the priority should be given to the creation of the front and not the party.[81]

However, the editorial of *Nabard-e Khalq* no.6 with the title 'Slogans of Unity', was somehow different from Ahmadzadeh's view. This editorial stated explicitly that a united 'anti-imperialist front' cannot be created until all its building blocks develop an organic relationship with the classes they represent.[82] But doesn't the organic relationship of communist organizations with the working class mean that the necessary conditions for forming a working-class party exist? The editorial does not provide an answer to this question. However, after stating the preconditions of forming a united front, it concludes that for now 'we must support the cooperation of revolutionary forces as much as possible'.[83]

For the OIPFG, the essential problem was not the formation of a united front, but the unity of all the Marxist-Leninists who believed in the armed struggle. Therefore, in the same edition of *Nabard-e Khalq,* Jazani's article 'The Question of Unity and the Strategic Role of the OIPFG' was published.[84] In this article, Jazani not only points out the necessity for unity of all the Marxist-Leninists who believe in the armed struggle, but emphasizes that if yesterday none of Marxist-Leninist groups accepted any force as the pivotal base of unity, today

> there is an avant-garde force which, to a certain degree, is competent enough to fulfil the leadership role and can become the focal point. This force is the People's Fada'i Guerrillas. The OIPFG have proven in practice that they are closer to reaching a revolutionary strategy than any other Marxist-Leninist group. They have proven the degree of devotion, integrity, and relentlessness necessary to fulfil their responsibilities towards the working class and liberation movements.[85]

In May 1975, news of the split in the People's Mojahedin organization was not yet made public. However, the slogans of unity in *Nabard-e Khalq's* no.6 indicated that the OIPFG were aware of the changes in the ideology of a section of the Mujahedin-e Khalq (OIPM) who had converted to Marxism-Leninism. *Nabard-e Khalq* in anticipation of the adverse outcome of this transformation, warned:

> Communists who join non-communist political organizations not only undermine themselves and the communist movement, but also cause internal conflicts, chaos, confusion, and uncontrolled vacillations to the right and left in these organizations... Communists should be prudent and recognize the authenticity of such organizations as an integral faction of the revolutionary forces and cooperate with them only in specific actions instead of trying to become members of such organizations.[86]

Despite such a prudent and sound warning, it appears that the writers of *Nabard-e Khalq* had not profoundly comprehended the ideological structure of the OIPM and the most probable paths of their transformation. But Bijan Jazani who had studied the Mojahedin 'phenomenon' in depth foresaw this transformation before the crisis broke open and the split in the organization took place. He was probably the first who coined the Mojahedin's ideology as Islamic Marxism or Marxist Islam. In an essay with the same title, he meticulously scrutinized eclectic ideologies from the perspective of a materialist, as well as a principled communist, and criticized the application of religious tactics in political struggle. Jazani cared about the fate of the OIPM as he considered them a 'friend' organization.[87] Subsequently and for 'tactical considerations', the necessity of avoiding 'conflicts and political confrontation within the ranks of the armed movement',[88] he decided not to publish his lengthy article (it was published in 1984, five years after the revolution, by the Rah-e Fada'i group outside Iran). Jazani foresaw the course of the OIPM's transformation as such:

> Without a shadow of doubt, a number of today's religious Marxists will remain religious, and a number will turn towards Marxism. We have evidence that the necessities of struggle and the importance of a having a correct understanding of the existing situation will canalize the militant forces towards an original Marxism-Leninism. The living example is Castro's movement in Cuba, where its forerunners, including Castro himself, were not Marxist-Leninist at the outset of the revolution. They adopted and applied Marxism during the revolution and by sheer exigency.
>
> Isn't it the same exigency that has led our religious friends towards Marxism-Leninism?[89]

Indeed, this essay did not stay hidden from the OIPM leadership in prison and from that day onwards they intensified their attacks on Jazani, openly undermining and portraying him as the source of contention and tension amongst progressive forces. Nevertheless, Jazani's predictions turned out to be very accurate. A few months after Jazani and his comrades were assassinated, in October 1975, the Marxist-Leninist Mojahedin announced their formation. Taqi Shahram's manifesto entitled *Bayaniyeh E'lam Mavaze' Ideolojik-e Sazeman-e Mojahedin-e Khalq-e Iran* (Manifesto of the Declaration of the Ideological Stance of the Mojahedin-e Khalq Organization of Iran) signalled the Marxist Mojahedin's sympathy towards the Stalinist take on Marxism-Leninism and also Mao Tse Tung's thoughts.[90] In March 1977, the discussions between the Marxist-Leninist faction of the Mojahedin and the OIPFG were circulated by the splinter group within the opposition movement to the Shah.[91] The discussions were mostly around forming an anti-imperialist front and the unification of Marxist-Leninists who believed in armed struggle. The focus of the Marxist-Leninist (M.L) Mojahedin's criticism was the OIPFG's editorial of *Nabard-e Khalq* no.6 (May 1975) concerning the slogans of unity which perceived the formation of a united front as premature. The Mojahedin defended not only the slogan of the united front, but also analysed the socio-economic situation of Iran and the pivotal place of armed struggle in the development of the movement, criticism of Khrushchev's revisionism and the significance of Mao's thoughts. They wholeheartedly sympathized with Ahmadzadeh's outlook and took a critical position on Jazani's viewpoints and distanced themselves from his thoughts. This is manifested in *Soalha-yi Darbareh 'Sho'arha-ye Vahdat'* (Questions about 'slogans of unity') which were posed by one of the OIPM educational groups[92] and also in a document titled *Shekafha-yi dar 'Sho'arha-ye Vahdat'* (Fractures in the 'Slogans of the Unity')[93] which was written by one of the OIPM groups.

Although the crux of Mojahedin's (M.L) discourse was the creation of a united front, in their negotiations with the OIPFG leadership they did not lay emphasis on the formation of such a 'United Front', but rather focused on the 'erroneous thesis' of the unity of Marxist-Leninists who believed in armed struggle. In this context they also criticized Jazani's emphasis on the strategic role of the OIPFG as another manifestation of sectarianism and superiority complex. The debates of the two groups on forming a 'united front' got nowhere. It is important to note that Mojahedin (M.L) insistence on the formation of a 'United Front' withered away, when the Mojahedin (M.L) rejected the theory and practice of urban guerrilla struggle in the winter of 1978, the question of a united front totally lost its relevance.

The split of Touraj Bigvand's group and refutation of the theory and practice of armed struggle

Touraj Heydari Bigvand, a member of the OIPFG wrote the *Theory of Armed Propaganda, Deviation from Marxism-Leninism* probably just before the 29 June 1976 event. The booklet was circulated in October 1977.[94] In his writing, Bigvand rejected the guerrilla struggle and called it 'deviation from Marxism'. On 4 October 1976 he was killed by SAVAK in a street clash.[95] His booklet, which had been distributed within the OIPFG, had found some supporters who split from the organization in November 1976.[96] Most of them later joined the Tudeh Party and consequently, the Tudeh Party published Bigvand's article with a foreword. It was distributed inside and outside the country. The focus of the essay was a critique of Jazani's book *How Armed Struggle Becomes a Mass Movement*.

Although Bigvand was the first known Fada'i who negated and rejected the OIPFG, he is not the first who criticized the political and theoretical foundations of the guerrilla movement and Jazani's views. In this respect the Tudeh Party was the forerunner. Notably after Jazani was killed and the first signs of the organization's shift to his views appeared, the prominent Tudeh figure Nureddin Kianouri took charge of re-evaluating Jazani's writings. In a series of articles in *Donya*, the theoretical organ of the Tudeh Party (*Donya* no. 3, June 1975;[97] no. 6, September 1975;[98] no.9, December 1975;[99] no.3, May 1976[100] and no.10, December 1976)[101] he challenged Jazani's point of view published in *19 Bahman Te'orik*, nos.2 and 3.[102]

Conscious of the different point of views within the OIPFG, Kianouri wrote:

> Two articles in *19 Bahman Te'orik* issues 2 and 3 were published by the OIPFG, both reflecting the position of one of the factions of the OIPFG until the fall of 1973. The reason we say one faction is because the content of these essays is very different from what is published in *Nabard-e Khalq*, which is the organ of the OIPFG.[103]

The pondering point in Kianouri's criticism is the approach he adopted to refute guerrilla struggle. This approach was essentially based on quoting Lenin's *What is to be Done* and *Left-Wing Communism: An Infantile Disorder*. The quotations were presented as sacred verses, or as Kianouri put it, 'general rules of a Leninist party'[104] by which one could evaluate the 'veracity' of the guerrilla way of struggle. The seasoning of his innumerable citations and quotations were an array of accusations and labels that would conflate right and wrong instead of concrete criticism and scrutiny of the writings produced by Jazani and the OIPFG.

In fact, Kianouri's approach in the refutation of armed struggle has many similarities with that of Bigvand, whose book is written in three long chapters: chapter 1, is titled 'Armed propaganda or provocative terror?' chapter 2 has to do with similarities between Russia (before the 1905 revolution) 'with today's Iran'. Chapter 3 is a critique of Jazani's 'How the Masses Will Join the Armed Struggle'.

In the first chapter, the viewpoint of the Narodniks, the significant movement of the Russian intelligentsia of the second part of the nineteenth century, is explained according to Lenin's *What Is to Be Done*, and in Bigvand's language 'armed propaganda' which is the very same tactic used by the anti-communist East Timorese Soibada movement's 'provocative terror' of 1900–2. In the second chapter, Russia's economic and industrial conditions are compared to that of Iran. As to why Russia in the beginning of the twentieth century is compared to Iran of the 1960s and 1970s, Bigvand has this to say: 'Leninist principles of propaganda and agitation are universal laws and inescapable.'[105]

The principle of 'concrete analysis of concrete situations', which was remarkable in the writings of all the Fada'i founders, is slandered as 'Trotskyism' and refuted: instead, a 'new form of reasoning' becomes the order of the day: comparative analysis is taken advantage to demonstrate symmetrical patterns and facilitate 'general rules' based on quotations from Lenin. This methodology stifles the power of logic at the expense of the logic of power. This same approach is seen in the third chapter, which was supposed to be a critique of *Chegouneh Mobarezeh Mosallahaneh Tudehi Mishavad*. There is no mention of the formation of the 'political leg of the armed movement', which was the most important concern, and one may say, contribution of Jazani's book. Instead of a critique of Jazani's concrete proposal for the advancement of urban guerrilla struggle in Iran, Bigvand opts to quote Lenin to prove that Jazani's 'armed propaganda' was not basically different from Soiboda's 'provocative terror', and as such should therefore be dismissed.

What is plausible in examining Bigvand's pamphlet is the fact that the refutation of the armed struggle becomes a new beginning in ideological confrontations of the Iranian left movement with the special characteristics of those who were to take distance from the concrete socio-economic and political conditions of Iran and the world, and relapse into the practice of comparing the incomparable and drawing analogies.

The Fourth Period: 1976–8

The period between 1976 and 1978 was the most challenging in the OIPFG's existence. After the decimation of the Jazani-Zarifi group in April 1975 and the blows of July 1976 which ended with the death of Hamid Ashraf and a number of its important leaders, the organization faced the threat of demise. It was solely the exceptional dedication and determination of remaining members and the high esteem OIPFG had earned – which was the outcome of years of resistance and struggle against the Shah's regime – which allowed the organization to revive its cells and networks. In the meantime, this revival emphasized the extent of moral and political influence of the OIPFG in the public opinion. This became more apparent in 1977 as public protests by the intellectuals and the sporadic popular unrest grew.

The reconstruction of the OIPFG after the mortal blows of 1976 and its increasing influence, especially from mid-1977 onwards, however occurred while the society was to embark on a radical transformation. The Goethe Institute's poetry nights of October 1977, vast mass demonstrations, meetings, strike and finally the February Revolution of 1979 all contributed to the revitalization of the OIPFG. A resurrection, one aspect of which was the acceleration of the process of turning away from Ahmadzadeh's viewpoint to turning towards that of Jazani. This change of heart was reflected in the student organ of the OIPFG, *Payam-e Daneshjou* (The Student Dispatch), no.3 (December 1977). In a statement delivered on the occasion of the 16 Azar anniversary,[106] three important points were highlighted:

1. The lack of objective conditions of revolution and the agitational nature of military actions:

   The evaluation of the blows of 1976 made it clear to the guerrillas that the objective conditions of revolution were not present and that it should not be expected from the masses to take up arms.

   The organization's analysis was that the 'objective conditions of revolution' were present (as explained by comrade Ahmadzadeh in the organization's theoretical pamphlet *Armed Struggle, Both a Strategy and a Tactic*), that is, the masses would respond to the call of the vanguard .... This view, which assumes that the process of 'armed propaganda' is short-termed, certainly cannot value tactics which bear fruit in the long term .... Despite facts that confirmed the lack of the 'objective conditions of revolution,' we ignored this contradiction and continued our way, having faith in our victory! ... The painful blows of 1976 left no room for the duality of positions and finally a period of tenacious ideological struggle within the organization, comrade Jazani's theories were accepted as fundamental pillars of our identity and activities.[107]

   Although the appeal to join the guerrillas was quite strong amongst the youth, students and intellectuals, the working class and other toiling masses were not yet ready to confront the regime militarily and their protests took place in the political and economic realms.

2. The importance of political and industrial demands and the construction of the second leg – namely the political wing of the movement:
   The recognition that the objective conditions of revolution were not yet present leads the OIPFG to conclude that the masses cannot take arms and take part in the military operations at present.[108]
   Thus:
   Paying attention to political and corporate (*senfi*) activities earns such an importance for the armed movement that we consider it as its second leg.[109] It is worth noting that in our view, for Jazani, the logic of the political wing of the

movement was the same as the one adopted by the Irish Republican Army (IRA) and Sinn Féin, the political movement associated with it.

3. Underlining the Shah's autocracy as the main contradiction of the national liberation movement.

Distancing from Ahmadzadeh's theory and embracing Jazani's went hand in hand with re-examining the main slogan of the National Liberation Movement. The OIPFG now believed that

> If we want to determine the main characteristic of the present movement, we should say: This movement is against the Shah's dictatorship. In the meantime, we should be aware that the Shah's dictatorship has an organic correlation with the dominance of imperialism and dependent capitalism .... At present, armed movement is an anti-dictatorial drive and a phase in the National Liberation Movement of the masses which, by relying on the slogan of 'Down with the Shah', and highlighting the economic demands of the people, tries to mobilize the revolutionary forces and take the leadership of the people's democratic revolution.[110]

Meanwhile, the OIPFG published a pamphlet explaining its differences with the Tudeh Party in fighting against the Shah's dictatorship. In that pamphlet the OIPFG took a clear stand against the Tudeh Party's slogan of forming 'an anti-dictatorial united front'. The pamphlet reiterates that the Tudeh Party's anti-dictatorial front has no constraints and can include any dissident in its ranks, even the 'realists' and 'farsighted factions' of the ruling clique. The OIPFG considered such a front dangerous and in the service of the ruling classes, not a vehicle to serve the Democratic Revolution of the masses – a revolution which would completely transform the lives of working peoples. In other words, even though the OIPFG had no problem sounding like a divergent array of political groupings in denouncing the Shah's dictatorship (including the 'realist' and 'far-sighted' fractions of the regime), it perceived the progress of the revolution only by taking distance and making its differences crystal clear with its adversaries.[111]

The history folds on its own term and bears no indulgence for deferred pronouncements and prolonged deliberations. As the OIPFG overcame its fundamental contradictions and ideological inconsistencies, society's socio-economic crisis evolved into a full-blown political crisis. Jimmy Carter, the new president of the United States (1977–81) took a different approach towards the Shah's regime. Within a short period, the crisis intensified and brought about the 'objective conditions of the revolution'. However, for the OIPFG it was not easy to admit this fact, nor reassess the situation. Qorbanali 'Abdolrahimpour (Majid) was among the first who, in May/June 1978, admitted that the objective conditions of revolution were present.[112]

In fact, the OIPFG adopted Jazani's thesis at a time when some of these theories no longer applied. Much later and only after the Jaleh Square massacre of 7 September 1978,[113] some cadres who had opposed 'Abdolrahimpour reached the same conclusion and adopted his position. In November 1978, the organization published a leaflet titled *Qiyam ra Bavar Konim* (Let's Believe in the Insurrection) written by Farrokh Negahdar who had joined the organization shortly after being freed from prison, emphasizing the 'presence of the objective conditions of the revolution'.

> The insurrection has started. Today at the peak of this revolutionary situation, when all Iranian people have become united as one and call for the overthrow of the Pahlavi dynasty, the OIPFG asks all freedom fighters to help in organizing the peoples struggle on the streets ... Let's believe in the insurrection.[114]

Jazani's viewpoint about the pivotal role of the armed struggle and the construction of the political organization of the movement had to do with the absence of the 'objective conditions of revolution'. The tragedy of history was that the acceptance of Jazani's point of view came too late. Jazani believed that in a 'revolutionary situation', when the masses were ready to rise, 'armed propaganda' by the vanguards would lose its significance and instead arming the masses would become pivotal.

Without a doubt, at a time when Mohammad Reza Shah's dictatorship was fighting for its survival and contact with the working class and various layers of the toiling masses had become feasible, one could not talk about 'armed propaganda' like before. In that crucial moment, the pivotal focus was to connect with the masses. *Fundamental Duties* did not take this important mission into consideration. However, the article 'More on Our Fundamental Duties' was not just about the necessity of people participating in the insurrection; in effect, it was yielding to the leadership of Ayatollah Khomeini and subordinating the Marxist-Leninist organization to the reactionary Shi'a forces whom they called the 'radical petit-bourgeoisie'. It should be noted that before the publication of the *Vazayef-e Asasi-ye Marksist Leninist-ha dar Marhaleh-ye Kunouni-ye Roshd Jonbesh Komunisti* (Fundamental Duties of Marxist-Leninists in the Present Stage of the Communist Movement in Iran) and *Baz Ham darbareh Vazayef-e Asasi* (More on our Fundamental Duties), no OIPFG theoretician had ever called the traditional Iranian petit-bourgeoisie and its clerical allies 'radical petit-bourgeoisie'. In fact, this term was first deployed in April 1978 to describe the viewpoint of Ayatollah Khomeini and his devotees and disciples. This term paved the way for Iran's leftist forces to support Ayatollah Khomeini in his crusade against the Shah's regime. It also presented a document which delineated all the principles of its ideology which later led the OIPFG Majority to follow Ayatollah Khomeini's line of thinking. This document, *Baz Ham Darbareh-ye Vazayef-e Asasi* (More on Our Fundamental Duties), promotes the necessity of alliance with the 'radical petit-bourgeoisie' at any cost and under the pretext of avoiding the 'unpleasant catastrophe' of the Tudeh Party's relationship with Mosaddeq. The letter concedes that the 'repressive measures of different wings of the petit-bourgeoisie' and its 'religious slant' should not be considered as an obstacle for the OIPFG to unite with them:

> Obviously, we are afraid that a scattering of Marxists who are fed up with the repressive measures of different wings of the petit-bourgeoisie – under the influence of such infantile disorders and mere imaginings of the present leadership of the non-working-class wing of the peoples' movement – will face the same deplorable disaster they went through with regards to Mosaddeq (national

bourgeoisie). A disaster that the working class is paying for up to today. There is only one difference: in those days, the leadership would consider other segments of the peoples' movement as reactionary and accused them of 'flirting with the Americans!' Today, they do this because of their 'religious inclinations'.[115]

The reason provided for this continuous effort to unite with the traditional Shi'a petit bourgeoisie was that the anti-imperialist struggle had priority over anti-dictatorship struggle.

It is evident that anti-imperialist struggle is not necessarily a struggle against capitalism, but rather, against the 'dependency' upon capitalism:

> In order to gain freedom, the contradiction between the masses and imperialism had to be resolved. Thus, it was more important to unite with the 'anti-imperialist petit bourgeoisie', or – to use the language of the text – the narrow minded, dogmatic, and religious, rather than approaching the liberals.
>
> Taking into consideration the little weight the liberal bourgeoisie carries within our movement, and the fundamental differences that exist between the petit-bourgeoisie and the liberal bourgeoisie, it is erroneous to confound the liberal bourgeoisie for the radical petit-bourgeoisie and to not recognize the distinct character of the radical petit bourgeoisie.[116]

As such, giving priority to the creation of the united anti-imperialist front meant that gaining freedom for the 'peoples' parties' should be hinged on raising slogans that do not intensify the contradictions within the front.

> Proposing and promoting the slogan 'Establishment of the Peoples' Democratic Republic' at present will only intensify the contradictions between non-proletariat currents and the workers' movement. No one with a sound mind could envision that intensification of animosities within the peoples' movement would promote friendship with the working-class.'[117]

The line of thought carried forward by Farrokh Negahdar was based on the slogan produced at the end of the open letter of the OIPFG to Ayatollah Khomeini on 18 January 1979, 'Let's Establish the People's Rule!'[118] In fact, Negahdar adopted the same slogan which appeared in the second foreword (July 1972) produced by the OIPFG for Ahmadzadeh's *Mobarezeh Mosallahaneh*:

> Thus, we strongly believed in the necessity of fighting for liberation movements in order to dismantle the puppet regime and establishing the People's Rule as an objective fact.[119]
>
> In the last half century, our country has witnessed the growth of this contradiction: the daily expansion of imperialist domination. Any form of transformation must resolve this contradiction. The resolution of this contradiction means the establishment of the people's rule and the downfall of imperialist domination.[120]

As such, political freedom is relegated to the moment in which the contradiction with imperialism is fully resolved. It is by the same token that anti-imperialist slogans of the traditional Shi'ite petit-bourgeoisie are vindicated. Subsequently, according to this strand of thought, little attention should be paid to the repressive measures of the petit-bourgeoisie forces in order to evade all obstacles for a future alliance with them.

Conclusion

The Fada'i Guerrillas had been at the forefront of the struggle against the Shah's dictatorship from the Siyahkal episode on 8 February 1971 through to the victory of the Revolution on 11 February 1979. They were also the founders and forerunners of a new communist movement in Iran. During those eight years, they maintained their political and intellectual independence from the polarized communist movement, avoided mimicking other global experiences and, based on Lenin's principle of 'concrete analysis of concrete situation', raised Iran's communist movement to a higher level. The military operations of this revolutionary organization always had a propagandistic character, despite the fact that in the first years of its formation, the organization was more inclined to Ahmadzadeh's viewpoint as opposed to Jazani's.

The OIPFG was not a homogeneous organization until 1974. The initiative to turn the organization into an ideological think tank between 1974 and 1976 played a role in strengthening the ideological identity of the guerrillas. Furthermore, it contributed to the internal cohesion of the organization. The execution and assassination of many of its cadres in 1975 and the fatal blows of 1976 threw the organization into a theoretical abyss. The formal acceptance of Jazani's viewpoints was only a posthumous antidote. It exacerbated the theoretical crisis of the OIPFG and its many supporters and sympathizers. With the rise of the popular movement against the Shah's establishment, the OIPFG lost ideological cohesion and the road was paved for a fierce contention to gain hegemony, the consequence of which was the final breakdown in the internal unity of the organization itself by 1980.

2

The labour movement in the words and deeds of the Iranian People's Fada'i Guerrillas

Touraj Atabaki

Introduction

The coup of 19 August 1953 was a turning point for the organized labour movement, which for more than a decade had cast a long shadow over Iran's political and social life. The years leading up to the coup had seen two different approaches towards organizing the labour movement. The first of these was taken by some of the early leaders of the labour movement, whose engagement with the labour activism and movement dated back to the time of Reza Shah. It included, for example, the organization of the memorable oil workers' strikes of May 1929 and the strike of the workers of the Vatan Textile Factory in Isfahan in May 1931. Among the early leaders of the labour movement were Yousef Eftekhari, 'Ali Omid and Rahim Hamdad. Benefitting from their experience in Iran's Communist Party and the labour movement of the interwar period, they sought to organize a labour movement that was independent from any political organization or party once released from prison in the aftermath of the Allied invasion of Iran in September 1941. Thus, they chose not to join the Tudeh Party or its affiliated union. The Trade Union of Workers and Peasants of Iran (TWPT) (*Ettehadiyeh-ye Kargaran va Barzegaran-e Iran*) was born out of this endeavour.

The second approach was that of the newly established Tudeh Party of Iran's union, the Central United Council (CUC) of Trade Union of Workers and Toilers of Iran (*Showra-ye Mottahedeh-e Markazi-ye Ettehadiyeh-ye Kargaran va Zahmatkeshan-e Iran*). The leader of this council, which benefitted from widespread Soviet-backed propaganda, came from within the Tudeh Party leadership and its members were loyal to the party.[1] After several years of unsuccessful attempts at organizing workers with no political allegiance, the TWPT could not continue competing with its rival union and was dissolved.[2] The destiny of CUC was not glistening either. Following the initial exceptional expansion of the Tudeh Party and its affiliated CUC by the end of 1940s and following the formal banning of the Tudeh Party in February 1949, the CUC continued its limited activities chiefly through its clandestine network. This led to the party's previously strong presence in the Iranian labour movement being weakened and at the end the CUC became nothing but a memory in the history of Iranian labour.

Post-coup crisis and the formation of the development state

One of the immediate outcomes of August 1953 coup was the wide-ranging repression overriding every corner of the political sphere in Iran. The coercive suppression of the Tudeh Party and its affiliated union, the CUC, resulted in party and union activists either being imprisoned or forced to emigrate. The years 1953–60 were a barren period: the labour movement hit rock bottom. Compared to the nationwide scale labour movement in the 1940s, in the post 1953 coup there are only fragmented provincial labour activities in some major labour-intensive complexes and industries. The strikes of the oil workers in 1957 and 1959, the brick-making workers of southern Tehran of 1957 and 1959, the Vatan Textile Factory of Isfahan in 1959 were among some of these salient protests. During these years, there was a union organized by the government under the name of the Congress of Iranian Workers Unions, representing Iranian government at the international podiums, including the annual conferences of the International Labour Organization (ILO).[3] However, the Congress of Iranian Workers Unions did not even feel obliged to publish, let alone convey the ILO endorsements for the improvement of the workers' living and working conditions to the Iranian authorities.

The economic recession of 1960–3 revitalized these disparate labour movements which had been hitherto poorly organized. Firstly, a number of political organizations which had been silenced following the 1953 coup, when the immediate imposition of martial law had led to widespread repression, were now able to organize themselves and once again come to the fore. The formation of the Second Jebheh-ye Melli (National Front) and the start of strikes and political protests are the hallmarks of these years, which were conducive to a deep political crisis. One of the consequences of this crisis was successive changes in the ruling cabinets. In May 1961, teachers organized a nationwide strike demanding a pay rise. During the protests of Tehran which took place in front of the parliament building, a teacher named Abolhassan Khan'Ali was shot dead by a policeman. This caused the resignation of the then-prime minister Ja'far Sharif-Emami. Nine months later, on 21 January 1962, the students of the University of Tehran, with the support of the National Front, went on strike. This protest was also coercively dispersed.

Surprisingly, in contrast to the 1940s, there was now no cooperation between the labour movement and other guilds or political movements. Each of these movements followed their own path, independent from and indifferent to other or others. The political movement's aim was to protest against the government which had seized power in the aftermath of the coup and against the repression which had ensued. Their goal was to open the window of opportunity just wide enough to let in a ray of light, allowing supporters of the anti-government movement to breathe easier and carry out their activities freely. The labour movement, in contrast, was indifferent to the turbulent political situation and remained focused on issues connected to ensuring the workers had money to put bread on the table. According to the Labour attaché at the US Embassy in Tehran, an assessment of the average cost of living for a worker's family was carried out at the request of the Ministry of Labour in 1960. The result was so shocking that the government refused to make it public. Though the average daily wage was 50 Rials, a family of four needed 178 Rials just to subsist.[4]

The result of the economic recession was an increase in labour protests and strikes.[5] The socio-political consequences of the economic recession worried the statesmen of the Pahlavi government. And, although the United States had itself played a part in the deepening of the economic recession, it now joined some Iranian government statesmen and similarly expressed its concerns. An atmosphere of concern had been discernible even before the Democratic government of John F. Kennedy had come to power in January 1961 but with the victory of the Democrats in the United States these fears became more apparent.

The post–Second World War period, particularly the 1960s, were the pinnacle of the 'anti-imperialist' movement, which was embedded in the ever-increasing tensions of the Cold War. The world coming out of the Second World War was characterized as the arena for new political realignment and economic and social reconstruction mainly through the agency of developmental states.[6] The United Nations called the post-war period and explicitly the 1960s as the decade of global and massive economic and political reform. In a language turn, the underdeveloped countries became known as members of the developing world and poised to leap over decades of economic stagnation and poverty. Authoritarian reform was chiefly confined within the boundaries of economic development aiming for a swift transition from hitherto pre-capitalist relations in order to avoid class and political conflict.

Following eight dark years of severe political despotism in Iran, a rally organized by the opposition, the National Front, in Jalaliyeh, north of Tehran in May 1961 called for an end to political exclusion and repression. Three months later, in August 1961, the Shah held his own rally in Doshan-Tappeh, east of Tehran, where he announced the introduction of a series of widespread economic reforms which he intended to implement.[7] A year and a half later, on 26 January 1963, a referendum was held on the Shah's initial program of reforms: a series of far-reaching socio-economic plans, later known as the White Revolution.

At the heart of the White Revolution was land reform. The state officials behind it hoped that this reform would upset existing pre-capitalist relations in rural areas and thus rapid capitalist economic growth would follow. Through this rapid growth, it was hoped that the pre-industrial stages of societal development could be skipped so that a society which was largely dependent on an agricultural economy might develop into a capitalist society capable of joining the global economy. Industrialization of the economy was fundamental for this process. The establishment of OPEC (Organization of the Petroleum Exporting Countries) in 1960 paved the way for the growing prosperity of oil-producing countries through increased oil revenues, and a smoother industrialization of their economies was also on the horizon.

On the objectives which brought OPEC into its existence, Fuad Rouhani, the first secretary general of OPEC, referred to the preamble to the Resolutions of the First OPEC Conference by saying:

> The desperate need for accelerated economic development amongst the so-called underdeveloped countries of the world is self-evident. Mankind has at its disposal today technical knowledge sufficient to ensure the necessary material comfort and security which we need for all. We must put this knowledge to work, and employ all our resources, both human and material, in order to combat the evils of hunger, sickness and lack of adequate shelter which still plague the majority of countries throughout the world. As a nation, we have the will power to do so. What we need now is to create a larger body of people familiar with already known techniques in agriculture, industry and commerce and to make the enormous investment required in each sector. The formation of these professional bodies and the investment of the huge sums required, will tax our financial resources to the utmost.
>
> ... In the face of these difficulties, the responsibility for channelling the resources of a nation towards economic development must lie with the government. Nowhere is this more true than in the great oil exporting nations, most of whom are members of OPEC, and earn almost all of their foreign exchange from payments by the oil companies exports of the nation's production of crude oil and refined petroleum products.[8]

The Third Development Plan (1962-7) provided the roadmap of this process. To register the land reform on his own record the Shah, however, insisted that the outcome of the reform should be detached from the Third Development Plan. The Third Development Plan, during its implementation, managed to secure national GDP growth of 8.8 per cent. Within this, the average annual growth share of industrial and mining sectors was 7.7 per cent.[9] In this period, migration of the workforce from rural to urban areas resulted in a decrease of the workforce in the agriculture sector and an increase in the labour force in urban industries. This, in turn, led to an increase in urban unemployment. Hundreds of thousands of villagers surged towards the cities. Of the total 950,000 newly created jobs, 623,000 were in the industrial and mining sectors during 1956-66. People employed in these sectors were predominantly from the excess labour force from rural areas. Between 1962 and 1968, from the total active labour force of the country (6.6 million in 1962 and 7.8 million in 1968) the share of the agricultural sector shrank by 6.1 per cent. This was despite the fact that the number of people employed in industrial sectors grew by 4.2 per cent to more than two million people.[10]

However, there was no trace of political development alongside the economic growth which occurred together with notable economic and social change. The exclusionary and coercive political practices was prevailing as before. While in the social sphere, change in the urban and rural relationship becoming more conspicuous, the political space was still suffering from the post-1953 coup repression. A strong female presence in all professions – including an increase in the number of female workers, widespread literacy programs, increased higher education opportunities, improved healthcare and communication networks among others – was the direct outcome of the practice of such a development state. The population mobility which was the outcome of these reforms led to increased rights of citizens whom the Shah, using leftist terminology, referred to as *Azad Mardan* (liberated men) and *Azad Zanan* (liberated women). Enforced top-down reforms together with increased powers of social forces from below resulted in demands from citizens for their rights. The political activists of this period could not ignore these developments.

With the start of the governmental reforms came great confusion among the various political parties and organizations which opposed the government. They were unsure on how to react to these governmental reforms, whether to support the reforms, oppose them or a combination of both. The protest slogans of the students from the University of Tehran at that time, 'yes to reforms, no to dictatorship', were soon adopted by many political organizations, including the National Front. The reaction of the Tudeh Party to the governmental reforms was influenced by the diplomatic relationship between the Soviet Union and Iran; it changed from rejection of the proposed reforms by Shah at the beginning of 1963 to welcoming it at the end of the same year.[11]

In words

In the autumn of 1967, when the Third Development Plan had ended, Bijan Jazani and his comrades published a study of Iranian society and the living standards of the different groups of workers and peasants. This study was later known as the *Tez-e Guruh-e Jazani-Zarifi* (Thesis of Jazani-Zarifi Group) or the Dilemmas of the Anti-imperialist and Liberation Movements of the Iranian Proletariat and the Main Responsibilities of the Iranian Communists. The main argument of this thesis was that:

> Following the coup of 19 August [1953], militarisation and the rule of a police state over socio-political milieus has become the regime's main underlying policy. This policy even at the peak of the regime's reform manoeuvres remained constantly in force .... The reform manoeuvres which the regime began since 1962 were not comparable to any previous reforms in terms of their form or content. When we use the word manoeuvre for the regime's reforms it does not mean that steps were not taken towards reforms .... Every manoeuvre leads to its own impact, depending on its depth and range and this impact in turn leads to change. A closer observation of the regime's current reform manoeuvres is important since some erroneously believe that the nadir of the political movement and silence of the people is due to these manoeuvres and this has hindered any progress the [political] movement might have made. However, in our opinion, although we do not refute some of the impacts of these manoeuvres, the main reason for the silence of Iranian society is indeed the unprecedented suppression and dictatorship which silences any opposition with bullets.[12]

Bijan Jazani, in the early years of the 1970s (probably 1974), in a treatise titled *Jam'bandi Mobarezat-e Si Saleh-e Akhir dar Iran* (The Conclusion of Thirty Years of Struggles in

Iran), discusses in more detail the effects of economic reforms of the 1960s on the class structure in Iran, particularly the working class at the end of this decade:

> The working class of today Iran has witnessed dramatic economic growth over the past two decades. The working-class of Iran can be divided into various stratums or subdivisions. These subdivisions specify the working-class as follows: unskilled workers, workshop workers and industrial workers are the three main categories. Agricultural workers are a new sector, whose numbers are growing ... The rapid growth of recent years has divided the working-class into two groups; new and old. Although both old and young workers, work in the same workshops or industrial complexes, in theory there are clear boundaries which divide them from each other. Old workers are distinguishable in terms of age, expertise, income, and family responsibilities. These older workers have experienced one or two periods of the economic and political movements. Despite relative conservativism and passivism, being less active because of their age and profession, they are relatively enjoying more class consciousness. However, their distance from the younger workers' groups together with their frustration caused by the unhealed wounds of the fruitless efforts of the previous two decades, pessimism and individual ambitions have all been huge obstacles to this consciousness being passed on to the younger generations. This binary opposition is largely apparent in the most important sector of the working-class, the industrial workers. These workers have often become professionals. While they receive better pay, they humiliate and look down on the new workers who lack any knowledge and culture of the working-class. The young generations of industrial and workshop workers have a higher level of education than those of the previous generation. Some of these workers come from urban and petty-bourgeoisie backgrounds. In contrast, the older generation often have rural roots. Although the young labourers lack the work culture, they have clear-cut socio-political demands which derive from their urban origins and the preferences have recently developed in the rural areas. The number of industrial workers of state and private sectors in manufacturing and mining (such as oil, electricity, energy, mines etc.) is nearly 350,000. While the workers of traditional workshops (such as masons, tailors/dressmakers, blacksmiths, print house workers, urban carpet weavers, workshop spinners and weavers) and non-industrial workers (such as railroad workers, transport workers, bus and urban drivers, hotel, hostel and restaurant workers, public bathhouse workers, barbers and hairdressers) are more numerous than the industrial workers and total at least 600,000 people. The unskilled construction and road workers fluctuate in different seasons but on average, the number employed in this sector is estimated at 400,000 to 500,000. In this respect, the working-class by economic definition makes up approximately 18 percent of the total number of the country's employees. If we add agricultural and seasonal daily paid employees to this number and add it into the countless number of unemployed, this would make up 25 percent of the total employed and those actively seeking employment. This means that the Iranian working-class never reached such a number. This labour force produces nearly 50 percent of the total national production.[13]

Masoud Ahmadzadeh (1945–1972), in his book *Mobarezeh-ye Mosalahaneh, ham Estrateji, ham Taktik* (Armed Struggle, Both Strategy and Tactic), which carries the date of summer 1970, discusses the outcome of the land reform programme and addresses the different stages of its implementation, an indication that his group, known as Pouyan-Ahmadzadeh-Meftahi cluster, had studied the economic changes of the 1960s prior to turning to armed struggle. In the words of Ahmadzadeh

> The goal of the so-called White Revolution was to extend the influence of imperialism in urban and rural areas …. [But] what was the reason that the regime consciously chose to eradicate feudalism which constituted its main social base? Does this mean that the end of feudalism was only a pretence? Or could it be said that feudalism was not the main social base of the regime? If feudalism was not indeed the main social base of the regime, then which economic power was represented by the government and which political will was persuaded by the government? The truth be told, the answer is that this power is world imperialism … Only a central power, supported and controlled by imperialism could safeguard the economic interests of the feudalists. This central power had to initiate the spread of imperialistic control, while at the same time suppressing the anti-imperialist movement of the people. In fact, feudalism changed into dependent feudalism and wherever this dependency was rejected, the central power [government] immediately acted. With the expansion of the authority of the central power and the influence of imperialism, feudalism was increasingly pushed out of the power bases. When the feudal economy conflicted with the interests of imperialism, without facing a serious problem or needing the help of people for the suppression of feudalism, the regime buried a feudalism which was already in demise.[14]

In Ahmadzadeh's view, the removal of feudalism was accompanied by the expansion of political strangulation:

> Here there are no spontaneous mass movements as there should have been expected, and if there are, they are limited and scattered in terms of time period, place and scope. Here, there are no noticeable working-classes or labour organizations. In general, the workers are not well-informed about any opposition movements. And if some elements of consciousness develop amongst some workers enabling them to form small circles of their own, in practice these circles, are not capable of propagating and promoting mass labour activities. The lack of widespread spontaneous movements which is inextricably linked with the harsh police state has practically distanced workers from any political views or actions. As a result of this situation, the workers lack any experience of fighting, class organization or even trade-union consciousness. Consequently, workers' groups who consider organising a political opposition movement are few and there is practically no significant relationship between the intellectual circles and these workers. Thus, in this respect the workers are not ready to accept political leadership and develop class consciousness. The worker would be ready to be

involved in political movement, accept socialist consciousness, and ready to be organized in political party and trade union, only after years of spontaneous economic and trade union activities. Here, where any labour movement is immediately suppressed, it is natural that the labouring mass avoids the political struggle. The Political activity requires consistency, organization, and an overall acceptance of discipline. It also calls for consciousness and altruism. In a situation where the workers are inevitably tied to cope with their everyday needs, it would be neither possible for them to accept political struggle, nor believe in it. In the absence of any notable spontaneous mass movements, it is not possible to witness the formation of widespread labour circles.[15]

In a note at the end of the treatise we read:

We do not deny the possibility of communication with the workers. We have enjoyed a great deal of cooperation from our workers comrades. We mean that there is no possibility of communication with the workers, in the real sense and in its traditional form. It is possible to work amongst workers. It is possible to recruit them, though of course with great difficulty and with very low outcome. But it is not possible to rally the majority of these groups of people. It is not possible to propagate and perform propaganda work.[16]

It is clear that the reference to the inability of mass work among the workers was due to the police state control that had cast its long shadow over workplaces. Later in his study, Ahmadzadeh further analyses the situation:

Discussing an independent labour movement in the current situation in Iran is nonsense. The main conflict in our society is between people and imperialism, and overshadows more minor conflicts such as the distinct contradiction between labour and capital. Moreover, the suffocating political pressure politicises any social movement and makes the emergence of an independent labour movement less probable. The political struggle in our society is inevitably an armed struggle. Therefore, a self-conscious working-class does not emerge from a labour movement; it is, rather formed out of an armed mass struggle. The purpose of the newly formed groups must be to unite not only the members of the working-class but every other member of society. Relying upon the entire community, these groups must be the voice of the common demands of people. Our terrain is where we can fight effectively and unite people most successfully.[17]

In his *Mobarezeh-ye Mosallahaneh*, Ahmadzadeh mentions the difficulties that he believes are obstacles in the formation of the working-class movement. These obstacles are all reduced to imperialistic policies, the oppressive practices of political establishment and the replacement of labour-capital conduction by the people-imperialism. However, a different analysis is offered by Amir-Parviz Pouyan in his treatise *Zarourat-e Mobarezeh-ye Mosallahaneh va Rad-e Teori-ye Baqa'* (The Necessity of Armed Struggle and Rejection of the Theory of Survival). The date of the treatise is the spring 1970 and was written a few months before Ahmadzadeh's work. In *Zarourat-e Mobarezeh-ye Mosalahaneh*, Pouyan does not focus on the socio-economic changes of the 1960s. He is instead more concerned with the consequences of these changes in influencing the behaviour of the working class and labouring poor:

> The process a worker goes through in his transformation into a disciplined revolutionary agent is a long, challenging and complicated one. Our experience indicates that the workers, even the young ones, despite being dissatisfied with their situation, are not very interested in political education. We can work out the reason for this. The lack of any tangible political contact and awareness has led to some degree of acceptance of the prevailing culture of society. Young workers, in particular, spend their limited leisure hours and few savings on despicable petty-bourgeois entertainments. Most of them have developed lumpen characteristics. During work hours, if they have the opportunity to have a conversation, they try to waste the working hours by vulgar gossiping. Those who read books are absorbed in the most sordid and reactionary contemporary literatures. By preventing any political mass movements and encouraging easily accessible entertainments, our enemy is trying to persuade our workers to accept despicable petty-bourgeois entertainments and in this way spread the anti-venom of any political consciousness …. In factories and wherever labour power has become a commodity, whether governmental or private, flagrant exploitation is rampant. If we express their agony using words, they feel this oppression with their skin and flesh. We write about their sufferings, but they must endure it constantly. Nevertheless, they tolerate this situation and patiently accept it. They try to lessen the pain by seeking solace in petty-bourgeois entertainments. Why? Several reasons for this can be summed up thus: they consider their enemy's power and their inability to escape the enemy's dominance as absolute facts. How can one be liberated with absolute weakness against absolute power? It is precisely this assumption that induces disinterest and even mockery to political discussions as a disapproving reaction to their lack of power amongst workers.[18]

In an addendum to this treatise, dated 10 June 1971, the OIPFG added: 'The fact that pioneer labour groups which have been shaped in connection with the proletariat and organized through spontaneous struggles do not exist, has made any relationship with the proletariat largely, does not mean that we cannot be in touch with pioneer workers individually. In our movement we have had many examples of pioneer activist workers.'[19]

Bijan Jazani too, in an analysis of the position of the revolutionary forces in Iran, without mentioning Pouyan's name, explicitly criticizes him:

> One of the social characteristics of our society is the position of the petty bourgeois in relation to the working-class. While, in relation to the historical weakness of the industrial bourgeoisie, the working-class in its true sense has not developed in our society, the urban petty bourgeoisie has significantly developed. The backwardness of workshop production, the size and the hierarchy of the distribution and finally

the extended bureaucracy which is in out of proportion to the productive force of society have caused the various groups of the petty bourgeoisie to grow. The social and economic weakness of the working-class has manifested itself in the qualitative retardation of this class in comparison to the national bourgeoisie and petty bourgeoisie. Therefore, the growth of a petty bourgeoisie has always been a prerequisite for the quality growth of this disproportionality, which is the undeniable characteristic of our society (and is often observed in dependent and oppressed societies) and has always been evident. This fact has laid the groundwork for significant development in various areas .... Despite this historical deficiency which has continued until today, the working-class in the years prior to its defeat [1953], had a much higher level of class consciousness and culture compared to the present-day. The economic and political processes which were launched after August 1941, and culminated in the coup of 1953, played an essential role in consolidating self-consciousness amongst the working-class. In fact, a working-class without its class consciousness and solidarity is a dispersed mass lacking revolutionary spirit. Working collectively with machinery in close proximity to others provides a platform for first economic and then political empathy and solidarity. The worker's culture which is the outcome of his/her material life does not develop immutably, as soon as a worker begins working in an industry or workshop. It is part of a long process together with economic, social and political processes in relation with other classes and groups through understanding his/her social status against other classes. Our working-class is aware of its own culture and possesses enough class consciousness; to undergo such processes. The most important part of the working-class in Iran, that is, workers who today are aged between 18 and 30 have had very limited class consciousness and yet their class culture has not been substituted by their previous culture (of peasant and petty bourgeoisie). This group of labouring class focuses mainly on their own personal problems and shortcomings. They are not aware of their collective power; they do not trust each other, and they attempt to solve their problems individually. Any small-scale collective actions that the working class has achieved over the past two decades have been so limited that they have failed to familiarise the new generation of working-class with any class consciousness or culture. Those who are talking about the degeneration of the working-class or about the influence of the non-labour culture on this class must realise that what is happening is not the degeneration or the substitution of another culture instead of the labour culture. It is rather the result of a young, inexperienced, and underdeveloped working-class culture. Unfortunately, without the development of collective activities of the working-class, the working-class will never miraculously acquire a well-developed culture of class consciousness. This development would in the beginning be predominantly economic (in the form of protests and strikes over economic issues). Without self-awareness, the working-class will be unable to achieve its historical mission. That is the objective root of the today's deficiencies in the working-class movement.[20]

A re-examination of the ideas of all three of the pioneering guerrilla movement theorists of the labour movement of the 1960s – Jazani, Ahmadzadeh and Pouyan – with regard to the labour movement in Iran demonstrates that in his analysis Jazani focuses on the history of this movement, the existence of various groups within this class and the culture of each group. These criteria are missing in Ahmadzadeh's and Pouyan's analysis. But what all three have in common regarding the class struggles of the workers is the fact that, for them, class struggle is nothing but an organized and structured confrontation. While evaluating the economic situation of the workers and the working class's spontaneous acts, Jazani's structuralist and political understanding of the labour movement is evidenced by his description of what he terms 'political movements or organized economic movements', which 'have connections to the working-class and its ideology and is the political or economic representative of this class'.[21] Such an interpretation of the labour movement means accepting the hegemony of politics and culture in the realm of everyday life. Of course, none of these theorists denied this hegemony, and what is more, by highlighting the political repression following the 1953 coup, they considered the 'destruction of the regime's suppression machine' as the main purpose of the struggle of the fledgling communist movement.[22]

In deeds

Before dealing with the deeds of the Fada'is, we need to mention the actions of the political activists prior to the beginning of the guerrilla phase. Contact with factory workers and poor labourers was a concern for many Iranian Marxist activists and intelligentsia in the 1960s and 1970s. This was not limited to the followers of armed struggle. Through contact with the workers three approaches were developed. First, to adapt the lifestyle of workers. Second, to better understand society from the perspective of the various groups of workers, in particular an understanding of the rapid economic and social developments that were taking place. In this context, there were reports of labour activities with the aim of creating better living and working conditions. And finally, the third approach was to encourage workers to be involved in various political campaigns. In the absence of any labour institutions and organizations, such as trade unions, it was necessary for left-wing activists who were non-workers (majority of them) to distance themselves from their class roots and join the army reserves of the labour force. In the narratives of followers of the guerrilla movements in this book some examples have been mentioned.

In contrast, the labour activities of the 1960s and 1970s took a different form than those that the political activists remembered or had recently heard about. In Iran in the 1950s and 1960s, the activities of workers to improve their working and living conditions can be identified by three features which date back to the years prior to the 1953 Coup: the first consisted of the unorganized workers' movement, which was itself the result of the vanquished labour organizations after the coup. The second was the limiting of workers' demands of the economic improvement and a move away from political demands. The third was the acceptance of a flexible approach. In many cases, the workers elected representatives who relied on administrative solutions to pursue their economic demands and were also successful in that regard. This process was prevalent especially in the 1960s, a decade of economic reform.

In 1959, the Supreme Council of Labour approved the bill for the registration of the workers' unions after debating about the general principles of the bill for many years. Subsequently, fifty unions were established in Tehran and Isfahan during a period of just six months. These organizations were mostly gatherings of the groups of workers who worked together rather than a union in its modern sense.[23] These unions were organizations formed with the approval of security services and the Ministry of Justice, and their leaders were trained in the syndicate-based courses which were organized by the US government in Iran.[24] In voicing their demands, workers sometimes used the capabilities of these unions. In Bijan Jazani's view,

> It should not be forgotten that these fake and regulated unions impose the idea of solidarity and unity on the working-class. For the young masses of the working-class, these unions represent their class rights for communal organization and struggle. Conscious workers and political movements connected to the working-class must use these possibilities carefully to initiate a movement and strengthen the working-class culture.[25]

By the year 1972, the number of such unions, largely established in large manufacturing complexes, including the oil industry, came to more than five hundred.[26]

The demands of the working class were not always pursued through these unions. The strikes of the workers of the Tehran Bus Company (1964 and 1965), taxi drivers (1965) and groups of workers of the oil industry (1965 and 1969) were among those which formed spontaneously and without previous planning. Pay raises and objections to being dismissed from their jobs were the general demands of these protests. In March 1970, more than four thousand workers of the Abadan Refinery and its related industries staged a strike to protest the Oil Company's scheme of classifying workers' ranks. The strike, which lasted twenty days, eventually came to an end with the demands of the workers being accepted and even the payment of salaries which had been deducted during the strike period being reimbursed. There are reports indicating that the workers held up photos of the Shah and placards with quotes from the Shah and the role of the workers in the White Revolution during the strike and the protest.[27] There is also a narrative that at their meetings the workers shielded themselves with large posters of the Shah to protect themselves from the onslaught of the police and security services, so that the attackers could only enter the meeting venue by tearing down his portraits.[28] Of course, not all workers' protests of this period had such an outcome. One such example happened in March 1972 – after a few days of strikes and demands for a pay raise, 2,000 workers of the Jahan Chit (Jahan Textile) decided to march towards Tehran from Karaj to protest in front of the labour office. This was due to the fact that Mohammad Sadeq Fateh Yazdi, the factory owner, had not paid attention to their protests. On the way to Karvansara Sangi (in the outskirts of Tehran), the gendarmerie forces stopped the marchers and opened fire on them. Three years later, on 23 July 1974, OIPFG guerrillas assassinated Fateh Yazdi while he was on his way to work. Following the assassination, the OIPFG published a statement in which we read:

The People's Revolutionary Trial condemned Fateh for the major role he played in the massacre of the workers of Jahan-Chit. He was condemned to death for his wrongdoings and suppression of the workers. The bloodthirsty Fateh faced justice for his appalling acts. With the execution of Fateh, the OIPFG declares its armed and unconditional support for the rightful struggles of the workers throughout Iran. The organization also warns the enemy that it will not remain silent when faced with any crime committed against the working class in Iran.[29]

The armed struggle began with Siyahkal following the growing oppressive political obstruction of the late 1960s. It is possible to categorize the phases of the OIPFG lifespan from the beginning until the Revolution (1971–9) from different perspectives. Sometimes these periods also overlap. The Fada'is' armed actions in relation to the labour movement can be categorized into three periods. First, the 'planning and strengthening of the armed action process', a period of three years, running from February 1971 to 1974. In February 1974, the first issue of the *Nabard-e Khalq* was published. The first issue was an internal publication of the OIPFG. Two months later, the second issue of *Nabard-e Khalq* was published, no longer internally. On its first page it heralded 'the beginning of a new era in the development of the movement'. This was an era which marked 'the end of the movement in its preliminary stage and the stabilisation of the pioneering armed organization in the society'.[30] The second period, 'the period of alliance with populace forces, including the workers', covered the period from 1974 to the massive assaults by the government on the OIPFG in 1976. And the third period lasted from the aftermath of the assaults of 1976 until the 1979 Revolution.

From the first period, besides the records belonging to the OIPFG, there are other remaining narratives that we have included in this book. During this period, among the pioneers of the OIPFG, there were workers who had previously been involved in armed actions. The forerunners included Hassan Nowrouzi (1945–1973); Sa'id Payan (–1974); Eskandar Sadeqinezhad (1940–1971), a member of metalworkers' syndicate; Jalil Enferadi (1940–1971), member of the metalworkers' syndicate and Yousef Zarkari (1952–1973). During the three-year period of the 'planning and strengthening' which included the first three years from Siyahkal to 1973 the main goal of the Fada'is was to reinforce the armed struggle strategy. They also encouraged the political activists to establish political-military organizations as a pivot to overcome political passivity and to pave the way for social struggle. Bijan Jazani was still in prison during this period, and his opinions on activity among the workers and labour movement were still not widely discussed among the armed movement's followers.

Hamid Ashraf, who was a disciple of Bijan Jazani, and at that time held a position of authority within the Organization, did not prevent the Organization from paying particular attention to the theories of Pouyan and Ahmadzadeh. In *Jam'bandi Seh Saleh*, we read:

> At the end of 1969, the [Ahmadzadeh] group was confronted with serious obstacles while promoting political activity in terms of attracting proletarian elements. The regime's coercive institutions ... prevented workers from engaging in political

struggle or even economic acts. During those days, the comrades who had reviewed the outcomes of their activities and had an in-depth understanding of the general mood and the suffocating situation of the workers in Iran, concluded that political activity by itself was ineffective in the current situation. They believed that solely political acts would not inspire the working class to fight. They assumed that what made the workers reluctant to join the movement was a feeling of complete inability among the working-class who were not part of a labour union to fight against the absolute power of the enemy. Furthermore, they sought new plans that would remove this binary opposition notion from the minds of the working-class and other potential revolutionaries. The aim of this plan was to revive new political hopes in the minds of the oppressed people of our homeland. Based on this thinking, the comrades considered guerrilla warfare a strategy to create a new political atmosphere in the society. After extensive studies and discussions in the triangle teams [teams of three people], the results of these studies were published in *Zarourat-e Mobarezeh-ye Mosallahaneh* and *Mobarezeh Mosallahaneh, Ham Estrateji, Ham Taktik*. Of course, throughout the spring of 1970, these two works were discussed, and most of the triangle teams, who were the best progressive forces of their time, confirmed the content of these two treaties.[31]

In terms of what directly linked the OIPFG to the workers, the treaties refer to plans which were not actualized due to logistics, such as: 'On 17 May 1971 a central meeting was held to assess the situation and it was planned that the Pars-Americ factory, whose workers were acquainted with comrade Jalil Enferadi, would begin operation the following week. This was postponed due to too many complexities.'[32] We do not know more about the Pars-Americ operation. Or in another case, we know that the Fada'is were seriously thinking to disturb the festivities associated with the 2500th anniversary of the Foundation of the Persian Empire:

> Of course, we had many ideas about this. For example, a primary objective was to attract the workers in numbers by occupying the factories and setting dialogues with the workers. We had also planned to address the specific needs of the workers of each factory. But in practice it was noticeably not feasible for these ambitions to be achieved quickly.[33]

It is possible to interpret such references in *Jam'bandi-ye Seh Saleh* as an intention to propagate armed struggle with the perspective of supporting workers' industrial actions. It is noteworthy to underscore that while this work is intended to cover the Fada'i activities over a period of three years (1971–4), it covers only a period of less than a year, the first in the Organization's lifespan. We do not know what has happened to the rest of the treatise. According to Heydar Tabrizi, the handwritten version of the treatise which he had read in 1975 was longer than what remains of it today. 'I do not know if other comrades had seen the full version of this essay. I have also not heard from anyone who had seen the full version of this treatise, but as far as I can recall, the handwritten copy of this treatise which I had read in 1975 was longer than the version that exists today and it also had more sections.'[34]

According to the Fada'is, the second period was supposed to be a period in which the armed struggle would be established among the political activists opposing the government. In this period Bijan Jazani was still in prison, and Hamid Momeni, who had joined the Organization with his followers, was gradually beginning to formulate the policies of the Organization, especially with regard to the labour movement, although the Organization's leadership was still in the hands of Hamid Ashraf. According to Heydar Tabrizi:

> 1974 was the year of some major armed operations. Later that year, the idea of … reducing armed operations and making changes in the structure of the Organization was raised by Hamid Ashraf. Hamid Ashraf's assessment was that the Organization had launched a military struggle, and that it was time to halt the armed struggle and focus on improving the quality of the Organization. Based on this assessment, in 1975 Hamid Ashraf called for an end to the period of large-scale operations and the beginning of a period of smaller but significant operations.[35]

In this period, according to Heydar Tabrizi, supporting the labour movement along with establishing a wide networking with the workers was increasingly highlighted in the internal discussions of the Fada'is. In particular, in analysing the impacts and consequences of Fateh-e Yazdi's assassination, the intra-organizational discussions focused further on the necessity of organizing political networks amongst the workers. In connection with these discussions Heydar Tabrizi also wrote a pamphlet in which he highlighted 'the need to expand the workers' political and trade union struggles to establish a link between the Fada'is and the workers'. Furthermore, he talked about the idea of 'sending out comrades to the factories overtly and creating unconcealed teams whose members could perform activities in the manufacturing complexes'.[36] The outcome of these discussions as reflected in the fifth issue of *Nabard-e Khalq*:

> Sure enough, there are workers that, under the influence of old-timers and crippled ancient opportunists, think that the [Fada'i] Organization is against any trade union, economic and political struggle of the working class. Hence, they believe that armed struggle can lead to separation from the masses. With such a presumption it is not strange that they think like that. But the fact is that we are not at all against the trade union-economic-political struggles of the working class, which would promote the revolutionary character of the workers, but rather, on the contrary, we believe the mass of workers by initially participating in this struggle, would regain their class consciousness. The objective observation of our comrades also confirms the view that the masses of workers must launch collective actions and economic strikes, to expand and develop their revolutionary movements. It is only by then that they would be drawn to a higher level of struggle.[37]

Another identifier of the second period is a shift in the position of Bijan Jazani's ideas in the OIPFG and the publication of his treatise entitled 'On the Unity and the Strategic Role of the OIPFG' in the sixth issue of *Nabard-e Khalq*.[38] The importance of this article, at first glance, could be in addressing the unity of the existing revolutionary movements of that period in Iran, whether specific or general ones, as well as discussing 'the Jebheh [Front] and the Party'. But another important point, which may have not been discussed sufficiently, was the emphasis of Jazani on 'using all the means of the labour movement':

> If in the past our major task was to start the armed struggle, if achieving this goal was worth paying any price for, even suffering very destructive attacks, today, the armed movement has become an objective process and despite the painful blows that the OIPFG have endured due to being the pioneers of this struggle, they will courageously continue their campaign. It is no longer possible to carry out their duties according to the previous plan. Today the duty of the OIPFG as the most progressive movement of the armed struggle is to understand the weaknesses and shortcomings of the armed struggles. This would help us to develop this movement and to direct the forces that have joined the movement, utilizing the best of the ideology of the working class and the revolutionary experiences of Iran and the world. Today, we try to unite and organize the revolutionary forces of the working class, using all the means of the labour movement, and establish the armed struggle under the banner of the OIPFG.[39]

What Jazani precisely alludes to by the 'use of all the means of the labour movement' remains very vague.

The execution of Bijan Jazani and his comrades in April 1975 coincided with other events. Discussions about these developments had already been under way for some time at this stage. According to Heydar Tabrizi, 'The views of Bijan, which leaked out of prison, played a very important role in this regard. Following the execution of Bijan and his comrades, Jazani was introduced as the author of works which had been hitherto published anonymously. Jazani's ideas were approved in the sixth issue of *Nabard-e Khalq*, which increased the importance of Bijan's ideas.'[40]

Heydar Tabrizi also notes that in a new strategy which the OIPFG had adapted with Hamid Momeni playing a leading role in proposing,

> the importance of organising the workers' trade union struggles became more important, and interaction with workers gradually played a major role in the deeds of the Organization. In summer 1975, the central organ of the OIPFG endorsed the Organization's strategy in relation to workers and decided that 80 percent of the Organization's efforts would be concentrated on the reinforcement of the workers' movement and special issues of *Nabard-e Khalq* for workers would be published.[41]

In late 1975, *Nabard-e Khalq Vizheh-e Kargaran* (Nabard-e Khalq for Workers) was published. This was different from the earlier *Nabard-e Khalq*. At the same time, the OIPFG published another publication, this time for the university students: *Payam-e Daneshjou*. Following the new political approach and paying more attention to the working class in 'The roadmap of the OIPFG for the university students' movement', which was published in the first issue of the *Payam-e Daneshjou*, we read:

Doing labour work during the summer holidays in urban and rural areas is the best way to observe the true situation of society. Indeed, it is useful to do all different levels of labour from unskilled work to that of skilled workers. But if working as an unskilled worker is difficult for those from comfortable bourgeoisie backgrounds, it is better that they learn some skills and then go to work.[42]

Later, 'the roadmap' suggests that the university students should organize a 'worker-student core'. This would enable them to individually go among the workers to establish a link with them if links with the Organization were weak.[43]

According to Qorbanali 'Abdolrahimpour, 'since the middle of 1975 some workers' team … with the aim of political activity and attracting workers were formed in the factories'.[44] As Heydar Tabrizi states, these teams were responsible to prepare workers' report, establishing connection with the workers, which was very hard, as well as observing the work environment for the distribution of the organization's declarations and possible military operations.[45] According to the same narrator, during this period, the reports of protests and spontaneous strikes were significantly increased in the declaration distributed by the Organization and later published in *Nabard-e Khalq*. Reports of labour protests and strikes in Tehran, Tabriz, Abadan and Mazandaran were also published on this issue.[46]

During this period, the Fada'i narrators make references on how the Fada'is carried out activities in the workplace amongst the workers. They all point out that they have been working hard to persuade the workers to move from a trade union act to a political one by circulating the statements at a time when workers were protesting and striking. This was mainly done by circulating statements in front of the factories by using a machine which became active by using gunpowder. According to Marziyeh Shafi' this task was performed by the female members of the Organization.

> We placed the machine in the populated districts or in front of the factories. This was mainly done by the female comrades who carried the machine under their veil (*chadors*). We estimated the time when the workers would finish their work and about ten minutes before the workers would leave the workplace, the timer of the machine would act, and the leaflets would be spread and circulated. We were very careful so that when machine acted it would not hurt the people. When the factory was closed, the workers would see the papers on the ground around the factory and many of them took them. At this stage, female comrades wearing *chadors* in the vicinity of the factory would pass through there in ordinary guise and observe the reaction of the workers.[47]

In another narrative, 'Abbas Hashemi, also a member of the OIPFG, recalls his activities in the factory with reference to the semi-overt connections of the workers' teams of the Organization. He mentions that in the factory they only carried cyanide and did not take guns. They performed more strict security considerations in connection to the workers.[48]

Examples of worker's reports from that period which were published in the *Nabard-e Khalq* refer to the new approach of guerrillas and their emphasis on their presence in workplaces and the not necessarily armed support of these protests. The seventh issue of *Nabard-e Khalq* refers to 'the strikes of the workers in Tehran':

> On the eve of May Day, at the same time as the bogus congress of workers, organized by the regime in Tehran, major strikes were staged in the factories in Tehran.[49] Our comrades from the Organization who were closely observing the strikes, informed the Organization about the desire of the workers to unite with the students and the people of the city. In response to this request of the striking workers our Organization immediately took action and with issuing a proclamation invited the students and people to support the rightful strikes of the workers in Tehran. In reply to this workers' proclamation of our Organization, university students staged a strike in support of the strikes of the workers in Tehran. Despite the severe police state control which make gatherings difficult the fighting students gathered together in *Meydan-e E'dam* [E'dam Square in Tehran]. They held up placards in supporting the rightful workers of Tehran. On the placards of the students this sentence was manifested: We have responded to our mentors and we are standing in support of the strike of the workers in Tehran.[50]

The aforementioned narratives of the OIPFG concerning the escalation of labour strikes during the second period are not groundless or imaginary. The year 1972 came to an end with two workers' strikes in the industrial section. But in the same section in 1973 the number increased to twenty and in 1974 to twenty-four, in 1975 to twenty-seven and finally in 1976 reached to the highest record of thirty-five.[51] The increasing number of the workers' strikes during the second period – the period that according to the Fada'is the armed struggle was approved among the opposition political activists – could prove the influence of the Fada'is on the workers opposition movement. It is worthy to note here that the number of workers' strikes dropped to fifteen at once in 1977 after suffering the knock-on effects of the blows against the Fada'i leadership of 1976.[52] One explanation of this decline could be interpreted as the impact of the Fada'is on the everyday life of labour.

The third period began with the knock-on effects of 1976 and lasted until February 1979. Since the final months of 1975, the OIPFG suffered very heavy blows and persecution. Despite the fact that the OIPFG issued a statement in October 1976 asserting that repression could not break the backbone of the armed struggle and that 'the armed struggle of the Iranian masses had gone through its first phase of planning and establishment of the armed struggle among the pioneer groups and is about to enter its second phase of its spreading among the masses'.[53] Nevertheless, the 1976 assault on the OIPFG turned to be the concluding moment in a period of its existence. Following the 1976 assault on the OIPFG, a new period in its history commenced, which could be characterized by incoherence both in the OIPFG organizational functionality as well as its political consistency.[54] In this phase, Bijan Jazani's guidelines became more popular among the sympathizers of the OIPFG. But the heavy losses suffered by the organizations on the one hand and the developing political events which led to the revolution of 1979 on the other did not yield any opportunity for a serious reconsideration of words and deeds of this Organization.

The first priority was that of preserving what was remaining of the Organization.[55] And then it is the day-to-day unfolding of the events of the revolution that threw the surviving elements of the 1976 blows from one corner to another. The OIPFG might have been able to better re-evaluate its past had the revolutionary process of 1978–9 not occurred.

Iran witnessed rapid, significant but uneven socio-economic growth together with the severely undeveloped political system during the 1960s and 1970s. This situation became the harbinger of crises which occurred in the mid-1970s. Uneven distribution of wealth, social services and opportunities which were the result of rapid but uneven growth, which in turn was conducive to the widening of sociopolitical gaps. In a report prepared by the International Labour Organization in 1972, Iran was one of the countries which had the most uneven distribution of income.[56] In 1972, the average income of the working population of the country was 1,248 Rials. This reached 1,569 Rials in the cities and 660 Rials in the urban areas in 1978. During the same year, the income of civil servants working for the government was 2.2 times more than that of workers employed by the government and 3.4 times more than workers in the private sector.[57]

Another indication of this uneven development was a large-scale migration of the workforce from rural to urban areas, which was conducive to an uncontrolled growth of squatter settlements. In the space of fifteen years, the population of Iran increased from 23 million in 1961 to 34 million in 1976. Cities experienced a double increase of population, from 8 million to 16 million, whereas rural areas witnessed a lower increase of 15 million to 18million.[58] The maximum growth occurred in Tehran with an increase from 2.7 million to 4.5 million in a single decade between 1966 and 1976.[59] Due to the high rate of migration, Tehran could not be an ideal destination for migrants, neither could it meet the demands of its own citizens properly. Reaching its climax in the mid-1970s, squatter settlements settled within the limits of urban economy but not involved in it. The exact number of squatter settlers was not published during these years, but based on all available figures and facts, the estimate would be between 500,000 and 1 million.[60] In the provinces the increase of squatter settlements was quite significant. In 1976, 11 per cent of the entire population of Isfahan and 10 per cent in Kermanshah were squatter settlers.[61] The growth of urban squatter settlers gradually indicated that although of a subaltern condition, their gradual prominence in society could not be ignored.

The approaching footsteps of revolution could be heard in 1977. Daily rapid incidents mesmerized them to the extent that they could not establish organized labour protests, rather they merely followed the existing ones. According to Tahmaseb Vaziri,

> the Organization [OIPFG] focused mostly on armed support of the urban communities, not workers necessarily. In relation to working-class protest, the Organization relied only on the presence of its sympathisers amongst workers. The relative immunity of the Organization's network in Tabriz from the latest government's assault made the city a better place to trace the presence of sympathisers in the industrial plantations such as Traktor-Sazi (Tractor Manufacturing) and Mashin-Sazi (Machine Manufacturing).[62]

Reports sent by the sympathizers of the organization from Tabriz included the different methods employed by workers in fostering their demands. For instance, the workers of Idem Company in Tabriz (manufacturing car diesel engines), while calling for accommodation facilities, held the picture of the Shah as a sign of loyalty to the monarchy.[63] Whereas two months later, the workers of Mashin-Sazi demanded for better life standards in an utterly different approach, crafted through more confrontational political initiatives.[64]

> The worker strikes culminated in August, September and October 1978 all over the country, including Tabriz. The related reports prepared by Fada'is are preserved in the documents of the Tabriz Revolt.[65] On 7 November 1978, a declaration was published by the workers of Tractor-Sazi and Mashin-Sazi in cooperation with Fada'is 'calling for wholescale strike for the abolition of the martial law through the country, the unconditional release of all political prisoners, the closure of all government sponsored labour unions, the divestiture of unjustified dismissal of workers, the reduction of weekly working hours from 48 hours to 40'.[66] Their demands evidently went far beyond the boundaries of trade union, indicating the current political environment of the time. The workers of the oil industries also shared this inclination. The numerous followers of Fada'is, especially the 'project workers' in Abadan,[67] started a rather late but widespread protest demanding 'the abolition of the martial law, the unconditional release of all political prisoners and the return of the exiled prisoners, the closure of existing the Union of Oil Workers, electing intellectual delegates and independent lawyers', and finally the 'Iranization of the oil industries'.[68]

The semi-clandestine network of Fada'is connected with the workers of the oil industries, transmitted in this way the details of the working-class protests to the OIPFG, and conveyed their instructions for a more organized and general protest of the workers themselves.[69] Furthermore, in another declaration published by the OIPFG, we read:

> Greetings to the vanguard oil industry workers and Mashin-Sazi and Tractor-Sazi:
> We the OIPFG, ... who have taken arms to liberate the working-class and other labourers since 1971 ... send our greetings to the revolutionary alliance of the oil industry workers across Iran, and the unification of Tractor-Sazi and Mashin-Sazi in Tabriz. With all our revolutionary power, we will announce our full support for these revolutionary workers.[70]

The declaration continued with a call for

> The Iranian workers! Join the alliance of the Iranian oil industry, Tractor-Sazi and Mashin-Sazi workers. Step out of the economic act' framework and walk into the realm of the political struggle against the dictatorship of the Shah and the bloodthirsty imperialism.[71]

In the final months before February 1979 and with the spread of the workers' strikes, strike committees were organized in many industrial units. The followers of the OIPFG in the oil industry created the 'Committee of the Oil Industry Workers'.[72] While it was possible to see the final fall of the regime in the horizon, it was nevertheless hard to imagine a substitute for it. The followers of the OIPFG were still waiting for the roadmap of the Organization's leadership to reach them:

> The OIPFG together with the mindful workers will try to organize the workers' struggles throughout the country, to unify the workers in the various factories and consolidate their being together. The OIPFG believes that through the creation of their own party the workers will be able to find their rightful place in the leadership of the revolution and steer the people towards freedom from imperialism. Our organization believes that the workers marching along towards all these goals should organize the first cells of the armed forces of the workers and peasants. They must move in the direction of preparing a mass armed struggle and get ready for a vehement and decisive battle. They must take practical steps to prepare this.[73]

Besides calling for supporting the striking workers, the OIPFG also supported the slumdwellers of the big cities. In fact, the first community who protested the uneven socio-political developments in order to receive a fair share of wealth were the slumdwellers. The slumdwellers, who mainly emerged from the rural areas, were not absorbed by the small or big industries and were in search of a humble shelter without a clear future in front of them, gave a different identity to their protest. An identity which eventually would attract them to any populist movement, including the Islamist one. Although the priority of the OIPFG was still that of supporting the movement of industrial workers, nevertheless, the same gradually turned somehow its attention to the protest of poor urban labourers in the shantytowns, using its own terminology.[74] *Gozareshati az Mobarezeh-ye Daliraneh Mardom Kharej az Mahdudeh!* (Reports from the Heroic Struggles of the Slum Dwellers), dated July 1978, is the last example of such an attentiveness:

> These reports are the result of the work of some clandestine and non-clandestine teams of the Iranian OIPFG which were prepared during the demolition of the houses of people in autumn of 1977 …. In the present situation, the masses who live out of the vicinity or the workers of the factories in the cities or villages have stood up and are struggling to get their economic and political rights, in a situation that the protests of the workers, students, guild and *bazaris* occurs in various cities of our homeland … The duty of all the conscious and revolutionary citizens is that of trying to organize people by using all available means. Among all this organising, the workers movement is of prime importance for us.[75]

One would wish that the Fada'is' prominence on organizing the workers could also represent their concern about the emerging political clergy. The clergy had come to exercise their hegemony over the revolution by conquering all its trenches one by one, including the trench of the labour movement that the Fada'is had striven to hold for more than a decade with their lives and passion.

Postscript

It should be noted that this essay does not present a comprehensive review of the ideas and activities of the leaders and followers of the guerrilla movements in relation to the role of labourers in social conflict during the decade prior to the 1979 Revolution. This essay should be considered only as a first step in the difficult task of producing a more comprehensive study.

A re-examination of the ideas and activities of the leaders and followers of the guerrilla movements in relation to the role of labourers in social conflict during the decade prior to the 1979 Revolution requires a broader and deeper study.[76] In this respect, analysing the actions of the Fada'i supporters especially in the months leading up to the revolution is crucial. Taking into account only the officially acknowledged actions of the Fada'is and disregarding the behaviour of the larger group of Fada'i supporters and sympathizers would not present a complete narrative of the OIPFG; its links with labourers and their social position. Reports such as documents concerning the uprising of Tabriz, the internal reports of the members and followers of the Organization, those from the Tabriz branch incorporated in this study all support these arguments. Accessing such documents, if at hand, especially with reference to the big cities, can shed more light on this history. On the other hand, it should also be noted that, even if such sources exist and are accessible, they are still paper documents. What oral history can offer in this field is significant. The importance of oral narratives of the Fada'i's followers during the period discussed should not be underestimated.

3

The foreign relations of the Organization of Iranian People's Fada'i Guerrillas: From formation to the Revolution of 1979

Heydar Tabrizi

The Organization of Iranian People's Fada'i Guerrillas (OIPFG) was one of the main organizations of the Iranian new left movement, which was formed in the course of the second half of the 1960s. From its inception the primary intellectual and political characteristics of this Organization were its emphasis on independence, refusal of subordination to any of the world powers (such as the USSR or the People's Republic of China, Cuba), and solidarity and support for revolutionary movements across the world and especially the Middle East. How did the OIPFG's relations with revolutionary and progressive political parties, organizations and movements develop from the Organization's formation until the 1979 Revolution? This is one of the chief questions pertaining to this historical period of guerrilla struggle undertaken by the OIPFG. The aim of this essay is to respond to this question by means of a cursory examination of the international activities of the Fada'i Guerrillas from 1970 to 1978.

Limited information has been published in the public domain regarding the nature of the foreign relations of the OIPFG. During the period in question, SAVAK and other security organs of the Shah's regime, which also collaborated with the intelligence services of the imperialist governments and their allies, such as Israel and Turkey, tried to benefit by striking at the OIPFG and uprooting the Organization. It was because of this reason that the observance of secrecy and the strict preservation of vital information were held to be essential. As a result, not only was information pertaining to foreign operations not published in the public domain, but within the OIPFG itself, information was shared on a very limited basis and very few comrades were kept abreast of developments in this regard.

The observance of clandestine activities under conditions of secrecy was an inviolable principle during the period and was completely observed both within the country and abroad. Because of blows against the OIPFG's domestic operations and arrests of its members some information would fall into the hands of SAVAK and thus obviated the need to keep it a secret. Consequently, the OIPFG could summarize the information of its relevant experiences and place them in the control of other political antagonists of the Shah's regime and the public sphere. *Jam'bandi-ye Seh Saleh*, or Three-Year Summation, penned by Hamid Ashraf is one such example. Foreign operations, however, were less susceptible to exposure[1] and limited information was uncovered by the Shah's regime. Thus, the rationale for keeping such information secret remained and thus was not published.

Until the major assault on the OIPFG of April–May 1976, there was a number of indications vis-à-vis the nature of the Organization's foreign operations. These included the following:

- The pamphlet *Tahlili az Takvin va Takamol-e Guruh-e Pishtaz-e Jazani-Zarifi* (An Analysis of the formation and Evolution of the Vanguard Group (Jazani-Zarifi)) by Bijan Jazani.
- The aforementioned pamphlet, *Jam'bandi-ye Seh Saleh* by Hamid Ashraf.
- The book *Az Jebheh-ye Nabard-e Felestin* (From the Battle Front of Palestine – The Memoir of Comrade Iraj Sepehri) and a biography of comrades who had gone to Palestine and lost their lives.
- The solidarity messages of revolutionary groups in the Middle East to the OIPFG and the Organization's messages to these groups published in *Nabard-e Khalq* in issues 5 (December 1974–January 1975), 6 (April–May 1975) and 7 (May–June 1976) were also indicative of the Organization's relationships with such forces. Between the assaults on the Organization in the first months of 1976[2] and spring of the same year,[3] especially the authorities' assault on the Organization on 29 June 1976,[4] every comrade who had information pertaining to the OIPFG's foreign operations up to that point had died. Moreover, all of the written documents pertaining to this domain of operations inside the country were destroyed.

Comrades at the centre of the Organization following the events of 29 June 1976 had no information regarding the nature and extent of the Organization's foreign operations, and for a protracted period, relations between comrades within and outside the country were severed. Only comrades who were outside the country, each varying in extent, were apprised of the nature and reach of these relations and operations.

On 23 May 1976, SAVAK published a letter in *Keyhan*, *Ettela'at* and *Ayandegan* newspapers through which it claimed to have discovered OIPFG safehouses.[5] In that letter there was a reference made to the Organization's international relations and based on it, SAVAK accused the OIPFG of dependency on foreign governments and spying on their behalf.

It is worth noting that during the years of struggle against the Shah's regime, SAVAK and the propaganda organs of the regime would always accuse the Fada'i guerrillas of 'dependency on foreign force'. Except for this forged letter, they were unable to provide any written documentation or confession, even through torture and interrogation, to prove this baseless claim.

A couple of days after the publication of this letter in authorized newspapers, and while Hamid Ashraf was still alive, the OIPFG published a statement revealing the forged nature of this letter and emphasized the relations of the Organization with revolutions across the world.⁶

After the 1978–9 Revolution, the intelligence and 'investigation' organs of the Islamic Republic which had SAVAK documents in their possession, as well as individuals willing to write for and cooperate with them, have written various books on the subject with the aim of distorting this period of the OIPFG's history. In recent years, mention has been made of the OIPFG's foreign relations in books which have addressed the history of the OIPFG and a handful of interviews and memoirs, but the published record remains limited in this remit. The limited nature of the information in the public domain has not only paved the way for baseless accusations, but perhaps more importantly, has provoked questions regarding the nature and extent of the OIPFG's relations with parties, organizations, liberation movements and some 'anti-imperialist' governments and their foreign operations during this period.

The present article is essentially an attempt to provide a response to some basic questions and a general overview of the international relations and activities of the OIPFG during the aforementioned period. For this reason, I have refrained from providing a merely descriptive account of events. Throughout the process of preparing this article I have tried to analyse contemporary texts and written documents as much as possible or where feasible contact those individuals who directly and indirectly possessed knowledge of the OIPFG's foreign relations. I have also tried not to approach the material selectively and have also benefited from the guidance of colleagues.

Despite the fact that I was active in the foreign relations committee of the OIPFG for three years, from December–January 1975 until January–February 1979, and have a fair amount of knowledge of its foreign operations, I was faced with a number of serious issues in preparing this article that are worthy of mention. Gaining access to credible written documentation was either very difficult or practically impossible. All of the relevant written documents inside the country were destroyed in the events of 1975–6 and 1976–7, and it seems that none of these were obtained by SAVAK. Except for the aforementioned letter, the SAVAK did not publish any other document and also after the revolution, SAVAK documents and interrogations of arrested comrades have been published in the book series *Chap dar Iran; Beh Ravayat-e Asnad-e SAVAK* (The Left in Iran; According to SAVAK documents) (Markaz-e Barresi-ha-ye Asnad-e Tarikhi-ye Vezarat-e Ettela'at); volume three of *Nehzat-e Imam Khomeini* (Markaz-e Asnad-e Enqelab-e Islami, Second printing, Autumn 1995) by Seyyed Hamid Rowhani (Ziyarati) and finally, *Cherik-ha-ye Fada'i-ye Khalq: Az Nakhostin Koneshha ta Bahman 1357* (People's Fada'i Guerrillas; from Inception until February 1979) (Moasseseh-ye Pazuheshha-ye Siyasi, 2008) by Mahmoud Naderi. Except for this letter and references to the interrogations of Safa'i Farahani, Houshang Nayyeri and 'Abbas Meftahi, there is scant evidence or clear-cut information on this matter. The main documents in relation to the foreign relations of the OIFPG in the days preceding the revolution were located in a house in Paris in which Mohammad Hormatipour, Ashraf Dehqani and Hemad Sheybani were residing. According to Hemad Sheybani (Mahmoud Akhavan-Bitaraf), at the time of the 1979 Revolution, when all Fada'i comrades outside the country returned to Iran, these documents were transferred to Lebanon for safekeeping with the Popular Front for the Liberation of Palestine (PFLP). They were, however, later destroyed following an Israeli bombardment and the destruction of the area in which these documents were kept. As a result, I was forced to rely primarily on various individuals' recollections, which unfortunately after some four decades have been afflicted by both forgetfulness and lack of precision. Additionally, on occasion these recollections can find themselves recast from a contemporary perspective or act to surreptitiously mask the inclination to justify one's past actions and thus find themselves distorted. In this regard, as the saying goes, human beings' memory conspires with their memories. Furthermore, unfortunately some individuals whose information could have enriched this article for various reasons refrained from sharing it with me, as well as those instances where I couldn't obtain access to relevant parties. The existence of multiple narratives, and even on occasion contradictory ones, and the lack of credible documents, in instances meant that drawing clear and explicit conclusions becomes very difficult. It is for this reason I refrained from drawing clear-cut conclusions at certain instances, and with the hope that in the future I might gather further information. In the composition of this article my main aim was for my narrative to approximate the truth as much as possible, but I must stress that the deficiencies and inaccuracies are not few, and I believe it will be necessary to amend and complete this research in the future. I hope improvement on this initial effort will become possible with the help of colleagues working in this field.

In this article the foreign operations of the OIPFG have been divided into four stages:

1. Prior to the formation of the OIPFG.
2. From the formation of the People's Fada'i Guerrillas to the summer of 1973.
3. From the summer of 1973 to the summer of 1976.
4. From the summer of 1976 until the 1979 Revolution.

I will address each one of these four stages with their characteristics. Before I begin, it is necessary to summarize the views of the OIPFG with respect to its international alignment of forces.

The view of the People's Fada'i Guerrillas regarding relations with parties, organizations, movements and governments

The People's Fada'i Guerrillas[7] was formed in March–April 1971 through the unification of two groups which had previously acted independently. The first group was known as the Jungle Group (known in Persian as *Gorouh-e Jangal*), a continuation of the Jazani-Zarifi group, which was founded by Bijan Jazani, Hassan Zia-Zarifi and a number of other communist militants in 1963. The majority of the original members of the original Jazani-Zarifi group had experience of political activism in the Youth Organization of the Tudeh Party and openly participated in the political movements of 1960 until 1963 and witnessed the events of the 1953 coup d'état and the subsequent repression and the massacre of 15 Khordad (5 June 1963). This group was identified as a result of the infiltration of Nasser Aqayan, a former member of the Tudeh at the service of SAVAK. Nasser Aqayan was a friend of ʿAbbas Sourki and joined the group through the latter. In the winter of 1967–8 an important number of the members and the primary cadres of the group were arrested by SAVAK, but a number of members of the group (including Hamid Ashraf, Ghafour Hassanpour and Eskandar Sadeqinezhad) were not identified by SAVAK and two individuals whose names were exposed (ʿAli Akbar Safaʾi Farahani and Mohammad Saffari Ashtiyani) could escape abroad and join the Palestinian movement. The uncaptured members of the group that were generally younger and didn't have the experience of the original cadre were able to reorganize the Organization and on 8 February 1971 attacked the Siyahkal military base.[8]

Group Two, which had become known as the Pouyan-Ahmadzadeh-Meftahi group, was formed in 1967 by the unification of four groups (Mashhad, Tehran, the North and Tabriz) by Masoud Ahmadzadeh, Amir-Parviz Pouyan, ʿAbbas Meftahi, Behrouz Dehqani and a number of other militants.[9] The majority of the members of the Pouyan-Ahmadzadeh-Meftahi group were younger in comparison to the Jazani-Zarifi group.

The two groups established relations in August–September 1970 and after a few discussions revolving around strategy and tactics reached an agreement in the same year and decided that together they would arrange a political programme for the future.

Both groups adhered to a Marxist-Leninist worldview but had serious criticisms with respect to the basic theses and policies of the Communist Party of the Soviet Union, especially following the Twentieth Congress of the Communist Party of the Soviet Union (CPSU). Despite different proclivities with both groups, they repudiated the Tudeh as an opportunistic party. They severely criticized the relationship between the Tudeh Party and the CPSU, as fundamentally one of subjection and dependence, and emphasized independence from the respective global poles in the course of the Cold War. Despite these shared views, theoretical differences between the two groups were discernible. In the Pouyan-Ahmadzadeh-Meftahi group the inclination towards the Chinese line was stronger and the criticism of the Soviet Union more pronounced.[10] In this group the view with respect to foreign relations and socialist governments hadn't been very ordered. In the Jazani-Zarifi group the tendency towards China was weaker and the criticism of the Soviet Union less intense, but there was a more systematic approach towards foreign relations and socialist governments.

In a text entitled *Masaʾel Jonbesh-e Zed-e Emperialisti va Azadibakhsh Khalqha-ye Iran va Vazayef-e Asasi-ye Komunist-ha dar Sharayet-e Kununi* (The Problems of the Anti-Imperialist Movement and People's Liberation of Iran and Chief Obligations of Communists under the Present Circumstances), composed by Bijan Jazani and Hassan Zia-Zarifi, a summary of the Jazani-Zarifi group's views in 1966, it was stated that:[11]

> The foreign policy of the Soviet Union and other socialist countries vis-à-vis the Shah's regime violates the fundamental principle of socialist politics. The issue is not one of having normal political, economic and good neighbourly relations. The issue is political, propagandistic, economic and military support of a corrupt, anti-popular (*zed-e melli*) regime … In our view the policies of the Soviet Union and other socialist countries regarding Iran is incompatible with progressive interests and the development of militant nations in Asia with imperialism and contravenes

the principle of proletarian internationalism and is contrary to socialist diplomacy. Political manoeuvring in international matters and differences in the international communist movement must not be the basis of the movement ... The diplomatic interests of the movement dictate that this policy be undertaken with a complete sense of responsibility and therefore refrain from uncritical following.[12]

In the pamphlet *Ancheh Yek Enqelabi Bayad Bedanad* (What a Revolutionary Must Know), which was composed in the summer of 1970, it was also stated that:

> A revolutionary individual in his relations with all foreign forces, more than governments or movements considers the national interests of Iran and the revolution and under no circumstances becomes a tool in the hands of foreign powers. In the use of foreign facilities, whether they be those of the Iraqi government and nation or Yemen or Egypt, the Soviet Union and China, does not forget that the character (*shakhsiyat*), independence, and authenticity (*esalat*) and interests of Iran must not be tarnished.
>
> A true revolutionary believes in an inviolable boundary between opportunism and noble cooperation with foreign forces. With these obvious precautions the revolutionary movement of Iran like all liberation movements of the world can benefit from international and regional facilities. Conversely, in the last third of the Twentieth century there has been a spread of international relationships and regional cooperation, both amongst political movements and in terms of the economic structure of countries, which increases everyday in importance.[13]

These two pamphlets show that the Jungle Group's views in this regard were to a considerable extent systematized.

There is no existent pamphlet or article by the Pouyan-Ahmadzadeh-Meftahi group on this matter. Two views exist in this respect. One is the pamphlet, *Azerbaijan va Masaleh-ye Melli* (Azerbaijan and the National Question), by 'Alireza Nabdel, in which Khrushchev-style revisionism is harshly criticized. However, it does not appear that this pamphlet is a summary of the group's views; perhaps it is an indicator of the Tabriz comrades' perspective. Another pamphlet, *Mobarezeh-ye Mosalahaneh, Ham Estrateji, Ham Taktik* (Armed Struggle, Both a Strategy and Tactic), which was written by Masoud Ahmadzadeh in 1970 and is considered a summary of the Pouyan-Ahmadzadeh-Meftahi group's views has stated:

> If during this period a distinction between Marxism-Leninism on the one hand, and revisionism and opportunism on the other, had not taken shape on an international scale, perhaps up to a point a loss of trust in the Tudeh Party had also led to a loss of trust in communism. But now it seems that the place of real Marxism-Leninism is empty and must be filled.[14]

Prior to the complete merger of the two groups in March–April 1971, the Forest group suffered several heavy blows, while the Pouyan-Ahmadzadeh-Meftahi group had managed to continue its activities unscathed. It is for this reason that after unification the majority of the members of the guerrilla teams were formed from the Pouyan-Ahmadzadeh-Meftahi group. Amir-Parviz Pouyan and Masoud Ahmadzadeh were considered the original theorists. Meanwhile, Bijan Jazani and Hassan Zia-Zarifi, who were the chief theorists of the first group, were in prison.

During 1971 the Fada'i Guerrillas endured a number of heavy blows. The theorists of the Pouyan-Ahmadzadeh-Meftahi group either lost their lives in entanglements with SAVAK, under torture or to the firing squad. In the middle of autumn 1971, only two guerrilla teams had remained. By early 1972, Hamid Ashraf had composed the pamphlet, *Yek Sal Mobarezeh dar Shahr va Kuh* (A Year of Guerrilla Warfare in City and Mountain), and in the spring of 1972 'Abbas Jamshidi-Roudbari wrote an introduction for the pamphlet, *Rad-e Teori-ye Baqa'* (The Rejection of the Theory of Survival) by Amir-Parviz Pouyan. But there is no reference to international issues in these two writings. It can be said that the beginning of the Fada'i Guerrillas' views of international relations and socialist countries continued to develop, even though we do not possess internal documentation clearly delineating the Organization's positions in this regard. After Hamid Momeni joined the Fada'i Guerrillas in 1972 until January–February 1976, most of the theoretical pamphlets and writings, pertaining to both internal and public articles and positions of the OIPFG, were written by him. Also, Bijan Jazani, who was in prison until March–April 1975, wrote numerous pamphlets. During this period, Bijan Jazani from prison and Hamid Momeni on the outside were considered the theorists of the Fada'i Guerrillas. Between the views of these two comrades there were serious differences surrounding the issues of 'socialist' countries, such as the principles of Stalinism, Khrushchev's theses and Maoism. Despite these differences, there were also basic commonalities which fit within the initial framework of the Fada'i Guerrillas.

With the rise in relations between the Iranian government and the People's Republic of China and China's confirmation of the Shah's regime, criticisms from within the OIPFG with respect to the foreign policy of the People's Republic of China increased in severity. A pamphlet entitled *Gerayesh beh Rast dar Siyasat-e Kharejeh-ye Chin* (The Right-wing Tendency in Chinese Foreign Policy) published in the autumn of 1974 was written by Hamid Momeni. This pamphlet was published internal to the Organization stated:

> Indeed, what we have said in this section, apart from showing completely the opportunistic position of the People's Republic of China regarding the vassal states of imperialism, specifically shows the reactionary and anti-popular (*zed-e khalqi*) politics of this country against the Iranian people and in this way we are obliged to decisively oppose its position. Every communist who doesn't decisively condemn this politics is a traitor to the masses.[15]

In the summer of 1975, the OIPFG published the pamphlet *E'dam Enqelabi 'Abbas Shahriari* (The Revolutionary Execution of 'Abbas Shahriyari, the Man of a Thousand Faces). It was a statement of the official position of the Organization in this regard and shows that the same initial views had continued. In this pamphlet it was stated:

> First issue – the difference between China and the Soviet Union: Propagating and enacting the new revisionism, incorrect views such as peaceful transition,

'social peace', opportunistic compromise with imperialism in matters of war, peace and the pillaging of colonies, the lack of necessity for the continuation of class struggle in socialist society, politicking with reactionary coteries. A radical position regarding the foreign policy of China and the Soviet Union must not come into existence. If we fairly examine the politics of the majority of socialist countries criticisms are feasible. We must courageously criticize those and must in this instance not become dependent on a particular side. Meanwhile we must remember that gripes without basis have no effect and do not penetrate the hearts of either friends or foes. We must bring the conditions into existence whereby the support of the regime by socialist countries is not possible in practice. This is an issue that will solve the growth of the movement ... On the whole, with regard to socialist countries within the communist movement, different views can exist and debate continue on this matter. However this debate must be bound by criteria which do not damage our communist movement specifically or more generally the revolutionary movement of Iran. On this score we must learn from the Communist Parties of Vietnam and Korea ... This is the official politics of our organization which we presented in the face of the "criticism" and 'offer of dialogue' from the vestiges of the Tudeh Party leadership. Honest revolutionaries concerned with the furtherance of the struggle should compare [our position] with the supine and opportunistic politics of the vestiges of the Tudeh Party leadership and comparable organizations and realize that the latter do not even have the courage to hear such words. Because of the existence of their organization and even their economic and material livelihood one by one the members of their organization were placed in danger.[16]

In a statement published on 23 May 1976 which is considered the final statement of the OIPFG before the assault by security forces of 29 June 1976 and the death of Hamid Ashraf and other leaders of the Organization, it was stated:

We clearly announce solidarity with and a feeling of closeness toward all true militant and revolutionary forces across the world and especially in the Middle East and we are not averse to any kind of support of these forces and are ready to accept any kind of help from revolutionary forces of the globe and the Middle East. The martyrdom of the fighters of our organization on the battle front of Palestine and Dhofar illustrates this solidarity is very close-knit and convivial.

After the strikes against the OIPFG in 1976 until January–February 1979, there is no internal or public pamphlet on the official position pertaining to this issue in our possession. After the deaths of the leading theoreticians no one emerged to take their place. However, the views prior to the strikes continued and the official acceptance of the views of Bijan Jazani by the Organization in 1977 did not mean the complete acceptance of the views of Comrade Bijan on this matter. Amongst the comrades of the Organization (both in prison and on the outside) differences of opinion and tendency existed and disagreements on this issue were accepted. However, the primary framework for the OIPFG's outlook continued to be based on independence, non-adherence to the will of the global powers and emphasis on solidarity, cooperation and aid to revolutionary forces across the world, especially the Middle East.

Of course, this important point must be considered that the official positions and theoretical writings, while rightly possessing their own important place, do not alone determine the identity of a political organization. In addition to these, the praxis and the activities of a political current perform an important and sometimes decisive role in bestowing substance to the identity of a political movement. The activities of the OIPFG in that period enabled them to establish their identity as an independent leftist force which did not adhere to the will of any of the global powers in the minds of public opinion.

Before the formation of the Fada'i Guerrillas

At this stage the People's Fada'i Guerrillas were not formed yet and the two groups, Jazani-Zarifi and Pouyan-Ahmadzadeh-Meftahi, partook in activities independently of one another. The Pouyan-Ahmadzadeh-Meftahi group didn't send anyone abroad and didn't attempt in practical terms to establish relations with non-Iranian forces and movements. However The Jazani-Zarifi group in early 1967 sent Manuchehr Kalantari, who was in need of medical treatment, abroad to investigate prospects and opportunities of organizational work.[17] However, this action did not yield any discernible results. In December–January 1967, SAVAK's assault on the group began and the central core and a number of active members of the group were arrested or forced to go into hiding. Sa'id Kalantari, Mohammad Choupanzadeh, 'Ali Akbar Safa'i Farahani and Mohammad Saffari Ashtiyani, whom had been identified by SAVAK went into hiding. After a number of months in hiding, because of the inability to carry on with their political activities and also due to their self-avowed lack of military experience, they decided to leave Iran and join the Palestinian movement and, after obtaining some relevant experience, return to Iran. The three people who had not been identified by the SAVAK remained in Iran and set about preparing forces and facilities. Despite the apprehension they had vis-à-vis 'Abbas Shahriyari, these comrades contacted the Tehran organization of the Tudeh Party. They wanted to use this channel to find a way of crossing the border and leave the country. 'Abbas Shahriyari, who was SAVAK's agent of 'a thousand faces' (Hezar Chehreh), and headed the Tehran organization of the Tudeh Party, was of course completely cooperating with the police.

In the spring of 1968, 'Ali Akbar Safa'i Farahani and Mohammad Saffari Ashtiyani by means of the same channel crossed the Iranian border into Iraq. Given that SAVAK knew of this plan, they set a trap for Sa'id Kalantari, whose capture the security forces valued considerably. They also sought to identify a third person, namely, Mohammad-Majid Kianzad, who remained unknown to them. So as to not raise suspicions, SAVAK permitted the first two individuals, that is 'Ali Akbar Safa'i Farahani and Mohammad Saffari Ashtiyani, to enter Iraq and did not arrest them. But when Sa'id Kalantari, Mohammad Choupanzadeh and Mohammad-Majid Kianzad began to cross the border into Iraq, they were arrested.

After crossing the border, Safa'i Farahani and Saffari Ashtiyani were arrested and imprisoned by the Iraqi authorities. The Iraqi government intended to turn them over to Iran, but in the aftermath of the Ba'thist coup of 1968 they were freed by the Iraqi authorities. After their release they then went to Jordan via Syria and joined the Palestinian Liberation Organization (Fatah wing) and continued their struggle amongst the ranks of the Palestinians. Over time Safa'i Farahani even reached the level of military commander. Bijan Jazani in his history of the Jazani-Zarifi group wrote in this regard:

> These two comrades upon entering Iraq were arrested ... the Iraqi government's intention was to hand them over to the Iranian government when the Ba'thist coup d'état in late 1968 took place, these two individuals were freed. After being freed they went to see Jalal Talabani (the leader of the progressive wing of the Iraqi-Kurdish movement and ultimately entered Palestine with his aid. They obtained membership of the Palestine Liberation Organization under the names of 'Abu al-'Abbas ' and 'Abu...'. Comrade Safa'i undertook armed activities and participated in several battles. Comrade Saffari partook in military preparations.[18]

Hamid Ashraf's *Jam'bandi-ye Seh Saleh* briefly alludes to this point:

> Two individuals successfully exited the border (Comrade Ali Akbar Safa'i Farahani, Comrade Mohammad Saffari Ashtiyani) ... These men who had crossed the border after a number of incidents were able to reach and join the Palestinian movement and until 1969 continued their struggle in Palestine.[19]

Hamid Ashraf in *Tahlili-ye Yek Sal-e Mobarezeh-ye Cheriki dar Shahr va Kuh* (An Analysis of One Year of Guerrilla Struggle in the City and Mountain) mentions 'Ali Akbar Safa'i Farahani's imprisonment in Iraq. The book *Cherik-ha-ye Fada'i Khalq: Az Nokhostin Konesh-ha* also addresses this arrest.[20] Thus this arrest and the imprisonment of these two individuals in Iraq is verified by several sources.

These two individuals, in order to escape the retribution of SAVAK and acquire military experience, left the country and joined the Palestinian movement. The remaining members of the group were not in a position to move towards the establishment of official relations with revolutionary and progressive forces or governments in the region. This was the reason why Safa'i Farahani and Saffari Ashtiyani did not attempt to establish official relations on behalf of the group with Palestinian forces, though the struggle within the ranks of the Palestinian movement allowed them to enjoy the support of this movement and in later stages smoothed the road to official relations between the People's Fada'i Guerrillas and the Palestinian movement.

The comrades from the group who had remained in Iran continued their activities within the framework of previously conceived programs and could until 1969 gradually renew their organization. They had prepared a number of used weapons and some quantities of explosives and had undertaken reconnaissance in forestlands.

In the winter of 1969–70, ʿAli Akbar Safaʾi Farahani secretly returned to Iran via the Iranian-Iraqi border and established contact with the comrades who had stayed in Iran. Considering the means at their disposal, he proposed operational plans and after some time went to Palestine and along with Saffari Ashtiyani returned to Iran with some weapons and explosive materials. The group's preparations and need for experienced individuals had now come to fruition.[21]

Hamid Ashraf wrote in this regard:

> In the winter of 1969-1970 Comrade Safaʾi crossed the border alone and came to Iran and established contact with comrades inside the country and considering the available means at his disposal, proposed operational plans. Later comrade Safaʿi Farahani went to Palestine and with Saffari returned to Iran with some arms and ammunition.[22]

Bijan Jazani also mentions this point:

> In the summer of 1969 comrade Farahani returned to Iran and for a time cooperated in the re-organization of the group. Safaʿi's return was effective in improving its state and speeded up its activities. Comrade Safaʿi once again returned to Palestine and along with Comrade Saffari came to Iran in the spring of 1970.[23]

Hamid Ashraf places the return of Safaʾi Farahani in winter and Jazani in summer, but due to Ashraf's more precise information, the date of winter of 1969–70 is probably more accurate.

Because the comrades were members of the Fatah organization and had struggled amidst its ranks for two years, in their comings and goings from Iran through Iraq they enjoyed various facilities and means afforded by Fatah in Iraq and the Middle East, though they did not have formal relations with the Iraqi government.

In the autumn of 1970 Saffari Ashtiyani with Houshang Nayyeri entered Iraq and returned to Iran with weapons and ammunition in order to secure more armaments. Neither Hamid Ashraf in *Jamʿbandi* nor Jazani in his history of the Jazani-Zarifi group have mentioned this trip. However this excursion is mentioned in the third volume of the book *Nehzat-e Imam Khomeini* ('Imam Khomeini's Movement') and in the aforementioned Naderi book.

I have conferred with Iraj Nayyeri regarding this trip and he knew of it. Houshang Nayyeri returned from this trip and prior to his venture into the jungle described the events of this trip in his final meeting with Iraj Nayyeri.[24]

In the biography of Mohammad Saffari Ashtiyani much has also been said about his numerous travels abroad:

> When the comrades arrived to Iran they came empty handed to the group of their former comrades, however, with faith and determination they began to prepare anew for armed struggle. Their military preparation consisted of some quantities of dynamite, a number of used weapons, but the presence of such activities gave the recently arrived comrades a renewed sense of hope.

After this, Comrade Saffari took on the responsibility for arming the guerrilla organization and had on a number of occasions come from Palestine to Tehran and vice versa under the most difficult of circumstances and with minimal provisions in order to provide his fellow fighters with decent and effective weaponry.

It appears that the reason for Bijan Jazani and Hamid Ashraf's lack of reference to this trip was probably due to their desire not to expose the Organization's facilities in Ahvaz, which had been used to make this excursion.

The Siyahkal group at this stage was still in the phase of preparation and reconnaissance in the northern forests and Sattari's trip was fundamentally for acquiring weapons and ammunition. It does not appear that in the course of this short trip they had sought to establish official and enduring ties and relations. If they had such an intent, they would not have returned to Iran so quickly and at the very least a comrade would have remained abroad in order to continue the relationship. The recollection of the events of this trip by Iraj Nayyeri as quoted from Houshang Nayyeri also confirm this.

The OIPFG based its international relations on the three points alluded to in the introduction. It is important to note that the OIPFG stood firm on these principles until the 1979 Revolution. It started its relations with the Palestinian groups not with the purpose of forging alliances or a united front but primarily for requesting ammunition and arms from them in order to advance the armed struggle against the regime of the Shah. This process occurred before the Siyahkal incident through 'Ali Akbar Safai Farahani and Mohammad Saffari Ashtiyani's trip to Iraq to obtain ammunition. However, the relationship expanded in a short span of time, when the PFG was in close contact with elements of the PLO, namely the Popular Front for the Liberation of Palestine under the leadership of George Habash. The Fada'is also started to have a relationship with the Democratic Front for the Liberation of Palestine under the leadership of Nayef Hawatmeh. However, this relationship evolved through time and the OIPFG developed the best of relations with the Popular Front for the Liberation of Oman and the Arabian Gulf (PFLOAG) who were fighting against the regime of Sultan Qabus bin Sa'id, a close ally of the United States and Britain. It is important to note that some of the guerrillas even fought in the Front against the Omani regime.

While continuing its support and solidarity with the Palestinian and other progressive movements in the Middle East, the OIPFG developed relations with the Revolutionary Left Movement (MIR) in Chile and the Tupamaros in Uruguay. Some ties were also developed with the Ejército Revolucionario del Pueblo, ERP, in Argentina.[25] The OIPFG representatives also took part in the activities of the exile radio stations which were put at the disposal of Iranian opposition groups by the Iraqi government.[26]

The overview of the Fada'i external activities presented in this chapter clearly depicts that what was announced by the OIPFG at the beginning of its political activities in Iran was persistently followed in deeds and as such opened a new chapter in the international relations of Iranian communist movements with their international counterparts.

4

A glance at the Organization of Iranian People's Fada'i Guerrillas (1976–9)

Qorbanali ʿAbdolrahimpour

In the decade 1961–71, the bulk of the politically inclined youth with leftist tendencies would create small circles which mainly featured as reading groups. From 1966 onwards, I started to read books and periodicals methodically with a friend and shared those works with other acquaintances for further discussion. Our two-person endeavors carried on until 1971 and expanded considerably thereafter. The majority of people with whom we interacted were university graduates. In our town of Sarab, in the East Azerbaijan Province, there were other circles besides ours which were engaged in similar activities. We kept in touch with them. These circles were mostly composed of teachers, university students and graduates encompassing all kinds of political leanings and tendencies. Some were sympathizers of the Tudeh Party, others were inclined towards the Toufan Organization or other Maoist groups.[1]

My Persian literature teacher, Hassan Ruzpeykar, had a decisive impact on the expansion of our activities. From 1967, myself and one of my friends became acquainted with Ahmad Riyazi. Ahmad was a student at the University of Tabriz and had contact with circles there, including those which included Manaf Falaki and Roqiyeh Daneshgari. Ahmad gradually handed us books such as the *History of the Iranian Constitutional Revolution* by Ahmad Kasravi, or of the *French Revolution* by Albert Mathiez, and suggested that we should write down our questions and comments after reading these works in order to better organize and structure the discussions with him. We did this even though I did not agree with Ahmad's proposal, because these writings could land us into trouble if any of us were to be arrested.

In 1968, I got to know Behzad Karimi through Ahmad Riyazi. At that time Behzad was a member of a group which had been established separately from the rest of the Tabriz circles. Behzad's circle was engaged in the same type of activity as other groups – providing books, attracting more sympathizers, creating a network of groups, participating in the broader student movement, occasionally taking part in demonstrations in larger cities, and writing and distributing communiqués and political flyers.

From the mid-1960s the question of the extent to which study and research should continue in its current shape started to make the rounds of the various groups and associations within the emerging New Left: 'What is the purpose, and what do we eventually want to achieve?' As these questions were posed, attention shifted from theoretical debates and study groups towards 'praxis'. Intellectual discourse became progressively associated with 'excessive verbiage' and 'lack of endeavour'. The belief that the 'age of theory' had come to an end and the time for practical action has emerged gained ground. From the end of 1969, the bulk of Iranian neo-leftist groups and circles who were hitherto interested in study groups moved towards more serious political work and praxis.

From the start of armed struggle on 19 Bahman 1349 (8 February 1971), thousands of Iranian youths who were seeking justice and freedom turned to the People's Fada'i Guerrillas. In this period, 'praxis' in its broad meaning of political, social and cultural activities was reduced to a narrow and limited interpretation. The principle of 'Armed Struggle, both Strategy and Tactic', which also featured as the title of the main work of Masoud Ahmadzadeh, dominated the activities of the People's Fada'i Guerrillas for the first two years. Therefore, the process of study, dialogue and reflection devoted to answering the pressing question of 'What is to be done?' and the emergence from the current (repressive) situation was heavily influenced by the points raised in Ahmadzadeh's booklet. In other words, the stance of Ahmadzadeh took precedence over the interpretations of Bijan Jazani and Amir-Parviz Pouyan in both thought and praxis. According to Pouyan, guerrilla struggle was a way to express political opposition, proselytize and engage in armed defence for confronting the repressive political order and the societal weaknesses in opposing it, as well as generating political influence within the workers and the toiling people and eventually founding the party of the working class.

Our group adopted Pouyan's outlook on political activism from the spring of 1971 and whilst proceeding with its endeavours also started to engage with the preliminary steps for commencing armed struggle. Some practical moves were taken before Hassan Pourreza (Behrouz) Khaliq and shortly afterwards Behrouz Armaghani were arrested in May 1971. Armaghani was arrested because of his connections with a formation known as the 'Engineers' Group'. His arrest was a tough blow to that group, but the rest survived and carried on their activities until 12 October 1971.

In the summer of 1971, our group decided to resort to activities aimed at exposing and undermining the 2,500-year celebrations of the monarchy, which started on 12 October. As far as I know, ten flyers in opposition to the festivities were produced and released in the cities of Tabriz, Tehran, Esfahan and the regions of Gilan and Kurdistan. The Persian service of Radio Iraq also read out these communiqués. On 12 October 1971, myself and Behzad Karimi were arrested in Tabriz whilst distributing these communiqués. I was sentenced to one year in prison and Behzad to two years. After being released from Tabriz prison, I went to the University of Rezaiyeh (Urumiyeh). I presume it was in January 1973 that I was arrested again in Rezaiyeh and sentenced to a year and a half of imprisonment. I was aware that I should not build connections, do organizational work or engage in clandestine activities soon after entering Rezaiyeh University. I decided instead to gradually establish ties with like-minded friends, form a clandestine group and establish connections with the Fada'i Guerrillas under the guise of overt student activities. But it appears that SAVAK got wind of my presence in the university environment. From what I can recall, the religious-minded student activists wanted to engage in an act against the anniversary of the forced unveiling laws of Reza Shah by printing a flyer and sticking it to the university walls. I was aware of this initiative through some of the religiously inclined and leftist students but they did not involve me in this action because I did not agree with this cause.

After this action, myself, a few religious activist students and a Tudeh Party sympathizer were arrested early in the morning in the campus dormitory which was located in front of the SAVAK office. I was aware that my arrest was not due to that particular action. During interrogations, which also included torture, I realized that SAVAK had informants within our circle of university friends. It was during imprisonment in various jails (Sector 3 of the old and common-law prison of Tabriz, the political sector of the new prison of Tabriz and the political prison of Rezaiyeh) that I became aware of the thoughts of Bijan Jazani.

It was around August 1974, two months after my release from prison, that Behrouz Armaghani, who had connections with the Fada'i Guerrillas, contacted me in the town of Sarab through Mohammad Haddad-Khiyabani and Mehri Memar-Hosseini (she was part of our own group). A week later I met Armaghani at his parents' house; he had not yet turned to clandestine life. We talked extensively about the continuation of activities and collaborating with the OIPFG. At the end of summer 1974, I travelled to Tehran in order to maintain constant contact with the Fada'i Organization. Until 22 February 1975, I had contact with Armaghani and 'Ali Akbar Ja'fari (Khosrow, a member of the leadership of the OIPFG) whilst working in a company which sold projectors and which was owned by a fellow Sarabi, Sadeq Fam. After working there for around four months, I noticed that I was under surveillance. Rahim Khodadadi, who also hailed from Sarab and was one of the sympathizers had been arrested there in January 1972 and condemned to a year of prison for having distributed flyers, was working in the same company. He had noticed that SAVAK was observing his movements. We talked about our situation. I had introduced Rahim to Behrouz Armaghani, without knowing that Rahim had previously been introduced to Behrouz through Behzad Karimi. Rahim was furthermore unaware that I had contacts with the Fada'i Organization. At any rate, I raised the issue with Armaghani and warned him that he should either interrupt his regular contact with me or bring about the circumstances of my entry into clandestine life. My rationale was that SAVAK could reach the OIPFG by following me. After several rounds of discussion, Armaghani finally accepted my stance.

The Rasht safehouse

It is important to note here that since the early days of the establishment of the Rasht safehouse, Mehdi Fowghani placed a slim booklet titled *Asasnameh* [founding charter] at our disposal. While perusing the same, I noticed that the term 'centralism' had been deployed instead of 'democratic centralism'. I first thought that this was a typing error, but as I progressed, I realized that there was no mention of democratic centralism which is a founding pillar of a Leninist organization. I approached Mehdi on the matter and he replied that our organization was a clandestine military one which could not practice democratic principles in the given circumstances. Before joining the Fada'is, I had become acquainted with the principles and structure of a Marxist-Leninist political party. I therefore remarked to Mehdi that we were in effect a Marxist-Leninist party, and that the principles of democratic centralism – such as criticism and self-criticism, party discipline and the minority heeding to the majority – all need to be included in the core principles of the founding charter. Since Mehdi could not provide a convincing riposte to my points, I wrote a letter to the Fada'i leadership and made my points clear therein.

Before delving into my personal experience of living in safehouses from spring 1975 to spring 1979, providing a general overview of joining and living in such locations might be of interest. The requirements for life in safehouses in 1975 were as follows: believing in Marxism-Leninism; accepting the outlook of the OIPFG; personal preparedness for clandestine life; complete knowledge of the individual by the leadership, which was particularly important in the security matter; previous political experience; and capabilities in organizational matters. In this period there was an emphasis on the quality of people's political abilities. At the same time, there were changes within the leadership of the Fada'is with regard to some of the principles of armed struggle. Excessive reliance on armed operations was criticized and more emphasis was placed on political activism. Other changes, particularly with regard to the kind of ties between the leadership and the sympathizers and the process through which ordinary members could participate in setting broader policies were also discussed. Between 1972 and 1975 the key principle for the formation of Fada'i teams was that the Organization was fundamentally a military one, and that teams were mostly ready for deployment. The key characteristic of a team leader was that of having considerable military and operational skills. From 1975 onwards, with the correction of the military course and the Fada'i Organization reconstructed as a political-military one being high on the agenda, the Fada'i cadres had to possess intellectual, political and organizational skills, particularly in view of the fact that a substantial number of political prisoners who had been released in spring 1972 had joined the OIPFG and entered the safehouses. The main task of the organizational units at this stage was that of reconstituting the organization as well as continuing and expanding its activities. However, errors committed through the recruitment of young and inexperienced militants made it difficult to carry on the new line at an acceptable pace. At any rate, from autumn 1975, a number of worker-based teams and printing houses were established in a number of cities. The creation of a theoretical team at leadership level also became the order of the day and all teams were mandated to devote more time and attention to political study at their weekly plannings.

This was the general situation prevailing within the Organization at the time of the creation of our safehouse in Rasht in a traditional white-collar area of the town. It was a relatively nice building, consisting of a living room, two bedrooms, a bathroom, a kitchen and corridor. In order to ensure security, the 'Girl' comrade would leave the house a couple of times a day to observe the surrounding neighbourhood. She also established ties with the neighbours and sought in this way to grasp their concerns and connections. We sought to align our behaviour and styles of clothing with the traditions and mores of the neighbourhood. We took turns in staying guard at night, and we had detailed escape plans which we would practice once a week.

A couple of months after the creation of this Rasht clandestine team, Esmaʿil Abedini, who had been recently released from prison, joined our team. We would then explain our relations to neighbours as follows: Mehdi was the breadwinner of the house, Golrokh his wife, I was the maternal uncle of Golrokh who was employed in a business.

Our safehouse underwent changes in the summer of 1975. Mehdi Fowghani and Esmaʿil Abedini were asked to create safehouses elsewhere. Myself (under the *nom de guerre* Behrouz), Golrokh and Asghar established a new team.[2] I therefore became the team's leader. Our team was instructed to engage in political work amongst factory workers and seek to recruit them. Asghar was from Azerbaijan. He was employed as a technician at the Toshiba factory in Rasht. Golrokh Mahdavi was employed in a sewing workshop. Despite being employed, both Asghar and Golrokh engaged in clandestine life and had been tailed by SAVAK for some time. An important point to note here is that the heads of branches had knowledge of the individual members of safehouses, but the same was not shared with the heads of the safehouses. Asghar and Golrokh therefore submitted the reports on their working environment to the branch heads, but not to myself. The branch heads also had the addresses and phone numbers of all safehouses under their purview. This was a major flaw of this kind of organizational structure.

Another team under my supervision was created in Rasht a couple of months after the creation of this new team, with myself at its head. This new formation had three members: Asghar Hosseini-Abardeh, an ex-political prisoner who came from Mashhad who would lose his life on 29 June 1976 together with Hamid Ashraf and the other leadership members, Farhad (Fereydoun) Shokri, who was the youngest member of the team from Mazandaran and Hossein Ghebraʾi, from Langaroud (in Gilan). Hossein was a member of our safehouse despite being a teacher. He did not live with us but occasionally visited us, albeit blindfolded. This was an educational team. I will now explain what the role and duties of such teams were.

The tasks of an educational team were as follows: delivering training on maintaining the security of safehouses (e.g. keeping information on a safehouse after arrest for a given period of time, clearing the safehouse if a member would leave and not come back, placing a health sign, so as to confirm that the safehouse is operating normally for those coming back); firearm training; getting to know the founding charter of the Organization and internal rules; distributing communiqués and devices and timers; providing first aid, including dressing wounds and injecting medicine in an emergency; getting to know how to use printing devices; detailed knowledge of cities, quarters and alleyways; knowledge of the habits and traditions of the local population and connecting team members in case of an interruption in communications. Signs were also placed in locations where meetings were to take place to ensure that it was safe to proceed.

In terms of how the daily activities of any kind of safehouse were established, it needs to be noted that every team had a set list of daily activities, such as supplying food, cleaning up, shopping, security checks around the house, preserving weaponry, study and theoretical education. All members of the team took part in these activities, which were planned on a weekly basis. Each team also had more specific duties.

Planning would occur with all safehouse members present and would be decided on together. If there was a divergence with the leadership's decisions, the latter would be implemented, otherwise there would be further scrutiny of the issue at hand and a majority vote of approval. In case a majority was not achieved, the head of the team's preference would be implemented. There was no mechanism for taking the views of a minority into full consideration, although if the issue was a serious one, the individuals involved could make their points to the branch head, or to the overall Fada'i leadership. The leaders were concerned about tasks being undertaken on time, any need for additional time would be discussed during weekly sessions, and a new schedule, if necessary, would be drawn up.

All safehouses had a small library. Given the conditions of clandestine life and armed struggle, a safehouse could not contain an elaborate library, particularly given the need to empty a safehouse at short notice if necessary. The books present were mostly Marxist ones – the works of Marx, Engels, Lenin, Stalin and Mao, books related to national liberation movements, especially ones related to Vietnam. The team members would study these books. However, there was more interest in praxis and little appetite for theoretical, social, cultural and political work inside and outside the OIPFG.

On one occasion the head of our branch, Behrouz Armaghani, came to our safehouse and after examining the situation ordered us to purchase chairs and tables. We had hitherto conducted all of our work, including night-time planning, on the floor. Two of our comrades spoke up in opposition to this directive and called it a bourgeois act and criticized Behrouz for proposing it. Esma'il 'Abedini and I, however, supported this proposal. In reply to the dissenting comrades, Behrouz said words to this effect: 'Comrades, why should workers and their supporters be prevented from consuming good quality food? For what reason is sitting on chairs bourgeois? Our lives are complicated enough, why do we have to make them even tougher? No one develops bourgeois tendencies through the consumption of good food and using chairs and tables!'

I had witnessed such debates and stances during my aforementioned imprisonment in the Tabriz and Rezaiyeh jails. Such extreme leftist attitudes also existed in those same years (1971–4) in Tehran jails (another example was criticism as to why the songs of two popular singers such as Marziyeh or Vigen were being sung), which progressively decreased through dialogue and discussion. The majority of people who were in jail from 1971 onwards were in touch with activists of all political persuasions and had left such extremist positions behind whilst becoming more measured and flexible.

The safehouse teams' budget was provided by the OIPFG leadership until spring 1975. From then onwards, the emphasis was on individual teams achieving financial independence and providing for their own costs. The teams under my supervision would cover part of their expenses through contacts with sympathizers and requests for financial assistance from them. After the 29 June 1976 blow, the financial autonomy of the teams increased as the bulk of contacts inside the Organization and external to it were interrupted. There were two types of budgets before and after 29 June. One was devised to cover the ordinary living expenses of the safehouses (e.g. rental, food, clothing, hygiene, medicine, cars …) and another for organizational matters. All safehouse members had 500 tomans with them at all times and could spend a small sum of it as deemed necessary. After 29 June 1976, the interruption of relations within and outside the OIPFG led to a deteriorated financial situation which resulted in that figure decreasing to 90 tomans.

Fulfilling security measures and stepping back from anything which would jeopardize the security of individuals and safehouses was strenuously emphasized. Anyone who would not respect the security measures would be criticized or punished. The latter consisted of being taken off guard duty, being deprived of firearms for a set period or, if the transgression was serious, relieving the individual of all duties. It was emphasized in this case that there should be no contacts with the family, due to the fact that the security forces were actively seeking individuals who had gone into clandestine life. For example, amongst the limited amount of SAVAK documents which fell into people's hands after the Revolution, a report was found stating that I had been spotted on the road between Tehran and Esfahan and Shiraz. And this was true. From spring 1977 to the proximity of the Revolution, I engaged in frequent trips between Tehran and Esfahan and other cities. I did not make use of a private automobile for these trips, but I would take buses from bus services named TBT and Iran Peyma. Some of my relatives who were going to Qom for pilgrimage saw me during one of these trips.

At around 4.00 a.m. on 18 May 1976, the sounds of explosion made us realize that a safehouse was under SAVAK attack. We learnt through newspapers at 10.00 a.m. on the following day that Behrouz Armaghani and a group of comrades had been killed. Given that our branch leader was Behrouz himself, this led to our section falling apart and our contact with other parts of the Fada'i Organization being broken. After being informed of this bitter development, Asghar Hosseini Abardeh, Fereydoun and myself tried to get in touch with the OIPFG leadership. We set up a meeting with Hossein Ghebra'i. I checked to see whether the 'safety check' was in place, but there was none. I went to the meeting spot nevertheless. But Hossein was not there. I tried again the next day, but Hossein did not show up then either. I later found out that Hossein had been arrested on that same 18 May in Rasht, but despite extensive torture by SAVAK, he did not reveal my identity or whereabouts.

In order to establish contact with the Organization, the three of us decided to go to Tehran. After managing to establish contact with Golrokh Mahdavi and Mohammad Reza Yasrebi near the 24 Esfand Square, Yasrebi delivered us to Nastaran Al-e Agha.[3] After discussing the recent blows, I reassured her that I have somewhere safe to stay. However, in reality I was forced to stay in a hotel in the Tehran central district of Nasser Khosrow, in contrast with the leadership's recommendation not to seek accommodation in such venues. Subsequently, Asghar Hosseini Abardeh took us to a kind man named Hossein from Gilan. A few days later, I went from that home to meet Nastaran. She took us blindfolded to a safehouse. I noticed Asghar's voice, and thereby noticed that he was there as well. I remained in that safehouse for a few days. Around ten days before 29 July, the new Fada'i leadership sent us to Mashhad together with two members of the Organization called Fatemeh and Farhad (Fereydoun). Mohammad Hosseini Haqnavaz (Mansour), a member of the Organization leadership and the branch head for Mashhad, took the three of us to a safehouse in the city. We were blindfolded in this house, which was under the purview of Hossein-jan Farjoudi

Langeroudi (Rahim), meaning that we had no information on the location of the house, or the identity of its team members.

The Organization's situation after 29 June 1976

I recall that sometime on 29 June the door of the corridor of the house opened and closed. Mehrnoush (Nahid Qajar) with a loud voice said: 'Comrades, Hamid Ashraf has been killed.' The news was brief, and the voice was interrupted. Mehrnoush gave some explanations later, with a grave voice and tearful eyes. Farhad then added quietly: 'Comrade Mansour is the same Mohammad Hosseini Haqnavaz who has been killed alongside Comrade Hamid Ashraf'. As the news broke, a deep sorrow and silence and heavy heart befell on each one of us. It was as if the walls became aware of the depth of our tragedy. Our house felt lonely and death was dancing on its roof. Mansour had said goodbye to each one of us in this very house two days earlier.

The sequence of blows against the OIPFG between May and July 1976 was conducive to the death of dozens of our dearest and best comrades. Hamid Ashraf had fled from several sieges, but this time he fell together with the rest of the leadership and a few prominent cadres. Our minds and bodies were full of wounds. But nobody was talking about it. Based on my prison experience, I felt the duty to break this leaden silence. Even though speaking was difficult for me, I gave a brief speech to this effect:

> Comrades, we have lost Hamid Ashraf and the other members of the leadership. These are unreplaceable blows. We all know that Hamid had an unmatched role in the creation and continuation of the OIPFG and the [anti-dictatorial] movement. We all loved Hamid Ashraf and the other [fallen] comrades and respected them. Hamid and the other comrades will always remain in our hearts. But we have to remember that we have joined the Organization because of our belief in the value system and historical mission of the Fada'is. We will carry on along this path. Each one of us can and will be another Hamid Ashraf!

Each of the other comrades took turns to speak. This was our standard procedure. As a comrade would fall, each of us who would have a memory of him/her would provide details about their life and times and recite a few lines of poetry.

Another bitter memory has come to mind: Shortly before the blows of 1976, Hashem and Hossein ('Ali Miraboun), a teacher who hailed from Zanjan, had gone to one of the garages of Esfahan to collect the equipment that one of the comrades had sent to us from Mashhad. As he was doing so, Hossein realizes that he is under siege by SAVAK agents and instantly bites his cyanide pill to avoid being captured alive. I had a meeting with Hashem on the same day. From a distance, I could notice that he was very grim. As we got close, he put his head on my shoulders and started crying. We cried in each other's arms and then left.

Given that we are discussing sentiments, I want to spend a few words on the issue of love and emotional relations between male and female Fada'i members, all of whom were young, in safehouses. As far as I am aware, there were no rules or regulations in place with regard to romantic relations between men and women within the OIPFG prior to the 29 June blow. On a broad level, the prevailing view within safehouses on romantic relationships was not a positive one. If such a relationship would blossom, the reaction to it would depend on the social and political experience of those inside the same safehouse. Even following the 1976 blows, there were no regulations in place. In this period, some romantic relationships did develop which wasn't hidden from my eyes and some other cadres in the position of leadership. None of these relations caused any problem. In a couple of instances, though, a critical or punitive reaction did take place. The punishment usually consisted of depriving the people involved of certain tasks or preventing them from being entrusted with higher responsibilities for a brief period of time. But one instance, the relationship between Edna Sabet and Abdollah Panjehshahi, regrettably caused the killing of Panjehshahi. This painful, disgusting and irresponsible act unfortunately occurred by the order of one of the leaders of the OIPFG and was not a collective, organizational decision.

It is not possible in this brief article to go in depth on the complex issue of sentimental relationships within the Fada'i Organization. But it should be said that in the years of our youth, and for the communist revolutionaries of my generation which was born after the August 1953 coup, romantic and marital relationships were considered as obstacles for progressing along the path of tough revolutionary resistance. Despite this nearly universal opinion and the atmosphere of ascetic life which was in place, there were individuals amongst us that would marry while carrying on political struggle.

The claim that my generation, meaning the communist revolutionaries of the end of the 1960s, did not cherish life and love, is baseless and absurd. The young and older men and women who created the Fada'i Organization were full of love and energy, thoroughly interested in life in its various forms including attraction to the opposite sex. On the other hand, they were full of optimism for the future and desired freedom, justice, a fruitful life and prosperity for their nation. They were ready to forego many of their personal needs for this purpose. Some waited a long time for expressing their love for their chosen man or woman; luckily some achieved their goal, others unfortunately did not.

Let us now focus on the everyday life in safehouses after the major blow of 29 June 1976. The members of safehouses came from different cities and social extractions. They had different forms of political experience and different interests and lifestyles. They would engage in communal life under one roof without prior knowledge of each other. They would spend most of their time together, and despite everyone being assigned his or her own task, they would necessarily witness to everyone else's behaviours and actions. Some of these would over time create problems. At times these were due to political or organizational matters, others due to simple lifestyle issues. People's attitude towards clothing, eating, health, study and research, criticism and tidiness is different and diverse. Some were not caring about their food, clothing or hygiene and considered this a proletarian or revolutionary way of life. But others considered such attitudes as necessary. Another example: in safehouses we would go through two series of relatively tough exercising every day. Women should not practice during their menstrual period, as it could be harmful for them, but young men would usually be bereft of knowledge about such things and would be troublesome for women: they would undertake exercising without explaining things to the men.

I need to emphasize that our women comrades were having the same rights as men comrades. They had the right to become team leaders, become part of the Fada'i leadership or engage in high-responsibility tasks. The key parameter for handing out duties was the individual's qualities and abilities, irrespective of their gender. The Fada'i woman member had this important characteristic of being able to perform certain tasks, including typewriting, stenciled carbon copy, and spotting agents in a particular manner. Women would also engage in better domestic management and discipline, hygiene and nutrition within safehouses.

These considerations are derived from my personal experience whilst living in safehouses run by the OIPFG in the cities of Rasht, Mashhad, Qazvin, Esfahan and Tabriz. I never lived in safehouses in Tehran but would briefly pass through some of the ones there. I believe that safehouses in Tehran ran similarly to those in other cities.

Until spring 1978 we had not yet settled on a clear political platform, and we did not place any faith in initiatives such as jurists, civil rights activists, National Front leaders' open letter to the Shah on demanding the full implementation of the Constitution, the Goethe Nights,[4] people's protests and the overt activities by the religious forces and the clergy. We progressively noted the winds of change within society and expanded the political activities of the OIPFG accordingly. In this process we did, however, bring about changes in the patterns of life within safehouses. But the activities of individuals and teams were subject to change. Fada'i participation in the protest and popular movement progressively increased. For example, in the city of Tabriz in 1977–8, hundreds of Fada'i sympathizers were active in the factories around the city, the university and the military college, and amongst schoolteachers. Each of these individuals organized their own cells, which were independent from one another and were indirectly in contact with the Fada'is leadership. It should be stated that the main roots for the semi-overt and semi-clandestine activities of the Organization were laid in this period. In 1978 Mehdi Fatapour and 'Ali Keshtgar proposed the creation of an overt organization as the political wing of the OIPFG.[5] The speed of revolutionary events prevented this entity from taking shape.

From the autumn of 1977, conditions arose for a new analysis of the general and political situation within Iranian society. The reality was that the fast pace of change within all layers of society were not compatible with our view, which was based on the lack of the objective conditions of revolution. The pace of change and transformation of our mindset was much slower than the changes which were occurring within society. At any rate, by spring 1978, the consideration that the viewpoints and assessments of Bijan Jazani were no longer matching the fast rate of change and the broad popular movement, began to take shape and momentum. There was the need to think about an alternative. I consulted with the other two members of the leadership, Mohammad Reza Ghebra'i (Mansour) and Ahmad Gholamian (Hadi), and impressed on them the need to prepare a new interpretation of the prevailing conditions of society. I presented my preliminary analysis of the new situation and the decision was taken to share this with other comrades.

In mid-May 1978, pursuant to the decision of the three-person Fada'i leadership, a session was held with 'Alireza Akbari Shandiz, Mehdi Fatapour, Akbar Doustdar-Sanayeh and Rahim Asadollahi, all recently released from the Shah's jails, for assessing the situation in the country. In this session, I raised the proposition that a revolutionary condition had indeed emerged. 'Alireza Akbari strongly opposed my evaluation of the situation and uttered words to this effect: 'Comrade Majid, we were claiming until yesterday that Masoud Ahmadzadeh's views on the presence of the objective conditions of revolution were not correct and we were therefore aligning ourselves to Bijan Jazani's stance instead. Are you now claiming that the conditions for revolution have indeed emerged?' I replied: 'You are correct. Such a condition did not exist until a while ago and we were therefore saying that the objective conditions of revolution had not yet emerged. But the situation has changed today and so has my opinion.'

After detailed discussion, none of those attending this meeting agreed on my point. But everyone concurred that the situation had indeed changed, and the Organization needed to expand its political activities amongst factory workers and the society at large and take part in rallies and other oppositional activities. I did however continue airing my views to other comrades in other teams and progressively gained acceptance for them.

The outcome of this important May 1978 session may be summarized as follows:

- The formulation of a new strategy based on active and broad political participation in the people's struggle and their everyday life, especially in the factories.
- Issuing directives to Fada'i supporters regarding their active participation in the people's struggle and street demonstrations.
- Broader and more active connections between the OIPFG and its support base: intellectuals and artists, students and other sympathizers of the movement.
- Broad communication with the freed political prisoners and attempts to recruit once again within the OIPFG.
- Deploying armed activities pursuant the current situation in defence of the people's struggles.

In the autumn of 1978, the Fada'i teams engaged in political activities within their own spheres of reference. From that point onwards, two new teams emerged in Azerbaijan. The branch leader for these teams was Hadi Mirmoayedi who had contact with a large group of overt Fada'i members and sympathizers. It should be noted here that the spiritual influence of the Fada'is within parts of the Tabriz population, its workers, intellectuals, teachers and university staff was due to many years of revolutionary activity of both members and sympathizers, particularly factory workers there.

Activities in other cities of Azerbaijan were also on the rise, especially Rezaiyeh. After my second arrest, I had become aware of the existence of two Fada'i supporter groups in Rezaiyeh prison: the Rezaiyeh group and the Naqqadeh group. The former was composed of forty-two people, twenty-four of whom had been arrested. Fourteen of these had been sentenced, thirteen of whom to between one and six years of jail. I do not have exact information on the composition of the Naqqadeh group. From 1977, some Fada'i supporters in Rezaiyeh, such as Rahim Yailabi, Hassan Hassani, Vahid Hassani, together with four others created a group called Rah-e Fada'i which was active under this name and published an eponymous journal too.[6]

Besides the aforementioned groups and individuals, a considerable number of Fada'i supporters were active in the years 1977–9 in the cities of Rezaiyeh, Naqqadeh, Salmas, Khoi and Maku. In Rezaiyeh they were active in the local university and between teachers, workers, and factory units, such as Pakdis, mosaic-builders, tobacco, sugar, and more.

At the end of autumn 1978, a team under the supervision of Iraj was dispatched to Khorramabad in Lorestan. Another team composed under the supervision of Tahmaseb Vaziri was sent to Ahvaz in Khuzestan. Tahmaseb Vaziri, who was the supervisor of the Esfahan team at the time, created a team composed of overt members prior to going to Ahvaz and handed over responsibility over Esfahan and surrounding areas to this team.

The Qazvin team, which was transferred to Tabriz, had contacts with Behrouz Soleimani, who had spent years in jail and was considered to be very popular amongst Kurdish opposition forces. After his release from prison in 1977, Soleimani created 'The Group Supporting the People's Fada'i Guerrillas' with Fada'i sympathizers. This group was composed of several smaller ones.

People such as Mohyedin and Bahram Toufani (who was killed), 'Ali Khaliqi (who has passed away), Nader Ayyazi (who has been killed), Enayat Modat and a few others who were living in Tehran and other cities had contacts with this group and would join it after the Revolution. Additionally, at the end of summer 1978, a small group named 'Tulu'' (Dawn) supportive of the OIPFG was created in the city of Baneh in Kurdistan. This group was involved in activities such as organizing protest rallies, producing communiqués and distributing the Fada'i ones across Kurdistan.

From spring 1977 until the February Revolution of 1979, none of the Fada'i branches had a permanent military team. Depending on circumstances, temporary military teams would be created. For example, in 1978–9, a few military operations were carried out by the OIPFG in Tehran, Mashhad, Tabriz and Zanjan with a view to giving military support to the popular mobilization. Even though the grave crisis across the country expanded, and the struggle of intellectuals, workers, and the urban poor was in full swing and the police force had been severely weakened, SAVAK would continue its targeted operations against the Fada'i Organization. For example, Yadollah Salsabili was killed in a night-time operation in spring 1978 in Qazvin, Mohammad Reza Ghebra'i was under severe pursuit in July 1978 and managed to escape the police dragnet in a skilful manner. One of the teams in Karaj was discovered and Soleiman Peyvasteh and Raf'at Memaran were killed in a shoot-out.

I do not have precise information on the teams of the branches led by Ahmad Gholamian (Hadi) and Mohammad Reza Ghebra'i (Mansour). But on a broad level, each of them had various networks in Tehran, Mashhad, Karaj, Gilan and Mazandaran.

A number of Fada'i teams were involved in military operations and armed actions in the rallies and defending them in the face of regime forces. The teams of my branch were mostly devoted to political activities in support of the popular mobilization and would engage in armed initiatives if necessary.

From autumn 1978, adherence to security protocols was not as strict as in the past, and some of the clandestine members would occasionally engage in overt activity and expand their contacts with the supporter base. We also circulated inside cities with less security precautions.

After taking into consideration the expansion and speed of the popular struggle against the Shah's dictatorship, the extent of the Fada'i sympathizers' participation being the same, and the need to expand our political presence within society, the three-person Leadership examined the plan for the expansion of the Leading organ which was initially proposed in the latter half of 1977 but which was not brought to fruition. As we were in the midst of executing such a plan, we temporarily brought about an expanded senior group consisting of 'Alireza Akbari Shandiz, Farrokh Negahdar, Mohammad-Reza Ghebra'i and, later on, Jamshid Taheripour and Behrouz Khaliq. The political helm of this group was taken by Mohammad-Reza Ghebra'i (Mansour). Mehdi Fatapour had relatively constant ties with this group, and I was also in touch with them. This group was based in Tehran but were not part of a single team or the leadership, with the exception of Mansour. This group did not have a pre-defined status or position within the Fada'i structures. However, this group would produce nearly all the Fada'i political statements and declarations in the last two to three months prior to the victory of the Revolution. The flyers would be written by Farrokh Negahdar and 'Alireza Akbari Shandiz under the supervision of Mansour.

In autumn 1978 there was a detailed discussion with the leadership and senior echelons of the OIPFG central organ regarding its expansion. The key takeaway point of the discussions was that the prevailing conditions – such as the expansion of the teams, the need to better regulate contact with the supporter base, expanding contacts within factory workers, the fanning out of the Leadership across various cities, and creating an official political overt organization, rather than an unofficial one – required a wholly new leadership. The previous autumn 1977 plan was therefore examined once more.

The following scheme emerged as a result of these discussions:

The creation of a Leadership unit based on the re-structuring of several other ones: the political unit, the organizational-executive one, and the military planning one.

The leadership would therefore consist of the members of these various units. This plan was finally approved by a central assembly based in Tehran but was not put into practice prior to the final stages of the Revolution.

On 10 February 1979, a meeting with the participation of a number of OIPFG veterans was held in a reserve safehouse. The two points on the agenda were the expansion of the leadership and the analysis of the new situation within society, the state of the regime and the Fada'i stance with regard to the crisis-laden situation within the country.

On this same date, a meeting and rally marking the anniversary of 19 Bahman (the Siyahkal event) was held. Mehdi Fatapour, the person in charge of organizing that meeting, was constantly on the move between our session and that gathering. The latter was the first public and overt move by the Fada'i Organization. Our internal meeting was suspended at 3.00 p.m. due to the proclamation of martial law by the government and was postponed to a later date; no decision had yet been taken.

At dusk, on 11 February, the radio and television headquarters fell into the hands of the revolutionaries and the Fada'i communiqué was read out by two or three channels. The following morning, the members and sympathizers of the OIPFG, under the supervision of Fatapour, proceeded to setting up a provisional political headquarters at the Technical Faculty of the University of Tehran. On that same morning, I reached it; there was a great commotion.

5

Military actions in the Organization of Iranian People's Fada'i Guerrillas: Scales and modalities

Hamid Nowzari[1]

On 8 February 1971, the People's Fada'i Guerrillas stepped onto the Iranian political arena with their first military operation in the Siyahkal jungle, and declared their genesis in April 1971. What did this organization, which played an important role in the struggle against the Shah between 1971 and 1979 understand by armed struggle? What military operations did they undertake? How did they merge 'armed propaganda' with political agitation, and what military chronicles did they leave behind? In the following essay, we will try to answer these questions and give a rather comprehensive list of this Organization's operations from April 1971 to 11 February 1979.

Guerrilla warfare: Its nature and justifications

Although the theorists of the PFG had different perceptions of armed struggle, they all stressed that political repression in Iran had deprived all oppositions from the possibility of pursuing any open or legal political resistance against the Shah's rule, and therefore had made armed struggle an inevitable necessity and also made the emergence of armed political organizations the order of the day. It should not be forgotten that by the end of 1960s, predilection towards the guerrillas' struggle was a powerful tide enticing intellectuals around the world, even enticing many radicals in the United States and in Western Europe.

Bijan Jazani was the vanguard theorist of guerrilla movement in Iran. In an essay titled *Nabard ba Diktatori-ye Shah* (Combat against the Shah's Dictatorship), he writes:

> Within the state of affairs in our society the possibility for any revolutionary movement to survive and grow through sole political struggle is not present; and based on a long political historical experience, fascistic grip (on society) and repression do not allow the growth and development of the covert political processes, and drive them to petty activities, decay, and eventual annihilation.[2]

Amir-Parviz Pouyan, whose name is intertwined with the Guerrilla Movement of Iran, was a prominent intellectual of his own generation[3] who postulated the 'two absolutes' thesis to prove the need for armed struggle: 'the absolute omnipotence of the enemy' and 'the absolute people's feeling of weakness to liberate themselves from the enemy'.

To explicate these two absolutes that according to him had blocked the development of political struggle in the 1960s Iran, he wrote:

> Our task is to challenge these two absolutes. The modus operandi of the compromisers and opportunists is the theory of 'we don't challenge in order to survive'. One must not wait for the 'appropriate moment'. There will be no 'appropriate moment' unless 'the revolutionary forces respond properly in each moment of their struggle to the necessities of history'. The revolutionary armed struggle is the response to such necessity: both in the dimension of armed propaganda and for the sake of armed self-defense.[4]

Pouyan insisted on this principle: 'In order to survive, we are compelled to strike.'

For Masoud Ahmadzadeh, whose views of the armed struggle was more prevalent among the advocates of the guerrilla movement in 1970–3, the political agitation feature of the armed struggle was not of essential importance. Unlike Jazani, he believed that the objective conditions of a revolution existed already in Iran and the masses' immobilization is the result of police suppression and the fear of SAVAK and their crackdowns. For this reason, he believed that 'any plan for organizing a party through political action among workers and peasantry in the current situation' is pure subjectivism. In the views of Jazani, who rejected the proposition of presence of revolutionary conditions in Iran in the onset of the 1970s, the first stage of the armed struggle, or more precisely the 'armed propaganda', was to shatter the dominant suppressive political conditions in the society, to mobilize the political sphere, and to set groundworks for development of the second flank of the movement, a political one:

> The propaganda characteristics of armed struggle is to boost the morale of masses to fight by striking the regime's military. Armed struggle should therefore choose those targets that will break down the image of regime's omnipotence in the eyes of the masses and thus, will put an end to the absolute weakness of those masses.[5]

However, based on his belief that objective conditions of the revolution were already existing in Iran, Ahmadzadeh saw in his turn a bigger potential for guerrilla militancy. For him, guerrilla actions could mobilize masses into a people's army 'not only from the military perspective and for the sake of defeating a conventional strong army, but also from the viewpoint of a political strategy'.[6]

The theoretical problems and disagreements did not have an important role in the development of OIPFG and its establishment as an Organization, although they were an important part of the dialogues between the two foundational groups, the Jazani faction on one hand and the Ahmadzadeh faction on the other. Hamid Ashraf bears an important testimony on this point:

The Forest Group ... believed that the armed struggle in both urban and rural areas complement each other effects, since the objective of first armed actions is to change the existing political atmosphere and making armed propaganda ... in other words, city could provide the rural movement with its technical, propaganda and preparatory needs and the rural movement could absorb the cadre members who had no opportunity to struggle in the cities. Moreover, the armed actions of the rural movement could make the enemy forces busy with itself in a vast area and as such, politicize those areas ... however, these are related to the stage of growth and development of the armed struggle. In the beginning though, the objective was to reach a wide-spread effectiveness of simultaneous guerrilla movements both in the mountains and in the cities. After long discussions, comrade Masoud's faction accepted however the thesis of the Forest group in Dey 1349 [January 1971] and it was agreed that the two fractions would make plans together for the future struggles.[7]

It must be noted that the IPFG, the Organization of the People's Fada'i Guerrillas (OPFG) and finally the Organization of Iranian People's Fada'i Guerrillas (OIPFG), never engaged in a single guerrilla action in the mountainous areas of the country between 1971 and 1979. The guerrillas often organized their military operations based on the idea of armed propaganda during those seven years. Their main target was the oppressive apparatuses of Shah's regime. There is no doubt that their radicalism, militancy, non-conformism and sacrifice gradually broke the rigidity of Iran's suppressive political atmosphere, gave credibility to Iran's leftist movement and empowered the anti-dictatorship popular movement.

The military actions of the OIPFG

We are not aware of all the OIPFG operations, although the Organization always published a statement or announcement after each armed action in order to explain why and how it was done, and to let the public know about the 'revolutionary appropriation' of a bank's holdings, attacks on police stations in this or that city, or the 'revolutionary terror [assassination]' of an official. However, we do not know all their actions, because the statements regarding guerrilla actions had first been distributed in the scene and then, 'the comrades, riding motorbikes, would distribute a lot of flyers in cultural institutions, universities, schools and urban neighborhoods'.[8] This was going on until 1974, when OIPFG started to publish *Nabard-e Khalq* (The People's Struggle) magazine. Before it, if a flyer or pamphlet of an action could not reach the political activists outside of Iran and had not been published in opposition media in exile, then it was possible that the only documentation of that action could be found in SAVAK or foreign intelligence services. In 1971, the OIPFG produced a booklet entitled *Pareh-i az Tajrobiyat-e Jang-e Cheriki-ye Shahri dar Iran* (Episodes from the Urban Guerrilla Struggle Experience in Iran) which contained details of the initial stages of the armed operations. This booklet was also distributed by opposition groups abroad, which were sympathetic to the OIPFG.

After the publication of *Nabard-e Khalq*, the documentation of guerrilla actions started in a regular manner, becoming more accessible to the public. This documentation went on until 1976, when the seventh volume of *Nabard-e Khalq* marked its final one. From June 1976 to November 1977, important members of the OIPFG leadership got killed and there was no significant armed operation. However, a few other military actions were organized after November 1977, and their flyers reached to the activists in exile, or were collected in one of OIPFG reports about the housing crisis (October 1978) or were published in the OIPFG newsletters (10 January–28 February 1979). It is worth to note that many OIPFG announcements related to its operations between July 1978 and 11 February 1979 (the day the monarchy collapsed in Iran) has been collected in a volume published by the Organization.[9]

The following list has been compiled through available information. It must be noted that military operation does not necessarily mean conflict between the guerrillas with the security forces of the Shah's regime. For the OIPFG, a military operation is a plan that is well-thought and evaluated before hand, past its preparation stage and performed within a specific framework. However, a few cases of unwanted and unorganized conflicts between the OIPFG and security forces have been included in the following list.

OIPFG military operations

1971–2

3 April 1971

A team from the Pouyan-Ahmadzadeh faction attacked a police station in Qolhak neighbourhood in Tehran to seize weapons. Nobody got killed or injured in this operation, but the guerrillas seized the machine gun of the police station. The Pouyan-Ahmadzadeh faction had not yet been completely unified with the Jazani group.

7 April 1971

After the execution of thirteen members of the Forest Group on 17 March 1971, the surviving members of the group decided to assassinate Major General Zia Farsiu, the head of the Imperial Army's Investigations unit. As they write in their announcement, 'the execution team successfully proceeded with the execution verdict of the people's court against this mercenary of the regime'.[10]

13 May 1971

At 10.00 a.m., an operational team of OFPG attacked the Eisenhower branch of the Bank Melli and seized 600,000 tomans of its cash deposits. Amir-Parviz Pouyan talked with the clerks and customers of the bank during this operation and explained the guerrillas' objectives to them.

16 October 1971

The OIPFG launches an ambitious plan to disrupt the distribution of electricity as the Shah's 2,500-year Persepolis celebrations got under way. The plan consisted of interrupting three main electric networks at a given time. One operation, the bombing and destruction of a pylon on the Tehran–Karaj Road, was executed successively with the use of four kilograms of dynamite.[11]

11 January 1972

In this Sunday, the Safaviyeh branch of Bank Melli was attacked by the OIPFG. The guerrillas seized cash again and the weapons of the armed guards of the banks, but Mohammadali Tashayyod, the manager of the bank, and Ibrahim Khalili Moghaddam, one of its guards were shot and killed by OIPFG members. The OIPFG explained the aims of this operation in an announcement on 13 January 1972: 'providing the expenses of the war' and 'the interruption in the banking and monetary system of the enemy'. The announcement also addresses the killing of those two persons: 'during such operations, intend to kill the armed guards, who themselves belong to the labour-force and must serve police under economic pressure ... a soldier shot at us and we only responded' but 'the armed policeman of the bank did not do this and he survived'. The manager was killed due to 'insubordination to the orders of the guerrillas'.[12]

1972–3

25 May 1972

A couple of explosions occurred in the offices of the traffic police. In their announcement, the guerrillas wrote: 'The attacks were in response to the bullying against the hard-working Tehrani drivers by traffic police officers.'[13]

29 May 1972

On Monday, a day before the former US president Richard Nixon's trip to Iran, the OIPFG attacked the Marin Oil company office and Iranian oil company offices in Tehran. Two days later, a twin bomb attack targeted the equipment of American advisers in Iran. The targets were not specific persons. The operation was performed in protest to the US military and economic support of Shah's regime and an announcement that Iran was no longer a safe place for them. In their announcement on 2 April, the OIPFG stated that 'these explosions neutralized all the expectations that the American pillagers had from their trip to Iran'.[14]

9 June 1972

An explosion occurred in the Shah 'Abbas hotel of Esfahan. According to the OIPFG, 'a bomb was set off by the guerrillas in this hotel that is the stomping ground for domestic and foreign pillagers and caused substantial of damage'.[15]

In the same year, on a date unbeknownst to us, 'the guerrillas attacked the Saderat Bank in Bozorgmehr Street in Esfahan and seized its cash'.[16]

1973–4

2 October 1973

Twelve revolutionary intellectuals were arrested and charged with an assassination attempt against the Shah and Empress Farah.

The official newspapers reported the incident as follows:

> The saboteurs wanted to kidnap members of the royal family and take them as hostage, request and hijack an airplane and exit the country with a foreign ambassador. Cinematographers, writers, newspaper employees, and trade company employees were among saboteurs. There are two women amongst the suspects ... The detainees are Reza 'Allamehzadeh, cinematographer and a nominee for an award for best children film, 'Abbas Samakar, cinematographer, Rahmatollah Jamshidi, Keramat Daneshian, construction company employee, Shokooh Farhang, newspaper employee, Ibrahim Farhang, trade company employee, Maryam Ettehadieh, newspaper employee, Morteza Siahpoosh, newspaper employee, Farhad Qeysari, employee, Manuchehr Moghadam Salimi.

Khosrow Golesorkhi, one of the main defendants of this case, was not included in this list.[17]

9 February 1974

On the third anniversary of the Siyahkal incident, the central office of the Iranian Gendarmerie was attacked by the OIPFG. In three explosions 'that were set off by a unit of the OIPFG ... the US advisors' gathering place and the center of Pahlavi puppet regime's conspiracy against the Iranian peasantry ... trembled'.[18] Specific individuals were not the target of this attack.

2 March 1974

Qabus bin Sa'id, the Sultan of Oman, travelled to Iran under the official invitation of the government. 'In order to declare the strong opposition of Iranian people and the armed vanguards of Iran's revolution against this conspicuous visit', The OIPFG 'did the following:

- Oman's embassy in Tehran trembled because of an explosion, in spite of a heavy police presence.
- In protest against the hypocritical policy of the UK in Oman's war and the direct and indirect intervention of this government in the liberation struggle of Oman, the headquarters of British Airways was damaged by a bomb in Tehran.

- In order to protest against the intervention of the international oil companies in the Oman civil war, an explosion went off in front of the Shell oil company.'[19]

1974-5

In contrast to the small number of OIPFG military operations in 1973-4, there was a significant increase in the number of operations in 1974-5. Nine successful operations were documented by the guerrillas of different OIPFG units. The military actions targeted regime's 'agents of suppression' in SAVAK, the army or university guards. The only exception was Mohammad Sadeq Fateh, the owner of Jahan Chit Tehran factory.

11 August 1974

Mohammad Sadeq Fateh was assassinated 'in an act of revenge for the massacre of more than 20 strikers in the workers' strike of August 1971'.[20]

In the announcement, the reason for this assassination was explained under two titles, 'who was the main agent of such a great crime?' and 'the history of the issue'. The guerrillas wrote: 'Fateh, the bloodsucking capitalist, and as the people of Karaj call him, the right eye of Shah, was the main agent responsible for that crime [the massacre of 20 workers].' In the end, they stated that 'blood is the response to blood'.

The announcement has also different sections: 'A short explanation on the life of workers and their increasing poverty', 'Who is responsible for this poverty and the bloody accidents that happened in the factories?', 'How do Iranian workers struggle against the increasing poverty?', 'Who was Fateh, the murderer owner of Jahan factories and what did he do?', 'The Shah's relationship with Fateh', 'The so-called charity-based actions of Fateh and its relation to the tax cuts', 'The full explanation of the Jahan Chit massacre, done through Fateh and Shah's government cooperation', 'The OIPFG's reaction in support of the workers' struggle, revenging the shed blood of martyred workers', 'On new armed struggles of Iranian people' and finally, 'What must workers and other revolutionary forces do in order to neutralize the enemy's conspiracies?'[21]

Monday, 30 December 1974

On 7.50 a.m., major 'Alinaghi Niktab, 'a senior officer in the intelligence service and the infamous chief investigator in the so-called Counter-sabotage Committee met with the consequences of his disgraceful crimes'. Dubbed 'the Scheme of Comrade Behrouz Dehqani', the operation was undertaken in Pasteur Street, Central Tehran. 'After the operation was performed, the specific explanatory announcement written for the distribution at the scene, was distributed and comrades left the area while shouting "Long live the people!", "Death to the intelligence service", "Death to the traitor Shah"'.[22]

Thirty minutes later, a bomb exploded in the personal car of Colonel Niktab and the people inside (SAVAK and police agents) got killed.[23] There are no more details on the incident.

February 1975

On the anniversary of Siyahkal, four operations were undertaken in Tehran, Mashhad, Babol and Lahijan. Some operations were mainly for propaganda without any casualties, but some others targeted SAVAK and the Gendarmerie.

- *8 February 1975:* A Gendarmerie station in Farzaneh Street, Tehran 'was bombed. It was a part of Bahman Operations series for the anniversary of Siahkal Insurrection'.[24]
- In the evening of *8 February 1975*: In Gendarmerie of Siyahkal in Lahijan, 'at the same time that the offensive operation of the Forest fraction of the OIPFG against the Gendarmerie of Siahkal in 1971 started', a bomb went off. 'The explosion destroyed a few enemy vehicles and caused a significant damage to the building and wounded a few mercenaries of the enemy. The infiltrated operational unit put a strong clockwork bomb in a way that the explosion does not hurt the citizens or the conscripts in the Gendarmerie.'[25]
- 7.00 p.m., *10 February 1975*: The bombing in Khorasan Province followed by a flyer that emphasized that the operation was a protest against 'the looting and pillage ... of the Razavi Holy Shrine Foundation by Shah and his servants' as well as in the memory of 'the executed comrades of this province, Masoud and Majid Ahmadzadeh, Amir-Parviz Pouyan, Hamid Tavakkoli, Sa'id Aryan and Mehdi Savalouni'.[26]
- 8.00 p.m., *11 February 1975*: An explosion hit Babol's police office 'in memory of the historical day of 8 February 1971, and in celebration of the anniversary of Iranian people's armed movement first action, and due to the infinite oppression caused by Babol police against the citizens of this city'.[27]

3 March 1975

On 6:50 a.m., Captain Yadollah Nowrouzi, the commander-in-chief of Aryamehr Technical University guards, was assassinated. The OIPFG wrote in its explanatory announcement that 'the hated commander of technical university guards was executed by a unit of OIPFG militants. The comrades of the operational unit targeted the traitor mercenary in front of his house with a machine gun, when he was getting into his car. They set fire on the car after the shoot-out.'[28]

In the evening of 5 March 1975

'Abbas Shahriari (aka Eslami), the double agent who caused significant damages to the militant groups, was killed by Fada'i militants near his house. In the corresponding announcement, one reads:

The revolutionary execution of 'Abbas Shahriari (Eslami), or as the traitor security Organization of Shah calls him, 'the man of a thousand faces', was in reaction to his numerous crimes against the militant groups and organizations of our motherland inside and outside of the country and to the damages he caused to the progressive movement of our people. The execution of this traitor was also a response to his spy works as one of the most nefarious mercenaries of SAVAK against the militant Arab nations.[29]

In the evening of 18 March 1975: Two SAVAK offices in Meykadeh Street and Firouz Alley (the west wing of the senate building) in Tehran were targeted by the OIPFG: 'In the first action, the guerrilla unit exploded a powerful bomb in the backyard of SAVAK office in Meykadeh Street … in the second action, a grenade was thrown into the SAVAK office in Firouz Alley after a booby trap was set in the office'. No one was killed in these operations. The operation 'was called the Operation of February 8 Martyrs, in the memory of martyred comrades who reached the high esteem of the revolutionary martyrdom on 8 February 1971.[30]

1975–6

21 May 1975

One month after the assassination of Bijan Jazani and eight other political prisoners by SAVAK agents, the OIPFG assassinated one of its former members who 'committed treason and served the enemy'. The announcement regarding this event reads:

> This operation was called Comrade Hassanpour Operation in the memory of martyred comrade Ghafour Hassanpour … Suffering under the brutal and barbarous tortures of SAVAK, comrade Hassanpour was confronted with immense information which was given to police by Noshirvanpour. The detainment of Forest fraction in Tehran and Gilan was made possible by this information … finally, in May 1971, the anti-popular spectacle was staged on National Television and Noshirvanpour, with his stunts and gags and subservience, appeared as the star and threw himself into enemy arms, disgustingly in front of the people's eyes.[31]

3 February 1976

Hossein Nahidi, a chief interrogator and the deputy manager of Mashhad's security service was killed by the OIPFG. The explanatory announcement of this operation follows the same logic as other important executions done by the OIPFG, including the execution of Fateh Yazdi. Nahidi assassination's statement starts with a summary: 'At 7:45am on 3 February, the revolutionary execution of Hossein Nahidi, the famous chief investigator of Mashhad's security service was performed by a unit of OIPFG militants.'

Then, a biography of Nahidi is given under the title 'Who was Nahidi?' The second chapter of the statement bears this title: 'Why did we convict Nahidi to death?' And the third chapter deals with this question: 'How was the traitor Nahidi executed?' The last chapter of the statement is 'a short explanation about the recent conflicts of Guerrillas in Mashhad'. Here we read about the logic of guerrilla operations in Mashhad and the reaction of different sectors of society (workers, students, old women, police officers) to the assassination of Nahidi and later, the Call of the Organization addressing 'the militant people of Khorasan'.

> The OIFPG has been formed in defense of the interests of hardworking, patriotic people and is struggling for the unity of toilers and workers before everything else ... We defend the right of those workers whose salaries are not getting raised, who have given little or no special benefits, and don't enjoy the right of choosing their real representatives. We defend those peasants whose backs are bent under the debts to banks or usurers ... we support students and intellectuals who have been shackled by the state and been deprived of their right to free expression and healthy thinking, their right to defend people and the human rights and the dignity of humans. We support the toiling craftsmen and shopkeepers who are under oppression by every side, those who are forced and threatened every other day with new taxes and tolls. And finally, we support the entire toiling and dignified people of Iran, in cities and villages, and we struggle for our compatriots' rights.[32]

It should be also noted that the guerrillas wrote another detailed statement after this one and published it in the seventh edition of *Nabard-e Khalq*. It was titled 'The Reactions to the Revolutionary Execution of Nahidi in Mashhad' with this subtitle: 'The Reactions from Mashhad Citizens and Some Counterrevolutionary Elements in the Ranks of Enemy'.[33]

13 February 1976

The governorate of Rudsar

> was bombed by a unit of OIPFG militants ... this bomb went off as expected sharp on 20:45 ... This action was performed in support of the right-seeking struggle of Rudsar's peasants and also in the memory of 19 Bahman 1349 (8 February 1971), the beginning of armed struggle in Iran ... As planned, this explosion did not hurt the people of the city. To save the life of the governor's family, who were living upstairs, we informed them through the gendarmerie and police office so that they evacuate the place as soon as possible.[34]

1976–7

In May 1976, in a date which is unclear, an explosion happened in the Mashhad labour bureau. OIPFG guerrillas were responsible for this explosion and wrote that Mashhad's labour bureau 'was destroyed by a bomb because of oppressing and suppressing toiling workers'. There is no more detail on this explosion.[35]

In two days, 16–18 May 1976, SAVAK strikes the vital network of the OIPFG in a surprise attack. 'These attacks started after controlling a part of our Organization's telephone network and the discovery of a few main centers, underlying the guerrilla's movement.' According to the OIPFG's report on that incident, '14 members of the OIPFG were martyred' and '70 agents of the enemy got killed'.[36]

On 29 June 1976, SAVAK finally succeeded in tracking down the leaders of the OIPFG in a house in Southern Mehrabad district and attacks them fatally from the ground and air during an important Organizational meeting. The official newspapers reported the incident as follows:

> After a series of continued measures, the central base of Iranian terrorist was discovered. The siege of this place, located in Southern Mehrabad district, began early morning today and by the sunrise, an armed skirmish between the officers and the terrorists started. After a 24 hours shootout, Hamid Ashraf, the leader of the group and nine other associates of him were killed. That way, the central command of Iranian communist terrorists was destroyed.[37]

After the death of Hamid Ashraf, Fatemeh Hosseini, Asgar Hosseini Abardeh, Mohammad Hosseini Haqnavaz, Tahereh Khorram, Mohammad Reza Yasrebi, Gholamali Kharratpour, Mohammad Mahdi Foghani, Youssef Ghane' Khoshkbijari and 'Aliakbar Vaziri, the Organizational links stayed broken for a while.

After a five-month silence and constant effort to rebuild the links of the OIPFG, the Organization published its first statement in October 1976. In this five-page statement addressing 'the Militant People of Iran', a report of May and June hits against the Organization is given:

> The armed movement of Iran's people has surpassed its first phase, i.e. the introduction and establishment of armed struggle among the progressive, self-aware and political forces of Iranian society and is at the verge of entering its second stage, the massification of the struggle. As we had hundreds of martyrs and thousands of prisoners in the first phase, we will have numerous martyrs in this next phase, which is a turning point in the struggle of our people ... martyrs such as the great comrade, Hamid Ashraf ... the martyrdom of these comrades, who were bearing the huge weight of the victorious people's armed struggle on their shoulders, is a great loss for the movement. But contrary to regime's claims, not only have there been no flaw in our belief and commitment to the continuation of our path, but also [the attacks] have made us more resilient and more aware in our struggle against the people's fully equipped enemy.'[38]

1977–8

- In the beginning of October 1977, a bomb was supposed to go off in Narmak's municipality, but it did not explode 'due to one of our comrades' mistakes in placing the bomb'.[39]
- 2 December 1977: Shahr-e-Ray municipality (district No.12) was hit by an explosion 'in support of the struggle of those toilers whose houses had been destroyed by the regime of traitor Shah'.[40]

- On 27 December 1977, the OIPFG bombed the Iran-America Society building as an act of protest against US president Jimmy Carter's visit to Tehran. The guerrillas wrote in their statement that 'to protest the looting by the American imperialism, we destroyed the Iran-America Society which is one of the dozens of centres of American pillaging capitalists for despotism and humiliation [against Iranians]'.[41]
- *8 February 1978*: Following the popular protests in Qom and Tabriz in December and January, and police violence against the protestors, the OIPFG attacked the Rastakhiz Party headquarters and a police station in Qom and another police station in Tabriz. The guerrillas published a 12-page statement following the attacks:

> While 'the traitor Mohammad Reza Shah, the policeman of the region, was travelling to Egypt, the mercenary regime attempted to defame the popular image of Ayatollah Khomeyni in its hired newspapers (Ettela'at and Rastakhiz) with an essay full of lies and libels. Regime's shameless behavior enraged the labouring people and the militant clergy.'

The Fada'is gave an analysis of Iran's political situation, the hard conditions of life for the people and the oppression and tyranny, and then explained the grounds for attacking the police station and the Rastakhiz Party building in the city of Qom. They asserted that 'a unit of our militants exploded these two centers with two powerful bombs ... As anticipated, the operation was performed in a way that the people of the city does not suffer any harms.'[42]

17 March 1978

The police station of Tabriz's third district was set to fire in an attack by the OIPFG. The guerrillas wrote in their statement that

> the dictatorship of the traitor Shah responded to the rightful protest of Tabriz people with live ammunition and killed hundreds of labouring people, whose families are mourning them ... In a show of armed solidarity with Tabriz people, our Organization decided to react to the massacre of oppressed Tabrizis and answer the executioner's bullets with bullets. Therefore, we attacked the police station of Tabriz's third district with bomb, machine guns and grenades.[43]

1978-9

1 April 1978

The OIPFG bombed a unit of Mashhad's police patrols in upper street between Chaharbagh street and Naderi crossroad. Regarding this operation, the guerrillas wrote:

> The militant people of Mashhad and especially those who protested against the regime on streets in recent days, know police violence and its role in

people's suppression very well ... our Organization decided to answer police's counterrevolutionary violence and aggression with revolutionary wrath.[44]

6 September 1978

An attack against the civic guard headquarters in Tehran's Eshrat Abad square. This was a response to the 'brutal massacre of Iran's militant people'. In the following statement, one reads:

> One of our units attacked a civic guard commando base in Eshrat Abad square with bomb and machine gun. They returned after damaging this centre of suppression, setting it on fire and killing a few of regime's mercenaries who had an active role in the suppression of people's struggles and shooting protestors.[45]

1 October 1978

Colonel Zamanipour, the chief police of Mashhad's sixth district, was assassinated by the OIPFG. The Organization published a three-page statement on the same day:

> In support of the civil rights struggles of Mashhad's militant people and in reaction to the massacre occurred against them by regime's murderous mercenaries in the recent demonstration, a unit of the OIPFG executed Colonel Zamanipour with a machine gun in the street, on October 1st. He was the commander in chief when guards shot at the people ... He ordered three protestors, who were arrested in the demonstration, to be raped in front of the public and hundreds of policemen ... According to the reports, two of them have passed away in the hospital. The murderous behavior of colonel Zamanipour, especially the recent case, filled the laboring, militant people of Mashhad with hatred. They filed collective petitions, addressing the governorate and the municipality to dismiss and punish him. Aware of the immense popular rage against this filthy element, secret service high officials promised to dismiss and punish him and announced it through *Keyhan* newspaper in order to restrain the momentum of the popular protests. But only a while later, it was revealed that he was promoted to a higher position in sixth district's police station.[46]

6 November 1978

The OIPFG called its sympathizers to 'help the people in their developing bloody insurrection'. The statement reads:

> Defend people's insurrection by teaching fight-or-flight tactics, blocking the communication lines of the mercenaries through sit-ins, barricading the streets, or disabling their forces. Defend the lives of protestors by blocking all roads against police and military caravans. Whatever means and tools you possess, whatever possibility you can think of, whatever tactic you are familiar with, whatever you

know ... offer all of them to the people! Wherever you are, try to assemble groups of people in a good opportunity and teach them how to deal with tear gas, to avoid enemy's line of fire, to find escape routes in besieged alleys, and other resistance tactics.[47]

25 November 1978

On 6:45 a.m., an OIPFG's operational unit attacked the Gendarmerie's office and its guards' base in Zanjan city. In the following statement, one reads:

> We attacked the Gendarmerie and mercenary guards' base in reaction to the counterrevolutionary aggression of Pahlavi's imperialist-dependent traitor regime, in a show of practical solidarity with the brave struggles of labouring masses, and of hatred and rage against the massacres done by the Shah's military dictatorship.[48]

4 December 1978

In the morning of 4 December, the guerrillas attacked the police patrol control station No.2 in Shahreza street in Tehran. The statement reads: 'The operation was performed in a way that does not conflict any damage on normal people and their property.'[49]

5 December 1978

Isfahan seventh district's police station was targeted, and a number of policemen were killed or injured in the attack.[50]

24 December 1978

A number of military personnel were killed by a hand grenade. In the OIPFG's statement regarding this operation, one reads:

> A number of military personnel who played a role in the suppression of popular demonstration in Nezam Abad were killed in our counterattack. We think that an active participation in people's struggles and armed operations against the despotic apparatus of the hated Shah's regime, particularly the army, is our responsibility in this situation. We fulfill our role as the revolutionary vanguard in directing the masses struggles, committing to and propagating armed struggle. We also call all revolutionary and militant forces to answer to this historical necessity and direct the organizational work of the people's movement.[51]

8 January 1979

Two operations in the day of general mourning for the victims of the entire anti-Shah movement: first, guerrillas armed with machine guns attacked an army base in Behbudi street at 11.10 a.m. in Tehran. In the statement, we read:

The operational units' comrade who were present in the demonstration and walking beside the people confronted with a unit of army special commandos, dressed in conscripts' uniform. This unit was intercepted a few days ago, when people's demonstration was brutally suppressed. The comrades followed them. After finding their base, the comrades threw two grenades and destroyed the base and executed those mercenaries.

The second operation was an attack on the army base in Park Street, southern Shahbaz district at 8.30 p.m. The statement regarding this operation reads:

In the day of general mourning for Mashhad, Qazvin, Kermanshah and other cities' martyrs, a comrade armed with machine gun aimed at a guard on a roof top from 8 meters distance. The guard retreated immediately and another comrade threw a grenade in the interior and destroyed it. Both comrades left the scene, while shouting slogans and distributing the pamphlets.[52]

9 January 1979

Demolition of an army unit in Anatole France street in Tehran. The operation is explained as follows:

At 10 a.m., a OIPFG operational unit attacked this army unit. The guerrillas were four comrades: comrade C was responsible for keeping the pedestrians away; comrade D was the driver; and comrades A and D attacked the soldiers with machine guns and after killing several of them, left the scene while distributing flyers.[53]

17 January 1979

Major Majidi, the chief of first district of Tabriz's police station was assassinated by an OIPFG unit at 8.00 a.m., Wednesday. The distributed flyer for this operation reads as follows:

The mercenary colonel Majidi had committed a lot of crimes to serve the interests of Imperialist-dependent regime of the traitor Shah such as the blood-red suppression of Tabriz University revolutionary students and using brutal methods of torture against these brave students ... A Uzi, a revolver and a two way radio were seized in this operation.[54]

24 January 1979

Attack on an army and police bureau in Sanandaj city:

On Wednesday night, a group of OIPFG supporters attacked a suppressive army unit ... based in Sanandaj central square to protect the mercenary runaway Shah's statue. We, the supporters and followers of the OIPFG committed this revolutionary act in reaction to the mercenary army's crimes in order to participate practically in the struggles of the labouring masses.⁵⁵

27 January 1979

The OIPFG warns its supporters:

> SAVAK agents, regime thugs and the former Shah's supporters may attack demonstrations and gatherings. We must fight against them until the end, with whatever means available. But if they attack with guns, we will follow fight-or-flight tactics. In any case, we will not start the conflict.⁵⁶

29 January 1979

An attack on the central gendarmerie command in Tehran's Simetri Street, after a number of demonstrators were killed on the previous day:

> In the evening of January 29, this centre of suppression and the tank in front of it was targeted by a OIPFG militant unit with machine guns and grenades. A number of regime's mercenaries were killed in this operation.⁵⁷

30 January–11 Februar 1979

OIPFG militants adjusted their policy of military attacks organically with the people's insurrection and continued to 'capture all the trenches' of the government. The highest point of this coordination and synergy was the occupation of the National Radio building in Arg Square on February 11. Qasem Siadati, a member of the People's Fada'i, was killed in this operation.

Conclusion

Through the careful evaluation of these operations, we realize that most operations during the first phase (1971–4) targeted the agents directly responsible for people's suppression or banks to meet the financial needs of the Organization adhering to the principle of preserving the Organization independence.

The highest number of military actions can be observed after the armed struggle was introduced and consolidated amongst conscious social forces, and at the threshold of the second phase, which consisted of the massification of armed struggle. The peak of this phase was in 1975–6. During this phase, well-known figures in the suppressive apparatus of the regime (including army officers, SAVAK agents and a factory owner) were still the targets of the OIPFG. Moreover, a SAVAK informer and a former OIPFG member were also assassinated. The latter had switched sides and collaborated with the government. Additionally, a few SAVAK head quarters, gendarmerie, army and provincial government buildings were targeted in this phase by the guerrillas.

The guerrillas' military activities ceased in the aftermath of the government momentous assault of June 1976, which led to the demise of the OIPFG leadership, and lasted until the autumn of 1977. The re-emergence of the OIPFG is almost simultaneous with the rise of a mass movement against Shah's dictatorship. In the beginning of this phase, the OIPFG's military actions are essentially against the centres of repression (such as SAVAK, Shahrbani, municipality, Rastakhiz Party, civic guards, army) and their agents. A few 'revolutionary executions' had been carried out in this period. We could confirm thirty-two operations from 1971 to February 1978: twenty-two bombings, seven 'revolutionary executions' and three 'confiscation of banks' where in one of those two individuals were killed, and in another the explosive operation thwarted.

From March 1978, when the popular movement against the imperial rule reached its revolutionary climax, until 30 January 1979, we could identify eleven military attacks and two 'revolutionary executions'. We don't have a clear record of the operations in last two weeks of the Iran's people movement against the government which resulted into the collapse of the imperial rule. According to available reports and documents, the dimensions and the complexity of OIPFG operations increased to an extent that one cannot easily count them. But one must note that the OIPFG's armed actions before and after March 1978 are different in many aspects. We can summarize some of the most important differences: (1) The spontaneous character of operations after March 1978 relate to the spontaneous movements of the masses. (2) The number of those who had been killed or injured during operations from March 1978 onwards are far in excess than those of the armed propaganda period. (3) Although only the high-ranking agents of the suppressive institutions had been targeted prior to winter 1978, the low-ranking agents also became the target of the OIPFG afterwards. The OIPFG formulates this point in the 'Warning' it issued in March 1978:

> We declare that if the low-ranking agents of the suppressive apparatus attack the people, they will be also our targets beside the murderous, shameless security service agents and high-ranking police and army officers.[58]

It is worth to bear in mind that the OIPFG had in particular insisted on keeping regular citizens out of harm's way and avoid injuring conscript soldiers during the armed struggle phase through to the eve of the victory of the revolution. They did not assassinate any foreign advisor, nor did they target European or American capitalists. Nonetheless, they supported the assassination of Harold Brice, an American military advisor, which was carried out by the People's Mojahedin-e Khalq Organization. This occurred at the same time when the OIPFG bombed two American company buildings just before Richard Nixon's trip to Iran. A number of British companies were also targeted by the OIPFG in 1973.

Therefore, before the beginning of the revolution in 1978 spring, the OIPFG military actions had been done often within the framework of armed propaganda, inspired by Bijan Jazani who insisted on the propaganda aspect of armed struggle and considered the Shah's dictatorship as paramount and regarded the institutions of the dictatorship and those imperialists who supported the dictator as legitimate targets. A few military actions in 1974 are an exception to this rule. The increasing numbers of military actions in this year, compared with previous ones, both in form and content, are not compatible with Jazani's ideas to establish the groundwork for the emergence of the second leg of the movement (a political front) and could be considered closer to Masoud Ahmadzadeh's idea of armed struggle. This fact might show the inability of the Organization in its transition to the second stage, the massification of the armed struggle. That could be the reason for the emergence of the 'People's Armed Propaganda Prototype' concept.

The OIPFG cannot therefore be accused of adventurism, blind terrorism and fearmongering. According to its record, the OIPFG was a progressive political Organization which took up arms for the purpose of effective opposition to the Shah's rule, and in defence of their militants, combatants, in the face of 'counter-revolutionary aggression'. More than being a military organization, the OIPFG in those years was a political one which coupled military operations with propaganda and expository undertakings.

6

From school to safehouse: A woman Fada'i's account

Marziyeh Tohidast Shafi'

I was born in 1953 in Tehran and grew up in a working-class family, entirely apolitical. Throughout my childhood I felt the poverty and injustices of the world around me first-hand and with all my soul. In my high school years, I became interested in reading books, but had no direction. At sixteen years of age, in tenth grade, I made friends with my classmate Zahra Aghanabi-Qolhaki. Soon this friendship became very close. Zahra too was an avid reader. She had grown up in a religious *bazari* family and would come to school wearing a black veil, whereas I did not wear a veil. Before attending Tehran Gowharshad school where I was a student, Zahra was studying at the Parvin High School in Tehran. In that school Zahra had a teacher named Nezhat Rouhi-Ahangaran. Nezhat was a mathematics teacher. This well-informed and progressive teacher had developed an excellent relationship with her students. She would have individual talks with her students and would lend them books as well. Zahra Aghanabi-Qolhaki together with Zohreh Modir-Shanehchi, both of whom joined the Fada'is, were students of Nezhat.

When Zahra Qolhaki's family noticed their daughter reading political books, such as Samad Behrangi's works, revolutionary novels, books on the liberation movement of the people of Algeria and the Cuban Revolution and the Vietnam War, the fundamental principles of philosophy and some of Mao's collective works and more, they became very worried. They were especially fearful because Zahra's uncle was a private driver for the Queen Mother. This was the reason behind Zahra's transfer from Parvin School to our school, the Gowharshad. It was our good fortune that our literature teacher, Ms. Parvin Sepehri, was also a well-read and progressive teacher. She too was from a family with brothers and cousins who had joined the Fada'is during the years 1970–1 and had been killed (Farrokh, Sirous, Farhad and Iraj Sepehri). When Ms. Sepehri noticed that Zahra and I were eager readers, she gradually introduced us to certain books, including those translated by dissident writer Mahmoud E'temadzadeh (Behazin) such as *Dokhtar-e Ra'iyat* (Daughter of a Peasant), or books by Bozorg 'Alavi such as *Cheshmayesh* (Her Eyes), or books by Samad Behrangi including *Mahi Siyah-e Kuchulou* (The Little Black Fish) and *Kand va Kav dar Masayel-e Tarbiati-ye Iran* (Studies on the Pedagogical Problems in Iran).[1] This committed teacher would take the time to speak with us and especially with Zahra, whom she had befriended. Zahra was an active participant in the February 1970 strike and protests by high school and university students against an augmentation in bus fares. She would write slogans on walls and doors and would distribute leaflets amongst people. Zahra and I used to have long conversations and she would give me books and tell me about the political situation and especially about the repression and cruelty of the Shah and widespread corruption amongst royals and the Hezar Famil, or a thousand families.[2] As mentioned, Zahra's uncle, who was Queen Mother's driver during that time, had first-hand information of the deep corruption among the royal family which he would talk about with his family, Zahra included. Zahra would relay that information to me. After a period, Zahra introduced me to Nezhat Rouhi-Ahangaran. Although her family wanted her to avoid having contact with Nezhat, Zahra had secretly maintained contact with her teacher, an enlightened woman with integrity. Nezhat, Azam (Nezhat's sister) and Bahman Rouhi-Ahangaran together with Hamid Momeni and a few others had become known as the Hamid Momeni group and were working in the Institute for the Intellectual Development of Children and Young Adults. They did important work at the Institute, including extensive research work on rural communities which was later published in a book.

I was in eleventh grade in 1970 when Zahra told me about a collection of handwritten materials including books and pamphlets that needed to be typed and printed. She asked me to learn to type and help with the typing of these materials. I welcomed the idea. The next day we went to the central Ferdowsi Street, where several foreign embassies were located, and bought an Olympia typewriter. Zahra paid for the typewriter, and we brought it to my room upstairs in my house. That summer I enrolled in a typewriting course, learned how to use the typewriter and received a certificate. I then began to type all handwritten materials that Zahra would bring to me. I had told my parents that I was typing other students' papers from school and was getting paid for it. In reality the money I was making was from tutoring elementary and high school students. Of course, my parents did not bother me about this, and I had a good degree of freedom which I would use in the evenings to sit in my room and type the handwritten materials brought to me by Zahra. I was in twelfth grade when Zahra told me I should learn to drive. I enrolled in a driving school and soon was able to drive.

In 1970, while I was preparing for my final exams, I typed a good number of pamphlets and books. I remember well the handwritten pamphlet by comrade Masoud Ahmadzadeh titled *Mobarezeh Mosallahaneh, Ham Estrateji, Ham Taktik* (Armed Struggle, both a Strategy and a Tactic). I also remember one day Zahra came to my house and told me: 'This handwritten material is the intellectual output of a highly valued comrade. You should take a few days in the house and finish-up typing it.' I accepted it wholeheartedly and typed it with utmost interest. At that point I knew that I was finally associated with a political group, and this increased my passion and interest in reading and typing the materials given to me. When comrade Nezhat explained to me who the guerrillas were and their altruistic goals and sacrifices, I wished one day to meet one of the guerrillas, maybe help her or him escape or give them shelter, and if they found me worthy and meritorious, to join their ranks to fight for freedom, justice and the welfare of people and against the Shah's regime. I was entirely fascinated by them.

My group duty at that time was mostly reading to intellectually develop myself. At that time, we were assigned a lot of reading either individually or as a group. Among the books that we were reading as a group was Samad Behrangi's aforementioned 'Studies'. I was also reading a lot of books on my own, including Maxim Gorky's novels such as *The Mother*, *The Lower Depths* and *My Universities*. I also read Jack London's *The Iron Heel* and *Grapes of Wrath* by John Steinbeck, writings about the liberation movements that were available such as Djamila Boupacha's and Sartre on Cuba, as well as the *Memoirs of Che Guevara*. I read books about guerrilla movements in Latin American countries including *The Manual of the Urban Guerrilla* by Carlos Marighella, *History of the Iranian Constitutional Revolution* by Ahmad Kasravi, Amir Hossein Arianpour's *How Did Man Become a Giant* and many more.

In addition to reading, there were other activities. Together with Zahra, Nezhat, Zohreh Modir-Shanehchi, Azam, and some other comrades we would go mountain climbing. Writing slogans and distributing leaflets were among some of our other activities. We would also go to the cinema and watch movies. I remember seeing *Grapes of Wrath*, *Guns for San Sebastian*, *Pancho Villa*, *Spartacus*, *Rome 11:00*, among other films.

In 1970 I did well in my final exams in twelfth grade. Zahra and I were eager to attend university. We registered to take the 'National University of Iran' entrance examination known as Concour. The following universities were on our list: Aryamehr University of Technology (Daneshgah-e San'ati Aryamehr), University of Tehran and Ahvaz Jondishapour University. I had selected law as my major. But I ended up not pursuing my studies and even lost my interest in going to university. The comrades in the group were emphasizing the need to work amongst workers, and that going to university now was a waste of time. We would have lengthy discussions about the conditions in the larger society, about the malaise and the passivity that had taken hold, about why every movement by the people would be met with severe repression by the regime, about the need for an armed struggle and why such a struggle is the solution to the dead-end the movement was facing. It was a period of anxiety. One part of me would go to bed every night dreaming of joining the guerrilla movement, while another part of me knew well that to step onto the battlefield I was woefully inexperienced and had to prepare myself in every respect. Despite all this, I possessed a strong revolutionary confidence, and I could see the strength within me to take that selfless step and to devote myself to the cause of liberating the masses. So more than ever I turned to reading. The comrades too, especially the more experienced and well-informed ones would bring me books to read and would address all the questions that occupied my young mind.

In the summer of 1971, a few months after the Siyahkal operation, one day Nezhat casually asked for my opinion about armed struggle. After hours of discussions with her I concluded that armed struggle is necessary. I then audaciously and without any hesitation announced my readiness to join the guerrilla movement as the only effective means to end the Shah's dictatorship and to bring about justice and freedom. In that moment, which I will never forget, an incredible feeling of lightness and contentment took over me. I thought to myself how fortunate I was to have such great opportunity to engage with my ideals. Nezhat was delighted when she heard that I am eagerly ready to fight for our sacred revolutionary ideals and was ready to give my life for the cause.

Yes, I was happy that I was willing to devote my life for the improvement of the lives of the oppressed. I was telling myself that I will always remain committed to my pledge, and I did remain committed. This filled me with a sense of freedom and liberation. Without any exaggeration and self-praise, I want to express that there were very few young people willing to sacrifice their life for the love of humanity, freedom and the welfare of others. For this reason, every single comrade or guerrilla fighter who was stepping into this path was valued immensely, and collectively we were willing to give our lives for each other. There was always so much joy at the news of someone new joining our ranks.

By this time, I had completely dismissed the thought of going to university. Of course, for my family there was the question of why I am no longer interested in going to university. Zahra and I had passed the national university placement exam, the Concour, with much excitement and effort fully intending to continue our education. Yet we were now telling our parents that we wanted to work for a while and help with family living expenses.

In 1972, based on the recommendation of comrades, I started working as office staff at the Azmayesh Factory, a manufacturer of refrigerators, air conditioners and water heaters, which was located near Damavand highway, east of Tehran. My family was delighted that I could help them financially with the comfortable salary that I was receiving. I quickly struck good relations with the factory workers and was gathering information and preparing reports for the group about the conditions and activities at the factory.

I worked at the Azmayesh Factory for about a year and during the entire period my connection with the group was through comrade Shirin Fazilatkalam (Mo'azed). Shirin, who was coming from a leftist family and her father was an ex-Tudeh Party member, was a kind and friendly woman. She was tall, very slim and pale. We would meet once a week for me to give her an update on the factory conditions and for her to tell me about the group's operations, skirmishes and leaflets. At that point, the group didn't yet have an organizational title.

The weekly meetings, an office job in the factory and connections with the workers, however, were not entirely satisfying to me. I was eager and full of excitement and wanted to focus all my time and pent-up energy on the group's campaigns and the revolutionary struggle. It was now I who was asking the comrades to help me go undercover. I should add here that I was not the only one who was eager to join the new revolutionary movement that had begun following the Siyahkal event. In that period, tens and possibly hundreds of committed, freedom-loving and justice-seeking youth were in a similar situation as me, desiring active pursuit of fundamental changes for the society. The world events at the time were also reinforcing these sentiments among my generation. Flames of revolution were blazing across the world, and we were getting influenced by the front-page news coverage of liberation movements in Vietnam, Palestine and many African and South American nations.. In Lenin's words, if you choose not to meddle in politics, politics will choose to intrude into your life.

How I went undercover

For an eighteen- or nineteen-year-old girl, to live separately from her family was taboo in those times. I needed to come up with a convincing excuse. I told my family that I needed to move to the Fars Province, in southwest of Iran, because I had been hired as a librarian in one of the cities there. In those days access to telephones and remote communication in general was limited and it was extremely rare for a family to allow their young daughter to move away. I promised my parents that I would keep telephone contact with them. However, for as long as I was undercover, I did not fulfil that promise.

It was an autumn day in 1973 when I left home feeling ecstatic. It was 1 o'clock in the afternoon. My mother, worried and teary eyed, was carrying my suitcase accompanying me to the street trying to hide her tears. When the taxi arrived, I kissed my mother and held her in my arms for several minutes. I had never been away from my family even for one night before then. I was twenty, the eldest daughter who had just engaged in her first white collar experience. That was an honour for the family. I was always an avid reader and was considered intelligent, and I was supportive of my family and friends. This entitled me to some sort of moral authority among my family members. These characteristics made it more difficult for my parents to agree to my moving away. For me too, it was not easy to leave my parents, though my new socio-political awareness and the belief that it's up to us to rise and bring about change, made it somewhat easier.

I left my mother and stepped into the taxi and went to the meeting spot to meet comrade Nastaran Al-e Agha. I had no idea where exactly I was going and what the eventual plan was. Of course, I wasn't permitted to ask questions about what I was assigned to do for our Organization. This was part of the elementary teachings and ground rules of life undercover.

I arrived at the meeting location with Nastaran, both of us happy and joyful. We took a taxi and went to the Fowzieh Square (presently Imam Hossein Square) and we got out in front of a large mosque known as the Imam Hossein Mosque. We entered the mosque's restrooms, put on our veils, then entered the mosque and sat among people in the mosque. The mosque was a safe place; women were busy praying and we sat in a corner and waited till the evening. As darkness arrived, we returned to the restrooms, removed our veils, left the mosque and caught a taxi back to the bus terminal. When we got off the taxi, Nastaran asked me to go pick up my suitcase and return to meet her at the same spot. After about ten minutes of waiting at the spot, Nastaran returned with a smiling comrade and without any introduction said: 'Comrade Tariverdi, our commander.' Comrade Tariverdi gave me a strong handshake. He had a kind smiling face with green eyes, of medium height and he had the appearance of a blue-collar working-class man. Much later I learned that his true name was Hassan Nowrouzi. Nastaran told me that we'll get on the bus and travel to Isfahan, a city in Central Iran, and that I had to sit all by myself pretending I don't know them. She said, 'if anything happens, you'll go to Isfahan by yourself.' I followed those instructions.

We got on the bus at seven in the evening and arrived in Isfahan early in the morning. Comrade Tariverdi disappeared in a blink of an eye. Nastaran said: 'I'll catch a taxi for us. You need to pretend you're not feeling well. Close your eyes and lay your head on my shoulder in a way that you don't see where we're going.' I accepted and did exactly as was instructed. After a while the taxi stopped, Nastaran paid the fare, held my hands and guided me out of the taxi, then walked a few steps and stopped in front of a house and rang the bell.

A tall young man with light-coloured hair opened the door and warmly greeted us. This was how I entered, for the first time, into an underground safehouse. After a few minutes I saw comrade Tariverdi again. He introduced the young comrade who had greeted us: 'Komsomol.' Komsomol is Russian for young communist.[3] Much later I learned that he was comrade Yousef Zarkari.[4] Yousef had dyed his hair because he was wanted by SAVAK.

I too had to dye my hair shortly after I started my underground life. One day comrade Tariverdi told me, 'Comrade, you either have to change your appearance or have fewer interactions with the outside world, because SAVAK is looking for you.' I later learned that my family was really worried about my safety and whereabouts since they had not heard from me for some time. They contacted one of our relatives who was part of the city police force to help search and find me. They were informed that I had gone underground. Here I should say that I did not have any contact with my family for six years thereafter and they did not have any information about me either. Throughout years of underground life, I worried about my parents' health, particularly my father's because he was suffering from ulcer. But I had come to believe that I do not belong only to my father and mother, but to the people and it is my people for whom I felt responsible. I had decided to leave my family and prior life and devote myself to personal growth through years of studying and contemplation. Furthermore, I understood that the average life expectancy of a guerrilla fighter is not much more than six months and therefore I must overcome worldly attachments and devote myself entirely to serve the revolution. There were also the constant and emphatic reminders by my comrades that underground members cannot ever have any contact with their families. There had already been enough instances of losses as a result of surveillance by SAVAK of the homes of the relatives of identified fighters.

The world of underground safehouses

Before describing the world inside underground safehouses, it is necessary to understand what criteria were applied when recruiting new team members as well as the process by which individuals were recruited for the Organization.

Members of the Fada'i Organization socialized within certain circles which included students, intellectuals, academicians and to a limited extent blue-collar workers. Through these contacts they would identify specific individuals who were considered sympathizers and who would then be approached over time. Typically, conversations would be initiated about social and political issues of the day, gradually leading to active collaboration through which the recruit would be better gauged. Those who would move to the next stage and would learn about the Fada'i Guerrillas, would still need to possess the requisite moral courage, principle and dedication before joining the Organization. Another important criterion was the impeccability of the individual from a security angle. There were different teams with different tasks. Some teams were involved with operations, while others were tasked with publications or logistics or training and yet others with reconnaissance.

The first safehouse I joined in Isfahan was a small house with two bedrooms which were separated by an inside door. The house had a small kitchen and a stairwell leading up to a small door opening onto the rooftop which provided access to check the surroundings. The house had a basement wherein typing of pamphlets, flyers and other writings was carried out. There was also a copy machine in the basement that we ran by pouring alcohol into its cartridge. The copies were nearly violet in colour, and we called them alcoholic prints. Of the two rooms of the house, one was designated for activities such as studying, building timers, sewing, mending the leather for gun holsters, reconnaissance of the city and physical exercises. We also slept and ate in this room. The second room was carpeted. We had put a few chairs and a table to make the room look presentable for any guests or stranger, such as the landlord, whom we could receive in a normal fashion.

We only slept six hours per day. Depending on the number of individuals in the team, we divided the hours of the night shift among ourselves to stand guard. Every comrade usually stood guard for one or two hours at night. During our shift, we looked around the house through the door opening on the top of the stairwell and in case of any suspicious activity, we would alert and wake everyone up.

The first house I lived in was cold and the furnishing was very sparse and modest. The floor was covered with cheap carpet and a few slogans and handwritten poems were hanging on the door and the walls. It was comrade Komsomol who was tasked with explaining the regulations and protocols of the safehouse to me and showing me the workings of the household. My main task in this house was to type the Organization's literature in the basement. I also learned to edit and prepare the pamphlets and was trained to sew leather as well. Group exercises and individual reading was also part of the daily routine. In this house we had a small library with a few books including the memoir of a guerrilla, written by comrade Komsomol, which I had read before. When I first saw him, I recognized him to be the author of the memoir. But we had no permission to ask questions about each other. After I lived in this safehouse for a period of two months, I was transferred to another one. My memory of an interesting incident in that house is worth recounting.

The Isfahan house was leased for one year costing 1,000 tumans which was a lot of money at that time. When we decided to move to a bigger house with two additional comrades joining us, Nastaran Al-e Agha and Hassan Nowrouzi who had left the house two weeks after my arrival to this house, returned to the house. These comrades, being the original tenants who leased the house, had to return to the house to renegotiate the lease with the landlord to terminate it several months before the end of the lease. A few days after their return, Nastaran told me: 'Today the landlord will be visiting us, and we must clean the rooms and make tea.' We then wore our hijab and waited for the guests. It was in the afternoon when the landlord and his wife arrived. Nastaran greeted them with charm and guided them to the guest room. I served them tea. Covering her face with a veil, Nastaran told them, 'We were just getting to know your city when my mother fell ill in Tehran and last week after about a month of bed rest passed away. I have brothers and sisters in Tehran, and I am the eldest daughter of the family and must return to Tehran and look after them.' Nastaran was telling this story while tears were rolling down her face, she was sobbing so hard that I too started crying. As she was crying, she told the landlord that I was her cousin and was temporarily staying with her, and that we must vacate this place soon and return to Tehran. The landlord seemed touched and sympathized with us and believed our story. He agreed to the termination of the lease and refunded our deposit in full.

That event was an interesting learning experience for me. I soon understood that female comrades played an important role in the affairs of safehouses. The presence of a woman – as a wife, a sister or niece – in a way helped guarantee the security of the safehouse. The Fada'i women had the heavy responsibility of making the safehouses appear normal to the outside world. Members living in a safehouse were usually depicted as a typical extended family with a wife and a husband, several brothers, uncles and more. The 'art' and role of the female comrades consisted of creating that impression for the outside world. To do this, we would socialize and establish friendly relationships with our neighbours, invite them to our house and accept their invitations in return, and help them with their daily lives. It was these skills of the female comrades that helped normalize underground safehouses and dispel any suspicions within the neighbourhood. Furthermore, shopping for important items such as stencils and typewriter parts, ink and other items like gunpowder and materials for distributing leaflets roller was primarily done by Fada'i women. We carried always under our chador "the leaflet distributor" and put it up in busy districts or in front of factories. We would time the leaflet distributor activation to coincide with the time workers would leave the factories. We would be very careful during the activation and distribution of the leaflets so that no one gets hurt. When the workers came out of the factories and saw the distributed leaflets around, many of them would pick them up. It would often be the female comrades who, while covered under their veil, would casually walk in the area and observe and take note of the workers reactions.

Love in safehouses

We believed that in a politically driven military Organization there was no room for romance and that a professional revolutionary must not spend time in romantic relationships. But love, this beautiful human instinct, was of course too powerful to be extinguished by even our dire living conditions. Whenever there was the smallest crack, the scent of this fragrant flower would overpower. Young women and men with the most tender, beautiful and deepest humanitarian and devotional affections were moved to express their love and affection towards each other. Alas, the conditions of the struggle created such a harsh environment that even a married couple would be challenged to maintain their relationship.

The case of Maliheh Zehtab and Masrour Farhang is but one example. They loved each other and while fully aware of the grave risks of the guerrilla lifestyle, joined the Organization. Less than a month after their marriage, they were forced to live clandestinely. The leadership decided to place them in the same safehouse, though not long after comrade Masrour was transferred to another city based on Organizational needs. In January 1974 he lost his life in an assault by SAVAK on the safehouse where he was stationed. When Maliheh Zehtab learned about the martyrdom of her husband and dearest comrade whom she loved more than her own life, she was stricken by grief that could not be described. She recounts:

> Instantly my entire body was gripped by a great pain. I became speechless. I could not express my feelings to anyone. We all knew we had stepped on a path where death was lurking around every corner … faced with the loss of my dearest and closest comrade and husband, I had chosen a life where I had to suppress my emotions and allow tears to flow only on the inside. Inside there were feelings of shock, anguish, and grief … but when I returned to join the two other comrades in the basement, I spoke in generalities only about the attack on the Gorgan, a northeastern city in Iran, the safehouse and the names of the martyred comrades.[5]

These were instances of the paradoxes and incongruities in the daily lives of the People's Fada'i Guerrillas. We were driven by deeply humanitarian and patriotic feelings strongly motivated by notions of freedom and justice, yet the conditions of our struggle prohibited us from shedding tears even upon the death of a loved one.

On confronting deep emotions and feelings, I can write a few words about my own first-hand experience with the death of a comrade. I should confess beforehand that as a person I have always been very sensitive, feeling deeply tender emotions that cause tears to well up in my eyes involuntarily. For this reason, I have never been able to speak in a gathering about the life of a fallen comrade.

In 1972 in Isfahan, after transferring from that small house to a bigger one, I joined the team of Yousef Zarkari and Khashayar Sanjari. We were later joined by Abdollah Panjehshahi. Once every two or three weeks comrades Hassan Nowrouzi and Nastaran Al-e Agha would come to Isfahan from Tehran to bring us various publications, communiqués and news, and to share with us the latest developments and decisions of the Organization. They would typically stay for a couple of days and then return. Comrade Hassan Nowrouzi usually rode the bus from Tehran to Isfahan at night to arrive in Isfahan in the morning. After going through the security protocol, comrade Yousef Zarkari who oversaw our team, would go to the designated meeting place to pick up and bring the visiting comrade to the house. One morning, an hour after Yousef Zarkari left to meet comrade Hassan Nowrouzi, he returned and told us that the visiting comrade did not show up at the meeting place. We waited for another couple of hours, then collected and packed all the critical items and left the building according to the safehouse rules. For such emergencies, male comrades had already rented rooms in different neighbourhoods in the city the whereabouts of which were only known to them. I did not have a place to stay. I accompanied comrade Yousef Zarkari to the room that he had rented. He introduced me to the landlord, an old lady who had other rooms to rent to single individuals. He told her I was Mehri his niece and that I was married and was arriving from Tehran to stay for a few days with him and would return to Tehran soon. I spent that night in the room Comrade Yousef Zarkari had rented and he left to sleep at another location. Next day at eight in the morning, I had a meeting with Comrade Khashayar Sanjari. Khashayar and I walked together and stopped at a newspaper stand. The large headline of the newspaper shook us both: 'Shoot-out between a terrorist and agents. The runaway terrorist Hassan Nowrouzi was killed in the clash.'[6] I knew comrade Nowrouzi and knew him to be a nice man who was wholeheartedly committed to the high ideals of the Organization. My tears started flowing. I turned into an alley and started sobbing. Comrade Khashayar was also very distraught. We wandered for some hours through the alleyways of the city talking about the dreadful news and returned to our safehouse. Comrade Hassan Nowrouzi was the first comrade I had lost. The condition of our lives and our struggle would not allow us to mourn the loss of a dear comrade. After such tragic events, the security precautions would leave no time for grieving, we had no choice but to immediately assess the situation in order to understand the point of failure, repairing the damage and taking necessary measures to limit and prevent further blows.

Hamid Ashraf (1946–1976)

Before going into hiding, I had heard Hamid Ashraf's name from many comrades. Hamid was well known for his courage and bravery and for his fierce struggles against the dictatorial regime of the Shah. He was always spoken of as a valiant freedom fighter with impeccable integrity. He, with his unshakable commitment to fight for justice and freedom, was a role model for the rest of us who dreamt of taking up arms alongside him and learning from him.

It was 1975 and it had already been two years since I went underground. I was transferred from Isfahan to Tehran. I was in a safehouse with two other comrades Mohammad Reza Yasrebi and Abdollah Panjehshahi. One night, after about a month I had joined the team, Yasrebi – the comrade-in-charge of our team – told us, 'Tomorrow night one of the comrades in charge of the Organization will visit us and help with our planning.' He was beaming when he told us the news. Comrade Abdollah and I looked at each other and smiled. We had both guessed that it would have to be Hamid Ashraf. We were just as happy if not more at the prospect of seeing comrade Ashraf. The next night at around 7.00 p.m., it was already dark when our comrade-in-charge left and after about half an hour returned with another one. A man of average built with broad shoulders and big bright eyes; the comrade was wearing a suit with a cap on his head. With a short beard and a rosary in his hand he looked more like a young haji, or pious *bazaar* merchant. He had a kind and endearing smile on his face as he greeted us warmly, firmly shaking our hands. After greetings, he asked if we were happy with the arrangements in the safehouse and the communal life. He was called comrade Mahmoud but from that very first moment we knew he was Hamid Ashraf. That evening we went through our usual routine; we exercised, had dinner, talked about the news of the day and the situation in the country, and he participated in our planning session. He also volunteered to keep guard at night-time. The next morning after exercise and breakfast he left the house. We had decided to introduce him to our neighbours as my uncle. From then on, Hamid Ashraf visited our house once a week, typically by himself and sometimes together with comrade Nastaran Al-e Agha. He would bring us books and other publications as well as equipment that were in need. When he was there Hamid engaged in all our team's daily activities including discussions and analyses of the politics of the day where he would demonstrate unusual maturity. During the night he would polish our shoes and prepare breakfast while staying awake and keeping guard. In the morning he would gently awaken us and we would together prepare for the morning exercises.

Comrade Hamid was a keen listener and like a student who is eager to learn, he would pay full attention to what any of us had to say, curious to hear and understand everyone's point of view. He respected the opinions of others and had a very engaging way of discussing and exchanging views. He believed everyone had something to teach no matter how young and inexperienced. During one of his visits when we were studying together, we talked about books, films and music. One of the comrades asked whether he had heard about a new movie called *Tangsir* which had received good reviews. Comrade Hamid responded, 'I have heard it is a good movie. You should plan to see it in pairs at a time.' We were taken aback and looked at each other with surprise. Could guerrilla fighters in hiding go out to the cinemas? In our minds such activity was not an option for us and certainly not authorized. But Hamid Ashraf's view was that with the right precautionary measure in place, going out to see a film that could inspire and spark a healthy dialogue is a good thing. Ashraf would encourage us to steer away from dogmatic thinking and would use every opportunity to help members of the Organization to learn and grow. His openness to new ideas and new ways of thinking helped with the growth of the Organization ideologically.

Hamid Ashraf was a patient and well-read man. It was clear that he came from a cultured family. He was also very active physically and was quick and agile. These skills helped him escape multiple close encounters with security forces of the regime. He felt deeply responsible for the Organization and the movement it represented. Anytime he felt any shortcomings in his ability to understand and analyse a concept or solve a problem in the Organization, he would organize study groups to discuss and try to find solutions. Together with two other comrades, Hamid Momeni and Farhad Sedighi-Pashaki, they planned a comprehensive study program on theoretical and tactical questions. He would spend hours and days reading and researching the topics at hand.

Hamid came across as a very calm, humble and earnest man who was also very self-assured in how he carried himself. The kind of human being in whose presence one feels not just seen and heard but respected and at ease. Because of these qualities, when you worked with him there was no sense of hierarchy. He very much cared for all his comrades including for their mental and physical health. I must recount this specific memory that is characteristic of his personality. At the age of nineteen, cavities had already destroyed three of my front teeth and I had to take them all out. I was without teeth in the upper front row of my mouth. One day comrade Hamid asked me, 'What happened to your teeth, comrade?' 'I had to pull them out because they went bad,' I replied. He said, "Abbas don't you repair your teeth?' The comrade-in-charge quipped with a chuckle, 'comrade, a guerrilla won't live past six months in the trenches, why worry about teeth?' We all laughed except for comrade Hamid who was quick to say: 'This is not a joking matter; you must arrange for her to see a dentist to have her teeth restored. It is not right for this young woman to go without front teeth.' That is who he was, a caring human being who had the respect of all around him.

Recalling those days, living with my comrades with all their strengths and weaknesses, was a warm and wonderful experience. Underground life in safehouses with all its limitations and difficulties taught me lessons I could have never learned any other way. I learned something from every one of my comrades. I consider myself fortunate to have had the honour of living alongside such fine human beings.

The last meeting with Zahra and Nezhat

In early 1975, I was told that I would be moving to another safehouse in Tehran. I asked the comrade-in-charge of our team that, if possible, I would like to join Zahra Aghanabi-Qolhaki and Nezhat Rouhi-Ahangaran. After a few days, they arranged for me to meet up with Zahra. It had been two years since I last saw Zahra. When we saw each other, we were very excited and happy and hugged and kissed for a long while. We walked around the neighbourhood for an hour or so and reminisced about the past and talked about our hopes for a better future. I didn't know this meeting was the last time I would see her.[7]

After meeting with Zahra, the comrades arranged for me to meet with comrade Nezhat Rouhi-Ahangaran. Meeting Nezhat was uplifting and encouraging for me. I was very happy to see her. After our initial greetings and sharing of our mutual excitement to be working together, she informed me that she had secured a place for both of us in the suburbs of Tehran in the Qasemabad Shahi district. I was very happy to hear this, especially when she said that she would lead our team.

Qasemabad Shahi was a working-class district in south central Tehran. Most houses had two rooms and a small courtyard. Many country dwellers who sought work in Tehran would settle there. A mostly religious community, comrade Nezhat had to wear a chador and present as a pious woman to be able to rent this place. Behzad Amiri-Davan was the make-believe husband of Nezhat to make the team appear like a normal household. When I moved in, I met another comrade who was supposed to be my brother. His name was 'Ali Dabirifard. We spent the first day unpacking and arranging the books on the shelves. The next day still unpacking and getting ready for lunch with 'Ali and another comrade, Amiri-Davan, we were surprised by the sound of the doorbell. I quickly ran and grabbed my chador and went to the door. It was the landlord. Apologetically, he asked to talk to my husband about a small matter. After speaking with the landlord, Amir returned with a concerned look on his face. He sat down at the lunch spread and said, 'Dear comrades we need to vacate the house immediately after lunch. This man wants to take us to the police tomorrow and introduce us to the agents there.' As part of a counter insurgency initiative, SAVAK had implemented a plan to stop Fada'is from infiltrating the working class; real estate agents and companies were instructed to register all new tenants with the local police station. Comrade Amiri-Davan promised the landlord that we would all be ready tomorrow around lunch time to go with him to the station. We wasted no time and quickly started packing. We had eleven suitcases altogether that included all the equipment for our operations. I used my chador to hide the bags one by one and carry them to the street. From there the four of us were able to get a van and travelled back to Tehran.

Comrade Amiri-Davan and I had a prescheduled meeting on the same day in the afternoon with comrade Hamid Ashraf. Hamid and comrade Amiri Davan, who managed the team's internal organization, discussed how to move forward, and decided I should go back to my previous safehouse. I had moved back to that house when one day as I was browsing the newspapers at a bookstall, I read the horrible news of the death of comrade Nezhat Rouhi-Ahangaran and others in an attack on one of the safehouses. While sobbing I made my way back to the house and broke the news to my comrades. The following is part of the report on the incident that was printed in the Organization's paper, *Nabard-e Khalq*:

> The Karaj training unit was run by comrade Nezhat Rouhi-Ahangaran. This unit was located at Dolat-Abad, a working-class neighbourhood of Karaj, a western suburb of Tehran. In this unit comrades Mahmood Azimi-Bolorian, a student at the Aryamehr University of Technology, and Yadollah Zareh, a worker at one of the factories in Tehran were undergoing systematic training for organizational and political/tactical aspects of the struggle. This house was discovered by SAVAK and once the agents of the enemy determined all were inside, on 27 June 1975, surrounded the building. Comrade Nezhat who was on her way to the house noticed the unusual circumstances in the area, readied her grenade around her waist and attempted to approach the house to alert her comrades. Before reaching the house, she was identified by SAVAK agents who pursued her. As she was about to be captured by the agents, she released the lever on the grenade and threw herself in their midst. Moments later the explosion killed martyred comrade Nezhat and brought down several of the enemy mercenaries. The sound of the explosion alerted the comrades in the safehouse … who quickly armed themselves and destroyed all sensitive documents by setting them on fire. With grenades and bullets … the comrades engaged in intense fighting killing a good number of the enemy agents. At this time … a fighter helicopter was deployed in the operation and within minutes was hit by the shrapnel from grenades, damaging and rendering it inoperative. The comrades took advantage of the disarray within the enemy ranks and manage to break the siege and get away. Multiple enemy agents chased after the comrades and finally managed to shoot them down.[8]

After the killing of Nezhat Rouhi-Ahangaran in 1975, all planning for our safehouse had to be scrapped. I returned to my old team. I was asked to find our next house and was told that we no longer could rent houses through agencies. I went through the different neighbourhoods asking random people for a place available to rent. I remember clearly that hot summer that I spent under my chador from morning to sunset combing through neighbourhoods asking people for a place to rent. So much so that some even remembered me and when they ran into me they would ask if I had found a place yet. And when I returned to the safehouse at the end of the day the same question was asked by my teammates, 'Shamsi, any luck?' During this time, I continued living on my own on the second floor of the old safehouse. I would see only comrade Hamid and the team leader. I was determined to accomplish what I was asked to do and find a place for my team. After endless research in Tehran with no result I decided to go to the southern suburb of Shahr-e Ray to look for a place. One hot day as I walked around Shahr-e Ray with my now torn shoes, frustrated and nearly hopeless, I asked a ten- or twelve-year-old boy if he knew of a rental place. To my surprise he said, 'There is a vacant apartment over there, let me show you where it is.' He took me to a man who owned the place. Upon meeting, the man said, 'No ma'am, this house is not for you, it is too small.' I told him not to worry, that we are not too many and the house was fine for us. He agreed to show the house. Once inside, I reassured the owner the house was perfect and that we wanted to rent it. I was to return the next day with my husband and sign the contract. I was relieved and filled with joy. When I got back to the safehouse, I saw comrade Hamid. With a big smile on my face, I announced that I had good news, I had found a house without going through any agency. A small place in Shahr-e Ray with two rooms and a kitchen, located in an old and religious neighbourhood of the city. The news made comrade Hamid also happy. The next day with comrade Behzad Amiri-Davan acting as my husband, we signed the lease.

In the beginning there were only two of us who lived in that small safehouse, comrade Behzad and I. After a week of residence, Nastaran Al-Agha brought two very young comrades who were introduced to the neighbours as my brothers. They were in fact brothers named Ja'far and Gholam-'Abbas. In order to develop a rapport with our neighbours, I made Friday *halva*, a religious ritual, and shared it with our neighbours. In the eight or nine months that we were there, I always wore a black chador. We were not assigned a particular task during that time. I spent most of my time reading and typewriting and did not know what others were doing. We all would ask comrade Nastaran for a more active role in the Organization.

It was late March 1976 when comrade Nastaran finally took me to another safehouse. This was a large two-story building with an entrance gate for cars. The house had a phone but otherwise bore almost no furniture. Until recently it had served as an important safehouse and a publication centre for the Organization, but it now served as a temporary base for the comrades who were in transit towards other locations. The comrades staying at this house were all blindfolded vis-à-vis each other. My primary task consisted of typing the Organization's writings in one of the rooms. After a while Behzad Amiri-Davan also joined us in the house and after him Ja'far Zarkari arrived. As members who were stationed in this house and not in transit, we were not wearing blindfolds and were engaged in various activities including group exercises, group studies and making handicrafts.

On 15 May another comrade by the name of Mojtaba joined. He had planned to go outside the city together with comrade Behzad to run some errands the next day on the morning of 16 May. On that morning at around 5:00 a.m., I was exercising together with three other male comrades when we heard a frighteningly loud explosion followed by the sound of machine-guns and then several other explosions. We assumed one of the Mojahedin-e Khalq safehouses was being attacked by the police. But soon this assumption proved wrong. I have already written about this incident:

We finished our morning exercise quickly and ate breakfast. I suggested to the two comrades who were planning to leave the house, not to go that day, but they said they would be careful and departed. I returned to my workroom and resumed typing and editing the materials from *Nabard-e Khalq* no.7, which were brought to me by Nastaran. Ja'far was also busy with his work. It was around 9:00 in the morning when the phone rang, and I picked up. I heard the agitated voice of Nastaran: 'Shamsi, whatever you've got, burn it and get out.' I had no time to ask any questions. I called Ja'far right away and ran to the kitchen. We always kept a bucket where we put important documents that were not to fall into the hands of SAVAK and were to be destroyed in the event of an assault or siege of the house. We had given the name 'double zero container' to this bucket of important documents. Together with Ja'far, I was busy burning the documents when Nastaran called again: 'Shamsi, hold on. Collect everything and get ready to leave, I'll come by to pick you up.' Nastaran made it to the house quickly and sat down on the corridor steps looking frantic. I asked, 'what happened comrade?' She said, with a trembling voice, 'We have lost everyone including Hamid.' Deeply shaken by the news, I asked, 'What are you saying, explain what happened?' She continued: 'Early in the morning I wanted to go to the house in Tehran-e Now district. The area was under siege and there were intense clashes. Likely all comrades who were in that house are killed. From there I rushed to the Kooye-Kan house. There too the area was under siege and armed confrontations were ongoing. On my way, I called the Kouye-Kan house and comrade Gholam-'Abbas Zarkari urged me not to go there, saying the situation there was very dangerous and that if I go, I would be killed.' It was remarkable that as Nastaran was sitting there explaining all this, she noted that attack happened because these houses had phones that must have been wiretapped. With alarm, she said 'surely, an attack on this house is imminent. We must leave the house at once.' I quickly took the necessary supplies and hid them under my veil and left the house together with comrade Ja'far and Nastaran. As we exited, I noticed for the first time that our house is in a blind alley. I did not know the area since I was brought there blindfolded. When we reached the streets around the house, the situation appeared unusual with lots of plain clothed people milling about who looked out of place. The circle of siege by SAVAK agents was getting tighter around us. But we stayed calm and alert and managed to leave the area. We later learned that not long after we left, the house was raided. As we walked away, at a nearby intersection we saw comrades Mojtaba and Behzad who were sitting in a pickup truck waiting for us. We got in the truck along with Nastaran and left the area. Nastaran said, 'We are now headed to a safehouse the location of which must remain unknown to you.' We were brought there blindfolded, and it was later that we learned this was the same Tehran Pars house, a recently built house in a middle-class neighbourhood. They took me to the basement of the house. That is where I saw comrade Kioumars Sanjari.[9]

It was in this house that we heard comrade Hamid was alive, and that after a long battle with SAVAK, while hit by bullets, he had managed to escape the siege. For a period, comrade Hamid was not allowed to move around. But as soon as he felt better, he began writing for *Nabard-e Khalq* no. 7. He would send handwritten materials to me via Nastaran. Comrade Kioumars Sanjari and I would then type the materials in the basement of that house, which became known as the Tehran Pars house. It was at this time that we learned about the details of the bloody and crushing blow of 8–16 May 1975, a short summary of which follows:

> These attacks began following the wiretapping of part of our organizational phone lines and the uncovering of several of our main bases behind guerrilla lines. ... Coordinated attacks by the enemy began with an intense siege of the Tehran-e Now base ... which was known as one of the bases behind the organizational front line. ...Only half of the comrades there were armed and for this reason militarily engaging the enemy was not feasible. ... At the same time as the siege of the Tehran-e Now base, Kouy-e Kan, another base behind the front-line which was in telephone contact with Tehran-e Now base, was attacked. There too, because of the shortage in military equipment, most of the comrades were unable to escape the siege and were martyred. The person in charge of this base was Fada'i guerrilla comrade Ezat Gharavi, a 55-year-old woman known as comrade Mother. Armed only with a grenade, she managed to kill several of the enemy forces before being martyred by the bullets of the enemy's machine-guns. With only a couple of handguns and a few handmade grenades, the rest of the comrades managed to kill several of the enemy forces before giving their lives to the revolution on that battlefield.
>
> Following these clashes, on the afternoon of Sunday 16 May, with fresh reinforcements of upwards of 500, the enemy surrounded another base in Niazi-Alley located between Sharegh Street and Qasem 'Abad-Shahi. Without any warning, the enemy attacked the base by throwing grenades and opening machine-gun fire. There were four comrades in this base, two women and two men. The four of them quickly executed the defensive plan of the base by burning all documents. With two machine-guns and one pistol (one of the comrades was unarmed), they attacked the enemy and managed to push the enemy forces back breaking through the first line of siege but faced another line of enemy forces. With the help of locals in the working-class neighbourhood, the comrades were guided away from the enemy house by house and alley by alley with skirmishes breaking out along the way. All four of them safely left the area and arrived at other bases.[10]

The printing of *Nabard-e Khalq* no. 7 was completed by comrade Kioumars Sanjari and me in the basement of the Tehran-Pars house. Comrade Nastaran Al-e Agha took the responsibility for its distribution. Under such dangerous and difficult conditions, she took *Nabard-e Khalq* to student supporters of the Organization, and this would disseminate the message of the Organization among different levels of the movement. Comrade Hamid believed it imperative that the Organization appear still alive and strong, that the guerrillas continued to be active and ceaselessly following their comrades' path.

It must be said that, during this period, the responsibility for all activities was with comrade Nastaran and she was the one managing all functions and appointments for comrade Hamid. Even under conditions of heavy police presence and surveillance, she would leave the house early in the morning in order to check on all comrades who were without a safehouse to see how they could be taken care of. Most communications were disrupted due to SAVAK's attacks and the subsequent loss of the safehouses. Nastaran once told me that her typical day included eleven meeting spots, and I understood well the risks she was taking and the sacrifices she was making. She finally lost her life attending to one of those meetings. On 23 June of the same bloody summer, she was gunned down on Qazvin Street a short while after meeting with comrade Golrokh Mahdavi and comrade Nadalipour-Naghmeh.[11]

It was after the martyrdom of comrade Nastaran when comrade Hamid decided to resume his outside activities despite warnings from other comrades. And finally on 29 June 1975, together with nine other members of the Organization, in a house at Mehrabad Jounubi, he was martyred in an unequal battle with SAVAK forces. Despite losing our entire leadership and large parts of our resources, our commitment to our comrades and the masses kept us on the path of the struggle for freedom, independence and emancipation of the people and the working poor. With very limited resources we started again, for the third time, persevered and made further progress.

After 29 June 1976

After the 29 June event we had lost our last remaining safehouse. Nine of us had lived in that house and most of us, including me, wore blindfolds to conceal our identities from each other. Comrade Khodabakhsh Shali was designated to be the so-called man of the house. Later, I learned that this house was in the Tehran Pars district.

It should be noted that, contrary to the recent claims and propaganda launched by former SAVAK agents outside Iran, SAVAK did not have any information on and could not trace Hamid Ashraf from 17 May 1976 until 28 June 1976.[12] The night before Hamid Ashraf was killed, he came to the same safehouse in which I lived. The next day when he set about to leave the house, members of the team insisted that he not do so. He left nevertheless, and never returned. All nine of us who stayed in the house remained safe. On 29 June, after hearing the news of the killing of Hamid and other comrades, at 2 o'clock afternoon radio news, we held a meeting to discuss the next course of action. We were in a tight financial situation, and it was decided that the so called woman of the house, Simin Tavakkoli, would seek financial support from a student sympathizer of the Organization. She left the house to visit the student, but she did not return to the house that night. We decided to vacate the house, still not knowing that she had been killed in a confrontation with SAVAK agents.[13] I went to the house of Khodabakhsh Shali's mother who was a very kind elderly woman. I stayed there for a period of seventeen days. Eventually, comrade Shali and other comrades decided to travel to Mashhad, a city in northeast of Iran, and connect with comrades in the Mashhad unit. Comrade Shali, another comrade (as far as I can remember, he was Siamak Asadian, whom we used to call Eskandar) and I went to Mashhad. We spent the night in a pilgrim lodge close to the holy shrine of Imam Reza. We were able to make contact which brought much-needed relief. The contacts and resources of comrades in Mashhad had remained intact because their safehouses did not have telephones. After much deliberation, we decided to retreat from Tehran for a period of time and reside in Isfahan, Mashhad or smaller cities, where the secret police were less present. Comrade Khodabakhsh and I decided to travel to Varamin, a suburb in southeast of Tehran, to explore establishing a safehouse in that town. We rented a room in Varamin from a property owner who was a young woman living with her toddler daughter. I helped the woman with some housework and care of her daughter and became very close and friendly with them. We went shopping together and visited the holy shrines in Varamin. My goal was to earn the trust of the landlord, neighbours and the local community, in order to gradually be able to rent a house and establish a new safehouse.

I must point out that it was around this time that some of the comrades started questioning the efficacy of guerrilla struggle and considering changing course and splitting from the Organization. Comrade Khodabakhsh was also one of those who had questioned armed struggle. After lengthy discussions with him, I started having doubts myself. During these discussions comrade Hassan Farjoudi, who also participated in our discussions tried to address my questions. At one point he asked, 'Comrade Shamsi, make your own decision, will you go with those who are splitting from the Organization, or will you remain with the Organization?' I replied, 'Comrade, I will remain with the Organization.'

I was transferred to Mashhad in autumn of 1976. I lived with comrade Kioumars Sanjari ('Ali) for two months in a rental room in a village outside of the city. During the days I would go with local women to work on the farms. I would ride with them in a truck, tie the chador around my head and work like other farm workers would work on vegetable farms, and at night would ride the truck back home.

Kioumars Sanjari was identified by police forces on 29 January 1977, in front of the Mashhad Telephone company.

> They charged at him, the comrade resisted arrest and started shooting at them, killing one of the regime mercenaries. He is then surrounded by SAVAK agents. The comrade reaches for and bites a Cyanide pill. One of the mercenaries tries to remove the pill from his mouth in order to capture him alive and subject him to torture ... and fails. Our comrade is martyred.[14]

After the killing of comrade Sanjari, I was transferred to a safehouse where comrades Kazem Ghebra'i (Kuchek Khan) and Qorbanali 'Abdolrahimpour (Majid) were living. This house was a small part of a bigger house owned by an elderly couple from Mashhad that comrades had rented. The house was in the Garage-Daran neighbourhood of the city, and we lived there for about a month. Later, we bought a small house for 27,000 Toman in Shahrak-e Sakhteman, a suburb of Mashhad. This house was in one of the working-class neighbourhoods of Shahrak-e Sakhteman. The house had two small rooms. We had water for only two hours a day, during which we would fill water containers and use them for days. I had developed good relations with the neighbours. Kazem would help the neighbours with our pick-up truck hauling their belongings and Majid would help them with electrical switch repairs, changing the lamps and such. We had lived there about five months when Majid left. We lived in the house for two more months until June 1977 when comrade Kazem Ghebra'i (Kuchak Khan) lost his life during clashes with security forces. We had no choice then but to vacate this house and rent another one. After Majid left for Isfahan and Kazem was killed, comrade Mohammad Reza Ghebra'i (alias Mansour, the elder brother of Kazem Ghebra'i), comrade Siamak Asadian (Eskandar) and myself created a new team in Mashhad. I was placed in charge of this team.

Following the arrest of Hasan Farjoudi in January and the killing of Saba Bijanzadeh (Hajar) in February of 1977 and the changes that occurred in rebuilding of the organizational teams and branches, I left for Isfahan and took charge of a team in Isfahan. We were renting a house with comrade Tahmaseb Vaziri. In total we were in Isfahan for more than a year. Comrade Tahmaseb had established a considerable number of connections with employees at Isfahan Steel factory, students in Isfahan University and other sympathizers of the Organization. Our team had many publishing projects which I oversaw. We republished *The Short History of the Communist Party of the Soviet Union(Short Course)* (1938) in several volumes and distributed these among the students of Isfahan University. In addition, we typed and printed the pamphlets of Tupamaros of Uruguay and the Movement of the Revolutionary Left (MIR) of Chile, which were disseminated by and amongst students. Some of Marx's works such as *The Eighteenth Brumaire of Louis Bonaparte*, Lenin's writings and the writings of comrade Jazani were also distributed amongst students. We were promoting the goals and aspirations of the OIPFG, which were well received by workers and students. In Isfahan I was in contact with several students. Based on the Organization's guidelines, these university students had formed teams of two or three members and were studying collectively and helping with printing materials. They were distributing the Organization's message. It is important to mention the name of a heroic comrade who worked in an underground cell and was instrumental in distributing the Organization's publications among the wider community. This comrade was Mojtaba Motale Sarabi, a medical student in the University of Isfahan, who was originally from Sarab. One day I had a meeting with him at Towghi Alley in Isfahan city where I gave him the book parcel which I had hidden under my veil. Shortly after this meeting, he was arrested with the books. I am aware that he underwent torture without divulging information. Otherwise SAVAK would have arrested me or put me under surveillance and perhaps all our teams and extensive networks in Isfahan which we had built with extensive efforts, would have collapsed.

It was in Isfahan that from the middle of 1978 we followed people's demonstrations and participated in them and distributed leaflets in strikes throughout the uprising. Approximately two months before the final victory of the revolution, for the purposes of organizing the sympathizers of the Organization, whose numbers were growing by the day and were becoming a notable force in cities like Ahwaz, Abadan and Aghajari: We went to Ahwaz, a city in southwest of Iran, along with Tahmaseb Vaziri and Ja'far Panjehshahi. After a short period of time, Behrouz Khaliq, Maliheh Zehtab (Simin) and Iraj Doustdar-Sanaye (Bahram) also joined us. We did all we could to organize, in as short a time as possible, all sympathizers of the OIPFG including workers, high school and university students and academics. By this time, it was these supporters who were leading the street protests as well as the strikes at their workplaces in order to advance the goals of the Organization. In coordination with the supporters, the Organization was also trying, with all its means, to carry out a series of political and military activities to further the revolution. The masses too, showed their interest and respect to the People's Fada'i Guerrillas wherever they heard the name of the Organization or saw the members of the Organization.

I was in Ahwaz for about a month, and with the experience I had gained on the printing projects, I was able to make good use of the extensive resources offered by our supporters. The communiqués and the flyers of the Organization which were disseminated extensively among the people, particularly in the oil refineries and educational institutions, together with armed attacks on the Shah's repressive institutions contributed towards the success of the final phase of the revolution.

Four decades later, when I look back, despite all the naiveite, youthful inexperience and mistakes of the 1970s, I deeply value and respect those struggles and aspirations. I cherish those years of my life, which were filled with moral courage and revolutionary passion, a time when we stood strong and said no to repression, to oppression, to despotism and to injustice, and the thought of surrendering to the enemy never crossed our minds.

My beloved Organization

Nahid Qajar

My childhood

I was born in the city of Gorgan in 1952. My father was a retired officer of the gendarmerie of Gorgan. I was eight years old when he passed away. I went to school there until seventh grade. Then we moved to Sari.

Our big house with a garden and a few old rooms situated in an old quarter of Gorgan was home to people of different spectra of society such as truck drivers, workers, public employees and architects. A Jewish man and a student also lived there as tenants. For years I lived a life full of friendship in the midst of this colourful community of different people. This environment enriched my spirit and character. We were friends with a lot of neighbours.

Thus, as a child I was already in contact with different kinds of people stemming from different social backgrounds. I was the only girl and second-born child of the family, living with my three brothers and mother in two rooms. Since my childhood I had a good relationship with my mother. Our income consisted of the small amount of money we earned from renting out the rooms and a small sum of money from my father's pension. It was in third grade that I became interested in reading books. I started going to the bookstore in Gorgan. In order to provide the necessary pocket money and pay the weekly rent for the books I borrowed from bookshop, I began to give classes to younger pupils and also pursued sewing and knitting. Thus, as a twelve-year-old girl, I earned my own money and even had the means to support my brothers.

The beginning of my political activities

I was sixteen years old when I first got acquainted with daily politics through my maternal uncle Rahim Karimian in Sari. From this moment onwards, my readings took a political flavour. All of the books and novels I read were formally defined as forbidden literature. I had to hide them from both strangers and close relatives, even my mother. Listening to clandestine radios also played a certain role. My mother, who had witnessed the suppression of the struggle of the previous generation of Tudeh and

Mossadeq followers amongst her own family and neighbours, was concerned by my studies and political tendencies.

From 1970 onwards, I became a sympathizer of the Pouyan-Ahmadzadeh-Meftahi group through my uncle Rahim. My political and organizational connections were interrupted with the arrest and sentencing of my uncle and Naqi Hamidian and the execution of Ahmad Farhoudi and 'Abbas and Asadollah Meftahi. From then onwards, I was compelled to pursue my political activities independently and on my own initiative. These activities included being in touch with the prisoners' families, setting up cells and poetry meetings, readings and book exchange groups. In those years, I also propagated the guerrilla movement as far as possible.

In 1973, I graduated in industrial chemistry at the Irandokht School in Sari. During this period my political ideas, revolutionary romanticism and spirit were intense and I was very much restless. However, I concealed my political activities from my family. I wanted to get in touch with the People's Fada'is. For such purpose, I had to achieve independence from my family and be able to pay my own expenses. In compliance with the recommendation of my uncle and contrary to my personal leanings, I decided not to go to university, even though it would have provided me with much desired liberties. He believed that it would be better to start a life among the people. Family restrictions, suspicion and hindrances that existed for a young woman like me constituted serious barriers to free choice regarding political activities. At the same time, I was very keen and excited about getting directly in touch with the people and society. In order to be independent from my family, I did not have any choice but to move to another region, far away from Sari. With such intentions in mind, I chose to voluntarily serve in the Literacy Corps.

In the course of six months of military training in the garrison of Gorgan, while being among female members of the Literacy Corps, I secretly began to do political work. I founded three different study groups. And outside of the garrison, in the city of Gorgan, I got acquainted with literary and artistic circles, as well as theatre groups and also collaborated with them as much as possible.

After finishing the training course, I worked as a teacher in the Literacy Corps and lived in a village called Hakimabad in Gonbad-e Kavus. I encountered different teachers there and tried to draw their attention to the necessity of teaching children and teenagers in villages how to read and write and especially draw their attention to social problems as well as to the existence of poverty and injustice through the books of Samad Behrangi. One of my teacher colleagues was Abdolhakim Makhtum.

I lived one and a half years in this village and built close relationships with different layers of the rural population and local government institutions such as the gendarmerie, as well as the organization of rural development, the office of electricity and water, the office of roads, the office of hygiene, social welfare, education, health and the development corps. As a result, I got acquainted with a variety of problems – misfortunes and sufferings of women, men and children in that area. It was also during this period that I became directly acquainted with the misfortune of drug addiction, the smuggling of drugs, the role of the gendarmerie in distributing it, prostitution resulting from poverty and distress, the hunger of my students, the lack of minimum hygiene and medical treatment, as well as with the poverty of agricultural seasonal workers. Personal contact with the people of this and other surrounding villages who had experienced different misfortunes had more effect on me than the hundreds of books and stories I read. It was during this period that my will to pursue political activism against a regime which claimed that the state of villages had improved in the wake of land reform became stronger and there was no going back from my decision to continue along the path I had chosen.

The relations with the Organization of the Iranian People's Fada'is Guerrillas

In the winter of 1975, I got into contact with the Fada'is via Ebrahim Kheyri-Abriz. He had been released from the prison of Mashhad and brought a message from Naqi Hamidian and Rahim Karimian to me concerning my potential cooperation with the Organization of the People's Fada'i Guerrilla. Before Ebrahim Kheyri, Mostafa Hassanpour had been released from prison. He immediately joined the Organization and attracted many ex-prisoners living in Mashhad to the OIPFG.

There was still one year left till the end of my civil service in 1975. In the course of this year, the Ebrahim Kheiri, 'Ali Akbar Ja'fari (Fereydoun), Shamsi Nahani, Mostafa Hassanpour and Bahman Rouhi-Ahangaran visited me in Hakimabad village.

In my first contacts, I expressed my readiness to join the Organization and go into clandestine life. The experience of my membership within the Organization of the People's Fada'is was as follows: In a meeting with 'Ali Akbar Ja'fari in Gorgan, I told him the main reasons for joining the Organization. I also informed him about my activities and political relationships within my private and professional life and the like. At the end of the winter of 1974, 'Ali Akbar Ja'fari made an appointment for me to meet a comrade in Yussef-abad Street in Tehran and clarify the questions they had about me. I went to the appointment and was looking for the special sign through which I was supposed to identify the comrade, but nobody came. I went there another day again, but no one was there. I lost hope. I decided to go there for a third and last time and in case the comrade did not show up once more, I would return to my working place in town. Suddenly, a young man carrying a journal called *Zan-e Rouz* (The Woman of the Day), which was our safety sign, called me up from behind. This is how we finally met.

The questions he asked me were diverse. Part of it consisted of the motives behind my decision to join the movement and the Organization. Another part was about political prisoners and their state of mind. He also talked about the belongings of group no. 2 (Pouyan-Ahmadzadeh-Meftahi), which he suspected had been put at my disposal during the years 1970–1. He also asked me about the methods used to communicate with the inmates, as well as how to contact the families of imprisoned Fada'is and Mojahedin. He asked with curiosity and I replied. When he asked me how I contacted the comrades inside the prison, I looked at him, waited for a while and told him that 'this is an issue that only concerns the prisoners and me. They are captive in the hands of the enemy and I would therefore not provide you with any information, even if you were Hamid Ashraf!' He grinned and said: 'Oh, I see!' His exact questions made me wonder whether he was Hamid Ashraf himself. Later I found out that he was indeed Hamid Ashraf.

Membership in the Organization

By and large, whoever believed in Marxism-Leninism and armed struggle could become a member of the OIPFG. In addition to that, one needed to be introduced by a person who was trusted by the Organization and be devoted to the people. Among the conditions of becoming a member, one had to voluntarily use all his/her time and energy into achieving the aims, programmes, policies and positions of the Organization and to be ready to leave behind any type of attachment. At that time, I fulfilled these requirements. My references were the comrades in prison.

Generally speaking, there was no distinction between men and women in the process of becoming a member in the Organization. In this context, the most important thing was acceptance of Marxist class struggle. At that time, women did not demand different rights and privileges vis-à-vis men. The Fada'i men and women believed that the real conditions for the implementation of women's rights in the society would be only achieved if freedom, democracy and social justice (a socialist order) was to be established. All the rules and regulations and the internal relations of the Organization were the same for both male and female members. Due to the pressure and brutal police persecution, there was no hierarchical difference between men and women members. During the time that I got into contact with the Organization, there was a more or less clear ranking amongst members and sympathizers, such as clandestine members, semi-clandestine members, overt members and the outside sympathizers. The general definitions of these three categories were written down in the internal rules and regulations of the Organization. What I experienced about how the membership and classification functioned is as follows: The clandestine members were those who were always at the disposal of the Organization and were organized in safehouses. Members in this category were not many.

The clandestine-overt members often worked and lived openly but they were linked with the covert activities of the Organization. They provided the necessary resources for the Organization. For example, they provided apartments, cars, facilities for printing and the distribution of publications, money and intelligence to the Organization. The Organization generally did not turn them into covert members as long as the Organization's security was not threatened.

As the name already suggests, the overt members lived an ordinary life similar to other people. But apart from their apparently common life, all their relations and activities were generally in the service of fulfilling political and propagandistic obligations of the Organization. They were very active in university circles, open corporate student activities like mountain climbing, sport activities, in libraries and in lectures, in dormitories, especially during student demonstrations and strikes. They collected financial aid and used every possibility they had in order to help the Organization. They also identified individuals who were prone to cooperate and acquainted them with the problems and needs of the Organization until they were finally recruited. The overt members were constantly under the exposure of the SAVAK secret police. There is no information about their exact number.

The sympathizers, who were a large group of supporters, were mainly to be found amongst students, the intelligentsia, artists and the other educated strata of the society. They helped the Organization in different ways. The number of supporters was very large and the most suitable and talented of these supporters were chosen for membership according to the needs of the Organization.

Before I became a member, I had been an active and experienced sympathizer of the Organization for some years. As a result of the arrest of my uncle, I lost any possibility to connect with the Organization. For over three years, I was active all by myself on my personal initiative, using my own knowledge and experience. In the spring of 1974, I announced my readiness to join the Fada'is. Subsequently, the Organization got into touch with me and I became a semi-clandestine member. I still did not belong to any safehouse. However, due to the many blows that the Organization suffered in Khorasan in early 1975, I experienced life within a safehouse for a limited period of time. The reason was that my comrades guessed that, in the wake of the above-mentioned blows, it was possible that SAVAK could have acquired some information about me. Thus, they brought me to a safehouse of the Mashhad branch with blindfolded eyes. I later found out that the house was situated in a street called Tehran Street. It was the comrades Saba Bijanzadeh, Mohammad Hosseini Haqnavaz (Mansour), Ahmad Gholamian (Hadi), Hamid Momeni,[1] Kioumars Sanjari, Abolhassan Shayegan Shamasbi, and Vida Goli Abkenari (Leyla)[2] who lived in that safehouse. Saba Bijanzadeh was the safehouse leader. It was the first stage in my learning on how to live in the safehouse. During the reorganization we rented a single house with Ebrahim Kheiri Abriz on Sarakhs Road in Mashhad. After it became clear that I was not in danger, I returned to Hakimabad. I was still a clandestine-overt member. I was also teaching in the village of Hakimabad besides being involved in organizing workers. In the meantime, I also did social work and informed the Organization about my acquaintance with the region, the local authorities and my work among the people, workers and peasants. This continued until Mohammad Hossein Haqnavaz, who was in charge of the Khorasan branch and my direct mentor, told me in one of the intermittent meetings of 1975 that the Organization needed my help and that I would have to become a covert member as soon as possible, so that I could participate in certain operations.

I immediately wiped out all my documents, photos and anything that SAVAK could use to find out about my appearance and background. I prepared myself for a covert life with no return to a normal one in mind.

The new comrades who entered the safehouse were equipped with grenades and cyanide. An educational schedule was implemented at this stage. It consisted of printing techniques, such as the layout of pamphlets and books, using explosives, distributing leaflets, using cameras and microfilms, producing cyanide capsules, making grenades, using arms and shooting, as well as becoming acquainted with the rules and regulations of the Organization, individual and collective study, obligatory sports, writing nightly or weekly programmes, getting acquainted with the city and the rules and regulations of life inside safehouses. These rules and regulations were printed in a small pamphlet which every new member of a safehouse had to study. Joint discussions also took place in order to clarify its contents. The rules and regulations regarding daily affairs were also consulted. A certain time was assigned to individual studies as well. The individual studies proceeded as such: a specific text was studied and discussed. The books that were mostly read in safehouses were as follows: the works of Lenin; the translation of the works of Marx, Engels, Stalin and Mao; books about the movement of freedom fighters and the guerrilla movements of South America, Palestine and Vietnam; and booklets written by the members of the Organization, such as the writings of Bijan Jazani, Hamid Momeni, Masoud Ahmadzadeh, Pouyan and Hamid Ashraf. In addition to that, the organ of the Organization, *Nabard-e Khalq* was also read. There was also a publication which was circulated only inside the organization which was called *Tabligh-e Mosallahaneh*, or Armed Propaganda, which reflected the opinions of the comrades of the Organization.

At that time, most of those revolutionary intellectuals of the left, who believed in armed struggle and the Organization of the People's Fada'i Guerrillas, set their hope in the existence and activities of the Organization. With the experience I had obtained from my activities among ordinary people, my idea of the overall activities of the Organization were more or less the same. I thought that covert members of the Organization were continuously engaging with the people and the workers and had direct contact with them. After I had gone underground, my comrades transferred me to the same safehouse in Mashhad with the same combination of people I have mentioned. At that time, I thought that, after one or two weeks, I would immediately start working among the people in the framework of a new operation. But after two weeks, there still was not any such operation in sight. I felt useless. Gradually the question came up why I wasn't participating in any operation and I wondered whether there was any operation going on at all?

I discussed my concerns with Mohammad Hosseini Haqnavaz, who was in charge of the Mashhad branch. I told him that I had the impression that I was locked up in this house and was not able to pursue any activity at all. He replied that the life of a guerrilla was just like that: 'The Organization has a general and thorough program, but you only consider your individual situation!'

I was not convinced and wanted to talk to another branch leader. Our house had a phone and one of the most famous and popular leaders of the Organization with the code name of 'Mahmoud' called our house (we all knew that Mahmoud was Hamid Ashraf, but we never mentioned it). I talked with Mahmoud about my concerns. He heartily told me that I could go back but then the comrades will change their minds about me. He meant that the Organization would lose its trust in me and the relationship would be cut off. This was too much for me to bear. I faced a dilemma: I liked the Organization and my comrades. Their judgement, as well as that of the comrades in prison was extremely important to me. I totally agreed with the armed struggle of the Organization. I propagated this idea in society and in my private networks. But their working patterns in the safehouse was not acceptable to me. I was of the opinion that a desirable and fruitful way of working would have been that, parallel to the activities of the Organization, I could have continued with the social and political work I had already been doing. Of course, I didn't think that there were any contradictions between the military, political and social work and the work among the people. At that time, I didn't want to choose between one and another but preferred to pursue both of them. Now, I had reached some kind of a crossroad, a dilemma, and I felt bewildered. Realizing that they could believe that I had retreated from the struggle was incredibly difficult for me. The fact that I had become a covert member was not because I was known by SAVAK and police and therefore had to hide from them. Even alone and without any relation to the Organization, I pursued relatively large social activities and was in touch with the people. I wanted to continue my activities within my favourite Organization. But this wasn't practically possible. At that time, I felt that I had been caught and was imprisoned in a narrow cell. The acceptance of a covert life deprived me of all personal and social relations. But I stayed and continued. I became a guerrilla member of the People's Fada'is.

Activities among the workers and others

In the years 1974–5, the leadership of the Organization reached the conclusion that during the four years of armed struggle, it had been able to establish and strengthen its position among the revolutionary intelligentsia. Therefore, it considered to act on another level. This stage consisted of working among the urban and rural workers. For this purpose, great efforts were undertaken so that some of the covert members of the Organization could go to factories and working places without the military belt, carrying only a pocket grenade and cyanide, not only to explore the workers' environment but also to do propagandistic and political work amongst them. I followed the roadmap accordingly.

I have to say that while I was still working at the Literacy Corps of Hakimabad, my comrades decided to assign me to one of these new political and propaganda cells. It was not in the same region I was working at, but somewhere in Khorasan. This problem had become a controversial question for me. In the meetings I had with Mohammad Hosseini Haqnavaz in Gorgan, I told him how I was practically doing the same work (as I had done before) and asked him why I had to go to another region and start from zero? Haqnavaz replied that 'the Organization has other plans for you!' So, I agreed.

In the spring of 1975, the specific plan for being active amongst workers and peasants of the area of Bojnourd-Qouchan and Shirvan was prepared and I took part as a covert-overt member in this operation. The person in charge of this operation was 'Ali Akbar Ja'fari (Fereydoun), a member of the central organ. But on April 22 of 1975, he was killed in a car accident on the Gorgan–Khorasan Road linking Gorgan and Khorasan. But Mohammad Hosseini Haqnavaz, who was with him, survived. With the loss of Ja'fari, Haqnavaz took the responsibility of the region of Khorasan and the plan I mentioned was implemented directly by him.

The plan was to take place with the participation of four members: Jahanbakhsh Paydary, Ebrahim Kheiri, a young man called Abolhossein Shayegan Shamasbi and myself. Kheiri and I were supposed to work in the sugar factory of Shirvan with forged identities and to also rent a house in one of the nearby villages. Jahanbakhsh would work as a peddling draper and move from village to village with his motorbike. Kheiri and I were equipped with cyanide and pocket grenades and Jahanbakhsh, who was a covert cadre of the Organization, carried a weapon and a military belt. Abolhossein was only assigned to our safehouse as a cover-up person.

Haqnavaz, Jahanbakhsh, Ebrahim Kheiri and me met in Kouhsangi Park in Mashhad to discuss our plan and prepare our operation. I agreed with the working program in the factory, but disagreed with the peddling draper. I disagreed because Jahanbakhsh looked more like an intellectual than a draper. In my opinion, this work was futile and wouldn't have any meaningful impact on the people. Haqnavaz said: 'Don't think that you know better than the Organization! The Organization has a holistic approach, when it comes to problems. But you only see your own logic!'

We were in the primary stage of being recruited in the factory and looking for a house when Jahanbakhsh, who was shadowed by the police, got killed during a gunfight. In conjunction with other assaults that our comrades suffered in the same area, our program practically got cancelled.

After this fiasco, another plan was proposed to work in the Royal Loom Factory of Mazandaran. It was composed of Abdollah Sa'idi, Ebrahim Kheiri and me. But this project also got called off in the first phase, as a result of the killing of Abdollah Sa'idi at the police station of Bandar Gaz.

The plan for working in the factories and living in the nearby villages in Khorasan and Mazandaran was called off due to several blows. The following mishaps occurred at intervals of six months between spring and winter 1975: 'Ali Akbar Ja'fari's death in a car accident, Haqnavaz's clash with the police in the cemetery of Gorgan and his subsequent escape, the killing of Jahanbakhsh Paydary and Abdollah Sa'idi, the seven-hour long pursuit of Mostafa Hassanpour by the police in Mashhad, Haqnavaz's, Zeynolabeddin Rashtchi's and Gholam-Reza Banezhad's clash with the police in the vicinity of the railway station of Mashhad and the death of Banezhad. Thus, the Organization was not successful in achieving any concrete results through its efforts in this region.

In my opinion, the entire work among the people which the Organization undertook in Khorasan and Mazandaran was a correct and essential operation which could have acquainted the Organization with the concrete problems of the people and society. But this operation did not become a plan that was independent from the Organization. The only people who were involved in this operation were those who either totally or partly lived in a clandestine manner. These kinds of programs could have taken place without the direct intervention of the Organization. The Organization's guidelines alone would have been sufficient to execute the operation. Individuals like me who didn't have a relationship with the Organization and were only acquainted with a general guidance could have done numerous projects without encountering any danger or making SAVAK suspicious of the emergence of secret networks and their relation to the activities of semi-clandestine or even overt members. The direct participation of the Organization and the guerrilla cadres who were on the wanted list by the police for other reasons were constantly under threat and were inevitably exposed to blows. It also has to be mentioned that due to the high level of secrecy in the Organization, each member could only be well-informed about the problems of the Organization in his/ her own area of activity. I have only alluded to my direct personal experience. As far as I see it, the basic work of the Organization in our region was that the overt members (like me) would go underground and would be assigned to work among workers with a forged identity in another region. This program could not have been successful. By and large, the Organization's operations among the people didn't reach a tangible outcome due to successive blows struck by the security authorities.

The living conditions in the safehouse

Life in the team/safehouse was based on a series of specific detailed operating procedures and regulations which each individual had to observe and adhere to precisely. The safehouses made up the structure of the Organization where most of the covert and overt members lived.

In most of the houses which I lived in, the team consisted of three to five guerrillas with usually a husband and wife couple as its nucleus. Having a couple as the nucleus provided cover as they maintained relationships with the landlord and neighbours. Everyone else would be introduced as a close relative of the couple. All of these relationships were fabricated and based on fake birth certificates. The required furniture and housewares were usually procured from either second-hand stores or were provided by the overt members. Each safehouse generally had a living room, appropriately furnished for the neighbourhood, in case of unexpected visits from the landlord or neighbours.

In general, each safehouse had a head and was organized for specific duties, such as publication, distribution, social work or communication. Both the head and the deputy for each house were assigned by the central organ.

The military work mostly consisted of recognising the targets for each operation, bombing, provision of funds (mostly by confiscating banks) and similar activities. The work of communication consisted of establishing contact with members of the Organization living outside the country, connecting with other revolutionary groups, relations with the sympathizers and so on. All these relationships were based on special security regulations. If a sympathizer of the Organization had a social or administrative position in a state institution, then the Organization would establish a special unidirectional relationship with this person. As a rule, the position of this person was strictly confidential.

Since the Organization was one of a political-military nature, these responsibilities were generally combined with each other. As an example, I was a member of the team in Mashhad which was simultaneously in charge of two responsibilities: military and publication. If a team suffered blows, detentions or murder of one of its members and in case the central organ felt the necessity to reorganize the teams, they would be changed accordingly. All the internal works of the team were organized attentively and with a clear division of labour. Each person was in charge of a particular task that resulted from the weekly and daily programming. The general obligations of the safehouse and the responsibilities were equally divided according to the capabilities of individuals amongst the male and female members. To give an example, Kioumars Sanjari, who was specialized in print and technical matters, was in charge of these responsibilities in the Mashhad team, where I was a member. Or Hamid Momeni, who was a skilled theoretician, was in charge of political discussions in the Mashhad team.

Every team member was in charge of a certain activity. The head of the house was always in charge of political and military matters. The head of the house lead the team especially during crises such as clashes with the police. Another team member was in charge of theoretical-political matters in every house that I lived at. Women were usually in charge of security and finances of the house.

Security was the most important issue of every guerrilla base. In order to maintain cover, an appropriate house for the planned duties of the team would be rented. For instance, a house in the working-class neighbourhoods would be used for teams assigned to social/political work amongst workers. The entire characteristics of the team, such as appearance, pseudonyms, the jargon and the dialect and the jobs each member supposedly held, were adjusted to fit the environment. On the other hand, if the safehouse was located in a wealthy part of city, then the characteristics of the member would be adjusted accordingly. Women were in charge of supervision and the security of the houses. They checked the appearance of comrades and carefully managed communication with the neighbours, maintaining an image of normalcy to prevent extra curiosity or sensitivity from the landlord and neighbours.

The person in charge of financial affairs managed the budget and supervised all expenses. The budget and rules for expenditures for each house was set with agreement of all team members. In 1975 the per diem food allotment was about 4.5 tomans for each team member. The minimum necessary food was provided with this budget. The team members in our Mashhad house were always hungry because we had three (morning, noon and evening), 30 minutes heavy exercise sessions each day since the team was responsible for both military (identifying and executing operational targets) and publication duties. Our financial means were scarce because we guerrilla fighters believed that the money bestowed to us belonged to the masses and should be spent for the struggle and the revolutionary movement, not for personal purposes.

From very early after the formation of the Organization, each member of a safehouse was required to have a backup residence. These were known as the 'single room'. The backup residence was another safehouse in case access to the safehouse was lost (due to loss of cover, an attack by security forces, etc.). This was essential for the safety of the members especially the female members as it prevented them from being left alone on the streets. The use of safehouse was meant to be temporary until the link to the Organization could be re-established. For example, after fleeing from prison, Ashraf Dehqani had been taken, blindfolded, to live in the same house as Marziyeh Ahmadi Oskou'i and Shirin Mo'azed. But when Ashraf had to leave the house after the two comrades protecting her had been killed, she not only did not know where she was but also had no place to go for protection. She had to live through a hard, dangerous situation (exposed to dangers of being homeless in addition to being a fugitive) until she re-established her links to the Organization.

The workroom

Every safehouse that I lived at had a separate room which housed all the political documents, communication equipment and firearms which belonged to the team. This room was known as the 'workroom'. The workroom typically included documents such as newspapers, archives of economic and labour reports, a small library of books and the Organization's published material. Pictures of Marx, Engels, Lenin, Stalin, Mao and Ho-Chi-Minh were to be found on the workroom walls. Beneath them were pictures of the fallen comrades of the Organization and those of the general arm struggle (Mirza Kouchak Khan, Sattar Khan, Bagher Khan, Colonel Taqi Khan Pesiyan, Khosrow Rouzbeh and Parviz Hekmatjou). The walls were also covered with slogans such as 'Prefer the movement over the Organization, the Organization over the comrades, and the comrades over oneself' and 'With faith in our victory'. The workroom also housed the typewriter, the explosives and if available a radio receiver which could capture the police's radio communications.

The Organization's classified files were at a corner of the workroom in a metal file cabinet. One of the team members was always assigned to burn the files, in case of clash with police and/or escape, with an incendiary bomb that was placed next to the file cabinet. The orders from the Organization were to destroy the files at any cost. The files were categorized according to their descending order of importance into 'double-zero', 'zero', 'one' and 'two' classes as follows:

A – The 'double-zero'-class files included the list of resources available to the Organization such as trusted doctors who would treat the guerrillas in case of emergency, people or companies willing to provide financial support, help with printing and distribution, required specialty materials, such as those necessary to make counterfeit stamps, a car or a safehouse. The list of current appointments was also classified as double-zero since it would endanger other comrades' lives if it were to be retrieved by the police.
B – The 'zero'-class files, which included a list of potential sources who could provide financial and logistics support in emergencies, such as an exposed cover story or other blows from SAVAK or the police.
C – The 'one'-class files included internal documents such as regulations, notes, letters, articles and analysis reports, as well as instructions for producing explosives. The safehouse's inventory list of the weapons such as handguns and grenades as well the available cash was filed under the 'one' class.
D – The 'two'-class files usually included papers related to the other equipment available at the safehouse such as typewriters, printing and binding tools, stencils, projectors, police receivers and more.

The 'double-zero'- and 'zero'-class files were to be burned immediately in case of an attack or if the house's cover was blown. As far as I can recall, at least two comrades were killed because of this requirement either due to panic or getting caught in the flames. As much as possible, attempts should have been made to save and take the 'one'-class files.

Military belt

As mentioned earlier, military rules and regulations were in place in the Organization. New recruits were equipped with grenades and cyanide to avoid getting caught by the police or the SAVAK in case of a clash with either of them. Members would be assigned appropriate firearms based on their experience, responsibility and rank in the Organization. Those responsible for communication, or information gathering, and exchange were usually equipped with heavier arms. The more recent recruits who did not have to leave the safehouse often would be equipped with a 22-calibre gun. My first assigned handgun, a 'Spring-gun', had been confiscated from a police officer.

Every team member had a 'military belt' to carry a weapon (a colt or a light machine gun), bullet cartridge, grenade, cyanide, knife, a wallet for pocket money (500 tomans for men and 1,500 tomans for women) as well as a first-aid kit. Each member made his or her own belt with leather covers for each item. The initial education of a guerrilla fighter consisted of the recognition of the area of residence, streets and city, typing, publication techniques, acquaintance with explosives, distribution of leaflets, production of cyanide capsules, construction of hand grenades, learning how to use arms outside the city, and how to move around in the city. It needs to be mentioned that education for all groups was not pursued at the same time. Before I went underground, I had already learned how to type, publish and use weapons. I had attained acquaintance with explosives and learned how to ride a motorcycle. In the first safehouse I went to, explosives and hand grenades were also made.

Planning

Each safehouse had a daily and weekly schedule for executing the specifically political and other general activities. Each house regulated its own weekly responsibilities. Therefore, one hour was set aside every evening for planning.

The working hours in the safehouse were from 6.00 a.m. to 11.00 p.m. Every minute of these seventeen hours were to be dedicated to the Organization. That left seven hours for sleep, but each member would be assigned guard duty for one of those seven hours. The guard duty period could extend to two hours if or when a small number of members were in the house.

Although each member was responsible to follow through on his or her daily plan, the responsibility to track and regulate the team's planned activities for each day rotated between each member on a daily basis. The daily plans included hourly details such as leave the house at eight, return at ten followed by an hour of reading from ten to eleven and an hour of printing and binding. We were supposed to actively follow the political news and events through the media.

The time after dinner, on nightly basis, was dedicated to review and discussion of members' daily activities, accomplishments and other events relevant to the house which included criticism and self-criticism, as well as planning. After planning, updates on Organization's broad plans, issues and events regarding other safehouses and news from political prisoners as well other groups inside and outside of Iran were discussed. These were followed by discussions regarding political events of the day as well as other political organizations such as the Mojahedin-e Khalq.

The internal rules of the Organization

The Iranian People's Fada'i Guerrillas had gradually developed and implemented a series of rules and provisions as the internal code of conduct for its members. I used to know them by heart but have forgotten many of them with passage of time. Here, I mention a few that I still remember.

One of the rules specified the dress code within the safehouses. In the safehouses, guerrillas generally wouldn't wear light-coloured or flower-patterned clothes. Furthermore, women were not allowed to wear tight clothes. Women usually wore tunic and pants. Men and women didn't wear sleeveless clothes. Women wore long stockings to cover their legs during sporting activities. All guerrillas wore sneakers (which we had nicknames as 'escape shoes') all day long and even slept with them. They took their shoes off during exercise for the sake of avoiding to make considerable noise. Women were not supposed to hang their underwear in an area visible to others.

Although female comrades adapted their appearance according to their roles and responsibilities (when necessary, young women plucked their eyebrows and wore a wedding ring and played the role of a housewife), women were not allowed to wear make-up while in the safehouse. If it was necessary to wear make-up outside of the house, they would have to wash the make-up right after arriving in the house.

One day Qasem Siadati and I had to pretend to be a married couple owning a big engineering company in order to by a copy machine from the Xerox sales office located in Northern Tehran. I had to go to a beauty parlour in order to have the right appearance for the appointment at the sales office. Neither one of us could look at each other while on the way to and from the sales office. I washed the make-up off as soon as I arrived back at the team-house as I didn't want my comrades to see me with make-up. I felt ashamed and reduced to a doll lookalike.

Another rule specified that every member had to bathe every other week. We usually had to use a public bath as the safehouses, generally, didn't have a bath. This rule made the situation very difficult for women during their menstrual period. Although no one would say anything, the reason was clear to others when one of the women didn't participate in group exercise sessions due to her monthly period. Personally, I didn't feel good being unable to do exercise in the morning and evening. For me, this was a weakness vis-à-vis men. Some women who were too shy or would not want to fall behind men would follow through with exercise routines under physical pressure due to menstruation. Typically, the difficulties with exercising started about a week before menses when the breast gets swollen and hurt. We used to wrap our breasts tightly with a scarf to make it easier to exercise.

The mental pressure from being down and bored, having back ache or being sensitive to the noise from the typewriter or the manual copy machine during menstruation was very annoying as women had to keep up with daily routines and could not express how they felt. These sort of period-related issues were usually only noticed by other women in the house.

The rules regarding night sleep required the safehouse members to sleep in the same room. Blankets were folded in sleeping bag form and everybody slept side by side with women generally sleeping next to each other. The wake-up routine in the morning or guard duty was to gently hit the sole of the feet. Those who were staying in the house behind the blindfold would sleep separately.

Overall, the rules and regulations had a strict military content and spirit. I will describe an event that I have witnessed as an example. It relates to our safehouse in Mashhad in the winter of 1975. The internal rules required each safehouse to have one member in charge of managing and regulating the daily planned activities. This person was also in charge of opening the door if the coded knock or ring had been used. Otherwise, the female member, as the housekeeper, was supposed to open the door in case the coded knock or ring had not been used. In any case, the protocol for opening the door specified that the person opening the door had to be holding a loaded and ready-to-shoot handgun.

One evening, a female comrade, who in her daily activity log had reported 'security negligence', confirmed that she had forgotten to follow the protocol and her gun was not ready to shoot when she had opened the door earlier in the day. The Organization's disciplinary rule at that time specified twenty lashes whipped with a black cable (usually hung in the workroom). I proposed to forego the whipping during the comrade's self-criticism discussion, I pointed out that since she had realized the mistake herself, she had learned her lesson and wouldn't repeat it. The other members not only disagreed with me but also assigned me to carry out the punishment. At this point, this decision was considered as an order from the Organization. I didn't agree with the decision and didn't accept the assignment. I told them explicitly that they could punish me as they wished, but I wasn't going to whip her. What I did was a clear act of disobedience vis-à-vis the orders of the Organization. My disobedience infuriated the comrade in charge of the team but I did not give in. There was no way that I could convince myself to whip a female comrade who was suffering from menstrual pain.

A few days before this incident, Mohammad Hosseini Haqnavaz and I had left the house to meet with a sympathizer. I put a brick I picked up at a construction site along the way in my handbag. Everyone at the house was asking me what I planned to do with the brick and the male comrades were jokingly saying that I wanted to hit them on their head. But the reason was that our female comrade always suffered from pain during her period and the painkillers were ineffective and we did not have a hot-water bag in the house either. I had brought the brick as an alternative to a hot-water bag to decrease my comrade's pain. The male comrades knew this but expected me to whip her.

I was boycotted by the rest of the team for two days as a result of my disobedience and had to write a self-criticism note. One of our male comrades eventually conducted the whiplashes.

During the 'two-day boycott', nobody talked to me and I was not supposed to do any other activity. This punishment was hard and intolerable. But the fact that I didn't punish my comrade gave me a strong feeling of pride and delight. I may have even considered it a personal victory. As for my self-criticism, I wrote: 'Self-realization of a mistake is sufficient to prevent it from happening again.' Later on, I pointed out the similarity between our internal punishments and what the enemy does. The enemy whipped our comrades in order to obtain information or a confession and we whipped them as punishment for not following rules. In reality, not only I had criticized myself, but I had insisted on the validity of my point of view. My note was not accepted by the group and caused a lot of discussion. They wanted my self-criticism note to reflect their point of view. My disobedience issue was put aside after a few days as our team got busy with other issues. Kazem Ghebra'i and I moved from this safehouse to a single-person house.

In the fall of 1974, Mohammad Hosseini Haqnavaz, who insisted on the rules and regulations, told me that my opinion on the disciplinary punishment had sparked discussions in the central organ and almost everybody had agreed to eliminate this aspect of the punishment rules. After the blows to the Organization in the summer of 1976 most of the punishments were eliminated from the rules and regulations.

Sportswear

There were too many members in the safehouse during one summer and that required a new form of organization. In our safehouse, we exercised three times a day, half an hour each time which led to a lot of additional sweating. One not so big room served as our living room as well as our bedroom, dining room, gym and study room. After each exercise session the strong smell of sweat would create a suffocating atmosphere. It was so bad that even opening the windows and doors wouldn't help much.

Seven people, Saba Bijanzadeh, Mohammad Hosseini Haqnavaz, Vida Goli Abkenari, Kioumars Sanjari, Ahmad Gholamian, Hamid Momeni and I lived in that house in Mashhad.

According to the rules and regulations of the safehouses, each member of the house was supposed to take a bath once every fifteen days. But a few of the male comrades wouldn't pay much attention to these rules and had to be reminded of their duties to change into clean clothes and/or taking a bath. On the contrary, the female comrades paid more attention to their hygiene. During their period female comrades were not able to exercise. The annoying smell of sweat had become a serious issue. The reason was that we exercised with the same clothes we wore every day. We had never used sport outfits. The two other female comrades and I discussed this matter and reached the conclusion that we needed sport outfits, so that we wouldn't have to do our daily duties in sweaty clothes. Saba Bijanzadeh proposed wearing blouse and pants similar to the grey outfit that the Chinese women wore. They had a loose design and were comfortable for exercising.

This proposal was not welcomed by the male comrades. Hamid Momeni calmly said: 'what difference does it make? Regular clothes and sport outfits do not make any difference!' Another one said that 'women always pay attention to everything, but you have to keep in mind that we don't have a normal life in this house! What is the problem with the smell of sweat?' Another one said that 'you are imitating the petit bourgeois women! The safehouse rules need to be identical. The rules and regulations do not mention sport outfits. Now our guerrilla women have found enough free time to search for sportswear!' In short, all the men somehow opposed the introduction of sportswear in the safehouse. Saba got very angry. The proposal for wearing separate clothes during exercise did not get much attraction that evening. But we were persistent and asked to discuss this issue in the next meetings. Several days passed, but there was no time to continue the discussion on sportswear. Saba oversaw the internal affairs of the team. She included 'Sewing sportswear!' in the weekly plan as a reminder and presented the male comrades with a *fait accompli*. This time Haqnavaz, who was in charge of the Khorasan branch and member of the central organ, adamantly opposed the issue and said, 'I'm not by any means in favour of introducing sportswear to the house because I think it's contrary to the life of a guerrilla, as well as the internal rules of the Organization. You want to impose petit bourgeoisie characteristics in the safehouse!' But Saba's stubbornness and our insistence on our demands turned created a tense discussion. We proposed in consensus that the matter should be turned over to the central organ when everyone realized that the discussion wouldn't lead anywhere. As I recall, Saba was very strong-minded and she privately told me that Haqnavaz thinks he is more revolutionary than the others since he is in charge!

Saba wrote a letter to the central organ, on the next day, in regard to sportswear, hygiene and health of the guerrillas, so that it would reach Mahmoud (Hamid Ashraf). After a while, we received a letter from the central organ with comrade Mahmoud's signature. The letter fully agreed with our idea and proposal. With this permission, Saba bought grey clothing without consulting Haqnavaz. There was an old sewing machine in the house. Saba and I sewed a few exercise shirts and pants in different sizes for each team member and hung them in the room.

Sewing and wearing exercise clothes did not affect any internal rules and regulations. Each member individually decided whether he or she wanted to use them or not. It is noteworthy that almost everyone used the exercise clothes and washed them once a week along with their other clothes. Haqnavaz, however, stuck to his opinion and never used any exercise clothes. We, the female comrades, were happy that we had succeeded in decreasing the sweat smell in the safehouse. I also have to emphasize that Saba Bijanzadeh's resistance spirit and persistence in winning our demands made me very happy, especially in light of the fact that I had only recently moved to this safehouse.

The mental illness of a comrade

I saw a picture of Mohammad-Reza Habibian, a Fada'i guerrilla, on a condolence note posted on a website in 2011. His scrawny face and white hair showed the passing of time. I stared at the picture for a long time. All the sad memories of what had happened to us and our rebellious and idealistic generation flashed by in front of my eyes. The wish for a free and thriving Iran still remains strong for the young generations of our country. Maybe one day they will attain this goal.

After the blows of summer of 1976, the Organization was confronted with the absence of experienced cadres. In 1977, a special plan for recruiting cadres from the released prisoners was initiated.

Mohammad-Reza Habibian was recruited as part of this plan. In December of 1977, he was brought to our safehouse in Gohardasht (Karaj) under the blindfold protocol.

The main members of this house at that time were Qasem Siadati, Mohammad-Reza Ghebra'i, Fati (Sheyda Nabavi) and myself. Ghebra'i knew Habibian from prison and it was through him that he was brought to our house under special conditions. Habibian, similar to Ghebra'i, sympathized with Bijan Jazani's ideas. At the beginning, Habibian was only allowed to see Ghebra'i and followed the blindfold protocol towards other members of the house. Ghebra'i was the only member who visited Habibian in his room. The other members communicated with him behind a curtain. He lived temporarily with us in order to get acquainted with and adapt to the conditions of the safehouses until he could transfer to another house.

Ghebra'i one day, after several weeks, inflamed and surprised us by stating that 'our blindfolded comrade is talking nonsense and seems to be confused. I don't know what has happened to him. He isn't himself.' We began to put him under intense observation and soon realized that his mental state was not normal. Habibian would say things like: 'I know where you have locked me up! We are in Karaj!' All members had to break the blindfold protocol in order to care for him.

His condition deteriorated as the days passed by. He would scream and shout and was not aware of his surrounding environment anymore. He only let few people come close to him. He thought that he was in a solitary cell and a 'young doctor' was his interrogator and that another was 'Azodi, the torturer. He accepted my presence because he thought that I was Mihan Jazani who would 'never betray [her husband] Bijan'. He literally would not sleep, even for a second. He talked all the time, screamed slogans and knocked on the door and wall with his fist. He even hit and kicked me and had imaginary political debates with himself. He would not eat anything. Only Ghebra'i and I could feed him a little by deceiving him. He quietly whispered in my ears about all the hiding places inside the prison, about the appointments untold to the SAVAK and the secret information about his former political activities.

We were tired of this situation. All the daily activities and plans in the house had fully ceased as we had to care for our sick comrade. The shouting and screaming had become a great problem since he would loudly insult the Shah, SAVAK and the torturers. We tried everything but couldn't prevent his voice from reaching Mrs. Mehri, our extremely nosey neighbour, whose house shared a common wall with our house and used to claim her son was helping SAVAK to fight the 'terrorists'. We had to tie up his hands and feet to prevent his violent attacks. The situation was emotionally very hard and painful especially for me, who was always at his side.

We decided to move out of the safehouse as a security measure. Every day, the comrades tried to find a new house but it was not easy. Our focus had changed to keeping an eye on our sick comrade and looking for another house. We had to move out all the military gear, files and documents as a security measure.

One day, when Habibian and I were alone in the house, Ghebra'i rang the doorbell. I neglected Habibian who was in his room as I went out to open the door. Ghebra'i was telling me about the difficulties finding a house as he entered the house and went to Habibian's room. Habibian wasn't in his room anymore. I was horrified as I thought what if Habibian had gone to the room where all the military gear had been kept, he could have blown up the entire house. Frantically I went to the workroom, but he wasn't there. In the short time that I was opening the door and was talking to Ghebra'i, he had dragged himself with tied-up hands and feet to the yard and sat near the pool. With his sweet Hamedani accent he said: 'Mihan, look how well I deceived you and escaped, but no one attempted to kill me while escaping!'

I approached him calmly and asked him to go in the house. He refused. We were afraid that the nosey neighbour would see this scene or that she would hear his 'death to the Shah' shouts. I eventually managed to get him back to his room. The reason we hadn't already taken him back to his parent's house was that Habibian knew where our safehouse was located. At the peak of his illness, he would mention political issues and information out loud. It had become impossible to look after him. We had to find another solution.

Therefore, Siadati, Ghebra'i, Gholamian, Fati, (or another comrade as I don't recall exactly) and I had an emergency meeting to discuss and decide what to do with him. We concluded that in the first opportunity, we would hand him over to his family for treatment. The day that we moved out of the safehouse, Gholamian and Ghebra'i took Habibian to his family in the city of Hamedan. They took him to their front door, rang the bell and walked away before the door was opened. They walked far enough to make sure he got in the house. I heard that he had recovered and regained his health after a while.

I saw Habibian, from a distance, at a rally on the campus of the University of Tehran after the 1979 Revolution. I was very happy that he had recovered. It seemed like he had returned to life. He did not recognize me. Along with the bitter memories of him in the safehouse, the vision of him attacking me with kicks and punches came to my mind for a moment. I quickly left the area.

Celebration of 8 March

One year Saba Bijanzadeh, Vida Goli Abkenari and myself, the women of the safehouse were so busy with the daily hustle and bustle that we forgot about 8 March, International Women's Day.

The plan was to develop the microfilms delivered from the European branch of the Organization after dinner on that 8 March. The microfilms generally consisted of declarations, reports, announcements of support of parties or revolutionary organizations in other countries, internal administrative or operational letters. We would take pictures of the enlarged microfilms first. The 'workroom' would convert to a darkroom for printing. A small gas grill was used to warm up the room and for cooking.

That night Vida Goli Abkenari and I were developing the films. A skewer with three carrots was on the grill as we entered the room. The pleasant smell of the grilled carrots filled the room. We both had to laugh when we saw that scene. At that time, carrots were the cheapest vegetable available. We commonly used it for our meals as it suited our low budget, I jokingly asked whether somebody craved for carrot kabab? Haqnavaz answered: 'Have you forgotten that today is 8 March, the International Women's Day? I have grilled these three carrots to present to our women comrades.' He, while offering us the nicely smelling grilled carrots, said with a grin on his face that he was adding carrot kabab to the other carrot dishes that Mehrnush (meaning myself) makes. We were caught off guard when a male comrade had remembered March 8 and the international women's struggle.

Vida Goli Abkenari and I surprisingly looked at each other and called Saba Bijanzadeh (Hajar) into the room. The three female guerrillas of this safehouse gathered around the grill with grilled carrots in hand to celebrate 8 March. Each of us talked or recited poetry about women's struggle, freedom of the masses and militant Iranian women, especially those of the Fada'is. Saba said: 'The day the masses are free, women will also have genuine freedom.' She then recited the 'I'm a woman' poem for the continuation of the struggle by Marziyeh Ahmadi Oskou'i in memory of Marziyeh and Fatemeh Sa'idi (also known as Mother Shayegan, who was in prison at that time). Vida talked about her immense love for her mother and expressed special respect for Marziyeh Ahmadi Oskou'i. I talked about the difficulties and misery of women in the villages, female workers and agricultural labourers who worked with crooked backs and bruised feet in the rice fields and with cracked fingers in cotton fields, about the forced marriage and the suicide among young girls.

Afterwards, Haqnavaz began to talk about his mother and her problems. He said: 'I will never forget that my father would get angry under life's heavy load and would whip my mother with his belt. I would throw myself on her to protect her.' Haqnavaz expressed a lot of love and devotion about his mother. Talking about our feelings and emotions was an unusual occurrence for us and we were touched by his display of so much emotion. His teary eyes were an indication of how deep he had drowned in his own feelings.

It was the first time I had seen a comrade speak so honestly and lovingly about his mother. Haqnavaz, who was very inexpressive in the struggle against despotism, oppression and the injustice of the regime, now talked with a heart full of affection for his mother and all the hard-working women of our country. He talked about the pain and difficulties that women were unfairly exposed to in their lives. He finished his words by wishing liberation and equal rights for women, and the hope that one day poverty would cease in our country.

Our team celebrated 8 March, that year, with three grilled carrots, by reflecting on the injustice inflicted on women by denying them equal rights, and by renewing, once more, our determination to continue the struggle against the double oppression of women 'with faith in our victory'.

The stray cat

During the winter of 1976, our safehouse in Mashhad consisted of Vida Goli Abkenari, Kazem Ghebra'i, Ahmad Gholamian, a comrade, known to us as 'Askar, under the blindfold protocol and responsibility of Mohammad Hosseini Haqnavaz.

A grey-and-white stray cat was passing by on the yard wall. As Vida wistfully looked at the cat, she said that the poor cat does not know where she has come. We have nothing for her to eat. I loved animals, especially cats and dogs, and therefore concurred with her. I had been deprived from having any pets as a kid. My mother used to say that cats cause asthma and dogs cannot be kept in the house. We both laughed when the cat jumped over the wall after we waved our hands.

It turned out that our male comrades had heard us talking affectionately about the cat, because that evening, after dinner, they criticized us for showing affection towards animals. They claimed showing affection for a cat indicated that we had not left our childhood emotions behind and had not become hardened.

They punished us both. They decided that I should write a self-criticism note and getting over my soft affection for animals. Vida's punishment was ruthless and cruel.

During the discussions it became apparent that Vida had developed some fondness for the cat as she had been feeding and caressing the cat from time to time. Vida had kept her fondness for the cat from everyone including me. After living in the safehouse for a while she had grown to like me like an older sister and would discuss certain issues with me. It was based on this feeling that she opened to me that day in the yard. She wanted to know how I felt about the cat.

That night Vida got skewered under a barrage of criticism. I felt so bad for the young girl that I couldn't sleep that night. Vida accepted the criticism that she had not conquered her emotions and agreed to follow through on the ruthless punishment. She agreed to kill the cat!

One day she shot the cat in the ear with a silencer-equipped handgun in the basement and left the cat's body there.

On the following day, Gholamian prepared stew. After we finished the meal, he said, 'It was a delicious cat stew.' I did not believe that the meat in the stew was from the stray cat. No one paid attention to what he had said and after a few silent minutes everyone went back to their work.

Lovely Vida wrote a self-criticism note, but she was not herself after she killed the cat. She would neither eat much nor participate in the exercise sessions for a week using menstrual pain as the excuse. She kept to herself and focused on typing and copying. One day when the two of us were working in the same basement, I asked her 'how goes it comrade?' Without looking at me, she put her head on my chest and said, 'This shall pass too. I am stronger this week and am committed to our mission and struggle.'

We never got a chance to share our real feelings with regard to this tragic event. A few months later we got separated. I got to see her a couple of times in the following two years, on the streets for very short work-related appointments. We found each other again after the revolution. She took me to her parents' house and introduced me as 'Comrade Mehrnoush, who is like my older sister'. Later, she told me about her marriage to comrade Hashem. She gave my name and number, as the next of kin, when she had awoke in the hospital after a horrible car accident in the Sari-Gorgan Road.

The split in the Organization created a large chasm between us. I saw her two other times in Tehran. She took me, under the blindfold protocol, to her house once. The close camaraderie was gone.

I heard of her death after I left Iran. The news saddened me for months. I put a girl's picture that looked like Vida on my wall and called her 'Leyla', her *nom de guerre*.

After all these years, I am reminded of Vida and the cruel pain we inflicted on her every time I see a cat.

The suiter!

A beautiful young girl with long brown hair was brought to our safehouse. She was called Ashraf but her real name was Raf'at Memaran-Benam. A few days before Ahmad Gholamian had come to our house for a weekly planning gathering and talked about a female comrade who does not get along easily with others and informed us that it had been decided to bring her to our house since 'Comrade Mehrnoush [me] has the ability to work with anyone'.

We had just rented this recently built house in Gohar-Dasht (west of Karaj). The main team members in this house were Qasem Siadati and me. Reza Ghebra'i, and one other comrade whose name I cannot recall lived with us. The house was part of a duplex in the middle of an open area. A woman, Mrs Mehri, and her only son lived side by side to our house. Mehri was extremely curious and knew everyone in the neighbourhood. I figured that getting close to her could give me an opportunity to know everyone in the neighbourhood. So, I befriended her. She, 'being neighbourly', would visit our house two or three times a week although her real intention was to figure out what was going on. We had to make up stories to justify her curiosity. Her visits became more frequent after Raf'at joined us. I had introduced Ashraf as my sister-in-law who was visiting from another town. Mehri had a young son and was apparently looking for a young and beautiful suiter.

Ashraf and I would visit from time to time a single room we had rented as backup, pretending to be teachers in a nearby village. A kind couple from Qazvin had rented the room to us. One Friday afternoon when Ashraf and I had come back from visiting the single room, Mrs Mehri opened her window and greeted us with a smile. I, without any hesitation, said that we were visiting my aunt and cousin who had delivered her baby. She said that she had been waiting for us as she had ringed the doorbell a few times. I got worried as I was unlocking the door; 'Had something happened while we were gone?' Even though all the security signs were checked out, I had my finger on the grenade pin attached to my belt and whispered to Raf'at to keep a distance after unlocking the door. Then, I turned to Mrs Mehri and said: 'Hamid must have been at work' (Hamid was Siadati's pseudo name in this house) as I carefully opened the door to enter the house. We found 'Hamid' ready behind the door. With the look on my face and rolling my eyes I told him it was all about the nosy neighbour.

The next day, Mrs Mehri came to visit us in the house with a big bouquet of followers. I asked Raf'at, who had braided her long hair like school girls, to bring some tea for our guest. The big bouquet was unusual since in the past, she had brought either delicious pastry or cooked meals when she came to visit us. So, I asked her with some curiosity what the occasion was and if someone was getting married? She said, 'God willing, there will be good news.' As Raf'at left the room, Mrs Mehri whispered in my ear: 'I have come to woo your sister-in-law for marriage.' I, in a surprised manner, said 'I am in no position to discuss such issues; my husband (Siadati, Raf'at's older brother) is not home and I am not her elder.' I then asked, 'Whom are you speaking for?' She said, 'Who better than my son, Mr Mehdi! I promise to be a good mother-in-law!' I asked about his employment. She explained that Mr Mehdi worked as an engineer and had a very good income plus he had another source of high income. I got curious about the other job and said, 'So, what is the other work? My husband may be interested to partner with him. we could use some extra income too. Maybe our situation would get better and we would not be so ashamed of our poor settings in front of neighbours and friends.' She asked me to keep what she was about to tell me between ourselves as she wasn't supposed to talk to anyone about it. Then she leaned over and whispered into my ear: 'SAVAK! Mr Mehdi works against terrorists in SAVAK. It is very lucrative.'

I was about to collapse and, in a moment, my whole body was drenched in cold sweat, but I quickly gathered myself and in a loud voice asked Raf'at about the tea for Mrs Mehri. Then, laughingly replied that I had no say in this and would have to discuss this with her brother and father. I explained that she had many suiters in her hometown and her strict father had sent her to spend some time with us to get away from all that. Then asked: 'Raf'at is a very humble and faithful girl but how do you know if your son likes her?' With a smile, she replied, 'But of course, I have pointed her when she was in the back yard to him many times and he has approved; never said no.'

I had the butterflies in my belly as I promised to follow up and get back to her so she could go to her 'parents' house'. She left us with a loving look at Raf'at. Siadati, Ghebra'i and another comrade named Nader who had locked themselves in the workroom throughout this ordeal came to the living room. Although I was sure they had heard everything, I told them what had happened yesterday and today and especially about Mr Mehdi's lucrative work against terrorists. It was a complicated situation. Our next-door nosey neighbour who had an eye on us wanted to 'join the family'!

Nowruz celebration

The psyche and the spirit of the Iranians changes towards the end of winter as spring and the new Iranian year arrives with spring, at the exact moment of the vernal equinox. One can smell the start of the natural renewal of life in the air. The rejuvenating atmosphere prepares people for the new year and new challenges in daily life. We observed the people's energized hustle and bustle of spring cleaning and their getting ready to welcome Nowruz.

I wanted to celebrate the arrival of spring in a corner of our small and dull safehouse but I would not dare to do so. I would only try to maintain the memories of spring in Northern Iran in my mind.

I remember my first spring living in a safehouse. I put some fresh grass, that I had cut, in my pocket and told myself, 'I have my spring grass, now that I am still alive.' I was saddened that we couldn't celebrate the Nowruz by simply growing the traditional wheat grass and having hyacinth in the house. Such issues were simply considered to be rudimentary, and a sign of petty-bourgeois tendencies, to be discussed.

Another spring passed. March of 1978 was my third Nowruz living in a safehouse. I was out shopping for lunch. I had to make meatless stew to keep the cost down. So, I bought a few small onions, potatoes and carrots. I also bought a few extra small onions as I had decided to grow some greens for Nowruz.

When I got back to the house, I put the ingredients in the pot with some water and oil and let it cook for lunch. I put the extra onions I had bought in water glasses and set the glasses on the window ledge. I told the comrades that 'this year we have both greens for Nowruz and we can eat the leaves as well. Luckily, no one complained about it either then or later that night while we were developing plans. I did not have to prepare self-criticism. I watched the onion leaves grow as if they were my mother's grass-wheat years ago in our old small house.

At night while on guard duty, I would watch the onion leaves in the glass. I would lose myself in the childhood memories as I caressed the leaves. I would remember the small, one square meter garden, under the fig and plum trees in our backyard in Gorgan when I was eight or nine years old. I used to plant herbs and beans in my little garden. I always kept up my green patch by weeding and watering it carefully. I could taste the ripe and delicious figs and plums that had fallen on my patch. Memories of my youth had been reduced to the onion leaves in those three glasses. For me, the onions in each of the three glasses had turned into symbols of the memory of my garden, the spring flowers (tulip, hyacinth and narcissus) my mother would set for Nowruz, and the memory of imprisoned comrades.

Undertaking armed struggle and living a covert life in safe-houses left no room for attending to routine aesthetics and emotional needs of normal life such as flowers, setting up for Nowruz or visiting parents and siblings. Our daily lives were so swamped in the struggle between life-and-death situations that we could not pay attention to such issues as aesthetics even if we wanted to. The path that we had chosen required true self-devotion and giving up all personal aspirations and longing for loved ones. Even married couples who would join the struggle would be separated in different safehouses or even cities so they would not be informed of each others' status. There was a stronger struggle within each one of us to not be distracted by personal desires. Even though we were ready to die in order to avoid being arrested alive, prevailing over personal desires, such as love and affection for others which is very natural in the early adulthood years, was very hard. Our love for our oppressed people, for our struggle for justice and liberation was the only factor which attracted us to the path we had chosen and helped us to overcome yearning for love and to deny ourselves any personal aspirations. The attempt to suppress our feelings was a temporary 'fix' as life would impose all the natural emotions at affections we had before taking this path.

This was my circumstance when I joined the Organization. I carried an untold and hidden love in my heart. I would try to forget this love and continue with the path I had knowingly chosen but it was futile as I would remember the one, I loved every opportunity I would get. He had been imprisoned and his release was like a dream. I thought that I could be killed at any moment without seeing him one more time. I yearned his freedom and luckily, he, along with thousands of other political prisoners, was released right before the 1979 Revolution. It was an unbelievable feeling when I, as an armed guerrilla fighter, secretly met him. On 25 June 1978 Naqi Hamidian and I were the first of our generation of guerrilla fighters who got married.

Abdollah Panjehshahi

There are painful memories in this story too. The account below does not represent my analytic views on what happened back then. I suggest and hope the reader considers the context and the spirit of those times when reading about the painful story of Abdollah Panjehshahi.[3]

In order to identify any remaining member after the major blows to the Organization and the killing of central figures such as Hamid Ashraf and his comrades in the Mehrabad Jonoubi shoot-out in the summer of 1976, SAVAK had required all real estate agencies and landlords to report the identity of all renters to the police. This had made it very hard for us to rent a house or buy a car. At that time, we had rented a house in Karaj based on a recommendation from our previous landlord without going through an agency or submitting any report to the police.

Saba Bijanzadeh and Behnam Amiri-Davan were hit on 27 February 1977. Qasem Siadati and I left the safehouse in Karaj on 28 February after we heard about Saba and Behnam. We took all the 'double-zero'-, 'zero'- and 'one'-class files with us alongside two machine guns, ammunition, money and a bag filled with a recently printed *Nabard ba Diktatori-ye Shah* (Struggle against Shah's Dictatorship) by Bijan Jazani. We bought a small car, an Iranian made version of French Citroen 2 CV with the little money we had. Without any connections to the Organization or a backup residence, we had become drifters who slept in car or in parks along the way.

Every member was required to have at least one backup connection to reconnect in such situations. At the time both Siadati and I had multiple backup connections. The backup connections were set up in a precise manner to keep the Organization from the reach of SAVAK in case the backup connection had been identified. Every connection had a 'safe' sign. A small mistake in the safe sign would nullify the connection.

At the time, we had to reach these back up connections, some of which were in different towns. For the next month, after Tehran, we tried our backup connections in Mashhad, Bojnourd, Gonabad, Gorgan and Semnan without any response. We read the news about the killing of Ghazal Ayati, 'Abbas Houshmand, Simin Panjehshahi and Nasrin Panjehshahi in the daily papers on 29 March 1977. We didn't know any of the names and were hoping none were our comrades.

We went back to Tehran as we had only one last backup connection left. We had decided to hide the firearms and the files, get a job and a house to save ourselves if we did not get any response from the last backup connection.

We were desperate and in the last bleak moments we got a response from a backup connection. Siadati with optimism and confidence followed up as I stayed in the car on Lorzadeh Street. Another comrade was with Siadati when he came back after thirty minutes. I recognized Reza Ghebra'i. I had met him through my contacts with the families of political prisoners in Mashhad. I surprisingly asked him, 'What are you doing here Reza and when were you released?' He quickly explained that Hamid doesn't know him, and his pseudonym was Mansour. He also explained that a comrade who thought we could still be alive had sent him to the meeting spot, although other comrades had assumed we had been killed or arrested alongside Saba and Behnam.

Mansour had been sent to follow up by a comrade in Isfahan. Abdollah Panjehshahi (Heydar) was the comrade who had sent Mansour and based on his recommendation, Siadati drove the car to Isfahan by himself. Ghebra'i and myself took the bus. I do not recall the exact date, but it must have been early April 1977.

Abdollah picked us up at the bus station in Isfahan and took us to the safehouse under the blindfold protocol. He was responsible for the Isfahan branch and was directly in charge of that safehouse. Ghebra'i was blindfold inside the house, but the members who lived there were not, whereas Siadati and I were blindfold to both the house and its members, except for Abdollah.

Although Ghebra'i was armed at the time, he seemed a fairly novice operative. Political theory was his strong suit. Ghebra'i endorsed and advocated Jazani's ideas within the Organization. It seemed like Abdollah would take Ghebra'i to internal meetings debating Jazani and Ahmadzadeh ideas. Abdollah thought that Ghebra'i should have minimal external operational involvement and be protected as the theoretician-comrade Hamid Momeni (Sadegh).

This assessment of Ghebra'i did not fit with the fact that he was sent to follow up with us in Tehran. Abdollah explained that Ghebra'i had been sent to Tehran for an important meeting when 'I asked him to check out the back up connection in case you were alive and luckily, we found you.'

Siadati and I were both impressed by Abdollah's capabilities to organize and deal with comrades after only one week of meeting them. We hoped the Organization would have a few more such capable comrades to survive the heavy blows it had taken in the summer of 1976. The Organization experienced multiple hits between July 1976 and March of 1977. We had lost many experienced comrades such as Hasanjan Farjoudi, Kazem Ghebra'i, Saba Bijanzadeh, Behnam Amiri-Davan, 'Abbas Houshmand and Kioumars Sanjari in few months.

Ahmad Gholamian had the longest tenure; he was the most experienced and the bravest of the remaining comrades that I knew at the time. I had much more hope about the Organization after meeting Abdollah as I figured the Organization must have more capable comrades unknown to me.

I looked sick and had lost a lot of weight and was down to 45 kg due to a bout of Malta Fever. Although Abdollah had associated these symptoms to malnutrition due to the lack of money and living in a car, he inquired about my health. I explained how I felt and told him that I needed a doctor. He immediately went to the other room and asked a female comrade to get a doctor's appointment for me. This is how I met Edna Sabet (Pari)[4] and the blindfold protocol ended between us.

I don't remember exactly how long but after some days had passed, Abdollah came home with two boys who were about ten and fifteen years old. The boys looked sleep deprived, shabby and extremely dirty. Abdollah was distracted. He opened the house door and without any introduction and security consideration brought the two boys into the house and said: 'I picked these comrades after the attack on the Panjehshahis' home.' The boys had escaped from their parents' house in the Narmak suburb of Tehran. They had lived in the parks until they connected with Abdollah and had come to Isfahan. Abdollah was both happy and agitated about finding the boys. Edna prepared the bath for them and washed the boys' clothes herself.

Abdollah was infuriated when he was with us in the evening. He questioned and complained about transitioning Panjehshahi's house to the frontline and utilizing it as a safehouse. He said the arrangement had been made for one sick comrade to rest and recover there, while the Organization found a proper assignment and a safehouse for him. The sick comrade he referred to was 'Abbas Houshmand (Parviz) who was one of the veteran comrades and had recently been released after four years of captivity. Abdollah objected Ghazal Ayati's decisions, which had led to using Panjehshahi's home as a safehouse. This was an ordinary home where a couple lived an ordinary life with their sons and daughters. The Organization was supposed to use the house as a back-up in extraordinary situations. Ensuring the safety of people who provided backup resources (such as financial help, residence, medical treatment, a private car) was supposed to be of utmost concern in utilizing their support.

He complained about the decision to send Ghazal to that house without consulting with him first. It was clear, from what he was saying, that it had been decided to avoid using that abode as a safehouse. He kept repeating, 'This was not our agreement.' I was neither clear then nor now on who was responsible for that decision, but Abdollah kept pointing to Ghazal and the 'central' comrades.

Such a decision could not have been made by the individual in charge of the team, which is why Abdollah blamed people further up the chain of command. His raging complaints were based on the detailed information he had gotten from the boys. I asked Edna about his rage. She explained that 'the two boys are his brothers and the two girls killed in the attack were his sisters' and that 'his mother and one sister have probably been arrested'.

Abdollah's rage was rooted in his worry for his mother and sister and the possibility of their arrest. He truly loved his mother and his family. Years later I met his mother and it was very clear that Abdollah had a special place in her heart.

As I explained earlier, Siadati and I were blindfolded to the other members of the house until I had to visit a doctor. We had to call every time we wanted to leave the room. One morning Ghebra'i, who looked distracted and confused, came to our room and said, 'I need to discuss an issue with you as I don't know what the rules are for such issues.' He explained that he had seen Abdollah and Edna sleeping together in the living room. Siadati, Ghebra'i and I used to sleep in the work room. Ghebra'i on his way to the bathroom in the middle of the night had heard strange noises and had looked in the living room.

Both Siadati and I were agitated and angry. After the recent blows, this infuriated me as a woman since I thought, may be, the situation is becoming insecure, open for abuse of women in the Organization. Siadati was angry that some comrades would abuse the Organization's weak standing. Protecting the Organization and its norms at that time were existential issues for those of us who had survived.

Siadati's first reaction was that of yelling and screaming while asking Ghebra'i 'Who does he [Abdollah Panjehshahi] think he is to behave in such manner in a safehouse.' He accused Abdollah of betraying the Organization and its ideals. We decided to not confront Abdollah or Edna directly on this issue since we were afraid that Siadati's prejudice and angry reaction towards Abdollah may lead to a physical clash between Siadati and Abdollah. So, we decided to discuss the issue with the 'central' comrades.

We made a request to Abdollah to arrange a visit but told him we needed to meet with someone from the 'central' comrades to discuss our future. He, unsuspectedly, arranged to have someone come to visit us.

When it came to female comrades and 'honour' issues I think Siadati's reaction was overtly emotional and beyond the cultural norms displayed by other comrades on such issues. He felt like he had to protect female comrades like an older brother. I should add here that Siadati felt guilty about the death of Mina Talebzadeh-Shoushtari in the Kou-ye Ziba clash. She and Siadati had been introduced, by the Organization, in early 1976 for a pretend but officially registered marriage. At the time Siadati was an employed engineer and she had finished her studies and was employed. They were 'undercover' members living in Kou-ye Ziba.

I did not discuss the issue with Edna as I did not have a close relationship with her, typical between female comrades. We had met very recently. She was usually very cold in her responses and would answer questions with a simple yes or no. Our first 'eyes-open' meeting was accompanied with a simple handshake when a sincere hug was very typical between female comrades. The coldness of this relationship was my first and last such experience in the Organization. I had assumed she did not want anyone in her personal space.

Siadati and I knew nothing about Abdollah's experience in political activities and this lack of knowledge had raised our suspicions under the circumstances. This had fuelled Siadati's rage towards Abdollah. His pessimistic view had left no room for any benefit of the doubt or healthy motivation. Instead, he doubted Abdollah's intentions by calling him an opportunist and traitor. For Siadati, the only saving grace was what had happened to Abdollah's family. We would have been even more angry if it wasn't for what had happened to Abdollah's family, but we had witnessed what he and his family had sacrificed themselves for the Organization and this would induce us not to doubt his motivation and intentions. This had reduced the rigidity in our view, especially for Siadati who considered Abdollah's action as betrayal.

I don't remember exactly how long it took for someone to come to visit us but one day, probably in late April of 1977, Abdollah brought Ahmad Gholamian to the house under the blindfold protocol. We had a meeting to discuss our future, Siadati's and mine, that evening. Abdollah, Gholamian, Ghebra'i, Siadati and myself were present. We first discussed our move to the city of Arak. At the end of the meeting, Ghebra'i brought up what he had seen. Abdollah had his head down and accepted everything without any objections. Siadati was furious and was cursing Abdollah by calling him, 'opportunist', 'traitor', 'filthy' and more as Ghebra'i was trying to calm him down. Abdollah, without responding to Siadati's verbal attacks or defending himself, frankly said 'we love each other' as he kept his head down and added that he would whole heartedly accept any punishment the Organization considered appropriate.

Gholamian said that he would raise the issue with comrades and we will make a decision. Either Gholamian or Ghebra'i had spoken to Edna as well. They told us that she had confirmed what Abdollah had said but not in terms which were as strong.

Gholamian stayed at the house, blindfolded, for two or three days after our meeting. Ghebra'i, Gholamian and Abdollah had multiple meetings in the living room. We could hear them from time to time as their voices would get loud.

We left Isfahan, after Gholamian left, to set up and facilitate activities for the Organization in Arak based on the discussed plans. Tahmaseb Vaziri was with us in Arak. We concluded that Arak was not an appropriate town for a safehouse after spending some time there. We went back to Isfahan to Abdollah's house. Ghebra'i, Edna, Abdollah, and his two younger brothers were still living there. It was decided for Siadati and I to go back to the same house we had left on 28 February 1977 in Karaj after assessing security and safety issues.

At Abdollah's request, we dropped Ja'far, his fifteen-year-old brother, in Mashad before going back to Karaj. Abdollah thought that Ja'far had technical abilities and could therefore fill Kiumars Sanjari's position in the Mashhad branch of the Organization after some training. Amir, Abdollah's ten-year-old brother, was going to stay with him in Isfahan.

It must have been late May of 1977 as I do not remember the exact date, when we got back to Karaj. I do remember that we were back in the house in June of 1977 after assessing security. We had not paid rent for three and a half months by then, but in order to make nice with the landlord we paid for four months. The landlord was happy with our generosity. Tahmaseb Vaziri joined us in the Karaj safehouse after we settled in.

Ahmad Gholamian, wearing a wig, came for a blindfolded visit to the same house in Karaj as my uncle, Rahim Karimian. I don't remember the exact date but he informed us of the verdict the Organization had passed on Abdollah. He said that 'he has been filtered out'. The 'filtered out' expression meant executed. Silence filled the room for a while. Then, Siadati asked if other forms of punishment had been considered. Gholamian authoritatively answered that it had been the decision of the Organization (or comrades, do not remember exactly) and we are to not talk about it anymore. He continued, 'if any comrade asks about him, we should say he has been hit' and emphasized that 'only the central comrades and you, because you were directly involved, are aware of this decision and this should not be discussed anywhere or at any time'. We considered this an order from the Organization and did not even talk to each other about it again.

Abdollah's mother and his younger brother Amir joined our last safehouse towards the end of summer in 1978 in Shahr-e Rey. Abdollah's mother and I got close after a while and she told me about the raid on their house which forced her to escape with her daughter, Zohreh, and led to the killing of her two other daughters. She somehow blamed Ghazal for that hit. She had never seen Abdollah after that day. She asked me a few times, 'Do you know where he was hit and why his name had not been printed in the daily papers?' I could not give her any clear answer other than he probably had not been identified and the Organization would not make any announcements regarding such issues. Reza Ghebra'i who also lived in that house endorsed my answer to her queries and said, 'This is a good answer, do not tell her anything more.'

A necessary note regarding punishments within the Organization

The Organization's policies had been published internally. The statutes probably never fell into SAVAK's hands as there is no reference to it in the book by Mahmoud Naderi.[5]

The part of the rules that has been published in this book is quoted from Zahra Aghanabi Qolhaki's interrogations. There was a time that I had the whole policy book memorized but I have forgotten most of the details.

The harshest punishment mentioned in the statutes for non-security-related matters was disarmament, expulsion, obligation to take up manual labour and one-way communication with the individual wrongdoer. As I recall, the details had been clarified. The person in charge of a unit or a safehouse would usually decide the form of the punishment for people working with him or her and the central organ would decide for those in charge of a unit (or a safehouse) or on very important matters.

We (Siadati, Ghebra'i and I) had some sort of disciplinary punishment in mind for Abdollah. We believed, as the policy book had indicated, that he should have been relieved of his duties, dismissed from the safehouse and the like and at the end be allowed back after writing self-criticism. I should emphasize nowhere in the statutes 'filtering' to mean execution had been mentioned.

Like most members, I did not know who and how many people formed the central organ. One, based on communications, could guess that a comrade may be in the central organ. Qasem Siadati, for sure, was not part of the central organ in the spring of 1977, as he was put in charge of our safehouse, for a short period of time, only in the summer of 1977.

Reza Ghebra'i, may have been part of the central organ due to his theoretical role in the Organization (and his opinion carried some weight). Ghebra'i was not known for his organizational capabilities except for his suggestion for a 'special membership drive' in the fall of 1976 which was very well received.

Abdollah was organizationally very capable and sensitive to the health and psychological status of comrades around him. He picked up on my health issues in the first week realizing that I needed a doctor soon. I found this very impressive. I was with Siadati through all those days, but he never paid attention to my health. Neither did Gholamian say anything about my weight loss or health status when he had seen me after about a year. I found Abdollah at that time to be stronger than Gholamian in the political domain and at least as strong in planning and execution. That led me to think that 'Abdollah was close to, if not in, the central organ.

The cause and motivation for Abdollah's execution is still not clear to me. Was the love affair between Abdollah and Edna the main cause of his execution? If so, why didn't Edna receive any disciplinary punishment? Was Abdollah's fierce criticism of those responsible for changing his parents' house to a safehouse the real cause of his execution? Could it be that Abdollah's criticism was pointed towards Gholamian and Gholamian used the love affair as an excuse to quiet him down? Was there more to the story that we don't know? Had Abdollah made some mistakes worthy of execution as punishment? Did a hidden tug of war for leadership lead to Abdollah's execution? Were there any special reasons for turning Abdollah's death into a security issue and covering it until after the 1979 Revolution? One cannot have a clear and precise judgement on the motivation for this internal execution which seemed to be centred on the love affair of two guerrillas until such questions have been answered. I believe that this case is still open and some people who can provide details on this unjustified death are still alive.

8

Female prison

Roqiyeh Daneshgari

The first detention centre for female political prisoners in Iran was established in the summer of 1971. Prior to this, before the guerrillas began their struggle against the Pahlavi regime, there was no need for a special prison. Rebellious women were confined alongside women serving sentences for non-political offenses. In June 1971, Dr Mastoureh Ahmadzadeh Heravi,[1] and two other medical colleagues of her were arrested by SAVAK. They were interrogated in Evin Prison and later confined in the medical room of Qasr Prison. Together with a young female student from the University of Tabriz, these were Iran's first female political prisoners following the Siyahkal episode.

Once guerrilla activities began, several Fada'i women (Atefeh Ja'fari, Ashraf Dehqani, Shahin Tavakkoli and myself) were interrogated and tortured in both police and SAVAK torture chambers. Neither the gendarmerie nor SAVAK had prepared any special detention centres for female political prisoners, even after the first women were transferred to Qasr, the first modern political prison in Tehran. After few days of moving these prisoners between the prison's courtyard and its visitors' rooms, they were finally confined to the prison's clinic.

The next step came when several more revolutionary students were arrested, five from within Iran, two from the Confederation of Iranian Students abroad who had come to visit their families. This group included an American called Sharon Laberking.[2]

During the first half of 1971, I was one of thirteen women imprisoned in that primitive clinic of the prison. It is worth mentioning that Atefeh Ja'fari was the first woman associated with Fada'i guerrilla movement who was detained in Qasr Prison. Detained after a bloody clash between SAVAK forces and her comrades, she was so heavily tortured in Evin that she hoped to be dead: 'On the torture bed I repeated to myself, lucky those friends of mine who were killed'.[3]

On 4 December 1971, after several months of interrogation and torture by the police and within Evin Prison, I was transferred along with my two other comrades Ashraf Dehqani and Shahin Tavakkoli to the same 'larger' one-room clinic in Qasr Prison. The three of us were arrested by the security forces. Ashraf Dehqani was the first female guerrilla fighter who was arrested. She was arrested on 13 May 1971.[4]

Shahin Tavakkoli was also arrested alongside her husband Sa'id Aryan on 24 May in Tehran. Shahin was directly taken to the 'Committee' police torture centre. I was arrested at midnight on 14 July 1971, while I was in my brother's house in the Javadiyeh district of Tehran, and taken directly to the Committee torture centre with my mother who refused to let me be taken alone.

We three Fada'i women, after going through torture and interrogation, were left in solitary confinement until the beginning of November 1971. We were kept in three cells out of the twelve in the basement of the Committee Shahrbani/police centre. For a while we were chained to our steel beds.

In Evin

During the first days of November 1971, on a cold autumn day, we were taken, wearing very little clothing, in a hearse to Evin Prison. The windows were tinted black so we could not see out and others could not see in. The hearse approached a place where we thought we heard gunfire. We were not allowed to look at each other or talk to one another. By then we believed we were about to be executed by firing squad. That, as it turned out, was not the case. The sounds were only the crows cawing from afar. Crows flew constantly over Evin's courtyard.

For almost a month the three of us were detained in the prison's public room. In Evin, we went through a series of interrogations. Fortunately, there was no torture this time. At this point, SAVAK had arrested a large number of Fada'is. Many of our comrades were now in the same prison in which we were in. They had all endured terrible torture and were now waiting in their solitary cells for trial. In Evin, we were able to meet our comrades and see our families for the first time. Shahin Tavakkoli visited her husband Sa'id Aryan and her brother Hamid Tavakkoli. Ashraf Dehqani met her younger brother, Mohammad Dehqani and I met my mother, Sorayya Daneshgari.

In Evin the food was better. We were also given two or three books and a small transistor radio, though we feared it was being used to eavesdrop on us. One of the books I remember was *Zardha-ye Sorkh* by Henry Marchant. Before my arrest, I was a student of pharmacology at the University of Tabriz and one of the hundred students on strike. I was one of the students in charge of distributing tracts and drawing graffiti. During the days of the action, when a number of strike leaders were arrested, Houshang Montaseri, the Dean of the University of Tabriz, immediately went to the prosecutor's office to ask why they had been imprisoned. He found out that one the books he had translated into Persian was being filed as criminal evidence against one of the arrestees. He then teased the officer by saying, 'The translator of this book is standing right in front of you.'[5]

In November 1971, many members of the *Sazeman-e Rahai Bakhsh-e Khalq-e Iran* (Organization for the Liberation of the Peoples of Iran) were arrested after attempting to kidnap the American ambassador. Around the same time, many members of the Mojahedin-e Khalq Organization were also arrested and tortured after attempting to kidnap Prince Shahram, the son of Ashraf Pahlavi, the Shah's sister. There was therefore no longer enough space in Evin for us. On 4 December 1971 we were transported to Qasr's women's prison. Once we arrived in the room which I described earlier, the number of female political prisoners reached seven. Some of the arrested students had been freed earlier. During the same year, some of the Mojahedin-e Khalq members joined us in the prison. On 25 March 1973 when Ashraf Dehqani escaped from prison, several religious women were transferred into the room where we were also held.

Eventually, the room that separated us from non-political prisoners did not have enough space anymore. The daily 20-minute walk in the prison yard was also not improving our respiratory and physical problems. The guards were left with no choice but to remove the wall separating this medical room from the small waiting room next to it.

Emergence of a political prison for women

The ever-increasing number of female political activists joining the new revolutionary movement, many of whom were guerrilla fighters, forced SAVAK to establish a separate section for women. Meanwhile, many women were arrested in the cities of Shiraz, Tabriz, Ahvaz and Rasht. Some were transferred to Qasr Prison after torture and preliminary interrogation. In autumn of the same year, they transferred twenty of us to the newly constructed women's prison. After that, we had female guards, some of whom were SAVAK agents or police officers. These female guards kept us under surveillance inside the prison and the male guards were usually outside in the yard. This was the beginning of a special section for female political prisoners.

As repression against the guerrilla movements increased so did the number of female prisoners. Eventually, this prison was not sufficient either. Another bigger prison was once again built for us. Between 1972 and 1979 the number of women's prisoners in Qasr increased fourfold.

The prisoners

Until 1974, by far most of the female political prisoners supported armed struggle as the major form of resisting the regime. They belonged either to the Fada'i guerrillas or Mojahedin-e Khalq Organization. After that year, the number of women who did not believe in guerrilla activity increased. They were either leftist students or left-liberal women. The majority belonged the Confederation of Iranian Students or to Maoist groups. A small number were members of the Tudeh Party of Iran. During the same period, several young women who were either followers of Dr 'Ali Shari'ati or teachers from the religious Refah School were also added to the prison. Later, some sisters and mothers of the activists who had escaped SAVAK's reach were imprisoned as well. In mid-1979 some followers of Ayatollah Khomeini and some Hezbollah women were also imprisoned. As mentioned earlier, although the number of prisoners who were against armed uprisings increased, the majority still believed in guerrilla struggle.

Almost all the women captured by SAVAK or the police were tortured, regardless of their beliefs or political orientation. Rarely were their bodies free from scars. Fatemeh

Amini (Bazargan) was the first women killed under SAVAK's violent torture in Evin on 17 August 1975. She was one of Mashhad's active and well-known teachers and a member of the Mojahedin-e Khalq Organization. Years later I discovered that her death was reported by the regime's press as 'an accidental fall from a cliff'. She had been arrested on 7 March 1975.

Later the SAVAK's agents also killed Mahvash Jasemi and Masoumeh Tavafchiyan, members of the Revolutionary Organization of the Tudeh Party of Iran. At that time, the reasons for their deaths were unclear to us. Later, after the 1979 Revolution, Bahman Naderipour (Tehrani) and Farajollah Seyfi Kamangar (Kamali) testified in the revolutionary court that Mahvash Jasemi and Masoumeh Tavafchiyan were also murdered by Nasser Nowzari (Rasouli) after they were taken into custody.[6]

Despite horrific tortures, many women remained true to the norms of secrecy necessary for the continuation of clandestine struggle, and never revealed anything which endangered their comrades and fellow travellers. A few who had family and children to bear, nevertheless displayed unbelievable tenacity under torture. These included Masoumeh Shademani (Kabiri), a Mojahed, and Fatemeh Sa'idi (also known as Rafiq Madar, Comrade Mother), a Fada'i.[7] Until 1979, when the regime was forced to open the prison doors and release all political prisoners, a total of 450 women were political prisoners. Sentences varied from one year, to life in prison. The first female prisoner executed was Manijeh Ashrafzadeh Kermani. In 1977 two Fada'i women, Azam Rouhi-Ahangaran and Zahra Aghanabi-Qolhaki were also executed by firing squad.

Most women, however, were sentenced to three to five years of imprisonment. Before 1975, the worst punishment was ten years. After that, with the worsening conditions, life-sentences were introduced and became common. Fifteen of my prison-mates were sentenced to life. Our trials were held in a military court. The first group of women tried a political-ideological defence. Most, however, used a juridical defence. Except for very special cases, the attorneys were court-appointed. Most of the female prisoners were between eighteen and forty years old.

I was arrested when I was twenty-four and had just graduated in pharmacology from the University of Tabriz. Most of us belonged to middle-class semi-traditional families. The women with religious ideologies were from urban mercantile backgrounds. Between 1972 and 1979, the vast majority of female political prisoners were leftists. Islamic women were only a small percentage.

Life in prison

For Fada'i women, life in the prison did not have a clear organizational structure. They also had no connection to the Organization outside prison. Nevertheless, we created a semi-organizational structure to promote solidarity. This network had a great impact on our lives in prison. Our prison life revolved around a commune which attempted to recreate the lifestyle of the Fada'i safehouses. We wanted our time in prison to reflect our ideas of equality and justice, which governed the life of the Fada'i guerrilla fighting units in safehouses. In these bases of urban guerrilla struggle against the Shah's regime, duties were divided between male and female members depending on their physical strength and mental abilities. Living expenses, food and weapons were also divided accordingly. No one was privileged over others. Fada'i women implemented the same lifestyle in prison. 'Commune,' therefore, meant equality for everyone. For example, the food and money received from the prisoners' families were collected and used for everyone. We shared daily chores. Together we cleaned, prepared plays and other cultural programs, and planned protest action. Sick prisoners were exempt from these duties. In other words, production, distribution and consumption were all communal. Everything was shared except for personal items such as underwear. In order to meet specific needs such as obtaining cigarettes or menstrual hygienic products, we used the money our families had sent. Only families which were relatively well-off could afford to send their imprisoned family members money, which went into the Commune's coffers in order to meet specific needs like buying cigarettes or menstrual pads or other hygienic products. Prisoners performed other chores such as sewing, knitting and providing for other day-to-day requirements in prison. During the first years of prison, knitting was done as a source of income for poor families outside prison. We cut our hair very short to keep it clean and spend less time on it. We would ask the prison guards for scissors when we needed a haircut. Sometimes they refused, since having any sharp objects was forbidden and getting them required great effort. The prison guards believed these could be used as means for murder or escape.

We took turns taking a shower and there was always a specific person coordinating it. After 1976, when we were transferred to a bigger prison, taking a shower was not such a serious problem anymore. In the new prison, showers, basins and toilets were in a separate section. There were four to five showers and that made everything easier. Cleaning the bathrooms and showers were our own responsibility. So was cleaning our prison, preventing fungal infections, fighting lice, flies and mosquitoes. Except for cleaning the visitor's room, everything was the prisoners' duty.

One of the most significant of these duties was looking after the sick or pregnant women before and after giving birth. Our prison-mates who were physicians took care of nutrition and looked after the ill. Mental traumas were often very severe, especially for those who had been tortured and raped. Our physician friends kept their secrets. They tried to heal their mental pain as much as they could. Among us, two had been raped and many had been sexually harassed by the interrogators. This was usually kept secret and not easily spoken about or revealed. Two of our prison-mates who were barely twenty years old had developed persistent infections and gynaecological problems after rape. One of them was driven mad due to sexual harassment and torture. Another girl kept repeating some unclear words for hours while hitting her head on the ground. Only once could she tell us what those words were: The SAVAKis had a coarse object and threatened to rape her with it continuously and then they hit her head so hard that she felt her brain 'was smashed'.

Amidst all the bitterness and terror, we had one pleasant duty: taking care of the new-borns. During my eight years of imprisonment three of my prison-mates gave birth to babies who changed the environment greatly and spread love and affection.

It is worth mentioning that the Commune included both religious and non-religious prisoners. However, the religious fanatics who were imprisoned in the last years of the Pahlavi regime had fundamental problems with our communal lifestyle and always kept to their own small separate groups.

The daily schedule

To optimize our time in the prison, daily life was carefully planned. The wake-up call was at 6.00 a.m. and bedtime was 10.00 p.m. Except for the sick and those who needed more sleep, most of the prisoners woke up at 6.00 a.m. From 6.30 to 7.30 in the morning warm-up and exercise took place. Those who were ill and those who had their monthly period did not participate in the morning exercise. Breakfast was a normal and traditional Iranian fare of bread, cheese, black tea and sometimes butter and dates saved from the previous night's dinner. Breakfast was divided equally between everyone.

After breakfast various classes were taught by the political prisoners themselves. These could take half an hour to two hours. Each person participated from morning to evening in different classes. Choosing the courses and classmates was based on preference and sometimes on the older and more experienced prisoners' recommendation and advice. In addition to these courses, prisoners who had not finished their high school diploma also took courses on high school subjects. Some of the prisoners who were educators accepted teaching responsibilities.

Lunch time was from noon until 1.00 p.m. To make food edible, time was spent for removing stones and dirt, which were commonly found in the stews and rice, as well as sediments of mud and sand which appeared regularly at the bottom of pots, pans and other containers in which the cooked food was delivered to the prisoners. We patiently spent time to get rid of all this. We sometimes found dead mice, pieces of fabric and even parts of soldiers' boots in the food. We strongly objected to such humiliating indignities and the lack of concern for our rights as prisoners. The quantity of food depended on the individual's needs. The sick prisoners and those with gastrointestinal problems followed special diets recommended by our physician friends. During the day we had one or two portions of seasonal fruits which were either sent by our families or given as a part of the prison's rations. In the afternoons, we resumed our educational classes, and the late afternoon, from 4.00 to 5.00 p.m., was devoted to light exercises and sports, including gymnastics or yoga and also volleyball and badminton.

With the increase of international pressure on the Iranian government, some reforms were initiated. Plans were made for a Red-Cross inspection of the prison. One of the consequences of these new developments was that we were also given a ping-pong table, and we also started to learn dancing. Dinner was brought to our cells at 6.00 p.m. and we had to eat by 7.00 p.m.; this was a light fare, which was mostly served cold. After dinner, we were free to do our personal chores. Sometimes we had special gatherings in which graduates of university, especially medical doctors and dentists, gave lectures about general and personal hygiene. The quiet-time began at 10.00 p.m., but often the lights were left on while we had to remain quiet in our beds. Some of us, however, continued whispering to each other under our blankets. Sometimes the theoretical and philosophical debates between religious and non-religious prisoners were carried out during this time and lasted into the middle of the night.

During the last years of prison (1977–9), we were given a television. Our favourite programs were the news reports, soap operas and music shows. Watching TV was also regulated both by prison guards and ourselves. These regulations had a twofold purpose: a form of censorship, and enforcing the rules of bedtime silence.

Theoretical studies

Most of our daily routine was dedicated to reading and debating. The most organized way to do this was in groups we formed and named reading sessions. These sessions took place regularly. Our reading materials were mostly legally published books and only occasionally did we have forbidden and censored material which were smuggled into the prison. Unfortunately, we did not have access to any of the literature related to guerrilla warfare in Iran, such as the works of comrades like Bijan Jazani, Masoud Ahmadzadeh or Amir-Parviz Pouyan. Nor did we have access to the written material of South American and French theoreticians such as Carlos Marighella, Régis Debray and others. However, we quoted them and referred to them time and again during our discussions. In defence of armed resistance, Pouyan's pamphlet which contained a dismissal of the Tudeh Party of Iran, *Rad-e Teori-ye Baqa'*, was an important resource. With regard to rallying the masses to armed resistance, we had handwritten notes on *Mobarezeh Mosallahaneh, Ham Estrateji, Ham Taktik* by Masoud Ahmadzadeh.

The imprisoned Fada'i women did not know much about the ideas of Bijan Jazani. It was only after he was killed by SAVAK that they came to know about his work. Apart from discussions about armed resistance, our theoretical work in prison had two basic premises:

- Studies related to criticizing or discussing the decline of discriminative regimes and political systems based on dictatorship and autocracy.
- Philosophical discussions on the decline of idealism and support for materialism.

Altogether, Fada'i women highly valued philosophical study and debate. Some of our religious prison-mates changed their point of view by participating in such debates. Later, some of them joined our groups. These conversions were never announced and were kept hidden both from the SAVAK and the Islamic prisoners. In those years, not one single leftist/Marxist was converted to the religious point of view.

Works of Lenin, Marx and Engels were not available in the women's prison. But some books of history, economics, philosophy and evolution were at our disposal and in need of repair due to overuse. We repaired them and some of us became excellent book-binders in due course. Some of the books I remember were *Tarikh-e Jahan-e Bastan* (History of the Ancient World) translated by Sadeq Ansari, 'Aliallah Hamedani and Bagher Momeni, *Islam dar Iran* (Islam in Iran) by I. P. Petroshevsky, *Mensha-ye Hayat* (The Origin of Life) by Aleksandr Ivanovich Oparin, *Tarikh-e Falsafeh* (The Story of Philosophy) by Will Durant, two books of Shakespeare and *Spartacus* by Howard Fast, *Hamsayehha* (The Neighbours) by Ahmad Mahmoud, *Don Quixote* by Cervantes, *Napoleon* by Yevgheny Tarle, *The Divine Comedy* by Dante Alighieri, *Amir Kabir va Iran* (Amir Kabir and Iran) by Fereydoun Adamiyat, The Quran, *Nahj al-Balagheh*, and some primary and high school books and some books related to university subjects.

We had access to only a few of the regime-prohibited books. Our families brought one or two thin books by hiding them among our clothes and personal items. Notes and pamphlets were also sent to us from male prisoners.

These books were treasures for us. We made compilations from paragraphs which included quotes from Marx, Engels, Lenin, and Stalin and copied them by hand. We also copied entire books by hand and hid them, then returned the originals to the library. However, these hidden copies were later discovered by the prison guards and removed. The confiscated notes and drafts included parts of Ashraf Dehqani's book, *Hamaseh-ye Moqavemat* (The Epic of Resistance) and other prisoner defences in court, a book of Azeri riddles and proverbs, a report about the living conditions of carpet weavers in Tabriz and a booklet of Azeri grammar collected and edited by prisoners. The booklet on Azeri grammar was the result of three years of teaching Azeri in the prison. We also translated a children's book from Spanish to Persian with the special contribution of Vida Hajebi-Tabrizi. We also serendipitously sent Ashraf Dehqani's critique on the novel *Spartacus* by Howard Fast out of prison. This precious body of work is currently available as published by the Fada'i Guerrillas. Inspired by François Truffaut's film adoption of the science-fiction book *Farenheit 451*, in which books are burnt systemically by a dictatorial regime, we also decided to memorize certain books. Unfortunately, we were unable to carry out this plan. Nonetheless, a few of us did succeed in memorizing some notes, poems and even important book chapters.

Reading newspapers was also part of our daily routine. Even the right to read the regime's newspapers such as *Keyhan* was gained by struggle. *Keyhan* was received most days from the prison guards who also deprived access to it as a form of punishment. For the most part, these newspapers, especially with news related to guerrilla struggle and workers' strikes, were censored before handed over to us. On the other hand, the news related to defeated street clashes and arrests of Fada'i and Mojahedin members were complete and intact. This policy was calculated to induce sense of hopelessness and despair in us.

Exception was the news related to the murder of Bijan Jazani and eight other well-known prisoners on the hills of Evin Prison and the attack on Hamid Ashraf and his comrades at the Mehrabad-e Jonoubi safehouse, which only parts of it were given to us. The women prisoners strongly objected to this ruse and took the related newspaper pieces from the guards. There was an especially designated group among the women prisoners responsible for archiving the socially and historically valuable topics and news.

Creative art

There was no access to poetry books in prison. But singing and reciting were amongst our favourite activities. We passionately recited and vocalized parts of famous contemporary Persian poetry and a few of the Chilean and Vietnamese revolutionary poets translated to Persian, such as Victor Jara and Touhou as well as verses from 'Alireza Nabdel's poetry, a poem of Mao Tse Tung called *Changsha* and poems celebrating Van Troy.[8]

During the first years in prison, since we were mostly guerrilla fighters and in favour of armed resistance, singing epic anthems and hymns was common. During those days we lost, in addition to our beloved friends, some close relatives: Ashraf Dehqani lost her brother Behrouz and Shahin Tavakkoli her husband and her brother. I lost my close and precious friend Manaf Falaki Tabrizi and Atefeh Gorgin lost her husband Khosrow Golesorkhi. Later, other women joined us, close relatives of whom were murdered by SAVAK.

When those who believed in political activism, rather than armed struggle, or women who followed no distinct political ideas joined us, our artistic activities became more diverse. We started to sing well known pop songs of the period. We also had some musically and theatrically innovative and talented prison-mates. Some of us remembered lines of Bertolt Brecht's plays and therefore with great effort put the scripts together in order to produce a scene. In theatre, the late Farideh Lashai's experiences were very useful to us.[9] At times, social problems were addressed in pieces we wrote and produced communally. Two examples that come to mind are Bertolt Brecht's *Mother Courage and her Children* and George Bernard Shaw's *Joan of Arc*. Other similar works produced by us were *About the life of northern fishermen*, written by one of our prison-mates, and *The Bazar*, which depicted the life of ordinary people. Sculpting was another favourite hobby. We shaped bread dough and stained it with dyes made from the prison pharmacy's pills and other medicines. These beautiful handicrafts such as animal figurines (horses and fishes) and ornamental beads were sometimes given to families as New Year gifts.

Revolutionary self-training

We Fada'i women prisoners took our revolutionary self-training seriously and worked to improve ourselves consistently. Focusing on the mental, physical, personal and practical aspects of our lives, we read, studied, and debated and discussed. For our physical and more practical self-improvement we practiced arts and sports, gymnastics and yoga.

During the first years, when there were only a handful of Fada'i women in prison, we continued a similar regime and schedule as those governing our life in safehouses. These practices were meant to maintain vigilance and willpower in the face of a terrible prison regime. We practiced asceticism by choosing night guard duty, staying awake all night, dressing sparsely when the weather was cold, eating very little, and walking barefoot on the hot prison yard tarmac. We volunteered for risky actions and willingly took part in difficult chores and duties. Criticism also had a special importance for us. We criticized each other often. However, the critiques were sometimes so harsh that they caused the debasement of people's characters and personalities. Nevertheless, our behaviour, habits and personal traits were routinely challenged and criticized;

sometimes it reached the point of questioning a person's intentions. Those who did not follow the prison-mates' norms and common behaviour were considered outsiders. However, only those who helped the police or spied on us were ostracized.

Later, we adopted a milder form of criticism, one which we called 'expressing feelings'. This took the form of either verbal advice or theatrical body language. That is, the person's behaviour was mimicked and sometimes resulted in laughter. Despite the problems with all this criticism, in my opinion, it made us better humans.

Political work and relationships in prison

In order to advance our goals in prison we had a semi-organizational structure. Precise and timely decisions on both theoretical issues and empirical self-development was one of our outstanding characteristics. We had sets of rules and regulations for when there were problems in the prison, or problems of communicating with other prisoners, and with the prison authorities. Communication with other prisoners did not usually mean attracting members for our semi-organization, but rather it meant having more friends and allies. Most of our efforts were directed to advocating for the righteousness of guerrilla struggle and armed resistance. In approaching people, we mostly considered their personalities. Characteristics like recalcitrance and tenacity, trustworthiness and secrecy, honesty, strong belief in revolutionary values, dedication and devotion.

Our relationship was especially close and friendly with those from the Mojahedin-e Khalq group, mostly because they too believed in armed struggle. This belief and revolutionary mentality were important for developing trust, friendship and collaboration between us. Jailed Fada'i and Mojahed women were united in strikes and protests.

Furthermore, Fada'i women respected their Mojahedin counterparts' beliefs and religious practices. The change of direction in some Mojahedin member's ideological leanings towards Marxism-Leninism did not significantly affect or alter our relationships. We did not hide our happiness when we witnessed some of our prison-mates discarding their religious views and joining the Fada'i women after the split inside the Mojahedin organization in 1975. This good relationship between Fada'i and Mojahed women persisted until the 1979 Revolution. We did not see any sign of hostility from them. Fada'i women also had a cordial relationship with other leftist women prisoners who were not in favour of armed resistance, although we did not have a particular friendship with them. Nonetheless, we respectfully engaged in theoretical debates with them. Despite all the diverging sociopolitical point of views and other differences, nothing really got in the way of our peaceful relationships in prison. Synchronization and synergy in strikes and protests was achieved after a session of persuasive discussion and a vote of the majority.

Our general approach in handling the problems which were created by prison officers was to discuss the same in our groups, inform individuals about our ideas or bring them to everyone's attention in a meeting. We then acted according to the opinion of the majority.

In sensitive cases such as hunger strikes or disputes with prison officers, planned procedures were handled with extreme care. One clear example of the collaboration between us and the Mojahedin was the escape plan of Ashraf Dehqani (Fada'i), Nahid Jalalzadeh (Mojahed) and Sediqeh Reza'i. The three women discussed the escape plan amongst themselves prior to the Nowrouz celebrations of 1973. At the time there were only seven women political prisoners. The three escapees kept the plan from others until it was executed. Even years later, I had no clue about the role of Sedigheh Reza'i and some Mojahedin families in the whole procedure.

We three Fada'i women (Ashraf Dehqani, Shahin Tavakkoli, and I) plus a fourth Mojahed woman, Nahid Jalazadeh, planned the escape. The first step consisted of preparing a face-to-face visit. We negotiated with prison officers to meet our relatives on the first day of spring, Nowrouz. They gave us the necessary clothing for the escape such as scarves and chador, shoes, money and likewise. The plan was to have Nahid Jalalzadeh as the only connection between us and the families. We decided to inform other prison-mates only under emergency conditions. The effort of Atefeh Ja'fari to get the chador and shoes from the changing room of the prison was admirable. She did not even know the reason for doing so, and never asked a question either. On the day of escape, we were suspicious about the presence of strangers among the visitors, so we reduced the number of escapees to two.

Finally, only Ashraf Dehqani and Nahid Jalalzadeh were supposed to escape. On 25 March 1973 this plan was executed through the participation of some women from the Mojahedin families. Only later we came to know that Sedigheh Reza'i played a key role in the whole plan. Those relatives of Mojahedin who helped the escape were arrested and tortured a few years later. Ashraf Dehqani succeeded to escape but Nahid Jalalzadeh was recognized by one of the guards and was returned to prison. After that escape we underwent a lot of pressure and interrogation, including a horrific irruption of SAVAK into our section in Qasr. It was only with collaboration of our friends that we could eliminate traces of the escape plan. We had no idea how the public and especially intellectuals inside and outside Iran reacted to this incident. A while after the escape, our families told us about the positive reactions of engaged intellectuals and other dissidents, who considered this as proof of the strength of the Fada'is.

Actions of resistance

Our daily behaviour was under the continuous surveillance of prison guards. Pressures usually increased on particular occasions, such as memorials or religious ceremonies. I cannot remember whether we had any special ceremony for International Worker's Day on 1 May or International Women's Day on 8 March. However, we observed moments of silence on occasions such as the day of Mao Tse Tung's death, the day of the massacre of the eight political prisoners on the hills of Evin by SAVAK and attacks on Mojahed and Fada'i families. On such occasions, reports from one or two spies resulted in prison guards' intrusions and them disturbing and disrupting the ceremonies.

Extreme care was needed on such occasions, because our rooms were always being checked by the guards. Surprise inspections were done every month or week. All of a sudden, a few sergeants and soldiers would raid our cells. They pushed all of us to one side and inspected all our personal belongings. The aftermath of their inspections felt like a battlefield.

To resist these raids, we had to be prepared for a physical altercation with the guards. How we got our belongings back later is another story. We also had to engage in a struggle with prison authorities in order to gain rights such as walking in the prison yard, possessing necessary living items, receiving visitors, writing letters, being able to engage in physical exercise, as well as obtaining medications and medical care or healthy and clean food. We were beaten with batons and placed in solitary confinement sometimes until we were close to death. We were sent to tight, dark and cold cells for solitary confinement. We were insulted, threatened and humiliated. We were often threatened with longer years of imprisonment or with being buried in the prison. However, we had no choice but preserving our identity and our dignity as political prisoners.

In order to make our requests we chose a representative who took these to the prison commander's office. Meetings with prison commanders were scheduled. When negotiations were possible, peace prevailed. Otherwise, we had to continue our protests in all sorts of ways, such as clanging on the prison bars and doors. There were also strikes and acts of civil disobedience. Sometimes such conflicts resulted in injuries on both sides and further punishments for the prisoners.

During the first years, because Fada'i and leftist women outnumbered the other prisoners, the aforementioned representative was often one of us. This was usually my responsibility. After my meetings with the prison commander, I conveyed details of whatever I saw, heard and experienced to my comrades. For example, while I was in the commander's office, I quickly skimmed through the uncensored newspapers – the same ones that were provided to us in a censored version. Often there was a newspaper on his table, which was either intentionally or accidentally placed there. The intentional cases took place when they wished to bring an event to our attention purposefully.

Hunger strikes

During eight years of prison, we went on three hunger strikes for the purpose of obtaining the basic rights of a political prisoner, such as the right to have books and newspapers, or family visits, which were often eliminated or cut short as a punishment, or the right for mothers to meet their children and, as mentioned, the right to basic hygiene or to spend time in open air.

Two of the strikes were long and were held in solidarity with those in the male political prison wards, which took place between 14 March and 13 April 1978. We held ten-day solidarity strikes with our male comrades during this one-month period. The main goal was to reduce everyday pressure in prison and to consume healthy food. We predicted this strike would be longer, therefore every morning we stored a number of sugar cubes and sugar grains and placed them in diluted teacups. To reduce the pressure caused by our hunger, we read Ahmad Mahmoud's novel, *The Neighbours* out loud, one by one. During the strike, several of us were sent to the medical room but none of us gave up or broke the strike. The strike only ended when our requests were granted, and our conditions met. The prison officers agreed with all our requests except for providing us with a radio. From then onwards, the quality and quantity of food improved and newspapers were given to us without censorship or cut-outs. We also received more books. Medical care and hygiene improved, and the imprisoned mothers were permitted to meet their children for the first time. Secondary relatives were also allowed to visit us. All of these improvements took place during the second half of 1977.

Our third hunger strike lasted three days and took place during the revolutionary fervour of autumn 1978. The objective of this strike was political, as it aimed to express our solidarity with the people outside the prison who were being killed every day in the clashes with security police, Immortal Guards, and other coercive forces. We wrote an 'announcement/letter of solidarity' and requested the prison commander to publish it in the national press. At the same time, we announced a hunger strike from 14 to 20 October 1978. The condition to end it was the publication of our declaration of solidarity on the national press. This time, because of the revolutionary atmosphere, our request was fulfilled faster. The letter was published in national newspapers. We stopped the hunger strike after three days. Everyone, both religious and non-religious prisoners, participated in this campaign. However, each group sent an independent letter. Islamically-inclined prisoners, including the Mojahedin, supported the leadership of Khomeini in their letter but Fada'i women refused to name Khomeini in their revolutionary declaration.

Among us there were two different views about the revolutionary momentum's political atmosphere. The majority of us, either guerrilla supporters or political activists, believed in the ongoing revolution and considered it as the expression of the will of the people. A small number of us believed it to be a conspiracy of superpowers. Before the start of the revolutionary process, our protests and strikes were met by violence and harsh condemnation from the prison authorities. By then the heads of prison were General Moharreri and Colonel Zamani. All the violence towards prisoners was meted out under their leadership.

Our united action and the Red Cross inspection

A year before the revolution in Iran, while Jimmy Carter was US president, public protest and campaigns for the rights of political prisoners started simultaneously with the efforts of the Confederation of Iranian Students and other groups of Iranian students abroad. The Shah and SAVAK decided to change the prison system and finally granted basic rights to prisoners. For the first time, the regime allowed the International Red Cross to inspect prisons. When the Red Cross representatives visited our prison, we were suspicious. We could not believe they were legitimate and therefore told them, 'We shall not talk to as long as the prison authorities are standing alongside you.'

The Red Cross agents promised us to come back one more time without the authorities by their side. We did not know when they would come back but discussed the issue and prepared ourselves for hours and days. We decided to choose one of the women political prisoners, who was familiar with or fluent in some foreign languages (English, French and German), to act as our representative and interpreter. We also agreed on the issues and points to be discussed with the Red Cross representative. We prepared witnesses who had been subjected to torture or harassment. We also gathered documents related to the executions of prisoners. Thus, upon returning to prison, the Red Cross agent was surrounded by women who were curious, eager and able to discuss crimes committed by SAVAK and other political policing apparatus. After hearing our reports and seeing the scars of torture on our bodies, the Red Cross agent was completely shocked and astonished. I remember one of her last sentences clearly. She said, 'The severity of tragedy in the prisons of Iran can be directly compared with Vietnam war crimes.'

Change in the composition of the prisoners

Just before the success of the revolution Islamic women with special uniforms and head to toe black covers and scarves entered the political wards. We named them 'sack-heads' or 'sack-wearers'. They had a destructive influence on the prison atmosphere. They negatively influenced the relationship between us and the Mojahed women. 'Sack-wearers' brought with them mistrust and pessimism from the beginning. If they were accidentally touched by a non-religious woman, they would wash themselves, as if we were 'untouchable'. They never participated in our established commune. Our Mojahed fellow prisoners also started to gradually drift into an increasingly conservative lifestyle. They separated their food cloth from the rest of us and our bonds of friendship and solidarity weakened. Relationships grew distant and cold as a result. This state of affairs grew to the extent that we could not collaborate during the aforementioned hunger strike of October 1978. They organized their actions independently and without consulting us. We were not aware of the reasons behind this coldness and distance for a long time, but we suspected that our Mojahed friends were commanded from outside the prison to keep their distance from leftists. We also heard that the Ayatollah Montazeri in the men's prison had issued a *fatwa* of keeping distance from leftists, in effect rendering us ritually unclean and therefore 'untouchable'. Some of us considered the threats from the Muslim fanatics to be the reason behind taking distance and avoidance.

It is worth mentioning that 'sack-wearers' threatened to report us to SAVAK when we tried to convert the newcomers to Marxism. These were by no means bogus or empty threats and at least in two cases were actually carried out. At one point I was actually in a physical confrontation with them and received a good pummelling as a result. They openly stated that 'even an alliance with the devil is justified against blasphemy'.

The history of women's political prisons in Iran can be divided into three periods. The first period was from 1971 to 1974, the second from 1974 to 1977 and the third period from 1977 to 1979. It should be highlighted that the relationship of Fada'i women during the first period was in its most dynamic and flourishing form. This flourishing relationship, though slightly faded, was still persisting during the second period. In the third period the relationship between prisoners lost much of its warmth, vitality and solidarity. For the first period, as mentioned, the majority of the women were those who believed in armed resistance and were Fada'i and Mojahed. During the second period, the presence of proponents of non-military political activism influenced these relationships. At the end of the second period purely political activists composed one-third of the population in prison. This was also the period in which two important revolutionary events significantly influenced the prison atmosphere:

- The crippling attacks on the leadership of Fada'i guerrillas which resulted in the decimation of its leadership.
- The split in Mojahedin's Organization and the founding of the People's Mojahedin Organization of Iran (Marxist-Leninist).
- The third period coincided with the popular uprising, when religious fanatics entered the prison. The aforementioned conflicts between female prisoners began at this time.

Despite the setbacks, Fada'i women kept their influential role, and because of the maturity of their behaviour and actions gained widespread respect by other prisoners.

The night of tears and laughter

On 26 October 1978, Captain Khoshsirat, the prison commander came to us with a piece of paper in his hands and asked us all to pay attention. Despite our disbelief he asked some of our prison-mates to collect their personal belongings and follow him out of the cells. When we shouted 'why?' and 'where?' were they being taken, he replied: 'These people are free to go.'

We followed the news every moment and could also hear the people's cries and protests behind the walls. We still could not rationalize the release of our prison-mates and were suspicious about it and worried: 'What if they were shot?' Therefore, when others were set free, they refused to go. They said: either everyone must be released or we would stay. These were some of the most unforgettable moments in my life, a manifestation of a colourful mixture of human emotions: happiness, doubt, sadness, worry, belief, disbelief, pain, sympathy and non-stop tears mixed with laughter. All of it crystallized in those moments. We called that evening 'The night of tears and laughter.'

Freedom, the outcome of revolution

After the first group of women were released, others prepared themselves to be discharged too. Fada'i women again sat down to discuss the situation, and we decided to prepare a speech to read out to the people who came to welcome us outside the prison walls. We decided to leave prison in our prison outfits, to symbolize the prisoner who is freed from jail as a result of popular will and the Revolution. We heard that our released friends were carried on people's shoulders all the way to their houses. This was the most valuable welcome gift for those of us who had spent the best years of our youth in captivity and had endured all sorts of stress and torture.

9

The Organization of Iranian Peoples Fada'i Guerrillas' prison organization

Nasser Rahimkhani and Nasser Mohajer

Like all other political prisoners, the left-leaning proponents of the guerrilla movement in Iran at the time of Mohammad Reza Shah Pahlavi, especially after the 1953 coup, once incarcerated, had to adjust to the new environment and find the means to organize their political activities in confinement. The leading figure of the Fada'is prison organization was Bijan Jazani. Jazani, along with a few of his comrades, was arrested in 1968 and tortured viciously during the first few months of interrogations before his transfer to Qasr Prison in Tehran. His charges ranged from inciting 'illegal activities' to initiating a guerrilla organization to evoke armed struggle against the Shah's regime. Once inside, they started building a network that eventually gave birth to the prison section of the Organization of Iranian People's Fada'i Guerrillas.

Soon after the inception of armed struggle in Siyahkal on 8 February 1971, the regime began its all-out offensive against the budding movement which attracted many intellectuals and thousands of students and youth. Prior to the Siyahkal episode, the two main prison facilities were Qezel-Qaleh and Evin, both near Tehran. These two facilities were primarily used for interrogation, which included physical and psychological torture. Prisoners often ended up in military tribunals and were sentenced from one year to life imprisonment. Dozens were also condemned to death by firing squad. Other than Qezel-Qaleh and Evin, prisoners were also held in the historical Qasr detention centre. In provinces too, many old and new penitentiaries were holding political prisoners.

When the Shah launched the Rastakhiz (Resurgence) Party in 1975, the urban Iranian population was surprised. Rastakhiz became the only legal political party, and all Iranians were required to join it. Consequently, Evin Prison was transformed into a long-term facility to meet the ever-growing political arrests. Interestingly, the Jazani group was the first to be transferred to Evin from Qasr only to be executed a few weeks later. Such transfers occurred frequently and undermined the activities of the OIPFG prison organization.

The narrative which follows illustrates the stages of the Fada'i prison organization from its inception and moves on to its expansion, operation, the presence of factionalism, its virtual dissolution and finally its rebirth. The narrative includes episodes of structural and disciplinary regulations imposed by prison officials. As such, we become acquainted with the context in which the OIPFG prison organization took shape in 1968 under SAVAK, the notorious secret police of Shah Mohammad Reza Pahlavi. It is important to note that the narrations are based on eyewitness accounts of prisoners and prison officials as well as SAVAK documents, monographs, prison memoirs, newspapers articles and reports by human rights organizations such as Amnesty International.

We would like to take this opportunity to thank all former political prisoners who accepted our request to be interviewed: Mohammad Farsi, Naqi Hamidian, Asghar Izadi, Mohammad-Majid Kianzad, Morteza Malek-Mohammadi, Amir Mombini, Parviz Navidi, Mehdi Same', Mohammad Reza Shalgouni and Jamshid Taheripour.

Mohammad Reza Shalgouni's narrative of his detention from 1969 to 1979 depicts different stages of the political prison complex during the last decade of the Shah's rule:

> The first phase starts in 1963 when the White Revolution was launched and continues until 1968. We understand the White Revolution as a milestone because it brings about the autocracy of the Shah and the total control of SAVAK over all aspects of life. In this phase, the number of political prisoners is at its lowest. Many older political prisoners were released soon after the White Revolution. The general condition of prison life, be it within the jurisdiction of SAVAK or police compounds, improved and prison sentences were reduced.[1]

Shalgouni expounds:

> The second phase starts in 1967 when revolutionary groups were in a preparatory stage to launch armed struggle. At the beginning of the 1967–8 academic year, university students staged demonstrations demanding an end to tuition fees. The demonstrations soon took a political turn. Many students were arrested and detained in SAVAK-controlled jails.
>
> It was during this period that some groups were arrested, each of which in a different stage of preparation for armed struggle. The most prominent of these was the Jazani-Zarifi group. Upon being taken into police custody, they transformed the atmosphere into one of learning and resistance. They created study groups, discussion circles and laid down the foundations of a clandestine prison organization. The discussion topics were usually the following: (1) the necessity of armed struggle as the main mode and most effective tactic to fight the Shah's dictatorship and (2) the position regarding the Soviet, Chinese and Cuban socialisms. Most of the criticism was aimed at the Soviet Union due to its establishment of good relations with the Shah's regime. On the other hand, most prisoners sympathized with revolutionary Cuba due to its perceived independence from the two pivots of the communist movement. It must be noted that most of the newly incarcerated had concluded that peaceful political activism by itself could not change the political situation. The secret police were aware of this fact and therefore one of the characteristics of this phase was the transfer of prisoners to different detention centres across Iran and particularly to regions with harsh conditions. For example, most members of the Palestine group[2] arrested in 1969 were sent into internal

exile and scattered across the country right after their trial in 1970. This occurred when veteran political prisoners were being sent back to Tehran from internal exile.

The first group of prisoners sent into exile in the second phase was the Jazani group. Its members were dispersed across Iran's penitentiary facilities after four members of the group attempted to escape from Qasr Prison in March 1969. It is noteworthy that the arrest of Jazani's group marked a new era in the policy of cruelty and torture of political prisoners in Iran. This era can be epitomized by the construction of a high-security Evin Prison and the transfer of radical dissidents to this facility. Evin was the first modern prison in Iran equipped with the most sophisticated apparatuses of torture applied by well-trained torturers of the CIA and Mossad.

Members of Jazani's group were sent to Qasr Prison after interrogation and severe torture awaiting trial. It was in Qasr that the foundations of a clandestine prison organization were laid by Jazani and some members of the group. Meeting after meeting resulted in the adoption of guidelines for handling problems of daily life in prison, drawing up a program for ideological study, political discussions and physical fitness.

Mohammad-Majid Kianzad, one of the early members of the Jazani group gives this account:

> Section 3 was a cold and harsh place. The inmates were not on good terms with each other. They kept their distance. Things changed when we arrived. We wanted to establish mutually respectful relationships and peaceful coexistence with members of different groups. In a short span of time, daily life changed from a passive existence to one full of life and enthusiasm. We suggested making a shower room and a volleyball court and the other political prisoners welcomed these suggestions. Bijan Jazani, our spokesman, obtained the consent of the prison officials and we started the project with our own money. Choupanzadeh was the architect of the team and we were the labourers. Almost all the prisoners took part in this project.[3]

Mehdi Same', who was arrested several times between 1967 and 1969, attests that no political formation had as much impact as the Jazani-Zarifi group in changing the prison atmosphere and empowering the prisoners:

> I was incarcerated in Section 3 in November 1969. Before Siyahkal, a number of supporters of the armed struggle from various revolutionary currents had been there ... However none could build a communal relationship amongst prisoners nor change the rapport between prisoners and prison officials. With the arrival of the Jazani-Zarifi people and later the Palestine Group things changed. To quote Hojjati Kermani of the Hezb-e Mellal Eslami (The Party of Islamic Nations); they disturbed the peace that existed previously.... Prisoners would sing revolutionary songs out loud together. The inmates formed a commune and lived life harmoniously within the prison walls. However Hezb-e Melal Eslami refused to join the Commune.[4]

The practice of singing revolutionary songs originated at the same time the commune was set up. One of the songs was *Ey Rafiqan* (Oh Comrades), inspired by the beautiful Azerbaijani song 'Olari-var'. In Ward 3 of Qasr Prison, it became a tradition to sing that song whenever a prisoner was being released or transferred to another prison. 'Oh, Comrades' was also sung in the second trial of the Palestine group right after the predetermined verdicts were announced before the startled judge, the prosecutor and the members of the jury could leave the military court.

With the attack of the Fada'i guerrillas on the Siyahkal gendarmerie post in February 1971, the prevailing prison atmosphere changed radically. Mohammad Reza Shalgouni recounts his observations:

> The news of Siyahkal, although not entirely unexpected, jolted the prison. The truth is that in the 1960s most Iranian political opponents of the Shah's regime had, in one way or another, developed sympathy for the notion of armed resistance ... [Yet, the Tudeh Party strongly opposed the guerrilla movement]. Nevertheless, as Che Guevara's *Guerrilla Warfare in Cuba* was translated into Persian by members of the Tudeh party, they [initially] had a dual approach towards the incipient movement. On the contrary, Maoist groups were diehard opponents of the guerrilla struggle. True, they believed in armed struggle and advocated a revolutionary downfall of the Shah's regime, but that was to be done according to the Chinese model and mainly by 'the People's Army'. All in all, apart from the Tudeh Party and the Maoists, all the younger prisoners showed real sympathy towards the guerrilla movement ...
>
> When the news of the Siyahkal episode reached Qasr, our court hearing had just come to an end and we were not allowed any further visits. By talking to other prisoners, we became aware of a military confrontation in the north of Iran followed by widespread arrests. It was at the end of February or early March of [1970] that the newspapers published the names of those who had been executed. When the police brought the newspapers to the ward, however, this piece of news was entirely cut out and censored. It took a couple of days to get the name of the martyrs. The prison was burning with anxiety. At our suggestion, a two-minute silence was observed.
>
> The arrest and execution of members of the Siyahkal group can be considered the beginning of the third phase of prison life. The prelude of this phase was the breaking up of the commune and sending us to different detention centres across Iran. This third phase that continues until 1973 is characterized by the 'emergence and consolidation' of the guerrilla movement. Subsequently, there was a spectacular increase in the number of political prisoners. Morale amongst the prisoners was usually very high. They were quite defiant in their interactions with prison guards even in solitary confinement in exile.
>
> ... The two main influential revolutionary organizations of the time were the OIPFG and the People's Mojahedin ... Both parties had a strong hand in the commune ... Those who did not join the commune were considered 'dropouts', 'burnt outs' or 'passive prisoners'. In the meantime, there were some excesses.

Amir Mombini's recollections shed light on another aspect of the commune. He recounts the harsh measures that were taken by several prisoners:

> A committee was in charge of the daily routine that we called '*senfi tasks*'[5] such as morning exercise, food and cigarette distribution, administering the diet of sick prisoners (people suffering from peptic ulcer), liaising with the prison control desk, collecting clothing, books, fruit and any other item brought by the prisoners' families. The cigarette ration was very limited ... Prisoners received only three single cigarettes per day. This led to complaints and protests ... The supporters of the guerrilla movement were quite strict about daily routine. For instance, they believed morning exercises were vital for physical fitness, so it became obligatory ... From time to time there were clashes with the police too.[6]

Recounting the tasks within the commune, Naqi Hamidian notes that efforts were made to establish a line of communication with women prisoners in order to exchange news:

> The commune was led by an elective committee composed of the Fada'is, Mojahedin, members of some other groups and also a few independents. Management rotated and was for a fixed term only. The commune officers liaised with the prison control desk for visits, purchased food, assigned kitchen duties and intervened in disputes when necessary. They were also in charge of setting quiet hours, scheduling morning exercises and sport activities such as football and volleyball, appointing a librarian, allocating rooms to new arrivals, making sleeping arrangements in the corridors ... Sometimes there were strikes for collective demands. For example, a sleep strike meant we wouldn't sleep....
>
> We also made some efforts to contact women prisoners ... Shahin Tavakkoli when was taken to stand trial at the military court, ... planned to leave notes and pamphlets – minutely written on small scraps of paper – in specific places of the shower room. The shower room was a common area and prisoners were taken there according to a specified schedule. Prison guards would inspect the shower room thoroughly each time common convicts used it .... During one of these routine inspections, the guards discovered the place where we hid notes and messages.[7]

After the Siyahkal episode, the People's Fada'i Guerillas and affiliated currents were detained in wards 3 and 4. In the meanwhile, some members of the Jazani group who had been dispatched to prisons in the provinces were transferred back to Tehran.

Simultaneously, the urban guerrilla movement was on the rise outside the prison walls. Political prisoners who supported the armed struggle felt it was their bound duty to help the organization intellectually, politically and practically.

Giving direction to various social and political endeavours during this period was no easy task. One needed to be informed about the modern history of Iran, political developments from the Constitutional Revolution onwards, and the class structure of society (particularly economic and socio-political changes due to the Shah's land reform at the beginning of the decade). The formulation of the theoretical views and the political program of the People's Fada'i Guerillas, as well as the prioritization of the necessities of the armed struggle hinged upon the above-mentioned intellectual tasks. These tasks could not have been accomplished without a methodical, political and theoretical struggle against other streams within the left-leaning movement.

Not only in the realm of theory, but also in the sphere of practice there were shortcomings and unanswered questions. As such it was imperative to organize the following:

1. Discussion groups to analyse political and theoretical viewpoints within the guerrilla movement,
2. To write and procure books and pamphlets about the guerrilla struggle,
3. Establish solid bridges with the OIPFG outside.
4. Organize correspondence with the leadership of the OIPFG by smuggling books and pamphlets and, thus, helping to inform and mobilize the Fada'i supporters abroad,
5. Recruit the most talented and steadfast political prisoners who were determined to join the guerrilla movement upon release,
6. Train the new recruits,
7. Attempt to reach politico-intellectual coherence and strive to unify all leftist groups and tendencies who believed in armed struggle,
8. Define the fundamentals of the political relationship with other streams within the armed movement, particularly the People's Mojahedin Organization of Iran (PMOI).

The presence of Bijan Jazani at Qasr Prison from the spring of 1971 until the winter of 1974 had a significant impact on organizing such tasks. Here former prisoners share their recollections. Mehdi Same', who was in Qezel-Qaleh in the spring of 1972, remembers Bijan Jazani's emphasis on the necessity of resistance and organizational activism inside prison:

> Bijan talked to me on the very first day. He said: 'we have to work here and we will -- at any price ... We have an organization in the prison and each one of us has to assume an organizational responsibility'. He would carry on with his political discussions and build up relationships while playing chess. With the arrival of Bijan, everything speeded up. I don't know if he had already formed an organization or if he had started it with us ... I assume it started in Eshrat-Abad, then Qezel-Qaleh, and Qasr afterwards. He continued it over there.
>
> In 1972, almost everything was organized. For instance, we were instructed to get information from our families during the visits ... Bijan used to say: 'When you have a visitor you have to pay attention to the morale of your family, what your family thinks about the organization, what kind of information they can pass on to us ...
>
> Bijan had a radio too. He had good ties with many of the prison guards. From time to time they would do him a favour. In Qezel-Qaleh, there were no routine inspections like in Qasr. Having a radio was really useful for us ...
>
> Bijan used to say: 'No matter what your rank is, you should never write a letter of remorse; you should not feed the regime's propaganda machine'. The [financial] situation of the families of political prisoners was also important to

him. Furthermore, he had talked to others about the importance of aiding the families of those political prisoners who'd lost their breadwinners.

In the second half of 1972, Bijan was taken to Falekeh (police headquarters). The apprehended were taken to Falekeh for a few days for identification purposes. Then they were transferred to Qasr Prison. Falekeh later became the Anti-Sabotage Joint Committee. Parviz Navidi was there at that time. Navidi remembers those days well:

> I had already seen Jazani at the Anti-Sabotage Joint Committee Jail … He arrived at the common ward of Falekeh on 18 November 1972. Nothing permanent could be created there as it was a sort of a transit station … Bijan talked to us for three nights in a row. Later, he told me that he was under the impression he had to be taken back to Qom Prison … That is why he wanted to communicate his ideas, reflections and all the work he had started in Qom in the very little time he thought he had with us … We were a very big crowd. He was afraid he wouldn't be able to put his thoughts in writing. In Bijan's words, he used that 'raw material' to get his ideas across. He rightly believed that if some of his words could be transferred to comrades outside or other prisons, it would be worth it. He wanted us to ask questions so that he could work on them at night and answer us in the morning … in writing or orally … I should mention that Bijan's wife, Mihan, was not his only channel of communication with the outside world. He knew some people in other prisons too. They would often join OIPFG upon release from prison and would relay his ideas to the organization. In November of 1972 we were transferred to ward 4 of Qasr Prison … Our arrival at the ward changed the situation.[8]

Parviz Navidi was transferred to Qasr alongside Jamshid Taheripour:

> In the winter of 1972, we were transferred from the Anti-Sabotage Joint Committee Jail to Ward 4 of Qasr Prison. Some newly arrested students and some Mojahedin supporters were there too …
>
> At the time, there wasn't an organization in Qasr. I mean an organization in the true sense of the word … Most of the detainees were university students. We would make a commune … it was a primitive commune by then standards.
>
> The Mojahedin held meetings in the big hall of Ward 4, they would study the *Nahj al-Balagheh*[9] and the *Quran*; their relationships were quite sectarian, they would only mix with people of their own kind or with their own supporters.[10]

Parviz Navidi confirms Jamshid Taheripour's testimony:

> From November 1971 to March 1972, I can't say that there was 'an organization' in the true sense of the word but there was some sort of organizational structure in Ward 4 of Qasr Prison. I mean we had created some cells to discuss certain issues. There was a sort of 'central organ' … In other words, there was a sort of hierarchy … For instance, we were the ones who decided what kind of discussions we should have; or what should be done. For everything we wanted to put into practice, we

would first study it. Of course, this period did not last long. I was in Ward 4 until 15 February ... Then, along with Jamshid Taheripour, I was transferred to Ward 3 where Bijan Jazani was. My court hearings had just closed.

Jamshid Taheripour and Parviz Navidi's narratives give the reader a broader view of prison life at that time. According to Taheripour:

> Parviz Navidi and I were both transferred from Ward 4 to Ward 3. Veterans from different political and ideological tendencies were placed in Ward 3. There were some prominent and established authorities there: the Coalesced Islamic Association the Jazani Group, some members of the Tudeh Party and the Mojahedin, and last, but not least, Safar Qahremani, an Azeri political prisoner who had been arrested in the aftermath of the collapse of the Autonomous Government of Azerbaijan in 1946 and was widely respected by everyone.
>
> When we first arrived at Ward 4, Masoud Rajavi invited us to his cell for dinner. I had been arrested in connection with Hamid Ashraf. Masoud was aware of this and of my political stance. That evening, he told us that, as well-known personalities of the guerrilla movement, we had to drive Bijan Jazani away from our ranks. He said: 'You must isolate him because he is an opportunist'. Rajavi's enmity towards Jazani was hidden from no one. I was in contact with Bijan from the very first day I stepped foot at Ward 3. Upon arrival, he welcomed us and held us in a warm embrace. We sat and talked for a while. He asked me about the organization and I told him everything I knew about it. Before being arrested, I only knew Bijan by name. I had a lot of respect for him as the leader of the Fada'is ... Then in March 1972, Bijan gave me a piece of paper with three names on it. He briefly talked about the prison organization. He said: 'You are a member of "the organizational committee" here and you are assigned to work with these three comrades.' He also said: 'You'll be our contact person with the Mojahedin. We'll inform the Mojahedin that you're our contact person from now on.' ...
>
> After a while I also became the contact person with the Tudeh Party comrades like 'Ali Khavari and Parviz Hekmatjou.
>
> ... There were no permanent members as prisoners were constantly being transferred to other prisons.
>
> I'm aware of the fact that a message had been sent from outside stipulating that Bijan Jazani had to formulate the theoretical framework of the left movement. As the OIPFG had entered a new phase of armed struggle, i.e. the mobilisation of the masses, it was deemed necessary to expand and extend the theory of urban guerrilla movement. Thus, Jazani was appointed to the task.

Parviz Navidi also depicts the situation in Ward 3 by comparing the 'real organization' in Ward 3 with the 'pseudo-organization' of young students in Ward 4:

> I should mention that the internal cohesion of the OIPFG was not Bijan Jazani's only preoccupation ... His criteria for recruiting new members were believing in Marxism-Leninism, believing in armed struggle under the leadership of the

OIPFG, having a combative spirit and an organizational discipline. He was also very sensitive to the relationship with other forces, especially the PMOI ... In 1972, Bijan noticed that the Fada'is and the Mojahedin outside were in contact with each other (Mehdi Fazilat-Kalam had given them dynamites). As soon as he found out about it, he undertook writing a pamphlet entitled *Islamic Marxism or Marxist Islam*. He said: 'We should have a correct understanding of the Mojahedin. We should know what kind of a political force it is; how close to each other we are; what our points of distinction and difference are.' When the critics of the guerrilla movement and the Maoists arrived at the prison, he reacted again by reviewing their theoretical underpinnings and political practice ...

Bijan had a profound knowledge of the political currents inside prison ... He was aware of its make-up; he knew how many people were for the guerrilla movement; how many were Marxists; what their social background was; whether they were intellectuals or students; how many were workers, etc. He updated this data regularly.

Educating political prisoners, especially the younger generation, was one of the priorities on Bijan's agenda. Mohammad Reza Shalgouni states that

Bijan was certainly the most charismatic person in prison and his influence on the supporters of the guerrilla movement was indisputable ... As a result, many leftist prisoners joined the guerrilla movement after being released. All in all, Bijan had greatly politicized prison life and did his utmost to sustain a vibrant political atmosphere. It wouldn't be an exaggeration to say that he worked 14 to 15 hours a day. He worked even during the darkest hours, when our discussions were regularly reported and we would be interrogated and punished under the pretext of undermining 'the regulations'.

Most of the educational programs in jail were done orally. Bijan would program 5 to 6 sessions per day. There would be two or three guys at a time, not to attract the attention of the prison guards ...

When I was in the same ward as Bijan in Qasr prison, writing pamphlets had become very difficult. Nevertheless, Bijan continued writing.

Parviz Navidi, too, has many memories of those regular teaching sessions:

I was in the same ward as Bijan, when he was writing *Tarikh-e Sih Saleh-ye Iran* (The Thirty-Year History of Iran) ... Bijan had just started writing on political parties which was a chapter of this work. He was writing about the things that were discussed during his three-night stay in Falekeh Prison, albeit in more detail and with more precision. He wrote and we made copies of his writings. This was the so-called 'overt period' of our organization. If someone paid attention, he would easily notice what the structure of the organization was. The morning meetings were held in the presence of Bijan. After two hours, each of us would meet our own group. Some of our sessions were semi-open. We would prepare crib sheets. We would write in extremely small letters with the finest ballpoint pens on cigarette paper.

Preparing crib sheets and 'minute writing' were the most important tasks of the Fada'i prison organization. Mehdi Same' who had participated in this sort of activity recounts:

> I would write the notes on a cigarette paper in minute letters. Yousef Zarkari was there too. Later, I found out that Bijan had worked on him a whole lot. He and I copied *Seh Maqaleh* (The Three Articles), *Do Maqaleh* (The Two Articles) and other writings of Bijan. I remember reading *Ancheh Yek Enqelabi Bayad Bedanad* (What a Revolutionary Must Know) at that time.

Organizational work, especially on a regular basis, was not easy after the events of June 1973 and the suffocating atmosphere thereafter. The seasoned cadres and activists of the guerrilla movement were facing harsh conditions. Many were sent into exile. Then Wards 3 and 4 of Qasr Prison were shut down temporarily and the prisoners were transferred to two separate entities. Wards 1, 2 and 3 were allocated to inmates with less than five years sentence. Ward 1 was completely separated from Wards 2 and 3. Wards 4, 5 and 6 were allocated to inmates with more than five years and lifers. Ward 6 was completely separated from the other two wards. Prisoners of Ward 6 were only allowed to go to Wards 4 and 5 for lunch and dinner, one hour a day.

In June 1973, confrontations with the guards backfired and led to surprise attacks and raids of the armed-to-the teeth police, who ruthlessly destroyed and looted the prisoners' belongings. This was followed by 24-hour surveillance, provocation, humiliation, threats and tortures. The worst being suspended by the manacles with the feet off the floor which took place at the police station and not in SAVAK's detention centres! Political activism diminished for a while. In the face of this deep despair and the prevalent passivism, Bijan Jazani developed this thesis: We should defend, more than ever, our *senfi* rights: 'From individual organized movements to collective movements'.

> Some supporters of the guerrilla movement regarded Bijan as a shy supporter of the Tudeh Party .... Disagreements led to fierce debates in some circles in Tehran prisons. On the Shah's dictatorial character, some believed that the monarch was totally dependent on the US and lacked any willpower. Bijan, however, believed that in spite of the regime's dependence on the US, the Shah carried a certain amount of weight. The second point [of contention] was the existence or absence of 'the objective condition of revolution'. Bijan advocated Lenin's thesis of ' Revolutionary Situation', whereas others supported Masoud Ahmadzadeh's theory. They believed that 'the objective condition of revolution' existed in Iran ... The third point was 'armed struggle' itself. Bijan considered it as the main tactic of struggle (nothing more than a tactic). By March 1974, he had even modified his understanding [of armed struggle] ... Referring to Ahmadzadeh's pamphlet 'Armed struggle both a strategy and tactic' ... Regarding the Soviet Union, some believed that Bijan was in practice advocating the same standpoint as the Tudeh

Party. Generally speaking, they would display sympathy towards the Maoist stance.

It is important to note that some of the supporters of Masoud Ahmadzadeh knew his book *Mobarezeh Mosallaneh, Ham Estrateji, Ham Taktik* (Armed Struggle; both a Strategy and a Tactic) by heart. According to Mohammad Farsi, Rahim Sabouri was one of them:

> He recited it to those who were interested and he would also train them. ʿAli Satari, too, knew Ahmadzadeh's book by heart. He was like an 'audio book'. He would recite the book word by word and inform the comrades who had never read the book of all the details of Ahmadzadeh's viewpoints. It made sense. Memorizing was the safest way of transferring the contents of these works. Another comrade, Morteza Malek-Mohammadi had memorized [Amir-Parviz Pouyan's pamphlet], *Zarourat-e Mobarezeh Mosallahaneh va Rad-e Teori-ye Baqa*ʿ (The Necessity of Armed Struggle and Refutation of the Theory of Survival).[11]

Jamshid Taheripour recalls the disagreements between the two tendencies within the armed movement and talks about the heavy atmosphere that was created:

> Despite enmities, we tried to revive our relationship with Ahmadzadeh sympathizers … but they showed no interest in having contact with us … The distance grew wider as the disagreements became more and more acute.[12]

We can learn about the pseudo-organization of Ahmadzadeh's supporters through the words of Asghar Izadi:

> I wasn't aware of the existence of a prison organization before arriving at Qasr … After the Siyahkal comrades were executed, our death sentence was commuted to life imprisonment … I was among the 23 people who were saved from execution … Not too many people were there at the time of our arrival. But by and by many others joined us. They were mostly Fadaʾis or Mojahedin. I guess there were about 200 new arrivals … The Mojahedin were quite organized and it was obvious that some of their leaders were there too. But none of the OIPFG leaders were present in Qasr. Almost all of our leaders had been executed.
>
> I can't recall when and how we started talking about the necessity of having an organization and well defined activity in jail. However, I remember that a few factors led us to organize ourselves and do some planning for effective activity. Firstly, resistance in the face of prison policies and prison authorities was crucial. So, we decided to gather the Fadaʾi members and all the inmates who supported the guerrilla movement. Secondly, it was the organized existence of the Mojahedin with a few of their leaders, including Masoud Rajavi, and many of their cadres in our ward. They were quite hierarchical … One day he told me: 'Asghar, you Fadaʾi guerrillas lost a big number of your leaders and cadres during armed operations and skirmishes with SAVAK agents. But see what we have done! We

have a hundred leaders, cadre, members and supporters inside the prison!' At the time, the Mojahedin were preparing themselves to begin armed actions and had not yet entered the military phase and politico-military structures. Actually, they had somehow reconstructed the same structures and organizational hierarchy they had outside, inside prison. For us the Fada'is what emerged from March to September 1972 in Qasr Prison was a sort of political formation and a kind of structure that brought about a type of organizational relationship between us ... there was neither a hierarchical structure nor a well-defined political framework among us. Except for the nucleus of the so-called 'central leadership', the existing relationship between the other comrades was like a network ...

Our activities revolved around several axes: 1) discussions we had among ourselves over a score of topics, from tactics of struggle to the history of the organization, etc. 2) analysing the news and information we received about the organization ... As far as I remember, we did not have any pamphlets at that time. Maybe one, and that was Masoud Ahmadzadeh's pamphlet. Let's play it safe! There might have been one or two other pamphlets, but I'm not sure ... We also had to communicate with the women's ward. Our contact person would put the notes or messages in a drop-spot in the shower room. Male and female prisoners used the same shower rooms, but on different days.

I need to emphasize a point regarding the formation of this 'semi-organization' we had. At no point was it clearly and plainly stated that we needed to have an organization in jail. We never sat down to discuss the question of having an organization or not. We felt as if we were outside prison walls ...

It is important to note that, at the time, we were witnessing the formation of small groups among the wide spectrum of prisoners. I mean, in that epoch, there was always an active political atmosphere and a multitude of relationships inside prisons ... The bigger commune which was in charge of handling prison affairs, too, had created an atmosphere of resistance and struggle. On the top of this was the effect of the ongoing struggle on society at large. Almost all groups and currents who somehow believed in guerrilla struggle gathered around the Fada'i movement; for example, the Red Star, The People's Ideal, the Palestine Group or members of student circles who ended up in jail because of their political activities. One could say there was no real boundary between these groups. I believe this was partly because of the name Iranian People's Fada'i Guerrillas. Whoever called himself/herself a leftist and believed in armed struggle was considered a Fada'i Guerrilla.[13]

Naqi Hamidian confirms Asghar Izadi's narrative:

Rahim Karimian and I were arrested in September 1971 and taken to Evin prison ... There, we learned how to make crib sheets. They were written in tiny letters on cigarette paper. First, the cigarette was emptied of tobacco. Then the paper was placed under running water to remove the film. Then we would write on the cigarette paper in very small letters. The paper was wrapped in a thin piece of plastic afterwards and thread was fastened around it. Later, it was 'stored' in the anus. In March 1972, on New Year's Eve, when Rahim Karimian and I were transferred to Ward 3 of Qasr Prison, Rahim took the crib sheet out of the 'storeroom'.

Regarding the prison organization. Each one of us was only in contact with a few comrades. It wasn't clear how things were organized. We, the comrades from Mazandaran, were used to working together before getting arrested. We were considered as political cadres. Rahim Karimian, Ahmad Farhoudi and I had prepared two socio-economic analyses and a report on the villages of Sari, a city in the North of Iran. In Qasr Prison, Rahim and I, rewrote those pamphlets from March to November 1972. The pamphlet got printed outside prison, under the name of Ahmad Farhoudi. Rahim Karimian, Reza Ghebra'i and I were in charge of the crib sheets. We would make copies of whatever we could lay our hands on even before reading it. We would make copies of some writings by Marx, Mao's *On Contradiction*, Ahmadzadeh's *Strategy and Tactic*. Some prisoners had brought with themselves a few of Bijan's writings on crib sheets. We didn't have a powerful organizing head, nor a seasoned veteran in Qasr ...

In Qasr Prison, our tasks and responsibilities were to read and discuss Ahmadzadeh's pamphlet, Pouyan's *Necessity of Armed Struggle* .... We would also recount the history of our leaders' endeavours, hold memorial ceremonies for fallen comrades, organize anniversaries, sing revolutionary songs.

Hiding the crib sheets in safe places in prisons was one of the organizations' biggest challenges. Pamphlets and books had to be hidden away. If discovered, the consequences were horrific. The punishment was harsh. To understand the hows and whys of hiding and transferring notes, it is imperative to talk to Mohammad Farsi, known as the 'God of concealment':

I started cooperating with the guys in Qezel-Qaleh. Bijan had just come from Qom to Qezel-Qaleh. Shokrollah Paknezhad[14] was in Qezel-Qaleh too; that's two prominent prison personalities of the time. We were there together for two months and then we were taken to Qezel-Hessar. In November 1972, I was transferred to the [Anti-Sabotage Joint] Committee, the temporary police headquarters. We decided to go for an ideological defence. Our trial was held. After the trial we were taken back to the [Anti-Sabotage Joint] Committee once again. Then ... I guess I was transferred to Qasr in May 1972. Bijan, too, arrived there, after a while. He gave me a manuscript and asked me to copy what he had written or rather rewritten. I had to write it in tiny letters and then conceal it. I noticed that some of the writings were different from what he had brought with him from Qom ... He had updated his writings according to new data and findings. Bijan gave me his notebooks and I would make many copies of his writings and prepare them for transit. Some were transferred to other prisons and others to the outside.

When I was copying his manuscripts, I noticed he had crossed out some parts or deleted something or rewritten it. I tried to precisely observe all those points. But we were always in such a hurry in doing that task and the security conditions were so tight that I did not practically have enough time to look over the manuscripts at my convenience and focus on all the changes and modifications. But one could assume that he had deleted his previous perceptions that were based on armed struggle in the mountains and the countryside. His focus now was on urban guerrilla warfare.

Here, I should mention that we ourselves would allocate rooms to inmates, not the prison guard ... When a newcomer arrived, we were the ones who decided where he should go. We did our best to have a 'wholesome' room. A room where all the guys belonged to the same group. It was in such a room that I'd copy the manuscripts in tiny letters by flashlight at night under the blanket while others kept watch. At 10 pm the prison imposed the bedtime policy. The lights were on all night long. We would spread our beddings on the floor next to each other ... We would lie in our beds. Sometimes when it was too hot, the comrade who was 'on watch' would lift the blanket every now and then so that I could breathe. Or I would press my comrade's foot to let him know that there wasn't enough oxygen and it was time to lift the blanket. But of course, the other guys backed us too. Whenever they saw the night watchman approaching the room, they would warn us. They would tell us if a suspicious person was nearby. As soon as they saw something, they would send us a signal and we would stop working. When a comrade was to be transferred to another prison or released, I'd assess the possibilities. I'd conceal the writings for him. At that time the police had not become sensitive to such operations. Maybe, the Qasr Prison guards didn't even imagine that we were smuggling writings outside. Sometimes I would conceal the writings inside a tube of toothpaste or in the bag the guys used to put their clothes in. I would pick a colour in the material used for the bag and then tried to find the same colour of thread. For example, when we were sitting, I would look at everyone's socks and would eventually find a pair of socks similar to the colour of the bag. Then I would tell one of the comrades, 'get so-and-so's socks. That guy would hand his socks without even questioning what I wanted them for. First, I would unravel the sock, then I would spin the thread. I would slit the handle or inner bottom of the bag carefully, then put the writings inside, and afterwards sew it with the thread. It would be as good as new. Sometimes there was cardboard tubing in the handle, and that would make it easier for me to hide the writings. But if the handle was made of leather, I had to remove a part of the leather, place the writings inside and sew it again. Sometimes, the difference of colours was noticeable. In that case, I would undo the whole thing and sew everything again with the same thread ... We were always successful. None of the comrades was ever caught! Later as the guards became more alert and there was more control, we used more complicated methods. Sometimes I would sew the writings into the clothes. We had a comrade called Jahanbakhsh Payedari. One day he told me, 'I want to take this pamphlet with me.' He had an American Air Force jacket. I started with removing the stitches, then I removed the lining. I found a large bed sheet made of high-quality material. It was tightly woven and was very light and delicate. I drew a set of grid lines with the same dimensions as an A4 sheet of paper, I numbered the pages, I put the sheet on a hard piece of cardboard I found and then I wrote the entire pamphlet with a blue ballpoint pen. I sewed the pamphlet to the lining of the jacket and then resewed the seamline. No one could even imagine what I'd done to the jacket! Anyhow, he was wearing the jacket when he was being released. Later Jahanbakhsh joined the Fada'i comrades.

The more the regime and the prison officials put pressure on us, the more creative we became. We used more complicated and complex techniques. The last technique we used was what was common among the drug addicts. We used the finger cots they gave us for bandaging our fingers. We would put the crib sheets in a finger cot and then put the finger cot inside another finger cot. We would swallow it like a capsule. We would pass it [after a day or two] and retrieve the writings. Even when we suffered harsh repression quite a few guys ingested those capsules to transfer the writings to Evin.

Concealment was more difficult in Evin Prison than Qasr Prison. Qasr was an old and rather run-down prison building with fewer options. There were lots of secret nooks and crannies. We would eventually find a place to hide the writings in spite of the tight control. We would take a brick out, put the writings behind it, and then put the brick back in. The problem was finding a material to fix the brick and put it back in its proper place. Something like plaster or cement were necessary so that it wouldn't look different from other parts of the wall.

In 1973, there was a weekly search and they would pillage our possessions whenever they wanted to. We had a comrade called 'Abdolhossein Pour-Yekta who was a member of the Red Star. Pour-Yekta made very nice decorative closets with beautiful legs out of cardboard. To make glue, he would add water to cooked rice, bring it to the boil, then separate the water from the rice with the sieves he would make out of old undershirts. After that he would add sugar to starch and that is how he made glue to stick the cardboards together and make those closets. We encased the pamphlets inside the closet, I mean in the frame of the cardboard closet. When we wanted to take something out of these closets, we had to make the room completely empty and block the guys from coming inside to let us recover the writings. Unfortunately, the policemen had fallen in love with these closets. During the raids, they would always steal our closets! After each raid and pillage, we had to start all over again.

In Qasr Prison there was a huge closet. Each one of the prisoners had a case. The cases were made of plywood. We would hide voluminous things in the cases. When the prison guards attacked, he would first go to the closet and turn everything upside down. Sometimes he would break a few cases … We had some documents that were very important and had to be kept safe at any price: manuscripts, reports, and analyses. There were different levels of classification. We had a special encasement for the documents that were classified as very important, such as Bijan's manuscripts, perspectives on the guerrilla movement, and a manual on underground activities. We had to keep several copies of each document in several places in case they were discovered by the police … Everyone was in charge of one thing; like in an organization.

Finding the right tools was quite complicated. We were always hunting for ballpoint pens with very fine tips that wouldn't bleed. Technical drawing pens had just come on the market and were scarce. If we got hold of one, it would exclusively be used for the crib sheets. Our tools were sharp knives and scissors, razor blades, strings, flashlights, batteries – which were very useful – different types and sizes of needles and glue. If we could get hold of a good glue like UHU, it would be like finding a treasure.

Parviz Navidi recalls:

We did it when the guys were sleeping. We would take some tiles out from different places round the rooms in the ward and had stashed the crib sheets behind the tiles. The notes that were supposed to be sent out were placed in the binding of hardback books. We would unbind them, put the very thin scraps of paper inside and then rebind the book. The books looked as good as new. We never talked about what would happen to the writings, nor where the books were going.

Contact with other prisons, communication with comrades outside, transmission of news and writings to them were of special importance. Parviz Navidi continues:

In April 1973, they called me and a couple of others. We were told we would be transferred to Qezel-Hessar. The pamphlets that I had to take with me were ready. They had been placed in books. Some had been transformed into capsules that we would take orally. Bijan met me in private and gave me the necessary guidelines. First, he explained to me the atmosphere in Qezel-Hessar, then he told me how many supporters we had and those I should have closer relations with. As a precaution, he told me who I should avoid and also gave me the names of those I should contact discreetly. He mentioned the name of those that I had to persuade to join the prison organization. He named someone, [Behrouz] Armaghani, who was to be released on September 5, 1973. He underlined that I should give the pamphlets to him so that he would take them out.

The pamphlets and other writings we took with us to Qezel-Hessar were: *Tarikh-e Sih Saleh-ye Iran* (The Thirty-Year History of Iran), *Tarh-e Jamehshenasi va Mabani-ye Esteratejik-e Jonbesh Enqelabi Khalq-e Iran* (A Schematic View of the Fundamentals of Sociology and the Strategy of the Mass Revolutionary Movement in Iran) *Cheguneh Mobarezeh-ye Mosallahaneh Tudehi Mishavad* (How Armed Struggle Goes to the Masses), Lenin's *Leftwing Deviation* ... He spoke highly of Behrouz Armaghani saying that he was a talented young man and a seasoned political activist. Bijan had really worked on him and as a result of hours of discussion, Behrouz had accepted our line of struggle. Bijan was of the belief that Behrouz would join the organization as soon as he is released! ... He would always say: 'We should work on guys with short prison sentences and who are going to be released soon.'

In my opinion, Behrouz Armaghani provided the OIPFG with the most accurate report on prison conditions ... We can see how fast Hamid Ashraf placed him in the central organ of the organization. I didn't exactly know how Bijan contacted Hamid Ashraf, but I was hundred percent sure they were in contact with each other. And we know that Hamid Ashraf who was at the helm of the organization, highly respected Bijan Jazani and truly believed in him … Behrouz had accurately relayed Bijan's takes to the leadership: his criticism of the line, the contradictions that were at work and the consequences of not correcting certain wrongs.

Mohammad Farsi also talks about the existence of prison organizations in the provinces:

> In Mashhad Naqi Hamidian and Rahim Karimian were in charge of such programs … They kept the works of Mao such as *On Practice*, *On Contradiction* and *On Protracted People's War* written in minute letters. These pamphlets circulated in their own group for educational purposes.
>
> Mohammad Ahmadian, who we called 'Zapata', was in Mashhad prison from 1972 to 1974. He says it was over there that he read *The Thirty-Year History of Iran*. So, we understand the crib sheets of that book had reached Mashhad Prison too … These guys had a radio they had tweaked. They could listen to the Radio Mihan-Parastan[15] (Radio Patriots). They would record the program, transcribe it, make copies of the transcription and give them to other guys. They were in contact with the Fada'i branch of Mashhad. They would even transfer the writings outside. They would record Ashraf Dehqani's *Epic of Resistance*[16] and lessons of struggle in Latin America. Naqi Hamidian who was imprisoned both in Tehran and Mashhad, depicts the organizational work of the Fada'is in Mashhad Prison:
>
> … we took some writings with us from Tehran to Mashhad. On arrival at Mashhad Prison, they did a body search and found Reza Ghebra'i's crib sheets. They added a new charge to his case.
>
> We later found out that there were some of Bijan Jazani's early writings, such as *Nabard 'Alayh-e Diktatori-ye Shah* (The Combat against the Shah's Dictatorship), *Ravanshenasi-ye Ejtemayi* (Social Psychology), *Tarikh-e Sih Saleh-ye Iran* (The Thirty-Year History of Iran), *Lenin's Leftwing Deviation*. We defined the tasks and assigned responsibility. The tasks were: listening to the radio, taking notes in shorthand, making a neat copy of the speeches and interviews of the authorities. We used to listen to *Mihan-Parastan*, *Surush* (Heavenly Voice), Peyk-e Iran (Iran Courier) radio stations broadcast from abroad.
>
> … The other tasks of our three-member group were to circulate pamphlets and crib sheets to other prisoners, contact newcomers, build relationships and talk about the guerrilla movement with them. Last but not least, there was the need to create channels and establish contact with the OIPFG branch in Mashhad. Through comrades who had short-term sentences and were to be released soon, we would introduce candidates for membership in the organization.

In Mashhad Prison, where a number of veteran Fada'is were incarcerated, the relationship between different currents were good. Mohammad Reza Shalgouni's account provides us with some valuable information:

> As far as I know, the first big crisis of the Fada'i Organization started in Shiraz Prison …

... in the early 1970s most of the political prisoners in Shiraz had lengthy sentences. Most importantly, the biggest number of Fada'i cadres who had been saved from execution were in Shiraz prison. I should also mention that most of the guys were under the influence of comrades Ahmadzadeh and Pouyan's views. As far as I remember, there wasn't anyone from Jazani's group before the prisoners of Borazjan[17] were transferred to Shiraz ...

... When we were transferred to Qasr Prison in Tehran in the winter of 1973, we noticed that the same kind of clashes between different currents of the People's Fada'i had permitted the police to take advantage of the situation. By imposing harsher measures on the prisoners, they had created an atmosphere similar to that of Shiraz. In Tehran we noticed almost the same factors that had brought about the dissolution of the prison organization in Shiraz culminated in the disintegration of the Fada'i grouping in Qasr. Although Bijan tried to reconstruct the Fada'i prison organization, he was confronted with a strong resistance. A resistance that was inflamed by the differences between two lines, Bijan Jazani's and Masoud Ahmadzadeh's.

Mohammad Reza Shalgouni, who was transferred to Tehran at the beginning of 1973, clearly sees the signs of an acute crisis among the Fada'i prisoners in Qasr:

In the winter of 1973 we arrived at Qasr prison in Tehran. The supporters of the 'movement' still had an 'organization' but you could see that there was a growing crisis among them ... I had the opportunity to see Bijan and talk to him regularly for about a year or so ... He tried hard to reconcile the differences but he couldn't succeed ... We would delicately slit the book cover, take the pamphlets that were written on very thin paper, and read them.

I should mention that with the passage of time Bijan changed and modified some of his views reflected in some of his writings. For this reason, some of his opponents (such as the Fada'i comrades who advocated Ahmadzadeh's thoughts) accused him of opportunism .... Even at that time this accusation seemed unjustified and nonsensical to me ....

Bijan was eight years older than me. He connected two sides of a tragic divide between two generations of leftist activists. Moreover, he stood head and shoulders above many political activists of the previous generation.

Thus, the ideological and political polemics among the imprisoned Fada'is, the intensification of contradictions between the advocates of the two main currents within the OIPFG, the consequences of heavy repression they were all subject to, the heterogeneity and dissonance in the manner of managing the non-political aspects of the commune and finally the relational crisis among the Fada'i forces led to division and dissolution of the Big Commune in Qasr Prison. As Shalgouni continues:

Actually, in the third phase, from 1971 to 1973, the relationship between the supporters of the guerrilla movement and their opponents had become tense in many prisons. For instance, in spite of the fact that most inmates lived in a unified commune, all existing problems were discussed and resolved between the Mojahedin, Fada'is and other trends within the guerrilla movement without consulting with and the consent of the others. This caused a lot of chagrin and ultimately the wound opened up at the end of that phase and the beginning of the fourth phase; i.e. 1973-1976 ... I should confess that I had taken sides against Bijan.

At the beginning of 1973, there were clashes between SAVAK agents and prisoners, both in Shiraz and in Tehran, that led to a period of intense repression in prisons all over the country. From then until 1976, prison conditions changed completely. There were frequent inspections, the guards became aggressive, many books were confiscated, and any resistance against the police was punished severely. Limitations were imposed on 'communal' life. Antagonism towards prisoners reached an extent that men and women who had served their terms were no longer released ... In comparison to the previous phases, torture was not inflicted for punishment, but to extract information or rather force prisoners to reveal their meeting spots.

In March 1975 when the Shah announced the formation of a single party, Rastakhiz, and made membership in it obligatory for all adult Iranians, Bijan Jazani and a number of prisoners of Wards 4, 5, and 6 were taken from Qasr to Evin Prison. The reason for this transfer, which was the prologue to the murder of Bijan Jazani, Hassan Zia-Zarifi, Aziz Sarmadi, 'Abbas Souraki, Ahmad Jalil-Afshar, Mohammad Choupanzadeh, Mashouf (Sa'id) Kalantari and two Mojaheds, Mostafa Javan Khoshdel and Kazem Zolanvar, is still a state secret. However, what was heard on the grapevine is worth mentioning. According to Parviz Navidi:

> One should not forget that SAVAK had become aware of Bijan's role in the Fada'i movement. They had precisely told him that if he wanted to turn the prison into a university [of Revolution], he would have to deal with them. This was a serious threat. SAVAK was of the belief that the revolutionary execution of 'Abbas Shahriari, an ex member of the Tudeh party who had become a SAVAK agent, had been plotted inside prison by Bijan. They were more or less aware of the accurate information that Bijan had given the organization about Shahriari.

Mohammad Reza Shalgouni points out:

> It was clear for SAVAK that Bijan determined the direction of the left resistance who supported the guerrilla movement both inside and outside prison. In my view, getting hold of Bijan's writings left no doubt for SAVAK as to the leading role of Bijan in the Fada'i Organization ... Bijan placed emphasis on combining armed struggle with political forms of mobilisation. Generally speaking, he wanted to get the guerrilla movement and specifically, the Fada'i Organization, out of the dead end they were stuck in .... In the summer of 1974, Bijan was taken to the Anti-Sabotage Joint Committee Prison for a month or two. He sent a message to Aziz Sarmadi, asking him to put away the pamphlets. One day a frightened Aziz told me that many of Bijan's pamphlets were in the hands of the police and by comparing handwritings they had concluded that Bijan was the author of them all.

Most importantly, they had found out that some of those pamphlets were used as the main educational source in OIPFG safehouses.

When Bijan came back from the Anti-Sabotage Joint Committee prison, he was extremely worried. He had found out that SAVAK had gotten hold of his writings and discovered he was in contact with the Organization ...

I was in ward 6 of Qasr Prison when we heard that Jazani's group and two members of the Mojahedin were executed. We were all shocked. There was some tension for a few days. Some guys swore loudly at the regime, but the police tried not to show a brutal reaction and let the tension die down. The event itself had scared most of the prisoners.

The murder of Jazani and his comrades on the hills of Evin changed the relations between the supporters of Masoud Ahmadzadeh and the followers of Bijan Jazani. Three months after that furious crime, all the prisoners who had been taken to Evin Prison in March 1974 were placed in Ward 2 of that modern prison. The leftists were on the first floor and the Mojahedin on the second floor. It was there and then that after years of division, the two factions of the guerrillas worked hand in hand and started some sort of cooperation.

In Qasr Prison, however, the relations between the two currents of the Fada'is did not undergo much change. Naqi Hamidian, who had been transferred from Mashhad to Tehran in March 1975 recalls:

Making copies of pamphlets did not happen anymore, nor did writing crib sheets. I didn't see any organizational relationship either. Book binding was done secretly and quietly. Comrades concealed the old crib sheets inside the binding of books.

As can be seen, the unique prison organization of the Fada'is which was not formed everywhere did not last long. Political developments in Iran and the world over, especially the protest movement against the Shah's dictatorship in the last two years of the Pahlavi monarchy, led to important political changes.

A new phase of prison life started in the winter 1977 which continued until the outbreak of the 1979 Revolution. The victory of Jimmy Carter in the US presidential elections in November 1976 had a hand in bringing about this new phase. The policy of violence and torture subsided to a great extent. Most of the prisoners who had served their sentences but were still incarcerated were released. The severe restrictions on visiting prisoners were relaxed. Those detainees of Evin Prison who did not have visitation rights were accorded visits. Prison conditions visibly improved in the spring of 1977 when the International Red Cross inspectors obtained permission to inspect detention centres. The visitors were authorized to bring books for prisoners and this further transformed the prison atmosphere.

Mohammad Farsi testifies that:

With the political opening of 1977 and 1978, we received the original version of the pamphlets. We could even find classic texts written by Lenin. The pamphlets and articles were printed on very thin paper, the size of the palm of hand ... I can still see with my mind's eye *The State and Revolution*.

The 1979 Revolution swept away the existing autocracy and thanks to the people's uprising, Mohammad Reza Shah's political prisoners were set free. Morteza Malek-Mohammadi's recollections capture the spirit of those days:

> During the fresh air time, inmates slowly approached 'The Committee to investigate prisoners' demands' in the corner of the yard. The person in charge of making a list of prisoners' demands constantly repeated: 'Yes, yes. I've written down the name of this book. Someone has already made this request. What else do you need?' The Committee was accompanied by one or two interrogators ...
>
> There was a stark contrast between the appearance of the inmates and that of the members of the Investigative Committee. The prisoners' shabby clothes, their ragged pants that were either too long or too short, the odd slippers. It was a pitiful sight.
>
> We were enjoying the sunshine in the yard of Ward 1 of Evin Prison. The comings and goings were a sign of new developments. The inmates were excited. The first breeze of 'political opening' was blowing inside prison ... The inmates jokingly called the open politics of Jimmy Carter 'Jimmycracy' ...
>
> Families brought parcels of books for the prisoners. In disbelief, inmates touched the books excitedly ... We heard in whispers that some literature by Marxist writers in foreign languages had penetrated into the prison. Antonio Gramsci's *Prison Notebooks* and *The Modern Prince* secretly changed hands. In each corner of the room, prisoners were busy reading books. Comrade Mahmood Navabaksh was reading Engels' *The Origin of the Family, Private Property and the State* for some people in French. It was said that Dr Rashidian was translating Marx's *Class Struggle in France* in Qasr Prison ... The cultural atmosphere of prison had become joyful. Families were feeling better now that they could bring books alongside meat and herbs for their loved ones.
>
> The interrogators and security officials were not happy with the new situation. The prisoners had met with the representatives of international human rights organizations and had discussed torture and violence with them. There were many prisoners who still had traces of torture on their body. The prison officials and SAVAK were trying to keep this group of prisoners away from international delegations. Hiding and transferring the prisoners had created confusion and chaos. In the midst of all these transfers, keeping the hidden books and pamphlets intact had become a major preoccupation for us. We had to find a way to encase them ... Work started rapidly. We tore out the pages of the onion-skin paper books, rolled them up into tubes and concealed them in packets of cigarettes so that prisoners who were being transferred could take them along. Some other books were separated into equal parts, rolled like German sausages, wrapped up in a piece of cloth and placed in the narrow pipes of the shower room. At that point in time, we couldn't imagine freedom or an end to our imprisonment. The encasements were done by calculating the return of transferees or new arrivals.

Reality overtook our imagination ... The storm of revolution shook the very foundation of thousands of years of monarchy in all its glorious splendour. After any political development or reform, a group of political prisoners were released. The last group of prisoners regained freedom on January 20, 1979, by the order of Bakhtiar cabinet. The end of imprisonment merged with the end of the Pahlavi regime. Ex-prisoners joined the people's demonstrations right after emerging from jail.

On 11 February 1979 Evin Prison was attacked by a revolutionary crowd. A large number of people were moving around the prison. In some areas there were scenes of fight or flight. The sound of gunshots could be heard. It was said that some SAVAK agents had barricaded themselves in Evin Motel and were shooting at people. All kinds of rumours were circulating ...

The crowd was looking for strange and terrifying things; chambers for torture, tunnels of terror, cages, ... things they had heard about in stories and tales. They wanted to know where the dungeons were. They wanted to know where the instruments of torture were and how those instruments were used. I had to tell the truth ... I had to say that the delicate flesh and soul of a human being can be shattered without dungeons and cages. Modern instruments of torture such as cables and the Apollo [an electric chair with a large metal mask to muffle screams while amplifying them for the victim] could even be more painful than one could imagine ... We entered the shower room of Ward 1. I was so excited. I couldn't believe that so many things had happened in such a short span of time. Weren't we encasing books in the adjacent rooms with anxiety and fear a few months ago? Now, hundreds of eyes were upon me. I pulled out a long wire with a hook at its end from behind the radiator and pulled the hidden books out of the shower curtain rods. The exultant crowd was staring at me with eyes wide open. Someone cried: 'What's that? Are those explosives?' ... I said,

'The truth that political prisoners were looking for, lies in these books. We were imprisoned and lashed for these books. But today we're all free ...'

... I don't know what else I said and how long the discourse lasted. Some people shouted there and then beckoning the others to join us. They said:

'This young man is telling the truth. He really was a political prisoner. He was detained here. He is a Fada'i guerrilla'.[18]

10

The Organization of Iranian People's Fada'i Guerrillas and the University of Tabriz: A personal memoir

Sorour ʿAli Mohammadi

My generation lived through turbulent times. The 1960s and 1970s were the most productive and at the same time the most violent years for us. The impact of these years on my life is so profound that I could never forget them. Reviewing this period is akin for me to recapping a movement which opened a new chapter in the history of the struggles of the Iranian people, a chapter which captures a life story in every page.

I was the third child in my family. My father was a contractor for the National Iranian Oil Company and my mother had a sixth-grade education. She had a beautiful handwriting and was good at composing my father's official letters and memos. In our household, boys were never allowed to order their sisters around. Freedoms and restrictions applied to all of us equally. We used to read a lot of leisurely newspapers and magazines, but my dad used to examine every book a thousand times to make sure, as he put it, it wasn't written by the Tudeh people.

Masoud Kimia'i, the movie director, is my mother's cousin. In fact, he was my first teacher and mentor. His father was pro-Mossadeq and always told stories about Tudeh Party's betrayal of the movement. My father blamed his aunt's cousin's (Zarar Zahedian, one of the few Tudeh members who joined the Jazani group) repeated imprisonment on their futile course of action, which according to him would result in only two options for youngsters who chose it: prison or death. My brother worked with Soviet engineers in the steel factory in Shahroud and had a good relationship with them. He believed that the only way to spread Marxism among the masses was through progressive Islam. The foundation of my way of thinking was based on these ideas. Boys and girls of my age were interested in the matters of the heart while I was trying to figure out the causes of Tudeh Party's betrayal of Mossadeq, the imprisonment of Zarar and coming to terms with the Islamic Marxism phenomenon.

During my high school years Mr Fakhri, our literature teacher, always encouraged us to read books. He and his wife were good friends of mine. I spent years exploring the stories of authors and writers such as Samad Behrangi, Sadeq Hedayat, Jalal Al-e Ahmad, ʿAli Shariʿati, and poets like Forough Farrokhzad, Akhavan Sales and especially Shamlou. When I was in ninth grade, I used to write for our school's student billboard which the seniors put together. I don't remember much of it now, but one memory sticks out. As a female senior high school student, I wrote a piece and posed a question: 'Why is it that in a country which exports oil, people die of cold'? The billboard didn't last more than two days and was taken down, and the coordinators of the billboard and I were summoned to the principal's office. All the teachers were present in the room. The principal and his assistant wanted to know who had put these thoughts in our heads. I thought that I was going to be punished, since I had written them. Greatly influenced by clandestine leaflets of the time, I gave them my reasoning. The assistant principal, a grumpy man whom I always disliked, then told me that I should tell my dad to lower the oil prices so people would not die of cold. I am not sure whether he was ignorant, or just wanted to belittle me, because it was common knowledge that the price of oil was set by the government. This happened during the finals that year and thereafter we were summoned to his office on a daily basis. It was only when Mr Fakhri took responsibility for the proceedings that things quieted down. He told me that from that point onwards I should be careful, and that he was the only supporter of the school's news billboard. Things were worse at home. Not an hour would pass without my father's pointless yelling. I could not understand why they were incapable of grasping such simple truths.

A few weeks after the Siyahkal episode of February 1971, the major headlines on state-controlled TV and newspapers were the clash in the Gilan forests, which naturally grabbed the attention of people of my generation. Even though the government tried to reduce the magnitude of this event to nothing but an incident involving a few young 'terrorists', there was no doubt in the minds of those interested in political matters that dispatching overwhelming number of troops and military helicopters for the clashes between those young fighters and the security forces which followed the attack on the Siyahkal gendarmerie station had deep roots in the Latin American revolutionary movements and especially the victorious Cuban guerrilla movement. This alone was enough to encourage my generation, frustrated with the inaction of the Tudeh Party, to passionately see themselves as members of a bigger family which was valiantly injecting new blood into the veins of a deteriorated left movement. They were the first group who engaged in urban guerrilla struggle against the monarchy. Two of its members lost their lives during the confrontation and the other thirteen were executed less than a month later. The government and security officials were under the impression that they had put an end to this movement, but in a few short weeks Lieutenant General Zia Farsiu, who was in charge of Iran's military court, was assassinated by other members of the 'Forest group', and this gave new hope to people like me.

In the autumn of 1971, the regime was organizing the celebration of '2500th Anniversary of the Monarchy'. While the state radio television and the government-controlled press were busy with glorifying propaganda for these upcoming celebrations, the young militants were writing about the homeless, the hungry and the sick in underground publications to inform what is happening around us. I will never forget one of these flyers which shook me to my core. I was constantly preoccupied with the stories of young persons like me who were from the shantytowns, toiling at brick factory ovens and who would never get to fully experience their youth.

The trial of Khosrow Golesorkhi and Keramat Daneshian in February 1974 brought me ever closer to the new revolutionary movement. The security forces had expected these prisoners to announce regret for their actions and beg for forgiveness, but Golesorkhi and Daneshian's solid defence strengthened our belief in the path that we had chosen. After hearing Golesorkhi's statement that young persons in Iran end up facing prison and torture for just reading books, my father, who always had an issue with my reading, tightened his control over me. My only refuge was my maternal uncle's house where I could read, or my literature teacher who had been asked by my father to keep an eye on me. Gholam-Hossein Sa'edi's *Chub Be Dast-ha-ye Varzil* and Jack London's *The Iron Heel* were amongst the books which opened my eyes to the painful realities of the world. Remaining at home under these conditions was nerve wrecking, not only because of the obvious and not so obvious agents of SAVAK, but because I also had to be careful around the house. I knew that Zarar's re-arrest was the most important cause of my father's worries. His arrest had caused hope in my heart and fear in my father's.

I entered the University of Tabriz during the second term of the 1974–5 academic year. Registration formalities were smoother and faster than I expected. I told my brother that I obtained my dormitory room on Shahnaz Street in downtown Tabriz. But he had promised my dad to get me a separate apartment. My father believed that the university dormitory was a place for rebellious students and with so many young people living under one roof, all that is needed for some form of provocation is just a few rebels. In response to my questioning, he would yell and tell me he is trying to take care of me but I just do whatever I wish. My brother and I decided to tell him we could not find a suitable apartment.

My stay at the dormitory lasted barely a couple of months. My father came to Tabriz, rented a room near the university and asked the landlord to report on my coming and goings. The landlord and his wife were very nice people as well as sympathetic to the Left movement, so they did not fully fulfil my father's request.

Choosing courses was not difficult. I was looking for Dr 'Ali-Akbar Torabi's classes.[1] The office clerk, a middle-aged man, underlined Dr Torabi's name, and then quietly told me Dr Zarshenas is as good. I selected both instantly. Classrooms were mostly empty except for the English class taught by Parviz Salehi who was Kurdish and had studied in Canada. Male students would not take his class often, because he referred to everyone as 'my dearest', although female students weren't too fond of him saying that either. I didn't mind that, and we became friends quite swiftly. He would only teach English in the first ten minutes and then start talking about societal inequalities. He was always in step with us and later became very active in the OIPFG. Torabi's class, however, was completely different. On the first day, even though I was fifteen minutes early I could not find a seat or a place to stand since there were so many students. What I remember from those days is a humble person who combined knowledge and awareness in such a way that made us think. He was close to Samad Behrangi, 'Alireza Nabdel and Behrouz Dehqani. His classes were so engaging that we could not realize how the hour passed by so swiftly. His teaching method in explaining the sciences in a simple manner was so unique that it truly satisfied our thirst for knowledge. At the end of the hour, we had so many questions that we would be either late for the next class or forego it all together. Sometimes our political views would differ, but he would humbly tell us that maybe we were right, and he would not want to completely disagree just because he had read more books. He taught us that it is always good to read more. He was a master instructor.

The presence of the security forces in our classrooms was one of the problems we had to persistently deal with. One of the tasks of more senior students was to remind others about complying with security rules. They would teach us how to behave during interrogations by the university security guard and to refrain from asking politically motivated questions in the classroom, and ask them privately instead.

As suggested by our professors, the National Library of Tabriz had become our hangout. We could enjoy reading books in the library. It was also a suitable place to distribute pamphlets and tapes. The director of the library, Mr Elyari, tolerated and supported us. He was a great human being who would turn a blind eye when we frequented the library at odd hours. His sympathetic view towards the OIPFG made our camaraderie stronger.

The Hiking Club was the only place where it was comfortable to be a female. It still gives me joy when I remember it. In the mountains far from the city, we could speak our minds easily and enjoy the companionship and friendships in the very first steps. I knew that we could find banned writings in these very same outings. The first hike was Eynali and it was an easy path. I realized that in the two-day immersion programmes, usually beginners would fall behind, but my problem was the language spoken. They would talk in Azeri amongst themselves, and I was the only one who could not understand a word. It was not a pleasant feeling. We were always together, but I felt lonely. At the rest stops the backpacks were opened and our lunch consisting of bread, cheese and dates was spread over newspapers. A smoke-covered kettle would make our hot tea.

There were mostly left-leaning students in the hiking clubs and hiking expeditions. I do not recall having any common expeditions with the religious students. We always had more members and if our paths accidentally overlapped, a brief hello and short chitchat would be all that would happen. They did not have more than two or three girls in their group, as opposed to our group which included many young women. We still had respectful interactions with each other on campus and on the mountain trails. They were supporters of the Mojahedin-e Khalq (People's Mojahedin) who also believed in armed struggle. We therefore judged them differently than other religious groups. When the subjects of Soviet Union and the Tudeh Party came up in conversation, there was a heavy silence among us which reflected our apathy towards the party. Ahmad and Fereydoun where veteran members of literature department's hiking club and believed in and supported the guerrilla movement. From the beginning of my enrolment at the university I realized that only the Confederation of Iranian Students (abroad) publications were distributed widely. I think it was during our two-day programme in Sahand mountain that I found an opportune moment to ask their opinion about why the Fada'i guerrillas' writings were not distributed under their own name. I asked even though the newspapers wrote about the arrests and the death of who they called 'terrorists', why wasn't there any mention of them here at the university, and why didn't we try to campaign on their behalf? They responded by stating that they receive these writings as they come and just pass them along to others. On that day our conversation was just limited to this exchange, but from then on, they were more cautious when interacting with me.

During one of the medical students' hiking programmes in winter of 1975, the OIPFG publication *Nabard-e Khalq* was given to me for the first time to read and redistribute. It contained material some of which I had already read but this time it had the name OIPFG under each page. Even though I had distributed the same writings before, this time I did it with much more interest and attention because it had the 'Fada'i' name included. That is when I realized that leaving out the name of the Organization in the past was done with the purpose of confusing SAVAK. After the 'revolutionary' execution of 'Abbas Shahriari, the SAVAK spy who had infiltrated the Tudeh Party in winter 1975, the name and reputation of the Fada'i guerrillas spread all over campus. It became clear that the university security guard was watching anyone who went up to the mountains. Lieutenant Javadi, the head of the security guard, knew the name of almost everyone who participated in the Hiking Club activities.

In the spring of 1975 before we even set foot on campus, a tremor shattered the quiet of the Nowruz holidays. *Keyhan* newspaper was passed around with shock. It had published the news of security agents killing nine prisoners 'while they were escaping' during a transfer from one prison to another. Their names were paraded in front of our eyes. The more we read this deceitful report, the more the flames of revenge raged inside us. While the new joyful spring season was yet to arrive, we were suddenly faced with the horror of the one of bloodiest seasons we had known. The oppressive control measures implemented by the university security guard had increased, and even when we went on mountain hikes, we felt this tense atmosphere between us. University cafeterias became the scene of repeated confrontations between students and the security guards, as they brutally and indiscriminately beat us with their clubs. But it wasn't the clubs which were hurting us the most, it was the magnitude of the catastrophe when it was revealed that Bijan Jazani's name was among the executed, which in reality meant that the mastermind of Iran's new communist movement had been eliminated. It became harder to pass around the pamphlets and *Nabard-e Khalq*. We knew what was published in the newspapers was fake news, and we knew we should point our fingers at SAVAK and tell people that we do not believe their lies. That year the May Day demonstrations were attacked by the security guards who battered the students. Then a deadly silence ruled.

The publication of the sixth issue of *Nabard-e Khalq* in May 1975 put an end to this guesswork. We got our hands on it towards the end of spring. Our speculation proved to be correct that the prisoners were executed and not killed during an escape.

In February 1976 the movie *Gavaznha* (The Deer), directed by Kimia'i, was released after a year-long review by the censorship bureau. Qodrat's character, which was based on Amir-Parviz Pouyan, was a representation of the Fada'i guerrillas' resistance. Every time we went to see the movie, I was surprised by the audience's reception and their interpretation of Qodrat (as a Fada'i) and Mohammad (as a Tudeh Party member). People compared the scenes from the movie to the newspaper coverage of the Fada'i guerrillas' street battles and wondered why Qodrat surrendered. Almost everyone was unhappy with the ending of the movie as in their minds a Fada'i would not surrender. Since I knew the real ending of the film and the fact that Qodrat resisted and blew up the house, I would describe it as such to the people I trusted.

On 7 December 1975, the day commemorated as University Student Day in Iran (16 Azar), there were clashes between the security guards and students who were shouting slogans about SAVAK's lies regarding the killings of Bijan Jazani and his comrades. In these demonstrations our main task was to try to connect with new students and if deemed trustful inform them about Fada'i movement. Chants of 'Long Live Fada'i, Long Live Mojahed' were echoing across campus when the security guards' attack put an end to the demonstration. There were always some arrests on these occasions. At the security guard's headquarters, they separated the freshmen to threaten or sometimes give what they called 'brotherly advice' to prevent them from being deceived by a 'bunch of traitors'. During one of these arrests lasting a few hours, Lieutenant Javadi once again labelled political prisoners as traitors, and then looking at me asked: What should be done with those who betray the homeland and the people? I remembered that during our mountain excursions the experienced students had cautioned us about these short arrests and interrogations and taught us not to respond as the questioning is just devised for scaring us. But on that particular day I was so distressed that I shouted, 'The Americans steal our oil and that is not considered a betrayal, but speaking up about people's rights is?' Javadi slapped me so hard that my last words never left my mouth. I spent the night at the security guards' headquarters and since they couldn't find anything but my study books in my room, I was released the following morning. These few hours I spent in prison proved to me that I had made the right choice, even though later on every single one of my hiking club members criticized me, saying a person who has not done anything should not get their name into the police records. I knew that some of the seniors were either in prison or were sent to military barracks as punishment. We often recited their names in our meetings and saluted them for their bravery. After a few arrests, I learned that the security guards exerted pressure to make us collaborate with them or even become their informants. I learned that in some instances the students stopped communicating with activists so that the security guards could not learn about the planned strikes or demonstrations, although there were some who did became collaborators.

The number of protests increased as we approached the end of term finals. As activist students, we did not participate in the exams and we also prevented other students from doing so. The security guards had to provide protection for those students who did want to take their exams, but we greeted them with rotten eggs and tomatoes. Those who lived at the dorms had it worse, as others would call them traitors. This walkout, which included religious students, was our most organized political action to date. After the walkout the university administration announced that all students must pass at least two courses before they are allowed to register for the next term, otherwise they would be expelled from the university.

The guidance from both Fada'is and Mojahedin organizations was to act in unison. The new mandatory university regulation was to pass six major courses but the goal was to sow division amongst students. This measure miserably failed because we all knew if they really wanted to follow up on the new regulation, half of the student body had to be expelled. We pulled together and steadfastly decided not to take the final exams and prepared to bear the consequences. Each day upon arriving at campus we were confronted by Javadi's inquiries. The final exams ended under the tight control of the security guards, and students who had a heftier security record were arrested or were suspended from school for a year. Those who had minor arrests, including myself, received a six-month suspension. In the letter sent to our families, organizing walkouts was given as the reason for our suspension, an infraction which applied to all of us. Before my father got home, my sister who was the first to see the letter panicked after reading it and told my brother right away. I had to go to Tehran and figure out a way to keep this information from reaching my family in order to keep staying in Tabriz. I rented a new place on Mansour Street and told my landlord, who was visibly upset, that he should not say a word to my father about it. I had to justify staying in Tabriz, so I took a drafting class along with my friend Mahrokh who had arrived from Sari. It was in this class that I met Maryam, who frequented Tabriz every so often and brought pamphlets and other booklets to read and redistribute. Besides materials by the Confederation of Iranian Students and the *Payam-e Daneshjou* journal, the student organ of the OIPFG, we mostly read Fada'i booklets and concentrated on learning about guerrilla struggle. We wanted to do our best to connect with the masses and raise their awareness about Fada'i viewpoints.

We did everything based on our own interests and abilities. I never heard that any of our comrades were forced to do anything. As directed by Maryam, I became the contact for three high school girls: Parvin, Shahdokht, and Mehran. One of these schools was located in the Armenian neighbourhood. In the beginning not only the students but also their parents wanted to teach me the Armenian language. I told them that we already have a common language we can communicate with, and I didn't really have the time to learn a new language. It was painful for me to learn they thought my disinterest in learning Armenian was for religious reasons.

Meanwhile we formed a basketball team from these schools and were thirty students in total. The best place to train was in the Armenian neighbourhood. During our breaks we talked about our restrictions at home and what to do about it. It was strange for me to find that they thought that I could not understand their daily restrictions because I was from Tehran. I explained that I couldn't even read at home, and this was the reason why I did not go to a university in Tehran. Our bond became stronger as they read Samad Behrangi's books with keen interest. Shamlou's poetry and revolutionary songs had replaced pop music for them as well. Everything was going well until one day one of the school principals prevented me from entering the school grounds and warned me not to maintain any contact with the students. A few days later one of the teachers alerted me that a student's father had seen me with his daughter on the street, and because of my short hair had thought that I was a boy and had scolded her. He later found out that I was expelled from my university. From then on, our meetings were moved to the city libraries. Even though my vast network had shrunk in size, I still had good connections with high school students. I left booklets in predetermined spots for them to pick up and knew who had got their books based on the kind of nuts (such as almonds or walnuts) they would leave in place of the books. One day when I went to drop some leaflets at the spot, I found a note that said 'almonds'! My immediate reaction was that the note was left by SAVAK. I alerted the students to be cautious and not get close to the site. Per our safety protocols we had to stay away from the site for three months. By experience these students had learned not to inquire about security matters. Later on, I learned that the note was left by one of our friends since she had forgotten to bring any nuts with her.

Fourteen months after the painful news of the execution of Bijan and his comrades, there was news of another strike against the Fada'i movement. Hamid Ashraf and nine other guerrillas were killed in a raid. Their house was surrounded and attacked from air and ground. As I walked towards the library, staring at the newspaper in my hand, I saw people were in mourning everywhere. That day, 29 June 1976 was such a tragically sad day that to this day it is still hard to write about. We decided to organize some form of protest at the university. We didn't have our student identification cards but were determined to pass the guards and get inside the campus. Mahnaz, a history student, passed her ID to me through the fence, as other students got their hands on some ID cards the same way. At the entrance, some students got into a heated argument with Javadi, and I took advantage of the opportunity and entered by showing the ID to a different guard. Mahnaz got her card back and walked away quickly. But Javadi and a group of security guards surrounded all expelled students. As we were escorted out, we started chanting 'Students are Victorious'. On that day this tactic of ours didn't work. Scattered protests continued throughout the city for the next few weeks, with the most organized being on 19 August, on the anniversary of the coup against Prime Minister Mohammad Mossadeq. It was met with a forceful attack by the security forces.

All my connections were severed after these raids. Maryam went into hiding and I lost touch with the Organization. I dropped the drafting class and left for Tehran. There I tried to find the Organization's perspective on the raid and the murder of Hamid Ashraf and his team. There was an atmosphere of terror and fear, clearly reflected in the televised and daily newspapers' coverage, all around the University of Tehran campus. I was in a limbo between Tehran and Tabriz as I couldn't stay in Tehran, and I couldn't just stand still in Tabriz. Newspapers were having a field day with the news of the attack and defeat of the OIPFG. I finally got my hands on the seventh issue of *Nabard-e Khalq* three months after its publication. It included various reports of the guerrillas' confrontations with the security forces in different cities. This news gave us hope that the Fada'i guerrillas were still around fighting the regime. This issue was quickly passed around in the dormitories and campus. I was impatiently waiting for the eighth issue of *Nabard-e Khalq* to learn more about the details of the confrontations but would only find out later, in the early days of the revolution, that this was to be the last issue.

These were the times that the number of underground student cells was growing. For us the underground student cells were an effective structure for well-informed students and supporters of the Fada'i guerrillas to actively work among students. In this manner, under the cover of student rights and grievances, we could also advance and expand our political goals. The tasks of these cells were virtually the same in all universities. By raising wide-ranging student issues (poor condition of the university cafeteria, Hiking Club, etc.), we then would always connect them to the students' lack of freedom and participatory rights at the university and the community at large. This also gave us the opportunity to proceed to more serious socio-political discussions. In addition to reproducing and distributing leaflets and pamphlets of the Fada'i guerrillas,

I believe that the most important role of these cells was that of reading and discussing the texts of Marxist theorists. The majority of Tabriz University students were from remote cities and deprived areas of Azerbaijan, hence their active presence in these cells was an important factor in exposing the inhumane character of the monarchist regime. It is important to emphasize that these student cells were constantly subject to brutal attacks during the Pahlavi regime's years of terror and repression.

In 1977 the university allowed suspended students to re-enrol, and at the same time the security guard increased their surveillance. These were hard times, and even hiking expeditions were an excuse to avoid feeling alone. And yet we would not just sing revolutionary songs, but rather would shout them aloud.

We were happy to be back on campus, but the year 1977 was the calm before the storm. The May Day student demonstrations were greeted with brutality by the campus security guards. Meanwhile many protests by students and workers continued sporadically.

Winter of 1978 was a very productive period for mobilizing, as our comrades organized labour forces and specifically workers at Tabriz Tractor Factory. The labour branch of the OIPFG was the most active of all political organizations during this period. This fact become clearly evident right after the victory of the Revolution in mid-February 1979, when large groups of labourers who had gathered in Tabriz University came to the OIPFG branch headquarters on campus as the place to voice their grievances.

With the election of Jimmy Carter, the suppressive political environment became less harsh. The 'Ten Nights of Poetry' organized by the Writers' Association and the Goethe Cultural Institute in October 1977 was amongst the events one could not miss. We decided to attend, show our support for the organizers and culturally enrich ourselves in the process. Maryam welcomed the idea but told us not to bring any pamphlets, as those were readily available in Tehran. About ten of us headed to Tehran. I was the only one with a place to stay in Tehran but taking everyone to my house was impractical as my father was not aware that I was coming to Tehran and he would have prevented me from attending the poetry nights. Hence, we all went to Masoud Kimia'i's house. Attending those poetry nights is when I felt the joy of being with and amongst the public at large. Sa'id Soltanpour's lecture and poetry recital was met with such rousing enthusiasm and outpouring that the Writers' Association had to warn everyone that the whole event could get shut down if it continued in that manner. Exposure to Soltanpour, who spoke fearlessly of the Fada'is, was like catching a pearl in stormy waters. That night myself and my fellow Tabriz University students managed to meet him and we spent an unforgettable time with him. We invited him to come and recite poetry at our university, and felt very productive as we travelled back to Tabriz. The many reporters present at the poetry nights wrote about what they had witnessed, and it didn't take long for the audio tapes of the readings and lectures to be distributed all across Iran and abroad.

Protests were now taking place beyond university campuses. The city of Qom saw its share of anti-government demonstrations. Tabriz erupted forty days later, on 18 February 1978. On this day, the protesters left the campus and headed for police stations, Rastakhiz Party offices, banks, luxury hotels, movie theatres and liquor stores. On a routine day, women could not go out or to the market without head covering, but on that day no one wore them. Yet, some reactionary groups took advantage of the uprisings as they set cinemas ablaze and harassed women. We misjudged these actions as public acts of rage and did not recognize the political force which was gradually creeping into the scene. Our understanding of Iran's society was very limited due to the extremely oppressive and restrictive environment we lived in. We were blind to the catastrophe that was shaping up right in front of our eyes. We even overlooked Bijan Jazani's warning that Khomeini might take the leadership mantle of a mass movement. We didn't pay attention to the power of the clergy in the public sphere and within the core of our society during the suppressive years of Shah's rule and did not even grasp it at the height of the openness in the period before the February 1979 Revolution.

The Tabriz protests lasted two days and our presence as students among the populace enabled us to make the catchphrase 'Unity, Struggle, Victory' popular. *Keyhan* newspaper published a 'list of the Tabriz detainees' and the pronouncement of 'up to ten-year prison sentences for 350 aggressors who were arrested' on its front page. Indeed, many students were among the detainees, while many were sheltered by the ordinary folks as they were fleeing from the street clashes.

By the end of winter of 1978 many banned books were being passed around freely. Works such as the OIPFG's *Vazayef-e Asasi Marksist-Leninistha* (The Basic Duties of Marxist Leninists), Maxim Gorky's *Mother*, Ahmad Shamlou's poetry and some of Bijan Jazani's writings were among them. We never thought we would have access to so many books that we could actually pick and choose from.

In March of 1978 there was a pro-government rally in Tabriz, as government supporters were bussed into the city for the rally and clashes ensued. Meanwhile memorial ceremonies for the fallen protestors of the Tabriz uprising of the previous month were being held in fifty-five cities across Iran. Our directives for that day were to strengthen connections between the recent events, the Siyahkal uprising and Fada'is supporters and also to covertly distribute the OIPFG's pamphlets and literature.

An expansive International Labour Day demonstration took place in Tabriz University on May Day 1978. I believe that we sang 'The Internationale' and chanted many political slogans too. We also printed and distributed Ahmad Khorramabadi's passionate letter to his mother (he was an OIPFG member who had been executed in June 1971). This was a very productive day for us, as we realized the strength of our organizing power. The following week another demonstration on campus was vehemently put down by the campus security guard in an unprecedented manner. They had hitherto usually resorted to tear gas and beating the students with clubs, but this time they charged us with carrying weapons to spread fear. We did not think that they would use their weapons, but they shot Davoud Mirza'i, a known supporter of OIPFG. We watched in disbelief as he fell to ground and his blood ran on the cobblestones in front of the Faculty of Literature. We could not believe what we had witnessed with our own eyes. Later when we were at the hospital, we heard that another student, Mohammad Gholami, had also been killed. Davoud was an enthusiastic student who wanted to use his education in the service of the downtrodden and deprived. The next day Davoud's father took his body to Zanjan. We had to go to Zanjan to show his family that he was not alone in his convictions, and also to show the authorities that they were not in control anymore. The cemetery was packed with people who were not shy to show their anger at the authorities. During the funeral a letter from Tabriz University students which demanded the prosecution of the university security guards who killed Davoud was read out loud. Davoud's uncle, who was related to the Diba family (the one of the Shah's wife) was also amongst the mourners. He spoke and claimed that Davoud had come to him repeatedly to seek help and that he was trapped by the leftists. He was interrupted by jeers and whistles from the crowd as well as Davoud's father who was furious and did not let the uncle continue. A few days later, a famous singer, Ashiq Hassan, composed and sang about the brutal attack at the university and the murder of Davoud Mirza'i. Events started happening at a much faster pace. The news of the university professors' protest against the security guards, the police's vicious attacks and the resignation of the university chancellor spread to all the campuses across the country. All our classes were cancelled, and at the same time the security guards and armed forces were making their presence known in and around the university.

Coordinated protests took place in early August 1978 in Tehran, Tabriz and Isfahan. The Isfahan protesters were confronted with violence. There were skirmishes in Tabriz with the police every day, and the public were demanding the prosecution of those who were responsible for the killings. The regime was not afraid of arresting and killing protesters and was now showing its true face. The fear among the populace had dissipated as chants of 'Death to Shah' became commonplace. One of the painful events during this time was the beating of the students in the Maralan neighborhood, a poverty-stricken district in the city of Tabriz. Most of the textile workshops were in this part of town, children who were deprived of education since the age of six or seven had to weave rugs instead of attending school. They had never got a taste of what it meant to be young. Our efforts to get connected to this neighbourhood often failed. We tried to encourage the children to go to school but their response was that the neighbourhood's mullah told them God will only reward the hard-working people in afterlife. They did not want us in their neighbourhood. During protests we saw them on the other side, confronting us and more specifically beating the women protesters in much harsher ways. The late Hamid Taslimi, one of the OIPFG activists, recounted his venture into this neighbourhood. He told us one day he wore shanty clothes and went to the neighbourhood's mosque to see what this mullah was preaching. The Mullah, after reciting the much-repeated stories of martyrdom of religious saints, warned them of the 'young students from schools and universities' who are communists and are coming to take their God away. Hamid then asked the mullah about communists, to which the Mullah replied: 'In the foreign language commune means God and we all know the meaning of '*nist*' ('is not' in Persian), so 'communist', means God does not exist'. Hamid then asked, 'Excuse me sir, in what foreign language? The mullah then shouted, 'He is one of them!' Before Hamid could escape, he got beaten up badly and his entire body was covered with bruises. These episodes still did not keep us from guiding our protests to go through the poor neighbourhoods as much as we could.

The protests that were organized under the direction of Fada'is, and Mojahedin organizations were quite successful especially in their first few days and caused a lot of confusion among the security forces. We used to come to the city centre more often during these times and had more open contact and engagement with ordinary people.

Following the events of summer 1978, on the first day of the school year in September, teachers found themselves bombarded by their students' questions. They could not restrain the students' profound enthusiasm as much as they tried, while they themselves could not express their own true feelings without the fear of repercussion. The students' only outlet to find suitable answers was to go to the streets. One of the most fascinating memories I have from those days is the never-ending questions the students asked me about the weapon that they thought I carried. When I told them that neither me nor my superiors were armed, they got disappointed and told me that we were not real guerrillas, although they still took our pamphlets and read them.

In November 1978 the prison gates were opened and political prisoners were being released. We travelled to Tehran and joined the large crowds outside the prisons, greeting them as they walked out into freedom. There was great commotion outside the prison gates every day, as crowds would gather to greet the exiting prisoners. We would make use of the opportunity to distribute the name and slogans of the OIPFG amongst those assembled there. We would also greet and congratulate the prisoners ourselves at the jail's entrance with a banner titled 'The Students Supporters of the OIPFG at the University of Tabriz' and even travel with them to their hometowns and villages in Azerbaijan. The political affiliation of the released prisoners was not of importance to us those days, to the extent that we accompanied the long-standing Ferqeh-ye Demokrat-e Azerbaijan (The Democratic Party of Azerbaijan) figure Safar Qahremani to Shishvan, his village of birth. The presence of a considerable crowd at Shishvan was very encouraging for us and a sign of the final victory over the Shah's regime.

Later on, back in Tabriz, on 16 January 1979, newspapers with headlines announcing the Shah leaving the country were being passed around on the streets. The University of Tabriz was a scene of pure joy, while the campus security guard was pondering its inevitable fate. The logo of the OIPFG was now visible on university entrance gates and even throughout the city. We were distributing pamphlets openly, and there were so many volunteers helping to distribute them and to write political placards that we felt like extras. People kept coming to the university, and there were huge demonstrations across the city and on campus. Even though the demonstrators wanted to march towards the city centre, we decided to remain on campus to prevent a confrontation with the military. Women, men, young and old were singing Ashiq Hassan's song in praise of Davoud and 'Long Live Fada'i' became a popular chant in demonstrations.

The month of February 1979 was a time of jubilation for workers and toilers. Factories opened to students. We were knocking on people's doors without any fear, and they were pleasantly receptive to what we had to tell them. On one of these February days, I went to see few households that I used to frequently visit. Young boys and girls were screaming with joy, and I couldn't hold back my tears. Men were now more kind and would admit that the suffering they had endured in their lives had shaped their behaviour. This was heartbreaking to hear.

I left for Tehran on 9 February. The police and military bases in the city surrendered during the mass demonstrations on 10 and 11 February. The Fada'i guerrillas sought to capture the main radio station in Ark Square with the support of ordinary people. As the jubilant crowds were ascending towards the radio station's stairway, the Fada'i guerrilla Qasem Siadati's heart was pierced by bullets shot by forces still faithful to the Pahlavi state. The sadness of this tragedy weighed heavily on everyone's feelings as they were celebrating the capture of the radio station, which was followed by capturing the main television station. Two of my relatives, Mir-'Ali Hosseini and his wife, were amongst the TV station's personnel who returned to work on that day after they had previously engaged in a long strike. I can confidently say the day the revolutionaries captured the main television station was one of the best days of my life. Hosseini, a famous TV presenter, appeared on screen and declared live on TV: 'This is the voice of the Iranian people's revolution.' That moment represented the final nail in the coffin of Iran's 2,500-year-old monarchy.

I returned to Tabriz on 18 February. The city was cheerful and joyous eight days after the final uprising. I took a cab and as we were driving along the city streets, I asked the driver about what had happened in the city in the last few days. I told him that I was in Tehran when the Fada'i guerrillas were leading the capture of the government's centres of power. When he realized that I spoke Persian and was a university student too, he told me that he had been to the campus several times in the past few days, and with tears of joy in his eyes, he said: 'We are free now, We owe everything to you folks.'

The city was filled with laughter, joy and music. I went to the National Library and found my friends there. We hugged and cried as I told them I had to come there even before going to the university. Mr Elyari told me that they always considered me like their daughter and embraced me warmly. They were eager to know everything which had happened in Tehran, while I was eager to know what had transpired in Tabriz, the city which had shielded my growing consciousness and the best years of my life. We went for a hurried walk around the city with the library's staff. All along the way they talked enthusiastically about the seizure of the military centres and the radio television stations by the revolutionaries and the people. They gave me the feeling that they had missed me being with them during these events, and I deeply felt this void inside me. It was February, but the city had the warmth of July.

I went to the University of Tabriz campus. Women, men, old and young were all gathered on campus. The OIPFG had turned the security guard building into its headquarters. Joyous life and passion ruled the space where students had previously been subject to punishment for years.

11

The Confederation of Iranian Students (National Union) and the Fada'i Guerrillas

ʿAli Nadimi

I left Iran on a sad day in the early fall of 1968. Before I did so, I spent time with a friend – a well-educated friend, who taught literature at a high school in Tabriz. He had recently been released from one of the Shah's prisons. We whiled away a few days in Maku. I did not want the regret of not having seen at least some of Iran's cities. I might never return and if I did, it would not be anytime soon.

These were heady times. Impervious to any individual, much less any institution, the Shah considered Iran as his lawful personal property. By the grace of a feared police force, he held absolute power in the domestic sphere. By the grace of a military armed to its teeth, he entertained regional hegemony abroad. In the Shah's lexicon, civil liberties and popular political participation held little to no meaning.

I was raised in a political household. My father and his older brother followed Mossadeq. My father's younger brother devoted himself to the Tudeh Party. As you might imagine, our home was home to relentless debate – all the more pronounced after the collapse of Mossadeq's government – of which I was an increasingly active observer. My father and older uncle on one side, my younger uncle on the other. Albeit with time and, after the formation of SAVAK (the Organization for Intelligence and National Security) in 1957, these debates waned in intensity. Albeit with time and, after the formation of SAVAK (the Organization for Intelligence and National Security) in 1957, these debates waned in intensity.

Towards the end of the 1950s and the beginnings of the 1960s, an opening emerged. During the national teachers' strike in May 1961, Abolhassan Khanʿ Ali died from wounds inflicted by soft-point bullets. The bullets were fired by Nasser Shahrestani, Baharestan's chief of police. In the ensuing fallout, Jaʿfar Sharif Emami's cabinet collapsed and the Shah appointed ʿAli Amini as prime minister. Amini's appointment, urged on with American support, increased peoples' hopes for achieving an open public sphere. Most notably, the parties organized under the National Front cautiously recommenced their political and organizational activities.

The newfound sense of optimism, however, didn't last long. Following a series of differences in opinion with the Shah over the national budget, Amini resigned to be succeeded by Asadollah Alam as prime minister. The Shah once more tried his hand at strengthening his pursuit of unparalleled power, calling for the suppression of democratic forces and putting an end to the political activities of any and all existing organizations and parties. The events that came to pass in this period, and their disheartening consequences, left a profound impression on not only popular consciousness but also society's more seasoned constituents. From then on, as the shadow of the Shah's dictatorship grew, open discussion, much less debate, gave way to a telling silence.

Fear ruled in the private confines of our family. We lost the motivation for debating. Family gatherings were fewer and farther between. Political squabbles invariably took place through innuendo. And as time passed, apart from exceptional circumstances, they withered away entirely. Our interactions with neighbours similarly tapered away. If a guest were to unexpectedly appear at our door, we passed inquisitive looks of distrust. A ceaseless stream of propaganda championing the Shah's 'peerless' rule had left its mark. It turned a culture of otherwise healthy and substantive dialogue into trite and futile disputes. Here and there, if some vestige of trust happened to lay about, conversations took place in private. And even then, they were tempered with symbolic and allegorical language-innuendo.

It was an atmosphere infested with despair and disillusion. Mohammad Reza Shah Pahlavi's government by merely heightening the intensity of political and cultural repression, had created an atmosphere of despair and distrust. The slightest misgiving about a gathering could result in arrest and imprisonment. In the worst-case scenarios, when SAVAK made an arrest, the experience would leave an immediate and often lingering impact on peoples' personal and public lives. When I was eighteen years of age, SAVAK arrested me for a series of purported 'crimes': membership in an intellectual group comprising young poets and writers, participation in that group's polemics regarding the absence of civil and political freedoms in Iran, protests against the Vietnam War. I spent eleven months in prisons in Ahvaz and Shiraz. When I was finally released, despite having participated in two separate entrance exams for which I'd earned the highest marks relative to my peers across the nation, I was prevented from enrolling in any of Iran's universities. Deprived of an opportunity to pursue a higher education and my chosen field of study, I ultimately chose to leave Iran and enter a state of exile.

The impact of Siyahkal

As soon as I settled in Austria and registered at the university, I became an active member of the Confederation of Iranian Students, National Union (hereafter, CISNU). It didn't take long before I joined the local student association. Shortly after that, I assumed a leadership role on its board of secretaries. And then again, a little over a year later, I participated in elections for the Austrian federation and became the secretary of the Iranian Student Association (ISA) in Austria.

At the same time, I established ties with the National Front in Europe. When the National Front underwent a series of changes in its internal composition (the details of which rest beyond the scope of this article), I became affiliated with the Middle East Branch of the Organization of the National Front of Iran Abroad (the Star Group).[1] My affiliation corresponded, for the most part, with the onset of guerrilla struggle in Iran. The guerrilla movement convinced Iran's younger, idealist generation of the futility of compromise. It pushed traditional doctrines to the periphery. It elevated movements in Algeria, Cuba and Vietnam to lofty heights. And it resulted in the formation of various underground groups brandishing weapons and adhering to the principle of armed struggle.

Siyahkal occurred at the height of the Shah's most perverted displays of power. The event irrevocably changed the political atmosphere in Iran, challenging the myth of 'absolute power' previously associated with the Shah's regime. In every discernible corner, progressive stirrings replaced a previous deathly silence. Through the force of arbitrary rule and the forgery of sham political parties tied to the whims of 'royal intentions', the Pahlavi state figured it had tamed Iranian society and tamed malcontents and opposition forces. Now, distressed and bewildered by a countervailing reality, it searched for answers in the intensification of repression. That is, instead of taking violent struggle by groups like the Organization of Iranian People's Fada'i Guerrillas (OIPFG) and the People's Mujahedin Organization (hereafter, PMOI) as a direct reaction to repression or the absence of political freedoms, it reinforced the authority of its secret police forces. The state could have allowed a measure of freedom and popular participation in political life, and in so doing reduced the perceived need for radical action against the government in public opinion. It chose, however, to establish a 'joint committee against sabotage' comprising the police, the army and the gendarmerie (acting under SAVAK's supervision). With all its might, drawing on experience from intelligence agencies like Mossad and the CIA, it proceeded to confront domestic guerrilla organizations.

From then on, its efforts were water under the bridge. The Pahlavi state vainly tried to reassert control over affairs, to present itself as having already anticipated everything the 'saboteurs' did. One vehicle – a popular television show featuring Parviz Sabeti, the head of Iran's security forces, as Maqam-e Amniyati, or Security Official – pawned colourful representations meant to sully militants through an array of accusations. They had no choice. In a short time, following the events of Siyahkal, the people formed near-mythic perceptions of the charismatic revolutionaries. These figures appeared as courageous, self-sacrificial heroes who, 'from the exalted threshold of their memory, leave the corrupt disgraced and ashamed'.

The events of Siyahkal spawned important and lasting works in literature and the arts. Poetry by Ahmad Shamlou, Nemat Mirzazadeh and Shafi'i Kadkani amongst others represent the most stellar works of the period. The effects of Siyahkal are similarly apparent in music and film. It all caused a great deal of excitement for an intellectually curious and unruly younger generation. In a very short time, a number of other armed groups embarked on political and organizational activities while the student movement in Iran's universities found new life. Increasingly well-received by students, it ultimately transformed the atmosphere on college campuses against the Shah's government and its false modernism.

Radicalization of the Confederation of Iranian Students

Anticipating tensions roiling society from below, the Shah's government made a bold tactical move. It banned CISNU. While the ban arrived on 8 February 1971, just before the overt declaration of guerrilla warfare, the state had laid groundwork for the decree well before. In a press interview on 28 December 1970, Sabeti made a futile attempt to link Taymour Bakhtiar – the first acting head of SAVAK, responsible for the deaths of hundreds of freedom fighters – with revolutionaries and communist forces. The interview, trumpeted by government propaganda for a time, alleged that 'Chinese communists and Maoists control the leadership ranks of Confederation of Iranian Students (CISNU)' that, 'in recent university protests, CISNU demanded a red revolution', and that 'CISNU, the National Front, and the outlawed Tudeh Party collectively published twenty-one separate newsletters and periodicals in various European and American countries'. Elsewhere, it suggestively asks, 'Where did the propensity for partisan acts by certain students come from?'

On 18 January 1971, in a radio-television interview given in the wake of the last defences delivered by members of the Palestine Group, the military's public prosecutor Siavush Behzadi declared CISNU illegal. 'In accordance with the penal code for those intending to perpetrate crimes against national security and sovereignty, members of affiliated federations, organizations, clubs, unions, and associations will be prosecuted and punished.'[2] 'The penal code for those intending to perpetrate crimes against national security and sovereignty' is the same ominous 1931 law, passed during Reza Shah's rule, that gave three- to ten-year prison sentences to 'anti-royalist' persons and/or individuals convicted of harboring 'communist ideas'.

Neither this law nor the warnings issued by General Behzadi – that families should 'heed the behavior of their children within and without the country to prevent them from deviating' – impacted CISNU's activities.[3] In fact, students increased anti-regime activism. A democratic atmosphere in Europe after May 1968 caused the retreat of right-wing forces and traditionally conservative political parties. These erstwhile formidable sectors of European society could only take measures against civil demands registered by Iranian students, or obstruct their struggle to realize democratic ideals, with great difficulty. The vigilance and insight of CISNU leaders played a role as well. Immediately after CISNU was banned, its acting board of secretaries wrote an open letter to authorities in the German Federal Republic condemning measures taken by the Iranian government and the claims made by Iran's military prosecutor. In the same breath, they presented CISNU as an organization that 'openly operates in accordance with democratic laws, anti-imperialist aims, the Iranian constitution, and the Declaration of Human Rights'.[4]

These measures were taken in step with far-reaching publicity campaigns. The most impressive of these campaigns was CISNU's boycott of the 2,500-year celebration of the Persian Empire in October 1971, which garnered support from eventual Nobel Prize winner Gunnar Myrdal, Simone de Beauvoir, Jean-Paul Sartre, Melina Mercouri and Mikis Theodorakis, among others. In response the March

1971 annual congress of German university chancellors issued a statement of protest against the Iranian government's banning of CISNU, a legally recognized student union in West Germany. The statement further called on West Germany's federal and state government to protect Iranian students from harassment and persecution by the Shah's regime.[5]

In March 1971, approximately 1,000 representatives from various chapters in Europe and North America participated in the twelfth CISNU congress. Their participation set to rest any lingering doubts about support for armed militants, who now appeared considerably stronger than the tricks and threats deployed by the Shah's government to silence protest.

CISNU's publicity campaigns regarding repression in Iran and its related efforts to defend political prisoners generated noteworthy endorsements from a range of progressive and democratic organizations, forces and individuals. A number of intellectuals and prominent international organizations – including Amnesty International, the International Commission of Jurists (ICJ) and related human rights groups – publicly offered support. I recall a hearing in Paris where CISNU members appeared in court. They had occupied a building associated with the regime – –its embassy, or the offices of the national airline, I don't remember exactly which. Yves Montand and his wife, Simone Signoret, attended the proceedings and defended CISNU's right to take action against the regime. The court acquitted the accused.

During the twelfth congress, a new slogan replaced the slogan originally adopted in CISNU's second congress (the Lausanne Congress). The latter had called for a movement to 'fully implement the constitution'.[6] The former now called for a 'movement to establish a democratic society [in Iran]'. The change augured ensuing transformations in theory and practice. Weekly meetings of the student union became more substantive; in opinions expressed and related political debates, a noticeable progression took place: despite their differences, proponents and critics of an armed movement were nevertheless in agreement on the need to struggle against the Shah's regime and to defend activists in Iran regardless of whether or not those activists took up arms.

In this respect, the armed struggle in Iran accelerated CISNU's radicalization. It gave the student movement an entirely different dimension. CISNU which had long supported the resistance by everyday people and activists in Iran, regardless of their views or political opinions, only now it listed defense activities for Iran's armed resistance at the top of its agenda. Support for militants who were prosecuted, imprisoned, tortured and executed in various forms appeared on a wide scale and in radical fashion, from holding announced and indefinite hunger strikes to occupying the regime's embassies and so-called cultural centres. The high point of these 'defence' initiatives came during the fourteenth CISNU congress in January 1973. In those proceedings, delegates passed an innovative plan condemning 'the severe and savage assault of the shah's puppet regime on the brave and heroic militants in [Iran]'.[7] Their plan called for 'the formation of an international tribunal to address the Shah's crimes':

In court proceedings before an international tribunal, Mohammad Reza Shah's crimes, and the mechanisms and tools of murder deployed by his hellish security forces, would be exposed. It would also reveal the nature of the regime's propaganda, the real conditions of workers in Iran, the state of health and culture in our homeland, and the uncompromising struggle of domestic organizations against reactionary politics and imperialisms.[8]

These initiatives spawned two concrete effects. For one, global public opinion came to perceive the Shah's government as a terrifying dictatorship. The notion, once prevalent, that Iran was an 'island of stability and security' feel subject to derision. This is despite the state's expenditure of an enormous budget on publicity and propaganda abroad. At the same time, CISNU gained notable esteem and credence in the eyes of other global revolutionary movements – in particular, the armed movement in Iran.

It was at this time that I established a correspondence with comrades Mohammad Hormatipour and Ashraf Dehqani. They were collectively responsible for the OIPFG's activities abroad. Over the course of the process known as 'homogenization' between the Star Group and the OIPFG – parts of which corresponded with my responsibilities as CISNU's general secretary – my comrades and I failed to neglect the slightest effort to defend these armed militants and the legitimacy of their struggle. In the midst of what was a truly historical conjuncture, we gave the movement everything we could.

Revising the charter

CISNU's fifteenth congress took place in January of 1974 in Frankfurt, Germany. It differed from any of the other congresses I participated in. In addition to solidarity messages from CISNU's traditional allies, it received, for the first time, a message of support from an organization fighting the regime inside Iran. The message from the Mojahedin [OIPM], and a moving speech by the mother of a slain Mojahedin guerrilla, stirred emotions and brought many participants to tears. There was a feeling that after more than a decade of tenacious efforts ... abroad, the Confederation finally had linked with a growing revolutionary movement inside of Iran. Another turning point was the passage of a resolution regarding the 'Iranian people's movement.' This resolution went further than the statements CISNU had previously issued – statements that had garnered support from all the various groupings and factions comprising the opposition. For the first time, a CISNU congress passed a resolution declaring that the opposition movement reflected 'the objective and historical demand of our country's progressive classes and strata for the overthrow of the despotic regime of Mohammad Reza Shah and the expulsion of imperialists from our country'. This amounted to an explicit call for the regime's overthrow, increasing divisions within the organization.[9]

Disputes between CISNU's various groups were so severe that the Fifteenth Congress could not select a secretariat reflecting the central tendencies represented by its attendees. In the end, the participants settled on an acting and provisional secretariat composed of three individuals. And yet, after the congress, CISNU's 'defence' activities continued with even greater intensity. In the late winter and early spring of 1974, CISNU organized defense campaigns for imprisoned writers and poets including 'Shari'ati, Gholam-Hossein Sa'edi, Fereydoun Tonekaboni, Fereydoun Tavallali, Houshang Golshiri and Nemat Mirzazadeh. It likewise threw its full support behind Khosrow Golesorkhi, Keramat Daneshian and their cohort, sparing no effort to save their lives. As usual, telegrams and letters of protest from organizations and individuals supporting CISNU's demands were sent to the Iranian government and its consulates and embassies. Demonstrations were held in the United States and several European countries. On January 9, hunger strikes were held by 150 students in Mainz, Germany and by 230 students between West Berlin, Vienna, Rome, and London. 6,000 gathered in Frankfurt to express support for the strikers. As these actions gained increasing press coverage in Europe, news arrived on February 18 that two of the accused were executed and three others received life sentences. The two executed men were Khosrow Golesorkhi, a poet and writer, and Keramat Daneshian, a film-maker … One day after the execution of Golesorkhi and Daneshian, six guerrillas faced a firing squad. On March 8, CISNU activists occupied Iranian embassies in Brussels, the Hague, and Stockholm in protest against the executions … They pulled portraits of the shah and the royal family off the walls and affixed pictures of Golesorkhi, Daneshian, and other victims of the regime in their place. Using the embassies' telex and telephones, CISNU transmitted demands to Iran and the mass media in other countries. At the same time, CISNU demonstrations in Britain, the United States, Italy, Austria, and West Germany demanded the release of those arrested in these actions … News of these actions were covered by *Le Monde, Liberation, Frankfurter Rundschau, New York Herald Tribune*, and London's *Times* and *Guardian*. Tehran's *Kayhan* and *Ettela'at* also gave these events front-page coverage, describing them as part of the ongoing international 'anti-Iranian' conspiracy orchestrated by foreign agents.[10]

A number of factors were converging at once: a series of sharp exchanges between CISNU and the Iranian government in the midst of acute societal transformation in the domestic sphere; a daily increase in repression and in response armed resistance; the radicalization of students who, especially after Golesorkhi's televised trial, sought higher education abroad; and a general sense of malaise, even repugnance, regarding the Shah's oppressive state in global public opinion. In this context, in January 1975, the Sixteenth CISNU Congress revised the student union's charter and reassessed its statement of purpose:

> In order to overthrow an absolutist Pahlavi government, to bring an end to the rule exercised by today's reactionary classes, to end once and for all imperialist influence, the peoples' movement in Iran and the student movement following from it are fighting to bring about an independent society. They fight to establish democracy and freedom on behalf of the Iranian people, in particular its toiling masses.
>
> The student movement comprises one part of the broader democratic anti-imperialist movement waged by the Iranian people. Its deep allegiance with and

support for that broader struggle arises from the fact that securing students' corporate, social, and political rights would be impossible without securing the social and political rights of the masses – without first freeing the millions of people in our nation toiling under the despotic yoke of reactionary imperialism. The completion of this task is only possible by virtue of actions taken by the masses of Iranian people, in particular its toilers. Consequently, the student movement believes it will only be capable of fulfilling its social duty when it acts in the service of the people's (and especially the toilers') movement …

… Insofar as CISNU gathers together students with different ways of thinking and divergent social perspectives, the student union cannot adopt a single, fixed ideology. Differences of opinion and perspectives in CISNU's various gatherings, seminars, and meetings will naturally occur. In fact, they must occur in order to (a) secure the more concrete, conscious, and expansive progression of our anti-imperialist and anti-reactionary struggle, and (b) preserve and fortify our unity.[11]

The new charter passed with a majority votes cast in its favour by representatives from chapters in Europe, America, India, and Turkey. The revisions marked an important turning point in CISNU's history. It was clear the various factions and political tendencies comprising the student union did not all approve the revisions or even the broader effort to adjust the charter in accordance with social conditions and movements in Iran. But then, in the midst of hundreds of solidarity statements from international organizations and liberation movements from across the globe, when statements by the PMOI and OIPFG were read, a palpable wave of pride rose amongst the participants unlike any I've ever seen. Excerpts of the Fada'i guerrillas' historic message merit attention:

Comrades, please accept our warmest salutations.

Because of your patriotic and global activism. Because of the part you play in giving testimony to the fact that the masses of our people, no matter where they may reside, will use all circumstances available to them to engage in an uncompromising struggle against imperialism and reactionary politics. Because of you, our people are content.

CISNU's efforts at gaining global exposure for events in Iran have consistently amplified both the regime's criminal deeds and the Iranian people's call for equal rights. Before the onset of an armed movement, when the enemy crushed political activism and liberation movements before they grew, a time marked by intense police repression and the absence of revolutionary organizations in the domestic sphere, CISNU's invaluable revolutionary activities supported the Iranian people and further revealed the shameful face of the Pahlavi regime … The conditions you and I live in are different. They call for different kinds of struggle. But all forms are necessary and complementary.

… Under the shah's command, Iran's reactionary forces seek to crush the seeds of our armed movement before it grows. At present, as a new and in suppressible movement spreads, these forces resort to unmitigated violence and (implicitly) fascist deeds. They attempt to squash the spirit of our political prisoners, to steer them away from the movement. But our comrades resist heroically. They continue to struggle.

You must deliver their revolutionary protests, their demands, to all who seek emancipation across the world. And you must do so in unison. Remove the mask imperialists use to cover the shah's bloodthirsty image. Come to know him from a different point of view. And use any means at your disposal for political publicity and propaganda. Present Iran's true conditions before those who value freedom. Make them aware. At present, 'Comrade Mother' – the mother of our heroic comrade, the martyr Nader Shayegan, whose arms were semi-paralyzed due to torture – is serving a twelve-year prison sentence. She not only refuses to relinquish the movement; she invites fellow prisoners to join her. At present, our comrade Shirin Mo'azed – her body burnt from shocks induced by lying on an electric brazier, her body riven from the blows of an electric cable used as a whip-- likewise continues the struggle. At present, our Mojahed comrade Simin Salehi, having lost one eye and given birth to a premature child, is under extraordinary pressure in the regime's prisons.

We've listed only a few examples of the regime's crimes against the rights of political prisoners. On a daily basis, subject to the tortures inflicted by imperialist mercenaries, hundreds of our fellow patriots are forced to defect – or lose their lives.

Under these conditions, who else but CISNU's patriotic, defiant, and organized students are likely to bring these tragic events to the attention of the world, to remove the veils covering the regime's detestable image, to reveal the truth...

... In addition to this message, we have dedicated one volume of the series of social researches we've undertaken regarding the prevailing objective conditions in our society.[12]

... On this sacred and dignified path, we are together. We move and act together. On this count, we warmly salute you, militant comrades. We send our best wishes for your sixteenth congress and your invaluable activism.

With faith in the victory coming before us.[13]

CISNU's sixteenth congress responded to the OIPFG in turn:

Comrades!

We have received your esteemed message. Its announcement caused considerable excitement during CISNU's sixteenth congress. We are honoured to hear our modest contributions to the movement waged by the Iranian people and its true revolutionaries has garnered such worthwhile results. We are likewise honoured that your organization has responded to our efforts with the prized gift of both your research and a message to our congress. Every member of CISNU undoubtedly appreciates the import of this outcome. In the effort to maintain our bond, we leave no stone unturned. As you mentioned: 'The conditions you and I live in are different. They call for different kinds of struggle.' We are aware that our struggle, the extensive efforts of students and intellectuals abroad, pales in comparison to your sacrifices and your tireless and revolutionary political activism. Our struggle is only effective when it acts in the service of a revolutionary movement within the country; when it is oriented in the service of the people's democratic and anti-imperialist movement; when it aids the movement in the task of overthrowing a reactionary despotic regime allied with imperialism. Following the reading of your message, the 1,500 individuals participating in our congress let out cries of joy and solidarity. They engaged in passionate debate and discussion in your favour. It's clear proof that the masses of students are prepared to render support to you … the People's Fada'i Guerrillas. With every day that passes, with every act of resistance and revolutionary striving on your part, with every militant effort, every demonstration of tenacity and perseverance, with every unforgettable epic account of your anti-reactionary and anti-imperialist movement, your unparalleled bravery exerts even greater influence on the whole of the people, Iranian students, and global public opinion. We know full well the difficult conditions in which you wage your movement. We are aware of the extent of help and solidarity you require from the masses of people, from the world at large. We intend to deploy our abilities and labours to the utmost to fulfill our duty on this path alongside the revolutionary movement. We will not be quiet as long as 'Comrade Mother', our guerrilla comrade Shirin Mo'azed, and our Mojahed comrade Simin Salehi struggle against the tortures inflicted by SAVAK's executioners, the mercenaries of the shah's apparatus. We will echo your cry, bringing it to the world's attention. We will make the militant call of Fada'i and Mojahed guerrillas reverberate in public opinion. We learn how to resist and struggle from you. We will tirelessly take steps toward your historic objectives: defeating reactionary politics and imperialism and overthrowing the shah's regime…For your battle embodies our people's refusal to compromise with a puppet regime. It exemplifies our nation's oppressed and exploited masses' refusal to compromise with the reactionary tyrant currently in power. Comrades! We will carefully implement your directives. We hold them dearly. Know that the students gathered in CISNU appreciate your revolutionary movement, your unparalleled resistance. They learn from it. They will not forget their duties. Let us proudly march under the banner of the Fada'i guerrillas' valiant struggle. Let us hurry forth with the help of our political prisoners. Let us announce to the shah's reactionary regime …: we will not spare any effort in the service of resistance and struggle. Allow us, in the name of the entire congress, to salute you in turn and wish you victory.

With joy, and a sense of honour, from your invaluable message.[14]

When bullying came to an end

The armed movement in Iran communicated a clear public message. It sought to mark in peoples' minds the fallacy of a despotic regime's mythical claim to absolute power. We can confidently say armed groups achieved their goals. This is despite the considerable blows delivered by the regime. The people took those blows, against the regime's intentions, as signs of desperation in the face of a mounting resistance movement.

There is much to regret on the fact that the discussion regarding CISNU's continued evolution went astray. How could its activism, its very existence, complement a new set of conditions facing the Iranian people's ever-expanding democratic movement? In particular, how might the student union best act in defence of guerrilla organizations? Dogmatism, factionalism and right-leaning tendencies accompanied useless disputes and rash, unmeasured reactions. These conflicts resulted in the sixteenth congress' inability to select a five-member board of directors as, once again, the congress brought its work to a close by selecting a three-person provisional secretariat. The efforts made over the course of the sixteenth and seventeenth congresses to bring about consensus were unable to fill the deep void that had emerged between the various groupings and tendencies gathered together. In the end, in its seventeenth congress, CISNU splintered and eventually suffered a final, definitive schism. Yet somehow, in spite of the separation that took place, the seventeenth congress was able to select a five-member governing board. It also identified a way to pursue even more influential forms of resistance against the Shah's dictatorial regime. The OIPFG's message was important in this regard. The message stipulates 'the duties of organizations' who benefit from 'relatively free conditions and access to public opinion':

> Over the course of its history, CISNU has always fulfilled its duties, supporting the movement within the country in addition to other parts of our people's anti-imperialist struggles. Given your sense of responsibility with respect to the movement within the country and with respect to undertaking these important tasks, we believe you will succeed. To close, we find it necessary to share specific recommendations for you to follow in light of the conditions provided for democratic and anti-imperialist struggle abroad.
>
> With respect to defence, CISNU's primary responsibilities include defending the people's movement within the country, proclaiming its support for the movement, and striving to secure for it the widest base of international support. The struggle against the shah's reactionary and criminal regime cannot succeed without these efforts. In defending the people's movement, you must strive to ensure a comprehensive strategy so that all parts of the movement are defended. In Iran today, the most brutal manner of state terror is directed against the armed movement's revolutionary combatants. On this accord, the intensification of your struggle, your support, and your defence of revolutionaries and the revolutionary movement in the country has been of utmost necessity. It is itself an intensification of the struggle against both the shah's regime and global imperialism. Extensive publicity regarding militants in prison, announcing your support for their continued endurance, and accruing international support in defence of revolutionary political prisoners should be a priority. Our comrades must strive to unabashedly reveal the terrorist-fascist Pahlavi regime for what it is. In collaboration with prominent progressive organizations and individuals, you must strive to organize public trials of the Pahlavi fascists and the person of the shah – trials akin to those that took

place on behalf of the heroic Vietnamese people against America's imperialist crimes. These measures will bring to bear the pressure of public opinion and in turn exert considerable influence on the conditions facing Iranian political prisoners. Regardless of their immediate impact, they are a step in the direction of further shaming Pahlavi fascism and mobilizing supporters in defence of the Iranian people's heroic struggles. Your organization must forcefully declare its position through material support for the families of political prisoners and combatants in the armed movement. The import of this act mostly lies in its standing as a symbolic display on the part of Iranians living abroad. In this regard, it would imbue those who have lost their loved ones, and now persevere under intense surveillance, with a sense of valour and self-sacrifice. You must strive to organize defence activities and support for revolutionary movements in the country, and in fact all anti-regime actions by various sub-groups, in such a fashion that democratic practices develop as they should. But you must also ensure that these practices are consistent with the transference of more precise political and ideological practices to the country's domestic sphere. You yourselves are well aware of the regime's policing tactics abroad – the instruments of terror and intimidation it regularly deploys. It is not our place, from within the country, to tell you how to adopt requisite procedures in response. You can better discern and discover solutions to these problem from within the field of operations. We believe you will take necessary precautions to not compromise or undermine the democratic struggle against the regime and global imperialism or limit the role played by the masses of Iranian students living abroad in that struggle, but rather move forward in a such fashion that both of these indispensable practices are performed abroad. Now is a time for the intensification of the struggle at all levels, not its attenuation ...

For years, the dictatorial Pahlavi regime has offered no viable alternative to the people's boisterous and unruly movement. In response to the formation of a single political party and its decrees of new laws, we must further intensify our anti-fascist struggle. The history of victories accrued by the toiling masses of the world teaches us the only response to reactionary violence is to fight back and exercise commensurate force. The only possible response to the shah's terrorist system is combat and conflict. Tighten your ranks. The revolution is irrevocably set on its path. It will progress. Support the movement to the best of your abilities. Expose the regime of terror. Use all the forces at your disposal to struggle against it. As far and wide as possible, champion a decisive and unwavering movement to obliterate the Pahlavis' puppet regime. At the same time, champion the movement against global imperialism under American stewardship. We wish you success. We rest content knowing there are forces abroad organized in the image of the people's movement, waging battle against the Pahlavis' bloodthirsty reactionary politics.

We salute you and wish the very best for your congress.[15]

CISNU failed to organize an international hearing on the Iranian people's complaints against the Shah's dictatorial regime. And yet, in the one-year interval between the seventeenth and eighteenth congresses, it did accumulate some stellar achievements in its defence of Iranian revolutionaries. Most notable among these were the occupation of a number of embassies and centres associated with the Iranian government including SAVAK's European headquarters in Geneva, which led to the confiscation and widespread publication of thousands of documents concerning the activities of SAVAK spies against political organizations. The portions concerning CISNU were published as a book. In its introduction, titled 'Why We Occupied SAVAK's European Headquarters', we wrote:

> When we first planned to occupy SAVAK's European headquarters in Geneva, we didn't imagine this level of success. It was however clear to us that, confronted with SAVAK's brutal attacks against the ranks of those struggling on behalf of the people and its numerous killings of revolutionaries from the Organization of the People's Fada'i Guerrillas, revealing and exposing its deeds would strike a blow against the shah's regime. No part of the regime is more sensitive than its security forces! SAVAK is a hall of mirrors … reflecting the various aspects of Pahlavi fascism … The documents we obtained in Geneva show this to be true. They likewise demonstrate how the nightmare casting a shadow over our people is propped up by thousands of strings – and how those strings are tied to American imperialism. Without a doubt, the thickest of those strings pass through the centre of the army, the police, the gendarmerie, and above all the 'security' forces. SAVAK's documents show that Geneva is one node in relations between SAVAK and imperialist spy agencies, most notably the C.I.A ….
>
> We're in good spirits. Having drawn upon all the resources at CISNU's disposal, we delivered a setback for the shah's fascist regime. We gave an apt response to its crimes. Our achievement is the product of CISNU's protracted efforts to reveal the truth. The victory belongs to the student union and the masses organized within it.[16]

The documents in this book and news of the action set off unprecedented repercussions across the globe. For the first time in modern history, opposition forces obtained classified documents regarding the spying agencies and security forces animating a dictatorial regime prior to that regime's collapse. We can appreciate the event's importance in light of its press coverage. The action was covered by all the major news outlets in the West and non-West, including in Iran. There were tens of newspaper and radio-television interviews with CISNU's board of directors. The most widely broadcast interview featured three CISNU activists (including this author) on CBS's *Sixty Minutes* with Mike Wallace. That program cast a spotlight on the Iranian security forces' overseas activities. After it aired, the Shah explicitly requested the extradition of the students who occupied SAVAK's headquarters. Diplomatic relations between Iran and Switzerland were severely affected when the Swiss rejected his request.

The end of the Shah's undisputed power, the moment when his bullying finally came to an end, corresponded with the end of CISNU's existence. Nevertheless, in light of the organization's rich experiences in struggle and its distinct democratic structure, we might reasonably assert one speculative possibility. Perhaps CISNU's legacy and the transfer of its experiences to an Iran in tumult between 1977 and 1979 might have configured the 'revolutionary' outcome otherwise – this time in the interests of democratic and progressive forces. Perhaps.

12

From Mehrabad-e Jonoubi to the technical faculty

Siavush Randjbar-Daemi

Introduction

The period between July 1976 and February 1979 is of significant importance in the history of the Organization of Iranian People's Fada'i Guerrillas (OIPFG). The assault by the secret police SAVAK on the hideout which was hosting the leader of the Organization, Hamid Ashraf on 29 June 1976 and the killing of this prominent figure and other members of the leadership effectively marked the start of a new chapter in the history of the Organization. The considerable presence of Fada'i cadres in the Shah's prisons and the continuing repression by SAVAK posed an existential challenge: preserving the very existence of the Organization, whilst carrying on minimal forms of political activity. Both Qorbanali 'Abdolrahimpour, who became a member of the three-person central leadership council after the 29 June incident, and Mehdi Same', who was freed from prison in November 1978, are of the view that the Organization's modus operandi until the autumn of 1978 was primarily of a defensive, self-preservation type. The Organization succeeded in preserving a minimal but visible existence until the collapse of the monarchical regime on 11 February 1979. In the days preceding this epochal moment in Iranian history, the Fada'is had effectively emerged from clandestine life to belatedly begin the overt phase of their existence.

The purpose of this chapter is that of providing an overview and assessment of the Fada'i reactions to the broader political and social developments of the 1976–9 period, such as the staggering acceleration of civil society protests against the regime from summer 1977, the Goethe Nights later that year and the progression of revolutionary activities throughout 1978. In order to meet this purpose, a broad range of proclamations and declarations produced and distributed by the OIPFG during that period will be drawn upon. These constitute both the proof of the Fada'is' continued ability to maintain a minimal political existence and provide a valuable, unvarnished perspective through which the group's contemporary stance on the critical junctures of that period may be examined.

The first reactions after the deafening blow of 29 June

As noted by the veteran Fada'i Asghar Jilou, '29 June 1976 has turned into the day in which the Iran People's Fada'i Guerrilla Organization lost all of the members of its central nucleus after over five years of bloody struggle against the government of Mohammad Reza Pahlavi and therefore became headless for the first time in its history'.[1] The Organization was therefore forced to change its leadership structure completely and move away from a single leader at the helm. The sole surviving member of the leadership councils of 1976–9, Qorbanali 'Abdolrahimpour, has emphasized in recent years that the minimal continued existence of the Fada'is became the priority following the 29 July incident.[2] The dual, at times conflicting, concepts of 'armed struggle' and 'political activism' and the patterns through which one was prioritized over the other became a fundamental theoretical challenge for the Fada'is and remained so until the victory of the Revolution in early 1979. This challenge caused a split from the Organization, when several members headed by Touraj Heydari Bigvand walked away from the Fada'is on a platform of renouncing armed struggle and eventually joined ranks with the Tudeh Party, which had rejected the guerrilla movement in Iran since its early emergence in the mid-1960s.

The Fada'i Organization focused on its internal restructuring for a relatively long period of time following the 29 June incident. It produced its first communiqué following the killing of Hamid Ashraf and the leadership in November 1976, thereby signalling its continued existence. The publication of the third and final issue of *Payam-e Daneshjou*, the Organization's main journal of the time, in December 1977 provided a digest of the internal thinking at the time with regard to the vexing question of the balance between armed struggle and political action. A long article at the start of this issue focuses on the group's internal situation following the 29 June blow, and proceeds along the lines of what had been previously discussed in the seventh and last issue of *Nabard-e Khalq*, the Organization's theoretical journal during Hamid Ashraf's leadership:

> Even though we observed the lack of the objective condition of revolution, we were nevertheless ignoring this and were moving forward based on that assumption because of our belief in the victorious march of our path! One should utilise Marxist-Leninist audacity in confronting the reality which sheds light on our theories. As we did not criticise ourselves courageously, we could not develop our theories and move forward based on a realistic evaluation of the situation.
>
> The leadership comrades were the first who noticed such a shortcoming. However, they took no firm practical measure in order to resolve this issue. But this matter, was conducive to the ideas of comrade Bijan Jazani gaining a greater influence within the Organization. This is because comrade Jazani's analysis was predicated on the fact that the objective conditions of revolution have not yet appeared [in Iran]. Given that his theories were proven right by the facts, they turned into a catalyst for a change of perspectives within the Organization. At the same time, however, we have attributed undue value to the initial inadequate theories and have therefore maintained our previous views! The sour reality of the

blows of 1976 left no space for duality in our positions and finally, after an active ideological struggle within the Organization, the theories of comrade Jazani were finally recognised as the main basis and guiding principles of our activities.[3]

These considerations led to an interpretation of armed struggle which presented differences with regard to the previous ones espoused by the Fada'is:

> The current phase, in which armed struggle proceeds through an armed vanguard, presents clear differences to a mass struggle which is conducive to the destruction of the ruling system, due to its inherent [numerical] limitations. This is because at present, the aim of armed operations is that of raising awareness and publicity and is therefore itself considered the preliminary level of mass armed struggle. This is the reason why the same is called 'armed publicity'. This kind of struggle, which precedes a revolution, does not require the objective conditions of Revolution ... However, resorting to such a struggle is, in certain specific conditions, a necessity.[4]

The clearest indication of the start of the 'political' phase can be noticed through the considerable number of flyers, proclamations, declarations and booklets which the Organization succeeded in publishing and distributing from its hideouts across Iran between November 1976 and the demise of the monarchy in February 1979. The printed matter was produced and distributed in a systematic and frequent manner and often made its way abroad, where it was reproduced by sympathetic bodies such as the Confederation of Iranian Students Abroad (National Union) – CISNU. At times, the aim of these publications was that of providing the Fada'i first reaction to important and broader events which were occurring in the political and social environment of that period. On other occasions, these proclamations consisted of open letters to personalities or political organizations external to the Organization, or even the landscape of the Iranian Left of the time, such as the letter, discussed below, which was addressed to Ayatollah Khomeini prior to his momentous return from exile in February 1979.

The first communiqués after the Mehrabad-e Junoubi incident

Following the demise of Hamid Ashraf, there was a hiatus in the production of communiqués by the Fada'i Organization. The first proclamation of November 1976, entitled 'The Communiqué of the Organization of Iran People's Fada'i Guerrillas with regards to the recent clashes with the agents of the Shah's regime' had the primary purpose of dispelling the extinction of the Organization and confirming its continued existence after 29 June. According to 'Abdolrahimpour, this communiqué and the following one, issued in December 1976 were prepared under the supervision of the first leadership council following Ashraf, which was composed of the female Fada'i Saba Bijanzadeh (Hajar) and Mohammad Reza Ghebra'i (Mansour).[5] Within the text of the communiqué, it is noted how

we have had a lot of martyrs this year, such as the Great Comrade Hamid Ashraf
... The martyrdom of these comrades, who carried most of the weight of the
victorious armed movement of the masses, is to be considered a major calamity
for the movement. However, the martyrdom of these comrades has not, as claimed
by the [monarchical] regime, created doubts regarding the continuation of our
path, but has on the other hand strengthened our resolve for facing the enemy of
the masses [the regime], which is armed to its teeth.[6]

Subsequently, the communiqué focuses on the reasons behind the 29 June blow:

[The security apparatus] has recently managed to uncover the OIPFG's telephone
network due to mistakes which occurred in our phone communications and reach
some of our bases after persistently tailing of some of our comrades.[7]

Elsewhere, the communiqué mentioned the challenges ahead:

Our Militant Fellow compatriots! The Masses' Armed Movement of Iran has
gone past its first phase, which consisted of setting forth and consolidating armed
struggle at the vanguard level and raising awareness of the same within Iranian
society. It is now on the cusp of entering its second phase, which consists of the
massification of the struggle itself.

This publication also noted the ongoing impact of the state's land reform initiatives which were launched in the early 1960s, mentioning as it did that the land reform project 'not only did not improve the condition of the lower strata of society, but worsened it by the day', and explained this statement by noting how 'the Shah's regime expropriated the farmers' fertile lands for the purpose of establishing agricultural stock companies and agricultural cooperatives, placing these at the disposal of foreign and domestic investors and in this way resulted in vagrant migration [of the rural population] to the cities'.

On the occasion of the anniversary of the 16 Azar (7 December) student protests of 1953, the Fada'i Organization reconnected with one of the main pillars of its societal support, the student body, through two brief declarations. In one of these, the Organization reiterated in direct terms how the 29 June blow was a serious and consequential one:

During the current [1976] year, the Organization, which had achieved a degree of
relative internal stability, was confronted by massive police assaults. The regime
was aware of the growth of armed movement and its attempts to connect with
the politically aware masses and made use of its own and world imperialism's
resources in order to repress this movement and deploy all of its forces for the sake
of neutralising the progressive organizations.[8]

The same text then proceeded to list the main aims of the new phase of the struggle which came about after the 29 June incident. These consisted of 'informing the masses on the aims of the armed struggle, ... mobilising the masses with the aim of obtaining their support for this movement'. The students were furthermore asked to 'reveal the plots of the [monarchical] regime aimed at suppressing the student movements, and in this way obstructing the dirty plots of the dictator Shah'.[9]

The security forces' offensive against the Fada'i Organization in the autumn and winter of 1976 resulted in the killing of Saba Bijanzadeh and the creation of a new leadership council, composed of Qorbanali ʿAbdolrahimpour (Majid), Mohammad Reza Ghebra'i (Mansour) and Ahmad Gholamian Langaroudi (Hadi), which would remain in place until the end of the monarchical regime in February 1979. The first flyer to be published under the new leadership trio focused on the pressing matter of the housing crisis in the shantytowns which had emerged just outside the urban boundaries of Tehran due to the rapid rural to urban migration which was alluded to in the Fada'i flyer of December 1976. According to Majid, the reason behind this decision was that in the summer of that year, the peripheral areas of Tehran had been the location for persistent protests and rioting due to the municipality's decision to destroy their precarious abodes. The Organization found it therefore beneficial to establish ties with an element of society capable of putting into practice strong resistance against the monarchical regime.[10]

The title of this October 1977 communiqué was 'May the Right-seeking struggle of the Mass of Iranian Toilers Be Successful', with the following subtitle: '1.3 million family units are currently homeless in Iran. The dirty and anti-popular features of the government of the dictator Shah are once again exposed'.

The text starts by placing emphasis on current economic shortages:

The shortage and high prices of housing are on the rise. Bread and meat and rice are scarce. The injustices meted out by government officials are increasing. Water and electricity are rationed. Educational centres and schools refrain from accepting the enrolment of students, due to lack of space and resources. Hundreds of similar problems afflict our people ... But the housing issue is what worries our people more than anything else these days.

This communiqué then refers to the much-publicized case of Moharramʿali Kordlou, a shanty town dweller who lost his life whilst trying to block the gendarmes from destroying his home, by calling him a *shahid*, or 'martyr', and adds:

You must be aware that more than half of the income of the toiling people is directed towards housing rental ... Why is it the case that 1.33 million Iranian households do not own housing and suffer from the high cost of foodstuffs and clothing? The reason is that the dictator Shah is spending its revenue for the purchase of tanks, warships and the latest military aircraft. He spends it on American military officers and his gendarmes. He then claims in a presumptuous way to be defending Iran and its people from foreigners through such activities!

In the concluding part of this analysis, the Organization issues the following appeal to the population at large:

The Shah and his associates call us the revolutionary guerrillas, who are your sons and daughters and brothers and sisters and who struggle for the rights of the toiling masses, saboteurs, terrorists and agents of foreign countries. Yes, we are proud of being saboteurs. We are intent on sabotaging the edifices of injustice and cruelty. Once the toiling masses will get to know us and realise that we are the defenders of their freedom and rights, we will together form a formidable force which will destroy the castle of injustice of the Shah and those of the dependent entrepreneurs which surround him. We will in this way free the nation together from the yoke of the Pahlavi dynasty and foreign plunderers, especially the Americans.

This communiqué concludes by stating the aim of replacing the Pahlavi dynasty with a *hukumat-e khalqi*, or rule of the masses, a proposal which had not yet been raised by either the armed or unarmed opposition, either domestic or abroad, as the only way for achieving higher welfare and quality of life.[11]

The Goethe Nights: A wasted opportunity?

The October 1977 declaration marked an attempt to establish ties between the OIPFG and the deprived sections of the society. During the same period, however, the Fada'is were also seeking to strengthen their bond with the student movement as well. The text which was prepared for the traditional 16 Azar student commemoration of 1977 contained ample reference to the efforts and the importance of the student movement in furthering the resistance against the Shah's regime after the August 1953 coup against Mohammad Mossadeq. This analysis notes that, following the coup, 'the university environment, which was one of the meeting points for the militant elements of society, was assaulted [by the state security forces] … but the university resisted against the aggression of foreign enemies and their domestic lackeys like a formidable bastion'.[12] The judgement on the current state of the student organizations was not completely positive:

> In broad terms, the dissolution of political organizations and the lack of a structured organization in the years following the coup were conducive to the rebellious potential of students not being deployed in the appropriate manner. Student militancy, which was supposed to maintain its coordinating bonds with the rest of the popular forces, became scattered and was muted by the blows inflicted to it by the enemy.

The apparent lack of presence of security forces inside the university campuses and the creation of a student body link to the ruling Rastakhiz Party was considered by the Fada'is as a conspiracy ordained by the Shah's regime. It expressed the following desire in the same communiqué:

> We ask all alert and militant students across university campuses to be aware of the Shah's plots and expose the anti-student nature of his regime through continuous strikes and other protest initiatives. They should ask for a genuine student organization which will tend to the real demands of the students themselves.[13]

This analysis of the student movement was presented at a time when the political atmosphere inside the country was in the throes of major changes. The steady production of open letters by members of civil society and old-time political activists, which picked up pace after the inauguration of Jimmy Carter in the United States in January 1977 and his human rights agenda, yielded new opportunities for dissident political activities.

The most important event of this phase was the Ten Nights of Poetry which were organized by the Kanun-e Nevisandegan-e Iran (Writers Association of Iran) under the auspices of the Goethe Institute in Tehran between 10 and 20 October 1977.[14] This epochal event provided an opportunity for dissident intellectuals to resume their public activities around a decade after the end of the final vestiges of pluralism in the Iranian public scene. In a report published soon after the Nights, the British Embassy in Tehran noted how 'not once did below about 5,000 - all serious, intense people ... The week's proceedings were described to me by one sober, if sympathetic, lawyer, as the most significant political event in Iran this decade', before concluding that

> There is no doubt that the activities of the Writers' Association are now more widely known than they were, and that there will be pressures for further such gatherings both from those who saw the proceedings at the German Club principally as a means of furthering a political objective, and from the equally large numbers who seemed to be attending purely because they wished to enjoy a rare cultural treat.[15]

However, the Fada'i Organization did not show any overt sign of appreciation for the importance of the Goethe Nights. These took place a few months after the liberation from jail of a number of Fada'i cadres, in August 1977. One of these, Mehdi Fatapour, established ties with a broad range of left-wing activists soon after emerging from prison. He describes the prevailing atmosphere as follows:

> The scene was an open one. The Fada'i communiqués would reach the university environment. The banned Fada'i publications would be spread on university grounds for all to read. The works of Bijan Jazani or Touraj Heydari Bigvand [the theoretician of the Splitting Group from the OIPFG] would be lined up against the wall, page by page; students would take turns to look at each. This mechanism ensured a broad distribution of such literature.

Fatapour's assessment of the scene at the time also includes the observation that previous groups were more active after a long hiatus:

> The activities of Tudeh Party and other formations which repudiated armed struggle and were promoters of [exclusively] political activism had expanded. They were previously absent, but when I was released from prison, they were on campus. We were all together in the university environment, there were no [ideological] barricades between us.[16]

At least one of the speakers of the Goethe Nights, Sa'id Soltanpour, had a clear inclination towards the Fada'i Organization and benefitted from the determined support of Fada'i sympathizers. According to Mehdi Aslani, who at the time was a teenage supporter of the Organization, Soltanpour's presence resulted in a considerable amount of his like-minded peers to crowd the Goethe Institute premises on the rainy night in which he was scheduled to speak. 'Ali Mousavi Garmaroudi, a poet with known Islamic tendencies, was scheduled to speak immediately after Soltanpour, but the crowd began leaving the premises as he was about to take to the floor, despite the pleadings of the organizers, leaving Garmaroudi's demand to listen to the words of their 'Shi'a brother' unattended.[17] According to Aslani, the Ten Nights marked the first occasion that a sizeable group of his like-minded peers were able to congregate in one place and extend beyond the very small groups which gathered to read clandestine editions of classical Marxist or guerrilla literature. Another Fada'i cadre who had been recently freed from jail, Esfandiar Karimi, also noted how he took part in all the Ten Nights with a group composed of other Fada'is such as Qasem Seyyed-Baqeri and Mohsen Modir-Shanehchi.[18]

Despite this varied interest in the Goethe Institute's initiative, a clear divergence emerged between the Fada'i supporters and the leadership of the time. According to the available information collected by this author, the presence of the Fada'i leadership in the Ten Nights was very limited. Neither Fatapour nor another young intellectual connected to the Fada'is at the time, 'Ali Keshtgar, considered the Ten Nights as an event which would bring about a substantial change in the relationship between state and society. Both refrained from attending the poetry readings and considered them as an initiative which was directed from afar by the Carter administration.[19] This opinion stood in contrast with the one espoused by other elements of the Iranian Left of the time. The *Haqiqat* periodical, which was produced in Europe by the Ettehadiyeh-ye Komunistha-ye Iran, a Maoist formation, in the midst of a strong criticism of the literary quality of the content of most of the poetry readings stated the following:

> This initiative highlighted the readiness and interest of the people (and especially the intellectuals) to seek a change in the current *status quo*. ... They make use of every opportunity, however small, and of any [socio-political] movement, if the regime's label cannot be found on it, as an instrument to express their opposition.[20]

Another Maoist publication, *Setareh-ye Sorkh*, the organ of the Revolutionary Organization of the Tudeh Party, published several of the readings in a special insert devoted to the Ten Nights and noted in its editorial article that 'people from across Iran participated in the Ten Nights. Old and young, women and men, from different social classes', and added

> If the first nights witnessed the attendance of 2-3,000 people, the last nights featured crowds of 15,000 or more. These were people who stood under the rain for hours and listened and express judgement. ... The poetry and the revolutionary discourse was met with the strong acceptance by the masses, and in reality, the people were a few steps ahead of the overall direction of these poetry nights.[21]

The reports contained in *Haqiqat* and *Setareh-ye Sorkh* highlight the impact of the Ten Nights on some of the Leftist forces. Their positive assessment was grounded on the considerable presence of youth and students with a high potential for carrying the protest movement further. However, the Fada'i cadres did not have such a view. According to Fatapour, 'There was little belief [within the Organization] regarding the opening up of the political sphere [by the authorities]. We thought this was all about the regime priming up to engage in a new wave of repression. This negative sentiment was compounded by the suppression of the poetry nights at Aryamehr Technical University and the arrest of Behazin.'[22]

The Fada'is did not produce any communiqué related to the Ten Nights. The commotion caused by the same persuaded Majid to visit the Goethe Institute on one of the evenings, when he was handed over the leaflets and booklets which the Fada'i sympathizers had produced regarding his fallen comrades which were rapidly circulating amongst the crowd. However, this did not compel Majid to promote the preparation of a communiqué of the event. It did however result, according to 'Ali Keshtgar, in an increased presence in the university environment, and the Fada'is had a positive appraisal of the student resistance to the authorities following the cancellation of Mahmoud Etemadzadeh (Behazin)'s speech in late December and the subsequent end of open dissident activities.

In December 1977, the Fada'is decided once again to address the student supporter body on the occasion of the 16 Azar anniversary, which coincided with significant demonstrations on campuses such as the University of Tehran. The communiqué published on this occasion notes:

> The wave of the thousands-strong student protest, in which rage and hatred [towards the regime] were on full display, featured slogans such as 'Death to the Dictator', 'Toilers, be aware that your Shah is a traitor', reached the working-class areas [of the capital Tehran], which highlighted the popular and anti-dictatorial nature of the protest themselves. Along the route of the protest, the windows of banks (this centre of oppression of the masses) were smashed. The destruction of the windows of the Lufthansa office and the expulsion of the university security guards from campus dormitories showed that no symbol of dictatorship and the interests of imperialists is safe from retribution. The students also marked their ties with the oppressed masses of the [Middle Eastern] region through slogans such as 'Death to [Anwar] Sadat' and 'Long Live Palestine.'[23]

Step by step with the revolution: The communiqués of winter–spring 1977–8

The start of widespread unrest following the publication of the scurrilous article against Ayatollah Khomeini in *Ettela'at* newspaper published under the pen name Ahmad Rashidi-Motlaq on 7 January 1978 occurred at a time when the Fada'i Organization was in preservation mode, with a considerable amount of its cadres still serving long prison sentences.

The Fada'is' first declaration regarding the initial reaction to the *Ettela 'at* article came in the form of a long communiqué published on 8 February 1978, on the occasion of the seventh anniversary of the attack on the Siyahkal gendarmerie post. This publication accepted responsibility for the bombing of Rastakhiz Party bureau in Qom and a local police station in Tehran, and contained an initial reaction to the Qom protests of 9 January 1978 which marked the first instance of 'revolutionary violence' following the publication of the article in *Ettela 'at*:

> In the present situation in which the Shah's dictatorial regime deceives our people through a thousand methods and silences any freedom-seeking voice with leaden bullets, the cry of the struggling people of Qom against the dictatorship of the Shah and the cruelty of its agents is rising high. In this situation, which occurred at the same time as the trip of the gendarme of the region, the traitorous Mohammad Reza Shah, to Egypt, the dependent regime and its client newspapers (*Rastakhiz* and *Ettela'at*) attempted to stain the popular image of Ayatollah Khomeini through an article laden with lies and smear. This shameful act by the [monarchical] regime generated the ire of the toiling masses and the militant clerics.

The communiqué then delved into more detail regarding the Qom incident:

> On the day of 19 Dey [9 January 1978], the people of Qom gathered in large numbers in front of the residences of the *maraje'-ye taqlid*, or Shi'a Sources of Emulation. The newspapers associated to the regime are set in fire as a protest against the [Rashidi Motlaq] rants. The crowds swelled in size. Alleys and streets, bazar and mosques and schools are also drowning in activity. The wave of anger and hatred [against the regime] enveloped the city of Qom. Teeth are gritted together; clenched fists go up in the air and chants by freedom-seekers can be heard. The bloody uprising of 19 Dey gets under way.

After providing a running commentary of the unrest, which contains some degree of exaggeration on the number of the dead ('over 50 people were martyred'),[24] this concluding analysis states:

> The bloody repression of the struggling people of Qom has caused the wrath of the freedom-seekers of the country. The militant university students across the country, these aware and bold offspring of the nation, have engaged in protest and strikes across the country in solidarity with the struggles of the people of Qom. ... The toilers must be aware that your Shah is a murderer, Down with this fascist regime.

The Fada'is then make the point that 'The violent suppression of the 19 Dey protests once again highlight the fact that the fist [of the regime] must be answered with the fist, and the bullet with the bullet', prior to tracing a symbolic direct line between the Siyahkal uprising and the Qom protests in the concluding remarks.[25]

A few weeks later, the Fada'is reacted through two proclamations to the severe unrest of 29 Bahman (18 February 1978) in Tabriz, which occurred on the fortieth day mourning ceremonies for the Qom dead. The first of these declarations was published in March 1978, and stated:

> Yet again the people of Tabriz, whilst clenching their fists and shouting the 'Death to the Treacherous Shah' or 'Either Death or Freedom' slogan, proved that they are ready, as in their bright past, to valiantly struggle in the path of the freedom of the Iranian masses.

It then engages in a direct comparison between the 29 Bahman events and historical episodes and personalities of Tabriz:

> The people of Tabriz have achieved such an epic result in this bloody uprising and brought back their previous champions, such as Sattar Khan, Baqer Khan, Heydar Khan 'Amuoghli, 'Ali Monsieur and other freedom-seekers of the Constitutional Revolution into public opinion.[26]

The choice to focus on known local figures of the Mashrouteh era and avoiding making any mention of Fada'i or leftist activists who had fallen in the struggle against the Pahlavi state in previous years, such as Samad Behrangi, Behrouz Dehqani, 'Alireza Nabdel or Behrouz Armaghani is a curious and unexplained one.

As the revolutionary activity was picking up pace in spring 1978, the Fada'i Organization started a political process which aimed to align the movement with the outside developments. In the words of 'Abdolrahimpour:

> In March or April 1978, the senior members of the Fada'i Organization held a session chaired by Majid, with the participation of 'Alireza Akbari Shandiz (Javad), Mehdi Fatapour (Khosrow), Akbar Doustdar-Sanayeh, Rahim Asadollahi ('Ali) and others in order to discuss the new situation emerging inside the country. Majid proposed that the country had now reached the stage of the *sharayet-e 'ayni-ye enqelab*, or 'objective conditions of revolution', however this was not approved during the session. But, there was a consensus on the Organization engaging in a considerable expansion of its activities in line with the changing situation.[27]

The practical consequence of this decision can be observed within the contents of a pamphlet titled *Vazayef-e Asasi-ye Marksist-Leninistha*, or the 'Fundamental Duties of the Marxist-Leninists'. According to 'Abdolrahimpour, this booklet was prepared by Shandiz after long internal discussions in August 1978.[28] This analysis claimed, in clear Leninist fashion, that the situation at the time in Iran was fulfilling the conditions of *sharayet-e 'ayni-ye enqelab*:

> The revolutionary situation is dominant in our society. The extent of the crisis is such that the oppressed masses do not want to live in the previous conditions and demand the change of the latter. The oppressors cannot rule in the previous manner.

The existence of revolutionary conditions shows that whenever the revolutionary vanguard is imbued with necessary quality, the revolution may be kick-started, and the masses can be directed towards the final and decisive struggle.[29]

The analysis then focuses on the middle class:

> We support the struggle of the radical factions of the petit-bourgeoisie, who are represent the broadest interests of the national and anti-imperialist forces within our society. We consider this support in the interest of the working class and the liberation movement. The scattering of the national forces has weakened the unity of the people's forces in the united front [against the Shah's dictatorship] and reduces the power of the working class in during the people's' democratic revolution.[30]

Finally, considerations are made with regard to the current state of the Iranian proletariat:

> The proletariat cannot fulfil its real role within the popular struggle without a militant vanguard organization. ... However, in the current circumstances, there is a considerable distance between the workers' movement and the struggle of other anti-imperialist groups. From the imperialist coup of 28 Mordad [19 August 1953] onwards, we have been faced with the stagnation of the workers' movement, except for scattered exceptions.[31]

The *Vazayef-e Asasi* booklet clearly highlights the fact that the Fada'i Organization had reached the conclusion, by summer 1978, that the continuous protest against the Pahlavi state was a serious and consequential event and the likely epilogue to the objective conditions of revolution. However, this text did not go as far as labelling the Organization itself as the ideal vanguard formation of the working class. In a briefer follow-up which was published a few weeks later, the unity of the revolutionary front was emphasized through a set of recommendations, which included avoiding to commit the 'major mistake' of lacking to distinguish between the radical petit-bourgeousie and the liberal, non-radical one and calls for refraining to impose Marxism on the political formations of the radical petit-bourgeoisie, and criticized the limitation of the concept of *khalq* or masses exclusively to the working class and thereby ignoring the momentum and aspirations of the other 'progressive forces'.[32]

The early flames of victory: From summer to winter 1978

The intensification of the popular struggle against the Pahlavi state from mid-summer 1978 onwards had a significant effect on the OIPFG outlook. The Cinema Rex arson attack in Abadan on 19 August and the Black Friday violence of Jaleh Square in Tehran on 8 September were conducive to the Organization leadership reaching the conclusion that the popular protests had achieved a revolutionary character. The Fada'is released separate communiqués after each of these critical junctures of the Revolution. Regarding Cinema Rex, the Organization's analysis shared considerable similarity with the rest of the opposition, particularly the religious forces led by Khomeini, in defining the tragedy as a conspiracy ordained by the Shah's government:

> The savage killing in the Cinema Rex in Abadan occurred a single day after the press conference of the butcher Shah with his pliant journalists, during which he stated: 'We pledged the Great Civilisation to the people, and they promise the great horror in return'. This proves that the mercenary agents of the Security Organization (SAVAK) brought about this historic crime upon the orders of the bloodthirsty Shah and in order to prove his point right. They now attempt to pin the blame for this historic crime to these righteous sons of the nation in order to create negative sentiment against them within the toiling masses.[33]

The same communiqué makes a likely exaggerated mention of '122 soldiers who joined the ranks of the popular martyrs due to the refusal to take the orders of their mercenary commanders'.

Following the Jaleh Square massacre, the Fada'i Organization expressed its disgust at the mass killing and made the rather bold and unsubstantiated erroneous claim that '373 of our resistant and revolutionary compatriots' were killed on the streets of Tehran on 'Black Friday'. According to Fatapour, the Jaleh Square events marked a turning point in the Fada'i Organization's assumption of the ongoing political developments as a revolutionary process.

On 6 November 1978, a day in which particularly violent protests caused the resignation of the Sharif-Emami cabinet which had taken over from the previous Amouzegar one after Cinema Rex and resulted in the creation of the military government of Gholam-Reza Azhari, the press entered its famous sixty-two-day strike, and the hopes of the moderate, constitutionalist opposition for a negotiated settlement of the crisis diminished considerably. It was then that the Fada'i Organization produced one of the most important and known communiqués of the revolutionary period, entitled 'Let's Support the People in this Bloody Uprising'. This proclamation would later be referred through its last sentence, 'Qiyam ra Bavar Konim' (Let's Believe in the Uprising). This communiqué notes:

> In this current climax of revolutionary opportunity in which the entire Iranian nation is united, and is asking in unison for the overthrow of the Pahlavi dynasty, the Fada'i Organization requests all the strugglers for the path towards freedom to assist in the organization of popular resistance in the streets.

The communiqué then moves on to offer practical advice borne from its own experience:

> Gather groups of people and instruct them on patterns of confronting tear gas, escaping from enemy fire, fleeing from besieged areas and other tactics which will result in less innocent victims ... the weapons which are used by the Shah to kill people should be handed over to the same.[34]

The 'Qiyam ra Bavar Konim' communiqué had the effect of accelerating the process for the creation of an overt political organization, which was provisionally called Pishgam (Forerunner). According to Fatapour, who was the main figure behind the initiative, 'the purpose was for Pishgam to collect membership in the university and intellectual communities'.

The first members of Pishgam were supposed to be extract from a list of names comprising figures including Fada'is such as Mehdi Sameʿ and Mohsen Modir-Shanehchi, who were released from prison by January 1979, the prominent former Tudeh Kurdish personality Sarem Al-Din Sadeq-Vaziri, Reza ʿAllamehzadeh and ʿAbbas Samakar, the latter two being young artists who had been arrested alongside Keramat Daneshian in 1973, the aforementioned poet Saʿid Soltanpour, the prominent writer Ahmad Shamlou and the academic Saʿid Rahnema.[35]

Alongside the plans for establishing Pishgam, another overt element in the Fada'i strategies in winter 1978 consisted of the considerable activities of the families of the Fada'i fallen, who engaged in activities such as sit-ins at the judiciary and Bar Association, photographic exhibitions regarding their loved ones or visits to the newsrooms of major national publications in order to raise awareness for the Fada'i cause.[36] These activities also had the effect of ensuring a new income stream for the Organization, through a considerable amount of donations paid to the families themselves.

The rapid advance of the revolutionary movement in January and February 1979 compelled the Fada'i to come to terms with yet another sharp turn of events. The departure of the Shah on 16 January 1979 was the occasion of a long communiqué by the Fada'is, which was read out by Mehdi Sameʿ in the *Ettelaʿat* newsroom on the same day:

> The Shah has fallen. This is a very valuable victory for the [Iranian] people who for over half a century have been under the yoke of one the dirtiest contemporary dictators and were deprived of all human rights. But the evolution of events and the destiny of the revolutionary movement is of utmost importance. Will the people's revolution achieve its final objectives? Is it capable of neutralising those who want to compromise [with the Shah's regime] and the opportunists? Will it be able to stand up to plots organized by the imperialist powers to block the revolutionary process? Are the revolutionary movement's leaders and the political activists who have had a leading role in providing a direction to the popular activism ready to take stock of past bitter experience and continue with the struggle until the complete collapse of imperialist rule and the transfer of state power and authority to the deprived masses is completed? Or will the road be paved once again for the defeat of the masses through the actions of traitors?[37]

A few days later, the Fada'i Organization reacted with predictable wrath to the appointment of Shapour Bakhtiar's government. The last prime minister of the Shah was compared unfavourably to previous nationalist figures such as his mentor Mohammad Mossadeq, the former foreign minister Hossein Fatemi and the firebrand pro-Mossadeq journalist Karimpour Shirazi, who were labelled as 'righteous national and resistant figures'. Bakhtiar on the other hand was defined as a 'sell-out character, who had opportunistically positioned himself within the ranks of the people's movement [in the Mossadeq era]'.

The Fada'i Organization could not remain indifferent to the remarkable return of Ayatollah Khomeini to Iran on 1 February 1979. Two weeks prior to this epochal event, the Fada'is produced an open letter in which they addressed their concerns and grievances to the cleric for the first time.[38]

The letter focuses in detail on Khomeini's role in the revolutionary process since the aforementioned analysis of the early Qom uprising in January 1978. It says in this regard:

> Considering the sensitive role that you played in this round of the people's struggle, it is evident that each of your decisions and *fatwas* ... have an important effect on the increase or decrease of the contradictions within the people's resistance front, on the unity of the people, and ultimately in the emergence or decline of the chances for complete victory of our masses against imperialism and its agents.

The Organization also expressed its concerns over recent developments in other parts of this letter:

> We want to express with utmost clarity that this revolution and what brought people to the streets in unison and unity ... is the expansive economic, political and national injustice. The current struggle is a liberty-seeking and freedom-oriented one, it's an anti-dictatorial and anti-imperialist and patriotic one. ...
>
> The struggle that is taking place is for freedom and liberation. It is an anti-dictatorial, anti-imperialist and patriotic struggle ... Real freedom and democracy will be gained only after the overthrow of imperialism a reaction is the most revered aspiration that has united all social strata and classes of the people from workers and students to office workers, the clergy and farmers and has brought them to a struggle to death against the regime.
>
> True freedom and democracy, which will certainly be achieved following the final collapse of imperialism and reactionary rule, is the most coveted ideal which unites all the strata and classes of the masses/*khalq*, from workers and university students to office workers, clerics and peasants, and has dragged all of these to struggle until the brink of death against the [monarchical] regime.

The letter then uniquely engages in a warning regarding current developments:

> If your understanding of the Islamic Shari'a and the Islamic movement means persistence in the anti-imperialist and anti-dictatorial struggle, we admire such an understanding because this struggle and sacrifice has been the highest aspiration and hope of all Fada'i martyrs and comrades and has always been a part of their skin, flesh and blood. But if, on the contrary, the purpose of appealing to Islam and its teachings is tantamount with repressing of every opposing thought, form and opinion, the chaining of thought and revival of an inquisition and instruments of

repression, the revival of the slogan of 'only one party" and the muffling of every freedom-seeking voice under the pretext of defending the Koran and the Shari'a, we are certain every liberationist patriot will condemn it and we believe that the people also will rise to expose and destroy it because they see it as a ploy in the hands of imperialism and reaction.[39]

The letter then presciently warns of the lack of tolerance for political diversity which was emerging within the ranks of Khomeini's most loyal followers:

> In the past few months our people have witnessed the increasing involvement of elements attempting to disrupt and destroy street-corner bookstands, and who have attacked with clubs and knives the gatherings of teachers, students and workers in Tabriz and Behesht-e Zahra, who tear up the leaflets and publications of the most militant fighters against imperialism and the dictatorship, and who shamelessly brand as traitors the martyrs who, in the dark years of the dictatorship and repression under the whip of the executioner, the torture chambers of the SAVAK have greeted the moment of martyrdom with cries of 'Down to the Shah'. It is not of concern that such provocations provide imperialist circles with excuses to misrepresent our people's magnificent movement. It is not of concern that forces participating in the movement be described as opposed to the liberation of women and land reform ... let them say what they please. But when a holy man look-alike orders to tear pictures of martyrs Samad Behrangi and Behrouz Dehqani, real holy men and patriots will not remain silent. They expose the hand of the enemy of the people with all the might and will put him, with all his lowly stupidity, up for people's judgment.

It then urges Khomeini to

> let all the people of our country know that we call such elements reactionary and ignorant because of their acts an insistently demand all true militants and our people to reform or purge these elements from the ranks of the people's movement. These elements are either those whose obscurantism and ignorance has denied them truth-reflecting eyes and need guidance, or they are a handful of the elements of reaction and afraid of people's victory inciting disorder and conspiring behind the cover of the Quran.

The Fada'i Organization also issued one of the earliest warnings regarding the extent of physical disruption of the activities of secular activists by religious ones:

> It is seen and heard that from time-to-time elements chanting 'the only party is Allah's party' attack people, passers-by, shops and public places, bookstores, freedom-loving speakers or popular gatherings and think they can impose their opinions and thoughts, their lifestyle and demeanour on everything and everyone.... we do not see any trace of progressiveness in these abominable actions. These elements should realize that our people, after 25 years of repression and coercion, have only

today found an opportunity and want to choose their own lifestyle. They should decide themselves about what to read, wear, say and believe..[40]

8–10 February 1979: The first public meeting and rally of the Iranian Left after the August 1953 coup.

The Fada'i Organization's attempts to create a separate and autonomous presence within the massive crowds which thronged the streets of Tehran on 1 February 1979, the day of Khomeini's return to Iran, bore little fruit. According to Mehdi Same', approximately 600 to 1,000 Fada'i sympathizers gathered in Navvab Street in central Tehran but were 'devoured' by the considerably larger crowd of generic Khomeini backers.[41] The increasingly overt activities of the Fada'i Organization and other elements of the Left remained concentrated on the campus of the University of Tehran. Alongside the rising revolutionary tide, the month of February held special significance for the Fada'i supporters, as it marked the anniversary of the Siyahkal episode of 19 Bahman [8 February]. On 7 February, the major national newspapers published special reports on Siyahkal which for the first time were bereft of government censorship and contained an extensive account of the lives and times of the Fada'i militants who took part in the operation. *Ettela 'at* newspaper published its own report on 7 February, and *Keyhan* and *Ayandegan* the following day.

On 8 February, the Fada'i Organization finally emerged to hold an overt event and openly engage with its broader support base for the first time ever. The sports field of the University of Tehran campus was host to the first-ever Fada'i public meeting.[42]

This event was managed by a restricted group of Fada'is who had returned to public life after their release from jail, such as Mehdi Same', Esfandiar Karimi, Qasem Seyyed-Baqeri, Hassan Arabzadeh and Mohsen Modir-Shanehchi and had been advertised in previous days via handwritten tracts distributed on campus.[43] However, the decision to hold a large rally in support of the new Provisional Revolutionary Government of Mehdi Bazargan on the same day persuaded the organizers to postpone the rally to two days later and hold a gathering within the university grounds instead. According to a report in the *Ayandegan* daily:

> A minibus was stationed by the [pro-Bazargan] rally's public order committee in front of the main entrance of the University of Tehran alongside the route of the rally and was frequently reminding the passers-by that 'the clergy are not holding any rallies inside the University of Tehran today'.[44]

The meeting on the sports field took place with a few thousand people attending despite this attempt to dissuade participation. It featured messages in support of the Fada'is by other sympathetic groups such as the Mojahedin-e Khalq, the Chit-Sazi (textile) workers of Tehran, representatives of Tehran truck drivers, of peasants from Karaj and of George Habash, the leader of the Popular Front for the Liberation of Palestine. Additionally, the resolution of the rally, which will be discussed below, was read out to the crowd by Mehdi Same'.

The first programmatic statement of the Fada'is

The first public appearance of the Fada'is on the grounds of the University of Tehran occurred at a time in which some of the cadres, like Farrokh Negahdar, Behrouz Khaliq and Jamshid Taheripour were still operating from within safehouses and were debating the future attitude and posture of the Fada'i Organization. The first inkling of such positions came through the document read out by Mehdi Same' in the 19 Bahman meeting, which contained the first programmatic statement of the Fada'is regarding the political path ahead.

In the latter part of January, Taheripour, who had been recently released from prison and was staying at a safehouse in the Shahr-e Rey area which was supervised by Nahid Qajar (Mehrnoush), was told to prepare the basic political programme of the Fada'i Organization and its proposals for the incoming revolutionary administration. The Fada'is were hitherto lacking such a document.[45] Nahid Qajar secured some of the writings which were circulating at the time, including those produced by European and Latin American Leftist groups, and one by the Tudeh Party of Iran. Taheripour handed his draft over to the Fada'i leadership by the end of January. Majid 'Abdolrahimpour and Farrokh Negahdar henceforth proceeded with amending parts of this programme and the edited document was forwarded on for publication.[46] The introductory part of this document confirms that the same was produced prior to the revolutionary finale of mid-February 1979. This programme does away with the previous critical stance towards Ayatollah Khomeini and his followers and instead states the following:

> In this glorious revolution of our masses, the righteous struggles and decisions of Ayatollah Khomeini in order to bring about the collapse of the monarchical system and the struggle against imperialism and its domestic lackeys are supported [by the Fada'i Organization] and we support his actions with all our forces.

Other demands made by the Fada'is in this text consisted of the dissolution of both Majles and Senate, the national army and other Pahlavi state institutions as well as the complete abolition of all anti-labour and anti-democratic laws. This programme also called for the Revolutionary council, which was tasked to form the provisional government, to include a broad range of representatives from within strike councils and other bodies which emerged from within society during the revolutionary upheaval. The council should furthermore be formed, according to this text, by representatives of urban and rural workers, white collar employees as well as intellectuals, clerics and merchants.[47]

The full publication of this programme on the first two pages of the 14 February 1979 edition of *Keyhan*, which followed its initial reading at the rally by Same', ensured that the same was read by a broad stratum of society at a time when other progressive groups, such as the Tudeh Party of Iran, the Mojahedin-e Khalq Organization and more had yet to formulate their own demands or programmatic statements with regards to the nature and aims of the future political system of Iran.

The start of a new phase: The technical faculty becomes the 'Meeting Place' for Fada'i members and sympathizers

The 8 February meeting on the campus of the University of Tehran marked the start of a new phase in the history of the Fada'i Organization. Two days later, a large rally featuring thousands of Fada'i supporters marched from the campus of Tehran University towards the eastern part of the capital, amid slogans such as 'We will convert the whole of Iran to Siyahkal', but the demonstration was cut short at Ferdowsi Square by news that the Homafaran air force officers had rebelled in the Eshrat-Abad garrison. The Fada'is asked all participants to head off to support the Homafaran. The last important phase of the final battle against the Shah's forces, the takeover of the radio building in Arg Square in central Tehran on the afternoon of 11 February was led by Qasem Siadati, a senior cadre who was killed in action.[48] At dusk of that fateful day, when the army had declared its neutrality and the last prime minister of the Shah Shapour Bakhtiar had fled from his office, the Technical Faculty at the University of Tehran came under the complete control of the Fada'is and their sympathizers. According to Esfandiar Karimi, the faculty was in Fada'i hands by the evening. Mehdi Same', who was also there, recalls that its halls were quiet that night, populated as they were by a few Fada'is who had turned up to deliver arms which had been seized across town.[49]

The Leadership Council member 'Abdolrahimpour reached the faculty on the morning of 12 February. He was initially prevented from reaching his comrades by the security team set up by Fada'i sympathizers, who had no way to identify one of their leaders due to Majid's persistently clandestine lifestyle until the previous day. He finally managed to clear security after showing a grenade he had been carrying, which had the Fada'i Organization's full title painted on it.[50]

The Fada'is produced two declarations between 11 and 12 February, both of which were broadcast by Radio Tehran, which was now using the callsign 'Voice of the Revolution'. The first proclamation of the takeover of police stations, military bases and the radio-television buildings was termed the 'greatest and most definitive victory of our heroic people ever'. The declaration then referred to 'militancy alongside the brave and heroic *homafaran*' as the Organization's greatest achievement and emphasized that the 'blood of Fada'i comrades' had been spilt in the final days of the revolution. In the final invocations, this declaration praised the sacrifice of workers, soldiers and *homafaran* whose combined efforts had neutralized the Shah's army and singled out Ayatollah Khomeini, Ayatollah Taleqani and the Mojahedin-e Khalq as the true vanguards of the revolution.[51]

The second message which was broadcast on the morning of 12 February contained practical instructions for the Fada'i sympathizers. The Organization asked the latter to 'exercise vigilance until the complete takeover of all the holdings of the enemy of the masses [the *ancien regime*] and the neutralisation of all the plots by the mercenaries'. This declaration also noted the first-ever creation of local headquarters for the OIPFG: 'The committees for coordination and communication [with society] are imbued with full authority' in all towns and villages. This development underscored the Fada'i Organization's intention to move over to the overt phase of its existence in a swift manner. Furthermore, the declaration noted the need for revolutionary masses to engage in military training in order to face off the counter-revolutionary forces. The declaration also calls upon people to avoid and prevent 'any type of destruction of private or government installations and property',[52] so that 'all national wealth be concentrated in people's hands in the future'.

The third and last Fada'i declaration to be read out over the radio contained a brief but very significant point: 'The People's Fada'i Guerrilla Organization of Iran announces to all militant comrades that the location for gathering and coordination of Fada'i comrades is the Technical Faculty of the University of Tehran.'[53] Following this announcement, a steady stream of Fada'i supporters and cadres made their way to the faculty and the overt phase in the existence of the Fada'i Organization finally got under way.

13

Poetry praising passion

Saeed Yousef

Siyahkal and poetry

Undoubtedly there will be some who would question the justification for having a chapter in a book like this on how a certain mode of struggle was reflected in poetry. Well, this can be attributed to their insufficient knowledge – not of a certain political movement, but of Persian poetry.

We might come closer to some sort of answer by asking another question: Will it be necessary to refer to the armed guerrilla struggle under the Shah in a book about Persian poetry? Our answer to this question cannot be a simple 'No!', because we should first know the answer to a complementary counter-question: How many pages is this book supposed to have and what periods of Persian poetry are to be covered?

Once this complementary question is posed, those familiar with Persian poetry already have their answer: they know that it is impossible to analyse Persian poetry of certain years (from late 1960s to at least the end of the 1970s) without considering the armed struggle and its impact, whether you like it or not, whether you find it positive or have a negative and critical approach to it. In other words, when discussing contemporary Persian poetry, one cannot ignore and skip the 1970s and jump from the poetry of the 1960s – years of proliferation of modern Persian poetry – to the 1980s and 1990s.

But what kind of poetry do we have in the 1970s? And what does this poetry have that justifies regarding it as some distinct 'period' in poetry? For it seems that ever since the constitutional revolution of 1906 we have had some sort of 'political' verse, with some ups and downs, labelled variously as poetry of *enqelab* (revolution), *moqavemat* (resistence), *ekhtenaq* (oppression); or called *mote'ahhed* (committed), *mas'ul* (responsible), *ejtemai* (social), *mardomi* (popular/people's), *siyasi* (political), *zir-zamini* (underground) or *ziraksi* (xeroxed).[1] Is the addition of the label *cheriki* (guerrilla) to that list in the 1970s enough to justify considering this period a distinct period in Persian poetry?

* * *

The armed struggle against the Shah's dictatorship – which started as sporadic acts from the mid-1960s and became a more organized movement after the Siyahkal event and in the years leading to the 1979 Revolution – was a movement that rose among and was nourished by intellectuals; the Guevara-esque kind of revolutionary romanticism that characterized this movement contributed to the poets becoming its ardent supporters.

The first generation of the Fada'is consisted predominantly of well-read intellectuals who mostly wrote and published as well. Among the Fada'i guerrillas who were executed or perished in armed clashes, there were some like Amir-Parviz Pouyan, Behrouz Dehqani, 'Alireza Nabdel and Mostafa Sho'aiyan who were published writers and each had many friends among other writers. For instance, Pouyan alone was a close friend of Esma'il Khoi, Ne'mat Mirza-zadeh, Mohammad-Reza Shafiei-Kadkani, Sa'id Soltanpour, Hormoz Riyahi, 'Ali Tolu', Asghar Elahi, Niyaz Ya'qub-shahi and many others. There were also published poets and writers among those also who spent time in prison for having either had contacts with Fada'i members or simply been sympathizers, like Sa'id Soltanpour, 'Ali-Ashraf Darvishiyan, Ne'mat Mirza-zadeh and Saeed Yousef, just to name a few. This can explain the wide support the armed movement enjoyed among the poets, writers and intellectuals in general. And that is how the poetry of this period became a predominantly political poetry that either directly and frankly (in underground poetry) or indirectly – using a symbolic, coded language – supported this movement and eulogized its heroes.

As it can be expected, this political tendency in poetry – though predominant – was not shared by all poets and critics. There were some who did not favour this trend, and they became especially vocal after this period had come to an end. They can be divided in three groups. The problem starts in fact as soon as one says that the poetry of this period was predominantly *political*:

1. There are some who say that all poetry is political; is there any poetry that isn't?[2] What is then so special about those years to make them a distinct period in Persian poetry?
2. On the contrary, some believe that 'political poetry' is a misnomer and there is no such thing; they say we only have good and bad poetry, and good poetry should stay clear of politics.[3]
3. And, finally, there are those who have political/ideological problems with this poetry – that is to say, they don't approve of the poet's views.[4]

This article, which is an attempt to explain the poetry of those years, would naturally not have enough space to deal with the above questions in detail, but I hope that the reader might find some sort of answer here all the same.

The Siyahkal event did not suddenly pop up out of nowhere, and such events as Bahman Qashqai's insurgency in the province Fars (1964) or Esma'il Sharifzadeh and Molla Avareh's in Kurdistan (1968) should be considered as the first premonitions of the political mindset of the intellectuals who regarded themselves as the vanguards of the masses. In the same way, the poetry written in the years following Siyahkal in praise of that movement had its precursors in the years before that event. Before Siyahkal, however, both such insurgencies and the poems were like scattered, short-lived sparks. There were poems inspired by international events or heroes with the intention of using these as symbols to indirectly show the need for similar acts or heroes in Iran – poems supporting the cause of Palestine, for instance, or the Cuban Revolution and the liberation wars in Algeria or Vietnam; poems in praise of international revolutionary heroes such as Che Guevara, Djamila Boupacha and Patrice Lumumba.

Calls for or praise of insurgency can be seen already in the poetry of the Constitutional Revolution (Mirzadeh Eshqi: 'I am not one who would die a natural death/ and waste this bowl of blood in a comfortable bed'), but these fade away later under Reza Shah, coming back to life after he is deposed (Fereydun Tavallali: 'The trumpet of the revolution/ resounding vigorously/ comes/ to ears/ from spots far-away'), then becoming scarce once again, until we finally arrive at the years close to Siyahkal. In the 1960s, such poems were mostly about international events (Cuba and Latin America, Palestine, Vietnam…) – events that inspired and influenced the political movement also – or dealt with certain domestic events like Shah's Coronation (1967), or the 2,500-Year Celebration of Persian Empire (1971) and so on.

On the 'political verse' front, apart from Siyavash Kasrai (of Tudeh Party) who still had a strong presence, some younger poets had started to appear, like Ne'mat Mirza-zadeh (pen name M. Azarm, with poems like 'Night-singing' and 'Exegesis'), Esmaʿil Khoi (with poems like 'Along the Khaki Street' and 'The North Too'), Mohammad-Reza Shafiei-Kadkani (whose poem 'Hallaj' was popular), Saʿid Soltanpour (with poems like 'My Iran'), Hamid Mosaddeq (with his 'Qasida of Blue, Grey, Black' which has the famous lines 'If I sit down,/ if you sit down,/ who is then to rise …') and Khosrow Golesorkhi. In the last years of this decade we have still younger voices who had just started to publish, like Mohammad Amini ('M. Rama'), ʿAlireza Nabdel ('Okhtay'), Niyaz Yaʿqub-shahi, Mansour Khaksar and Saeed Yousef.

This is not to say that committed or political poets were limited to those mentioned above; I only named some who were writing more daring poems, using a more direct language, without always caring for getting printed or minding their 'bond' with 'leaden types'.[5] Otherwise, how would it be possible not to mention poets like Shamlou and many others? It is, for instance, in those years that Mohammad-Ali Sepanlu depicts the milieu of Iranian intellectuals against the backdrop of a world sunk into wars and revolutions ('Amid piles of smoke in vague cafés/ we drink a cup of tea/ and the radio brings the news of a revolution/ in a far-away horizon/ following a hail of bullets') and asks, 'What is the national anthem in the country of slaves?' He views the poet as a 'battlefield reporter'.[6]

The poem 'Another Vietnam' by Siyavash Kasrai, written for Che Guevara (as even the title makes it clear) and published in *Khanegi* (a collection of his poems, 1967), can serve as an example here – a poem already heralding guerrilla warfare, a poem in praise of 'a man and a gun/ a man and a backpack of bread and pride:'

> Despite all those weapons,
> despite all that fatigue,
> all those bullets that riddled your body,
> Ernesto!
> your death was again a lie.
> Those who are in such a hurry to bury you,
> those who clean their hands with the corners of your banner,
> exclaiming: 'It's all over now, everything as we wished' –

they are cowardly, ill-starred criminals
they are ignorant morons. [...]

And this is only one example, by a 'Tudeh poet' who should normally not support violent methods – but one should not forget that in those years even some Tudeh members were beginning to favour armed struggle in Iran, although the majority were against it.[7]

Shafiei-Kadkani is the first scholar to recognize Siyahkal as a start or turning point, first in his academic teachings and later in the book *Advar-e She'r-e Farsi* ('*Periods of Persian Poetry*'). In an attempt to periodize the contemporary Persian poetry, he considers the Siyahkal event (late 1349 = February 1971) the starting point of a new period. He rightly mentions that the armed struggle that began in Siyahkal (by Fada'is, later joined by Mojahedin) 'changed the meaning of struggle and the social attitude of the younger generation, which constitutes the majority of our society'.[8] This approach could naturally not be shared by the Islamic government, which preferred to minimize (or rather erase from memories) the role of the leftist groups in the years before the revolution. Ironically, it was first someone from the ranks of the Tudeh Party who challenged the validity of Shafiei-Kadkani's periodization.[9]

The section or 'period' devoted to Siyahkal in Shafiei-Kadkani's book hardly exceeded a few paragraphs (while citing a few lines from poems[10]). And since the appearance of this book, no serious attempt has been made to explore the poetry of this period except my book (*Now'i az Naqd...*[11]) that appeared in 1987 and has remained ever since the main source on the subject, often quoted by other researchers.[12] A shorter version of this, of course, had appeared in February 1982 in *Kar* (official organ of the 'Minority' Fadai's, special issue for Siyahkal). And, just for the record, that was in turn an expanded version of what was to appear in *Kar* in 1980 – that is before the 'Minority/Majority' split[13] – but was not published, apparently because it was not in line with the policies of the Organization.

* * *

Debates over 'committed art' and 'art for art's sake' among critics were no novelty, but they became especially heated from the early 1960s in literary journals and magazines and, just as in politics, here more radical trends were becoming dominant – which in turn influenced poets and their poetry also. The young revolutionary generation had even started to regard some outspoken, committed writers like Jalal Al-e Ahmad as more or less 'safety valves' of the regime; this generation seemed to believe in underground literature only. Committed poets like Shamlou were discovering in events like 'Khusheh Poetry Nights'[14] that they were no more radical enough for a young audience. In the *Khusheh* event, Sa'id Soltanpour, a younger poet with fiery poems, stole the show from the organizers and got the loudest applaud – something that both worried and infuriated poets like Shamlou and Baraheni, causing them to react in the weekly Ferdowsi (and later in the foreword of the anthology published on the occasion), condemning *sho'ar* or 'slogans' and cautioning the readers, albeit without mentioning Soltanpour's name, 'not to count the *slogans* uttered on one of these evenings as *poetry*'.[15]

This kind of approach that contrasts *slogan* with *poetry* was challenged by other critics. In 1969, Mohammad Azimi, who was in charge of the poetry section in the periodical *Jahan-e Now*, wrote in an article:

> The *poetry* vs. *slogan* debates have become vulgarized now, because in Iran's literary milieu the distinction between the two has become more or less clear, but the applicability of the terms in each particular case is subject of dispute. Let us not forget that many of the 'slogans' can be preferred to some of the 'poems'.[16]

In the next issue of *Jahan-e Now* – in which there is a poem by me also, as well as one by Mohammad Mokhtari – Mostafa Rahimi writes:

> It's not clear who first started to circulate this wrong thesis that poetry and slogan belong to two different worlds – not to mention the fact that, to quote Siyavash Kasrai, some of these [critics] forget to attack the negative slogans also: they point their swords to positive slogans only.[17]

It is interesting that this same issue has a review of Ja'far Kushabadi's collection of poems *Saz-e Digar*, in which Shafiei-Kadkani writes that 'this directness, in almost all cases, is an enemy of beauty'.[18]

Whether these were good or bad poems is not the point here, but one thing that even the critics of directly political poems have to admit is their influence and their ability to become widespread. Faramarz Soleimani writes about the years close to Siyahkal:

> It was during these years that banned books and those with no distribution permit secretly circulated and went from hand to hand, books like *Sohuri* by Ne'mat Mirzazadeh, *Sedaye Mira* by Sa'id Soltanpour, and Golesorkhi's poems, were distributed in great numbers. These poems, which looked more like political articles, were able to exert immense influence.[19]

The poets who were seen, rightly or wrongly, as having some distance from 'committed political poetry' were either followers of the 'new wave' in poetry and Yadollah Ro'yai's 'spacementalist' school (labelled as 'formalists' by the committed front, with some wrong understanding of 'formalism'[20]) or they were poets like Mehdi Akhavan Sales (M. Omid) known as 'pessimist' poets or poets of defeat. In the book *A Sort of Criticism of a Sort of Poetry* I had written:

> One of the important consequences of the poetry of this period was that both the formalists and the defeatists were forced to either shake themselves up and align themselves with the new trend or to declare bankruptcy and close their shop. The majority of them chose the second option. ... Even [Sohrab] Sepehri, the only representative of the 'new mysticism' trend in contemporary poetry, almost stops writing poems from around the same years.[21]

It is interesting that Esma'il Nouri-'Ala, one of the founders of the 'new wave' trend, also says the same thing in his *Theory of Poetry*, only put differently and with some sort of regret:

> The 1970s, too, could have been a flower-bed for the growth of dozens of fresh and promising talents in contemporary Persian poetry, and the genuine 'new poetry' trend could have reached its full bloom. But our historical destiny wanted it otherwise. Very soon the shah's rabid government closed *Ferdowsi* and some other magazines, [the secret police] SAVAK started to kill poets, the Intelligence Ministry made a list of banned writers, and the so-called all-encompassing party Rastakhiz decided to go the whole hog. There was an atmosphere that everything was moving fast towards absolutism. Most of the poets of the 'poetry workshop' either joined underground political organizations or drowned themselves in drugs. And I was witnessing with regret the annihilation of a young generation in which I had invested so much hope.[22]

The point is that if a poet chose in that particular period not to align himself with the needs of the majority of his audience (in the case of modern poetry, an audience consisting of college students and young intellectuals), if he chose not to write 'the poetry of his own time', he would have alienated himself from his audience and had no use any more. Therefore, if someone like Nouri-'Ala feels 'regret-stricken' (asaf-zadeh), is he feeling sorry for this simple rule of the relation between a poet and his audience or for the course of events that was taking the society in that certain direction?

Not unrelated to commitment becoming increasingly widespread, one can observe a change also in how meaning was to be understood. It seemed as if for being considered a committed poet it was no more enough to be against tyranny and to uphold the cause of the people, but the poet had to demonstrate in his poems (if not directly, at least by using symbols and codes) that he supported the armed struggle – what can be understood as a change in value criteria (or 'tahavvol-e me'yar-e arzesh-ha', to use Shafiei-Kadkani's expression[23]). And that is how even in a poet like Siyavash Kasrai, who had been an uncompromisingly committed poet even before Siyahkal, we observe a new development in those years. And perhaps this kind of change that starts with Siyahkal is easier to observe in the poetry of Kasrai than in poets like Sa'id Soltanpour.

In 1976, Tudeh Party published a collection of poems in Europe, titled *Red Like Fire, Tasting Like Smoke* by a certain Shaban Bozorg-Omid, a pseudonym under which Siyavash Kasrai had hidden his identity. Both the poems in this collection and the preface written by Ehsan Tabari can serve as the best proofs of Siyahkal's influence. According to Tabari, the first two poems in this collection ('lah-lah va tanaffos' and 'Degar Be Jukhe-ye Atash Nemi-dahand Ta'am', both written apparently before Siyahkal) demonstrated the poet's disillusionment: 'In this collection, the first two pieces reflect those spiritual moments in the poet when he was suffering from the apparent lethargy in the society.'[24] Then Tabari refers to some change in the poet and his poems and since, as a major leader of the Tudeh Party, he can't possibly approve of armed struggle, he has to write about the poet's 'change of mood' with an understanding but not quite happy fatherly tone, using some the poet's images:

The Siyahkal clashes and the fearless confrontation of some young people with the blood-thirsty wolf of tyranny lash out at the disillusionment that was caused by impatience .... The onslaught of spring on scorched lands immensely moves the poet and fills him with joy. Now there is a new turning point here .... He is no more a night-stricken meteor or a coffin buried in the dark, but rather he sees people who owe nothing to death. Hopelessness and tiredness cause him to set his heart on some sort of 'revolutionary romanticism' without giving a serious thought to its 'philosophy'. He talks with ecstasy and amazement of 'fighting to the last bullet and dying with one's last bullet.' The excitement and hope of change and its burning craving leave no room for political deliberations in the young and passionate poet. Would the method chosen by these brave people be capable of breaking open the dark ramparts? He is merely mesmerized by the courage of the young heroes who enter an unequal battle against a dragon with seven heads, armed with nothing but the magical gems of their hearts, and he feels rejoice and is surprised to see how flowers of fire blossom in the shadows of a bleak house and wonders how these self-sacrificing heroes could be raised in this 'orbit of darkness':

Say, Mother! Down in this broken house,
How can flowers of fire
Blossom in the garden of your lap?
By which leopardess were raised
These brother and sister of mine?[25]

This 'change' ('*tahavvol*') starts in fact, most directly and powerfully, with the third poem. In the previous poem, the poet was saying ironically:

They no more feed the fire squad
Nor put a blood bud on anyone's chest;
The martyr dies blue in our country.[26]

But now, referring to the '15 Siyahkal martyrs' and blaming his own previous ignorance, he says (using a woman singing a lullaby as the speaker):

O my dear, my desert flower!
O fiery poppy of many petals!
O blessed bloodied fifteen petals
Blown away from the crown of this young stem!
I nourish you in my garden of memories
I plant the scent of your hopes
In my heart, this red ceramic.
I carve your blessed white name
On the old tree of Esfand on New Year's Eve[27]
O Siyahkal, fallen so young!
I said they no more kill anyone
I said they no more take anyone

> To the fire squads
> I said the color of martyrs of love is blue
> And I was ignorant, Comrade!
> May your sad glance forgive me and my nonsense.[28]

This kind of 'blaming oneself' can be seen in other poets also – for instance, in the poem 'In the Mirror' by Esma'il Khoi ('Lies had deceived me to the extent that/ I could no more believe/ even the mirror of dawn ...'[29]) or in 'Confession' by Shafiei-Kadkani, a poem written after Khosrow Golesorkhi's arrest:

> Living thus, with no trust in sunshine
> Living thus, with no trust in soil and water
> [...]
> In an alley, where you can admit
> The purity of fellow-travelers
> Only
> At the moment of the leaden bullets
> At the height of fury
> And that – with tears
> In the corners of your eyes.[30]

But we are not finished yet with Kasrai and his book *Red Like Fire, Tasting Like Smoke*. In another poem – both the date (Khordad 1350 = 22 May–21 June 1971) and the name of this poem ('Pouyandegan' = 'farers' or 'seekers') betraying that it was written for Pouyan[31] and his fellow-combatants – the poet says with admiration and awe:

> They owe nothing to death:
> They, who drank the whole life in one gulp
> They, who drove away fear
> Behind the frontiers of time.
> They hoisted [their own] names
> Atop the roofs of daring
> They fought
> To the last bullet
> They died
> With their own last bullet.
> Yes, they owe nothing to death –
> They, the lovers of our age
> Farers of treacherous, hopeless paths...[32]

And there is no need to cite more examples from this book, which includes many.

By giving examples from poets who were not specifically 'Siyahkal poets' or 'Fadai poets', I am trying to better demonstrate how widespread and all-encompassing the influence of Siyahkal was.

* * *

In *A Sort of Criticism of a Sort of Poetry*, Shamlou's poetry is analysed in detail to show how it changes after Siyahkal – changes evident not just in mood but also in language and choice of words, apart from poems that have clear references to Siyahkal, using the symbols and codes common in those years. As in the long poem *Ziyafat* (Feast, 1971), which first appeared in the collection *Deshneh dar Dis* (*Dagger on the Plate*, 1977), and in later reprints after the revolution Shamlou made it clear that it had been written for 'the epic of Siyahkal forests', and the following lines are from that poem:

> Men descend
> from green trail.
> They bring love
> as moss
> – inseparable from rocks –
> on their bodies
> and wounds on their chests.[33]

Or see his poem 'Hejrani' ('Che hangam mi-ziste'am...') written in exile, in which he talks about 'the roaring of tigers in Deylaman [= Siyahkal]' and considers bonds with his homeland and its ongoing struggle a necessary condition of his own being:

> Let me feel the soil of homeland
> under my feet
> and hear my own growth:
> beatings of blood's drums
> in Chitgar[34]
> and roarings of impassioned tigers
> in Deylaman.
> Or else, when have I been living
> which unbroken string of days and nights?[35]

The influence of Siyahkal can be observed in almost all poets. As we saw, in the poem by Kasrai the name Siyahkal was directly mentioned (in an underground poem, of course, that was not meant to be published inside Iran, nor could it have been with that harsh censorship), while Shamlou was using the name Deylaman (though in poem written in exile), and in the poems written by other poets around that time we have words that function as symbols and codes for Siyahkal. Suddenly the word *jangal* (forest) becomes a code name for Siyahkal, as well as *bahr-e khazar* (the Caspian) and anything that could be associated with the location and surroundings of Siyahkal. For this reason, when analysing the poems written in those years, it is necessary to find the exact dates when the poem was written in order to be able to decode the hidden messages; even the numbers play a role here, like the number 15 in the poem by Kasrai that was cited earlier – a reference to the 15 Siahkal guerrillas fallen in battle or executed – or numbers that refer to years and dates.

Shafiei-Kadkani mentions *darya* (sea), *mowj* (wave), *sakhreh* (rock), *bisheh* (thicket), *arghavan* (Judas-tree), *shaqayeq* (poppy), *setare-ye qermez* (red star), *tufan* (storm), *tofang* (gun), *enfejar* (explosion), *dar ham shekastan* (breaking down), and the like, as the 'building blocks of the poetic images of this period',[36] which should be seen as a change in the poetic language of this period (at least in choice of words); what is more important, however, is the change in symbols and codes in Persian modern poetry, a poetry whose dominant school bore the label of 'social symbolist'. This meant giving new meanings/significations (absent before Siyahkal) to words that appeared to be the same 'signifiers'.

The first underground poem that began to circulate immediately after Siyahkal and the March 1971 executions was a very passionate one whose poet was never known, and it started like this:

> Whoever said, 'All movement
> died in this dark, silent land!,'
> must be ashamed of himself.
> Cry, O Caspian!
> Tear your garment [in mourning], O red forest of Gilan!
> Slash your heart, O hard peak of Elburz![37]

And soon we see an outburst of such sympathies, praises and mourning in poems written by other poets. Shafiei-Kadkani speaks of 'the strong buds of the silent forest'[38] and of 'wave after wave of the Caspian' all 'wearing black in mourning'.[39] Sa'id Soltanpour stays 'with bloodied mane/ in the thickets of anger'[40] and tells of 'the nightmare of blood and anger and street'.[41] Khosrow Golesorkhi says, 'The enemy's deep, deadly wound/ marked your chest/ but you/ O standing cypress tree/ did not fall/ you always die standing,' and 'your name is Iran's flag/ the Caspian lives on through your name.'[42] And 'Ali Mir-Fetros addresses the 'red spirit of the wakeful forest' which is blowing 'from the wounded Siyahkal' and 'through the nearby woods'.[43] And so many others. Some of these poems remained sealed in drawers until after the revolution, as it must have been the case with this poem by Houshang Ebtehaj [Sayeh], a once Tudeh poet who after the 1953 coup devoted himself to lyrical ghazals and songs for the official radio. However, he suddenly writes 'Marsiye-ye jangal' ('The elegy of forest') in March/April 1971 – to be published in 1981:

> O forest, O wrath!
> Aflame like the lightning with shredded garment!
> Tell me of the story of that massive white poplar
> that fell, like a piece of sky, with the cry of thunder.[44]

Another change that is observed in many of the poems of this period is a change in atmosphere in the sense of the setting and location: the atmosphere is now often of guerrilla warfare (first rural and then urban), of underground safehouses, of torture chambers and prison cells and execution fields, often written by those who have either experienced these or know those who have, and this gives some unique originality and sincerity to the political verse in this period that is hard to find in other periods. In classical Persian poetry we had the prison poems of Mas'ud Sa'd Salman (eleventh century), under the first Pahlavi (Reza Shah, r. 1925–41) we had prison poems by Mohammad-Taqi Bahar (1884–1951) and some scattered references to prison in the poems of Mohammad Farrokhi Yazdi (1889–1939), another poet who had spent time in prison and was finally killed in prison. Under the second Pahlavi (r. 1941–79), there are initially poems in the form of letters or messages sent from prison – most notably a traditional *qasida* by Shamlou addressed to his father,[45] or a few poems attributed to Tudeh officers who were executed after the 1953 coup. In poems like 'The hour of execution' (1952) and 'Death of Nazli' (1954), Shamlou successfully introduces such themes and locations in modern poetry.[46]

In the years around and after Siyahkal, this category of verse grows significantly in number and diversity. In poems like 'Gozaresh-e goman-shekan' ('Report revealing lies') and 'Zan-su-ye dard' ('From beyond pain'), Ne'mat Mirzazadeh talks of his own tortures in Mashhad Prison.[47] In the poem 'Zendan-e falat' ('Prison of plateau') which was written in prison, a poem from the collection *Avaz-ha-ye Band* (*Songs of Prison*), Sa'id Soltanpour is reminded of 'the tired prisoners of this soil' who 'are in the prison of work and cruel labour' and says:

> We
> these small roofs of storm
> the song of prophesying the sudden storm
> with hot brands of torture
> flowers of wound and skin
> from parched chests we sing
> and from every row of cells in the dark bastion:
> Freedom, O bleeding change!
> O near revolution![48]

Another example is the poem 'Zakhmi' ('Wounded', 1971) by Shafiei-Kadkani, which pictures the tense, militarized atmosphere of the society after the armed resistance started in the cities:

> They search
> every street and alley
> they smell
> every man and woman.
> Listen!
> These are the howls of search dogs
> looking for him
> and the soil
> the thirsty soil
> and drops of blood.
> Where will that free wolf
> wounded by gunshot

find a refuge tonight
in the city of the cities
or how will he find its way
to the thickets
under the thunder of raging bullets?[49]

Shafiei-Kadkani favours, however, a more indirect and symbolic language, as can be seen in the poem 'Dar Jost-o-ju-ye qarre-ye eshq' ('In search of the continent of love') written for Pouyan (known to friends as 'Amir'), but the person addressed twice in the poem is 'Mira' ('ephemeral/dying') rather than 'Amir' – a word play that involves changing the position of one letter:

In search of the continent of love
the eighth kingdom of the firmament of Earth
you sail on waters of awe
Mira!
with no provisions and no compass.
In the heat of the sun
your look dissolves in darkness
like salt in water.
Before you, Eliases and Alexanders
had lost their way in this polar night
but this will suffice you as provisions
Mira!
Chant this spell time and again:
'Storm
knows no retreat...'[50]

Some of the poems written either under direct influence of Siyahkal or influenced by the general ambiance it created in the society are among the best poems of the period – if not in Persian poetry. And why shouldn't one mention here the poem 'Khatabe-ye tadfin' ('Eulogy') by Shamlou – a poem he may have dedicated to different people at different times and then taken it back from them, as he sometimes did – but there can be no doubt that he could not have written such a poem at a different time: it was in Ordibehesht (April/May) 1975, at the height of guerrilla warfare and only shortly after the murder of Bijan Jazani and eight others in prison.[51] This is a poem for 'the humble discoverers of the hemlock' who 'stand before the thunder,/ light the house,/ and die.'

And allow me to name a few more poems, of which, I believe, this period has every right to be proud: the poems 'Shaneh-be-shaneh ba felez-tavan, zamin-kavan' (1976?) ('Shoulder-to-shoulder with iron-smelters and soil-diggers') and 'Jahan-e komunist' ('The Communist Jahan/world', 1980) by Sa'id Soltanpour, and the poem 'Yek chehreh az Said' ('A portrait of Sa'id', 1981, a eulogy for Soltanpour) by Esma'il Khoi, and by Khoi I can still add the poem 'Falsafe-ye Don Kishot' ('The philosophy of Don Quixote') written a few years later in exile, an incomparable poetical achievement contemplating this whole period of armed resistance, passion and hope for change.

Siyahkal and a poet

The second part of my book *A Sort of Criticism of A Sort of Poetry*, which in fact constitutes two-thirds of the whole book, is devoted to the poetry of Sa'id Soltanpour, whose poems, I argue, are the most representative examples of the poetry of this period, without always being necessarily the best poems of the period. In the book I have written about this paradox in detail. Now, without ignoring for a moment the role and significance of Soltanpour, I want to write about my own experience as a poet of that period. I hope it wouldn't appear as self-praise; my goal is showing the impact of Siyahkal on a poet, and therefore it would be necessary to know this poet better (especially as viewed by others).

Even before getting to know at college some students who belonged to the first generation of Fada'is, my poems were sometimes political to different degrees, as it fitted the times (late 1960s) and in moderation, using the symbolic language common for that type of poetry. These poems were occasionally published in the local papers of the province Khorasan (like *Khorasan, Aftab-e Sharq, Hirmand*), and a few were later published in Tehran (in *Jahan-e Now, Muzik-e Iran*). I, too, had written a poem for Che Guevara ('In ast agar tamami-ye budan', 'If this is the whole being'), or a poem influenced by the Vietnam War while using the stories of Shahnameh ('Faje'eh', 'Tragedy'):

> In your sight, the wind
> will carry tons of ashes
> from one region to another.
> If it's not true that the likes of Sudabeh
> have come back to life
> how is it then that the likes of Siyavash
> are galloping bravely
> in the red of distant horizons?
> The tragedy, however –
> the tragedy is when the fire is fire
> and Siyavash no Siyavash.
> In your sight, the wind
> will carry tons of ashes
> from one region to another.[52]

This poem even lacked the directness of an average poem by Kasrai, and for me, a young poet relatively familiar with the debates on poetry in Iran, this meant a deliberate choice of language and mode of expression. Once Shamlou had come to Mashhad (in 1969?) and I went to the lobby of the hotel where he was staying to meet the great master for the first time. I showed to him a few of my poems, including the one I just cited; he said it was good (which could have been a polite 'taarof' only) and had some suggestion also. Then I asked him how he found Soltanpour's poems. 'Soltanpour?' he asked with a scowl, and one could sense some contempt, if not disgust, in his voice. 'What he writes is rubbish, sir; this is no poetry.' This is not the first time I am writing about this meeting and exchange,[53] and the reason that I am repeating these here is to give a picture of those years – after Khusheh poetry festival – and to show the fronts and where the lines were drawn; I also want to show that Sa'id Soltanpour was a familiar name for someone like me in the province; and finally this shows how important it was for a younger poet like me to know how much politics (as well as directness) was allowed in poetry.

In spite of the recommendations of Shamlou and other critics, my poems were moving towards more directness, and this was certainly not unrelated to my increasingly closer friendship with Fada'i students in my college years. For instance, the poem 'Dar foru-rikhtan' ('On collapsing', March 1969) uses the same symbolic/coded language but talks more directly about 'an underdeveloped swamp' and the fact that 'the fortress walls are all weak/ and castles crumbling and soaked.'[54] The poem 'Ruz-e fath-e kabutarha' ('Day of victory of doves', May 1969) uses an ironical to sarcastic language:

> We need to erect arches of triumph –
> your sacrifices were not in vain, O brave soldier!
> We won! We uprooted and threw away
> like useless weeds
> our most dangerous enemy: freedom.[55]

The poem 'Ma gom nakhahim shod' ('We won't get lost' or 'we won't lose our way', early 1970), in spite of its heavy meter and the quiet on the surface, is in fact a battle cry:

> We will leave many a fellow-traveler
> on the road with slashed skins
> heavy with lead [from bullets]
> and we'll keep going and going
> but
> we won't get lost;
> we are steadfast;
> we won't get lost;
> we have no fear of night nor of the dark forest;
> we won't get lost…[56]

Some poems I wrote around that time were already 'underground' literature, not meant for publication but for circulation among friends and going from hand to hand. In fact, I even stopped writing poems for some time, believing that those were not the best times for writing poems. It was Gholam-Reza Galavi (from Fada'i students) who encouraged me to continue. The result was a poem like 'Veda" ('Farewell'), which, I know, Bahman Azhang and Hamid Tavakkoli[57] liked; a poem about a garden 'watered with the blood of the youth' (a reference to a song from the times of the 1906 constitutional revolution) and 'fertilized with gunpowder'[58]… These fellow students (named above) were very well-read and cultured and to them poetry, or art and literature in general, was very important. When asked by a team member why they didn't make 'better' use of me,

Azhang, who was the most insightful among them, responded (as I heard later): 'What Saeed is doing right now is more important.' According to another anecdote, when a Vietnamese poet was being praised for a poem he had written for Nguyen Van Troi (a Viet Cong executed in 1964), Azhang had said, 'We too have Saeed, who is as good.' They probably thought the same about Sa'id Soltanpour, though they must have regarded him not very fit for underground activities due to his undisciplinable character as an artist and intellectual.

To have a picture of my cultural milieu and political surroundings in those years, we can look at a real picture: a group picture of the students of Mashhad University (the present Ferdowsi University) in Autumn 1968, on the occasion of Prof. Rajai's end of term as Dean of Faculty of Letters. He is the one in the middle (1). And, of course, Mohammad Mokhtari (2), the poet and researcher who was one of the victims of 'chain murders' in 1998, is well known. Among the others in the picture, two are SAVAK informants. Two became college professors (Horri and Azad; both deceased). Six of them were arrested in late spring or summer of 1971, of them three were executed on 2–3 March 1972 (Azhang (7), Tavakkoli (9), Galavi (5)), two got 3 years each (6 and 11), and one spent a year or two in prison (8). And all this in one small picture; you can guess the rest.

I was arrested in June 1971 (just as I had finished my BA with honours); in the graduation ceremonies they had called my name to get my award from the hand of one of the Shah's brothers, not knowing that I was already in jail. And from here a period of prison poems and songs starts. Soon after I had been transferred from solitary cell in Evin Prison to a larger room with a group of prisoners (in summer 1971), I composed – using some themes from Rimsky Korsakov's *Scheherazade* – a song which came to be known as 'The Song of the People's Fada'i Guerrillas' and was later adopted as the official song of the Organization. You couldn't sing revolutionary songs in Evin yet in the summer of 1971; so it came with me to Jamshidiyyeh Prison, where we had a chance for group rehearsals (supervised by 'Abbas Houshmand, later killed in 1977). Five members of the 'Arman-e Khalq' (People's cause) group, a team of guerrillas loosely associated with the Fada'i Organization, were executed in October 1971; they were the first to sing this song at the time of execution. Then the song went back to Evin through transfers and reached the founders and high-ranking members, almost all of whom were later executed. But they were the ones who sang this song in the military court:

> The bright sun of revolution
> rose from behind the mountain;
> the dark night is being chased
> by the glorious sun;
> I am a Fadai guerrilla of the people,
> I sacrifice my life for the people...[59]

This song became the integral part of almost all ceremonies in Iran's prisons under the Shah where political prisoners (most of them sympathizers of armed struggle) were being held. But was it a good song? Not really; it only answered an urgent need at that time.

Eight of the songs which became part of the repertoire of political prisoners of those years had been composed by me. We are fortunate to have recordings of Hamid Ashraf (leader of the Organization; killed in gun battle in 1976) singing songs, though recorded with poor quality, and he wasn't a good singer either. Four of those are my compositions. 'Ali Tolou' had also composed a song in that period which became very popular. And let us not forget that these were epic, hymn-like songs to be sung in prison ceremonies. Not comparable in any way with the songs created later by Sa'id Soltanpour which, though uplifting, were capable of being enjoyed by wider masses of people, as proven by their recording in the cassette 'Sharareh-ha-ye Aftab' ('Sparks of Sunshine'). (I have more songs after the revolution also, some of them recorded by Kargah-e Honar.)[60]

I wrote many poems also in prison (not all of which were necessarily 'political'). Some of them found their way in all prisons and became integral parts of the ceremonies. One such example was the relatively long poem *Az yek-do qatreh ta oqyanus* ('From a couple of drops to an ocean'). Despite its being close to 400 lines, many tried to memorize the whole poem, so it could be transferred to other prisons or outside of prison. This poem was a look at the history of class struggle from an internationalist perspective, starting from the ancient times and coming to its manifestation in the current struggle of Fada'is. I remember that Ayatollah Rabbani had sent a message through the Mojahedin in Qezel-Qal'eh Prison (Tehran) that he wouldn't attend the prison ceremonies if this poem were part of the program. (He was against references in the poem to the khalifs in Baghdad, etc.) This poem alone, which was on everybody's tongue in prison, shows how prevalent the internationalist sentiments were among the leftist activists ('Cyrus took me to plunder Babylon/ and Darius/ in Susa/ exploited my children's forced labour/ Shapur pierced my shoulder…'[61]) – mostly replaced now, sad to say, by Persia-centred and chauvinist feelings.

In my prison poems I sometimes record certain moments of life in prison, sometimes try to keep alive the memory of those fallen in struggle – mentioning their names in the poem, without minding the critics who usually said this could reduce the poem to an occasional piece and decrease its general appeal, poeticity or endurability. Some poems were instant reactions to events, like a poem I wrote after we heard that 'Abbas Jamshidi-Roudbari had been killed,[62] and in a ceremony on the same day this poem was recited by Asghar Izadi in the 'large commune' of Qasr Prison No. 3:

O fallen vanguard!
Praised be your fight and your path!
May no one see anything but combat from your comrades-in-arms
Nor hear anything from them but battle songs![63]

These poems should not be seen as merely balled fists and slogans; they often reflect the reality of life as experienced in prison. The poem 'Bagh-e albalu' ('Cherry orchard'), for instance, while being a poem written for Bahman Azhang ('Antoine'), depicts a memorial ceremony in prison, and here is the beginning:

When the news came, we sat down
hugging the knees and stunned
silent and mute –
we said nothing.
We did not until evening break the silence.
Until evening.
The evening was all about you,
    Comrade Antoine! ….[64]

The relatively long poem *The Bomb* is about the impact of armed struggle in the society, about life in underground safehouses, torture chamber and also includes an imaginary dialog with a prisoner awaiting his own execution.[65] The poem 'Bedrud dar zendan' ('Farewell in prison') is simply about a farewell in prison when a prisoner is being released.[66] And many more like these.

I still believe that poems can treat such themes, even using a direct language, without being mere 'slogans' – it all depends on 'how' they manage to do this, and it is this 'how' (and the genuineness of their emotional and intellectual experiences) which can determine the value of a poem, should there be any. While in prison, I wanted to write political poems using a language as simple and naked (i.e. undecorated) as possible, without, however, ignoring what Akhavan-Sales used to call the 'attraction lassoes' of poetry.[67] It was my ambitious hope also to perpetuate through these poems the memory of my fallen friends, whose names often appeared in the poems. Nevertheless, when I was released and went back to peer poets with dozens of poems – some very long – committed to memory, I wasn't quite sure of my success. Mohammad

Mokhtari, who knew me from college years in Mashhad, seemed to be only amazed by the incredible amount of passion he found now in these poems. It was in response to such friends that I wrote the rubaiyat 'Haman khakam ke hastam' ('I'm the same soil that I used to be'),[68] alluding to a poem by Sa'di of Shiraz (thirteenth century CE), and this is one of them:

> A red rose withered and in this worthless soil
> there's still some of its fragrance left.
> O, that he were here to see how, after so many years,
> whoever I talk to gets drunk from his scent.

The approach of some peers, like Shafiei-Kadkani, was a mixture of disbelief and fascination with these fresh moods and new experiments in poetry. Had he not read my poems, we probably wouldn't have had the 'Siyahkal period' as a distinct period in his book *Periods of Persian Poetry*. He was the one who encouraged me to publish the poems in the months before the revolution, and they were finally published as *She'r-e Jonbesh-e Novin* ('The Poetry of the New Movement') by Tus publications in 1978 in tens of thousands of copies. If I remember correctly, Shafiei-Kadkani even suggested the book's name as well as the pseudonym 'Safar Fadai-niya' for the 'compiler'. I had typed the poems myself with a cheap typewriter and done the clumsy layout job, and since the SAVAK was still there I had chosen nine different pseudonyms for my poems, mixing in a few poems by Soltanpour, Golesorkhi, Azarm, Shafiei and so on.

For the information of those who might have or come across a copy of the book *She'r-e Jonbesh-e Novin*, it would be good to know that all the poems that mention the following pseudonyms as authors are by me: F. Pashaki (five poems), S. Payan (eight poems), S. Yousef (two poems), M. Rashid (eleven poems), Shangarf (seven poems), and also the pseudonyms Tondar, B. Rayat, Qoqnus and Kargar (one poem each).

These pseudonyms caused some problems also. For instance, in Shafiei-Kadkani's *Periods of Persian Poetry*, the pseudonym *S. Payan* changed to *Sa'id Payan*.[69] This not only led to my being represented twice on the list of poets in the Siyahkal period (as both Saeed Yousef and Said Payan!), but also made some readers (even some in the Fada'i Organization) believe that Sa'id Payan had really been a poet.[70]

In spring 1981, Faramarz Soleimani published the book *She'r Shahadat Ast – Naqd va Barrasi-ye She'r-e Enqelab* ('Poetry is Martyrdom Critique and Review of the Poetry of the Revolution'). The first chapter after the introduction is devoted to my book *She'r-e Jonbesh-e Novin* and bears the same title. Although he personally does not approve of political directness in poetry, he still admires the poem and admits their power and effect:

> [These] poems are national anthems. Slogans on walls in the cities and trenches to provide a moment of calm for the soul in the ups and downs of a struggle full of fire and blood, a calm that gives rise to a new storm and gives you the strength to return to the battle. These 'verse-slogans' are poems of the day, turning the back to yesterday and having the eyes on tomorrow; and although that kind of reach might

seem unlikely, their effect on the current poetry and especially on the minds of the people of our time is undeniable.[71]

Throughout the whole chapter Soleimani uses images from my poems, cites directly or makes indirect references. In a part of the passage quoted above, for instance, he has one of my poems in mind: the poem 'Rah-ha'i digar fekr konid' ('Find other ways'), in which I say, 'Our job/ is breaking with yesterday and fixing the eyes on tomorrow.'[72]

I mentioned above Akhavan's expression 'attraction lassoes of poetry', and the lassoes in my poems included a touch of humour, some playfulness even in the face of tragedies. Humour had always been present to different degrees in my works, and I can cite Shamlou here who, though not approving my style that too closer to Akhavan's than to his, admitted in 1967 that 'the language and form you have developed fits perfectly well the taunting, humorous mood present in your poems'.[73]

This touch of humour continuous even in my later political poems, even in those written for fallen friends, as some device to achieve a certain estrangement effect or artistic distance, whereby to avoid both heroization clichés and the sentimental mourning tone. One example is a poem for Sa'id Payan ('Sa'id was wounded when a bomb exploded/ and for a second or two the smile fell from his lips'[74]), or in the poems written for the other Sa'id, namely, Sa'id Soltanpour:

> 'Today, however, Sa'id reminds one with his car
> of Don Quixote and his nag again:
> he constantly hits the car
> against bumps and potholes
> God knows whereto he's driving again
> hitting the gas and, as always,
> starting in second gear, driving fast...'[75]

Sometimes this humour is in the service of self-criticism and advice; this is, for instance, how the poem 'Payam-e yek kargar' ('A worker's messge'), a poem addressed to the Fada'i Organization, ends:

> You have said and keep saying that you are the 'armed arm' [of the people].
> That's great, excellent –
> and that's how you are, it is obvious.
> (I wish you were always so humble.)
> But an armed arm needs a body.
> Where are its body, chest and eye and mouth and foot and head, where are all of these?
> So long as he is not organized
> a worker is no more than a zero.
> A lion with no mane, tail and belly you can't even find in Rumi's book.
> It never existed.[76]

Until darker times arrive and with them poems that are sometimes dark and bitter (although I have never totally surrendered to despair) and sometimes questioning and doubting, the latter group showing some influence of Brecht:

> Yes, we were the first to pick up arms.
> But who will be the first to hit the target?
> Yes, we were the first to engage in that glorious task.
> But who will benefit from it, once it is finished?[77]

But such poems, and what I wrote later in exile, belong to a different period, beyond the scope of this article.

Summing up

For lack of space, I did not allow myself longer citations from poems or more examples, nor did I mention some more of the poets who deserved to be named or discussed. The task of doing a thorough research on the poetry of this period and the poets that formed it will remain one of the challenges of future researchers who are both familiar with the poetry of the period and are politically unbiased. Such research will show still more clearly the important role of Sa'id Soltanpour as the most representative voice of protest in the political verse of this period, even if some do not recognize his as the 'best' voice.

In between the Khusheh poetry festival in 1968 and the 'Ten Nights' event in 1977 we have almost ten years which constitute the most decisive years of this period, and it is interesting that no one can deny the significant and dominant role of Sa'id Soltanpour in either of these two events – even those who do not approve of this type of political verse or do not particularly like Soltanpour have to admit this.

I have already talked about Soltanpour's role in the first of these two events, citing Shamlou and Baraheni; for his role in the second event also I prefer to cite someone who is not a Fada'i and certainly does not approve of their way of struggle. And if it was Ehsan Tabari who talked earlier about the impact of Siyahkal on Kasrai and on the society, let us hear now Behazin (Mahmud E'temadzadeh), another prominent Tudeh writer, talk about the 'Ten Nights' and Soltanpour:

> [On the 5th day] Sa'id Soltanpour scares all of the organizers of the event – Iranians and Germans alike – by reading poems in a loud and rousing – and inciting – manner, poems that talk about prison and blood and bullets and executions and revolution. The secretaries of the [Iranian Writers'] Association feel concerned not only about the continuation of the event, but also about the existence of the Association. Why does this young poet, whom I like and whose craftsmanship I admire, act so rabble-rousingly in spite of my instructions a week ago in my own home? The enthusiasm of the huge crowd of young listeners – most of them sympathizers of the People's Fadai Guerrillas – knows no boundary: they applaud and shout bravos and ask for more poems:

> 'What happened to my country
> that prisons are filled with dews and poppies…'[78]

Behazin then cites lines from different poems that Soltanpour had read and writes about their effect on the audience:

> The words in the poems of this young poet are like red-hot metal, heavy and burning. They pierce the heart and settle therein. …
> He started to read another long poem. He was applauded with passion. The crowd sitting on the ground stood up and, applauding and shouting, asked for more poems.[79]

Let me end this article with my deepest respect and appreciation for my fallen friend and fellow-poet, Sa'id Soltanpour.

14

Reflections of the guerrilla struggle and the Siyahkal incident in literary prose and fiction

Nasim Khaksar

Introduction

Before Siyahkal, which has come to symbolize the capability of a small group of combatant intellectuals to shatter the concrete walls of despotism in our political culture, our history has borne witness to many groups both large and small, arising in defiance of despotism and struggling for independence, justice and freedom. Perhaps the first link in this chain originates in Fereydoun's mythical struggle and the way that his mother, Faranak, concealed the young Fereydoun with the cow Barmayeh so that he could return in the future to lead the Iranian people's struggle against the unjust Zahhak. Over the course of history, this manner of struggle has also been associated with the names of many figures who struggled as the representative of the common people – figures such as Mazdak, Behafarid, 'Abu Moslem Khorasani, Sinbad, Babak Khorramdin, Yaqub Leys Saffari – as well as with the struggles of the Ismaili sects against the 'Abbasid caliphate, the Sarbedaran uprising against the Mongol invasion and the many injustices that accompanied it, and, from the Constitutional movement of the early twentieth century onwards, with the names of Colonel Mirza Taqi Khan Pesyan, Mirza Kuchak Khan Jangali and Heydar 'Amu-Oghli.

Thoroughout its history, Persian literature has always welcomed the recording and preserving of these popular struggles with open arms, whether in the form of poetry or prose. And it has not only played a role in protecting these memories from the blight of time; rather, by reflecting the existential realities of those struggles in the mirror of imagination and thought, literature has been able to present a more vivid image than what one encounters in historical reports. It is with such a view in mind that I review the impact of the Siyahkal episode and the ensuing guerrilla struggle on our fiction.

Literature gives testimony that mankind has lived, matured, been ruined and rebuilt, has encountered the world and learnt from it, all at specific points in time. And this testimony is not the same as the one found in historical accounts. The what and the how of historical accounts become raw materials for the literary writer to toss into a different furnace and with which to cast a new mould. These moulds and shapes come in various forms; in each, one encounters hues and traces of release from or attachment to the reigning socio-political, cultural and traditional bonds at the specific point in time when these moulds and shapes have been forged.

This brief essay is divided into two sections. The first section considers the movement from the outside while the second segment considers it from within. In the first section I take up the stories and writings which coincide with the moment leading up to the Siyahkal incident and the years which followed. In the second section, by turning to the stories that I have written, I will endeavour to sketch a portrait of the figure that the guerrillas in those years had impressed on our minds, my experiences from that period and my impressions of my generation's activities, actions and thought.

Part one: An outside look at fiction. Literary criticism. Socio-political writings

1. Allegorical veneration of the guerrillas as reflected in short stories: *Mahi Siyah-e Kuchulu* (The Little Black Fish) by Samad Behrangi.

Mahi Siyah-e Kuchulu is an allegorical story written for children and adolescents. In this story, a small black fish, a character that comes to allegorize the life and theoretical formation of a guerrilla during those years, decides to leave the narrow stream where he lives and find a way to the sea.

On this path that he has chosen for his own life, the fish is confronted with tense, demeaning and threatening encounters with other fish, each of which represents a different social type; however, he never backs down. With the help of a dagger given to him by a lizard, the little black fish frees himself from a prison where he is held, a pelican's throat, and then once again continues on his way. At one point in the book, Samad Behrangi writes in the fish's voice:

> Death could easily fall upon me now, but, as long as I am able to live, I must not go forward to welcome death. Of course, if one day I should inadvertently find myself face to face with death – and I will – it doesn't matter. What does matter is the effect that my life or my death has on the lives of others…[1]

2. The critical reflection: *Hey Hey Jabali Qom Qom*, Reza Daneshvar; *Mirrors with Doors*, Houshang Golshiri, *The Tembi River*, Khosrow Davami

In the story *Hey Hey Jabali Qom Qom*, written in 1970, Reza Daneshvar predicts, in the form of a fictitious account, the bitter consequences of the rebellions and insurrections carried out by individuals or by armed groups made up of a few individuals. The writer maintained a friendship with Pouyan and Ahmadzadeh and offered his verbal support for the struggle. Daneshvar constructs his story around characters such as Kalb Hajji and Hassan Zolfu, both of whom participated in Colonel Taqi Khan Pesyan's uprising as his fellow combatants and friends. These are people who, following their defeat, live entirely within their own thoughts and memories of the past and who, in the end, are crushed by life's realities.

Years later, people had forgotten even Kalb Hajji's name; the same went for Hassan Zolfou. Hassan Zolfou settled in a tailor's shop in Mashhad. He would work the needle. He was the only one who did not try to forget. Though he would talk about how in a few years' time they would send an artificial moon into the sky and he'd talk about how they were building bombs that would turn the whole fabric of the earth into a tangled mess before a person could even say his prayers, even with whatever else he wanted to become, Hassan Zolfu was not one to forget. Not the retreat to the mountains, not the Colonel, not his refrain of *Hey Hey Jabali Qom Qom* and 'This is what becomes of nationalism' and not the cursed liquor.[2]

Several years later, Houshang Golshiri adopts a different method, namely, conversations between characters, to place that same period under his microscope. In his long story *Ayinehha dar Dar* a character from one side says, 'Sure, but ultimately, we also had to experience it; we could not sit around waiting for the world to change on its own or, as the reformers would have it, for 'the instruments of socio-economic development to accumulate."' From another direction, someone says: 'These people playing at guerrillas deprive everyday citizens of many things.' It turns out that these were guerrillas who were required to transcribe a single book ten times in their team's safehouse. And their paradigmatic female martyr was 'a woman veiled in black, tall, of course, and beautiful, as they had seen them in movies; an insurrectionary paradigm'.[3]

In the same story, when a female guerrilla wants to give a sense of her guerrilla husband, she says:

> When I was carrying our daughter Pesi he never even once put his ear on my belly to hear her heartbeat. I said it was as if he used to sleep on a rug at night and pull a thin blanket over himself. He would make fun of high-heels, saying 'and if they show up right now, then what?' One day I went to a meeting wearing a chador and when he recognized me, he laughed and said 'in Algeria they used to transport machine guns under this same type of chador.' Well, if he were around now, he would see hundreds if not thousands of young people dressing the same way.[4]

Khosrow Davami's *The Tembi River* was written in early 2002. The story revolves around the unsolved case of the murder or disappearance of an individual named Khosrow who took part in a guerrilla organization and whose disappearance some blame on internal disputes within the group. The narrator is a friend of Khosrow's and fellow member in the guerrilla organization. In an emotional language and with a pained tone, he slowly unravels the story's many strands until he arrives at the thread of the romantic relationship between Khosrow and Leila, another member of the organization. The story does not develop in a linear manner. Rather, the story circles around guesses and conjectures in order to arrive at its bitter truth. The story's narrator speaks directly to Khosrow's daughter. Her father was murdered during those years of guerrilla struggle as a result of an organized plot, a plot in which the narrator played an important role, because of his involvement in a romantic relationship with a fellow member. The narrator recounts these events years after they occurred and makes every effort not to tarnish anyone's reputation for it seems he remains unsure whose side Khosrow's daughter or others in the future will take. In the end, relying on figurative language and on the story of the King Kaykhosrow's occultation, a legend from the *Shahnameh* (Persian national epic), he writes:

> I wrote this for your mother, my lady. Who really knows Khosrow's true fate? Maybe he really did go into occultation; maybe he really did go into hiding and then join a group of shepherds or maybe he dressed as a foreign pilgrim and entered a faraway city and lived there, far away from the rest, for years; or maybe he was secretly killed in a conspiracy led by Tus or Guive or Bijan. What does anyone know? For many of the others also met a fate resembling his.[5]

3. Realist portrayals of the combatants' emotional and ideological worlds in novels as a way of revealing certain angles of Iranians' lives during this period: *Jazireh Sargardani* (Island of Bewilderment) by Simin Daneshvar and *Majerah-ye Sadeh va Kuchak-e Rouh-e Derakht* (The Short and Simple Adventures of the Soul of the Tree) by Shahrnoush Parsipour

In her novel *Majerah-ye Sadeh va Kuchak-e Rouh-e Derakht*, Shahrnoush Parsipour relates the adventures of the generation at the end of the 1960s and beginning of the 1970s who want to change the world and yet who do not acknowledge women. The members of this generation, even with all their shortcomings and faults, are portrayed as honest and sincere people. They are people who share the pure bearings of ascetics like Mansour al-Hallaj and 'Ayn al-Qozat Hamedani and, like them, are prepared to give their lives to defend their ideals.

Hossein is one of the representative figures of this generation. He is beloved within his circle of friends and serves as a sort of spiritual mentor. Before he is killed in a confrontation, which the writer leaves ambiguous, Hossein leaves a note at a friend's house in which he writes:

> I want to say that I know there is something missing in me. I live in a gray zone. Among these compiled cruelties and kindnesses, it must be me who possesses many shortcomings. Frankly, it's very strange that I can't find anyone in this world to be my partner, anyone to bond with. I'm sorry. I have accepted my solitude for some time now.

At the end of the note, he writes:

> I do not know kindness. Maybe that is the problem. I want to change the world without any humble perception of kindness.[6]

4. Figurative and metaphorical reflections: *Khurus* (The Rooster) by Ebrahim Golestan; *Mosalsal-e Posht-e Shisheh* (Machine Gun behind the Glass) by Samad Behrangi; *Ba-ham* (Together), *Mahi-ye Ba'di* (The Next Fish) and *An Rouz-e Barani* (That Rainy Day) by Qodsi Qazi Nour; *Bakhtak* (Nightmare) by Houshang Golshiri; *Qazal* by Nasim Khaksar.

Even though it was not published until after the Revolution, Ebrahim Golestan's *Khurus* was written in 1968–70. In the introduction to the second edition, published in 1995, he writes: 'My intention was to show my perspective and thoughts on the prevailing times.'[7]

This is a story about a rooster that hatches from an egg placed in a wall clock rather than from a batch of eggs with a chicken sitting on top of them. In the book, the narrator, Hajji, who owns the rooster and presides over the house and the surrounding land, reveals that

> It hatched right in here. I had a bowl in my damn hand. I wanted to put it in there. Then I got distracted. I forgot I had set it down inside the clock. I completely forgot about it until the day the little bastard started making a racket.[8]

The rooster in this story implants itself in the reader's mind as a symbol for the guerrilla struggle of the Fada'i and Mojahedin Organizations in the 1970s. When the rooster matures, its role becomes crowing and squawking at the wrong times or, aiming to dispel fears and invalidate the ruling power, leaving its droppings on a goat head that has been mounted above the door of the house, a talisman that symbolizes the house's protection and oversight (i.e. a symbol for the ubiquitous personality of the Shah). As a result of the conflict that develops between Hajji's servants and the rooster or, in other words, the war between them, the servants pelt stones at the rooster while he sits on the goat head and break the goat's horns. Hajji's situation quickly deteriorates. Finally, everyone in the story is mobilized to capture and cut off the head of the rooster who raises its wake-up call during the day and at all the wrong times.

At another point in the story, the narrator says:

> I started thinking of the rooster. There's something in the air that the rooster is aware of. He knows that morning is near or that noon has arrived when he crows. Morning arrives regardless of the rooster's crow. But the rooster has this special virtue of knowledge that the morning is arriving. He's in tune with time. In the star-filled solitude at the night's end, the rooster was sorely missed. The hollers arising from the neighbours' houses could not fill the void of his song. They emphasized the void. It felt as though this house was empty. It felt like this house was in need of the morning song.'[9]

And in an even more explicit expression of praise for the roosters, he says:

> In the half-light that made the darkness seem even darker, you couldn't see anything more clearly ... the roosters were carrying their dawn anthem from one house to another.[10]

In Houshang Golshiri's *Bakhtak*, which was written in 1975, the story of young men who went into hiding in a safe house, because of the prevalence of censorship at the time, takes on a figurative and symbolic form in the story of the disappearance of a boy from a single family. The father tries to console his wife and explain to her that their son had gotten lost once before as a child and afterwards was found again. But the wife and mother of this lost boy who would pick lilies from their branches every evening before they could blossom with the rise of the following day, places a different, tragic reality before the reader's eyes.

In *An Ruz-e Barani* which she wrote as a children's story, Qodsi Qazi Nour tells the story of a little girl named Zari who one cold and rainy day sees a young man who resembles her brother Mehdi's teacher. Mehdi's teacher is a good man. After having a conversation with him, Zari delivers the young man's message to Mehdi, her playmate and brother who is in fact in contact with the guerrillas. Then, as he is under threat of arrest, she lets him take refuge in the basement of their house and spend one night there. Since it was published after the revolution, the story's depiction is explicit.

The young man asks her: 'Zari, why did you help me hide?

I said, 'you looked like Mehdi's teacher.'
--Just because I look like Mehdi's teacher?
--Well, he is a really good person.[11]

5. Symbolic use of venturesome activities like smuggling and individual acts of revenge against one's immediate oppressor for the sake of having the reader exalt fearlessness, the cultivation of a militant spirit, and guerrilla struggle: The Screenplays for *Qaysar* and *Gavazn'ha* (The Deer) by Masoud Kimia'i and two short stories of *Shab-e Jadeh* (Night Road) and *Giyahak* (The Embryo) in the collections of stories *Giyahak* by Nasim Khaksar.

In his film *Qaysar*, Kimia'i depicts an act of injustice committed against a family and, through the two distinct reactions from the members of that family, contrasts two separate courses of action that can be taken in response to despotism. On the one hand, we have Khan Da'i's reaction and on the other Farman's and Qaysar's. Khan Da'i is not a man of action. He keeps his head buried in books and tries to prevent Qaysar and Farman from acting and taking revenge. But the two of them do not pay Khan Da'i any mind. Farman goes looking for his enemies unarmed and ends up getting killed. But Qaysar arms himself and ambushes his enemies, killing them one by one. This film was produced and screened in the same year that the idea of guerrilla struggle began circulating widely among militant intellectuals. When Farman calls out Qaysar's name as his enemies stab him to death, it announces the arrival of a new movement that manifests in Qaysar's life.

Nasim Khaksar centers his *Shab-e Jadeh* on the smuggling activities of a vagabond and cripple. The smuggler in this story is a fearless individual who sets out on the desert roads in the cold and dark of winter. After battling with gendarme agents and making a daring escape, he successfully delivers his contraband to its destination. The bus passengers' admiring glance at the smuggler who has escaped from the agents on his hobbling foot and has returned unscathed symbolizes the people's admiration for those individuals who do not fear the police or the gendarmes and who treat the government's military power as nothing more than a game, even in a period when fear presides.

6. Praise for heroism and rebelliousness through personal uprisings against individual acts of injustice and historical events: *Tangsir* by Sadeq Chubak; Sa'edi's dramas published under the pseudonym Gowhar Morad on the popular struggles in Tabriz during the Constitutional Period; Sa'id Soltanpour's Drama *Hasanak*.

In the dramas collected and published under the title *Panj Namayesh Nameh az Enqelab-e Mashruteh* (Five Dramas on the Constitutional Revolution), Sa'edi depicts the eagerness of the youth in Tabriz to join the Constitutionalist fighters and the people's disgust with and hatred for the government agents in an attempt to create some distance from the prevailing climate of defeat in the era following the 1953 coup d'état.

In the play *Az Pa Nayoftadeh-ha* (Those Who Remained Standing), Mullah Monaf flees from Mir Ghazab and takes refuge in the tomb of a local saint where an armed opposition fighter (*mojahed*) emerges from the shrine and rescues him. Mullah Monaf then joins the opposition fighters. In the play 'Naneh Ensi', the people cut off their ties from Naneh Ensi and constantly berate her on account of her son who works as a low-level government agent. After her son abandons the government agents and joins the opposition fighters, they treat her kindly once again and start buying the boiled potatoes that she sells as her means of livelihood. In the play's final scene, when the agents come to arrest Naneh Ensi, who has become a symbol of the people's united opposition against the government, the people form a line to protect her and in doing so build a fortress out of their bodies to provide her defence:

Second Agent: Come out from there, you old hag. (Naneh Ensi doesn't move)
Second Agent: Hey old lady, I'm talking to you. Start moving and come here!
The agents slowly close in with their guns drawn. The people calmly form a line in front of Naneh Ensi while they stare straight at the agents.[12]

Sa'id Soltanpour's drama *Hasanak* makes heroes out of the common people through the story of the eleventh-century Sultan Mahmud's vizier, who, after the Sultan's death, was disgraced by his son, Sultan Masud. In the conversations occurring between the people of that time while the vizier Hasanak is hanged, Soltanpour recreates the debates taking place at the end of the 1960s and beginning of the 1970s among militant and political intellectuals. One of those people is a rebel prepared to die for his cause who angrily says of his own lack of action:

The movement is taking hold in Bahrain, Yemen, and Iraq. The regime in Bahrain is about to fall. But we are just beginning here and we can't draw in the masses on our own.

He laments the fact that, because the objective conditions of revolution do not exist, he is obliged

to risk my life to free opponents like Hasanak.[13]

Another character warns him that

> they must not act hastily and unilaterally.

And in the play, they also talk about mobilizing the masses to gather weapons.

> The second man: We need to dispatch some people to Herat. Beyhaq is ready to revolt. A thousand blades have already arrived from Iraq but it isn't enough.
> The fourth man: We have to work on accumulating weapons right here. The craftsmen in Syria took several armaments in one day. The foundations of this regime are shaking.[14]

7. The guerrilla as savior and mythical figure in the novels of *Khosrow-e Khuban* (The Virtuous Sovereign), by Reza Daneshvar and *Hadis-e Mordeh Bar Dar Kardan-e An Savar Keh Khahad Amad* (The Story of the Hanging of the Knight Who Will Come) by Houshang Golshiri.

Khosrow-e Khuban is an allegorical novel whose foundation lies in faith in the arrival of a messianic figure, hope for a saviour, and belief in the Hidden Imam, all of which are prevalent in our religious culture. Reza Daneshvar employs Iranian mythology in this novel to give a different account of our contemporary situation, an account of a nation that, every time it aspires towards its own salvation and hopes to emancipate itself from despotic rulers or governments, selects a virtuous sovereign under whose supreme leadership and guidance it upraises, but who never obtains its own liberation. In this novel, the guerrilla struggle and the incident at Siyahkal appear as one instance in a continuum of expectation for a saviour's arrival that marks our national history. And the people of Kohandezh, the area where the guerrillas attack the gendarmerie outpost, have in fact been counting the days in anticipation of a knight's arrival long before Bahram and his friends show up there. Daneshvar writes:

> According to the SAVAK report, the people of this village were eagerly awaiting the rule of the Hidden Imam and every Friday the village as a whole would send two horses and each area within the village would contribute an additional horse so that a group could set out as a welcoming party and receive the Hidden Imam on his imminent arrival to the village.[15]

This village's history also extends as far back as the mythological era of Fereydoun, for the people had imprisoned the demon-king Zahhak in the caves of the surrounding areas. Alexander also passed through that site. Likewise, the warriors from that village in every era, based on their geographic location, would take up another group's cause and dress themselves for battle.

> The latest manifestation of the warrior-descendants of those guards at the cave who took on the responsibility of keeping watch over Zahhak appear in the time when the cursed Yazid beheads Imam Hossein – peace be upon him – and all the

young men from the bastion dress themselves for battle and go to Karbala to aid the Chosen One in his uprising for vengeance.[16]

8. Rereading of literary texts in light of the guerrilla struggle: *Jahanbini-ye Mahi Siyah-e Kuchulu* (The Worldview of the Little Black Fish) by Manouchehr Hezarkhani, and *No'i az Honar, No'i az Andisheh* (A Type of Art, A Type of Thought) by Sa'id Soltanpour, published in 1970/1 (1349). *Taziyaneh Bahram* (Bahram's Whip) by Morteza Saqebfar and a drama by Arsalan Pouriya with the same title. Date of publication, cited from memory, 1972 or 1973 in *Jahan Now* and *Hamlet dar Mehvar-e Marg* (Hamlet on the Axis of Death) by Nasim Khaksar, *Seda Quarterly*, 1972.

Hezarkhani's reading of Behrangi's *Mahi Siyah-e Kuchulu* starts as follows:

> The story of *Mahi Siyah-e Kuchulu* is a story for children. But within that story, there lies another history and another lesson for adults. The story is not meant to entertain but rather to educate.[17]

In his interpretation of this work, Hezarkhani writes, 'The black fish's story is the story of a conscious and formulated rebellion.' This rebellion, in Hezarkhani's view, 'disarms the conservatives and the pragmatists' so that, in the end, the little black fish

> has two paths before him. Either he can go and study all the types of possible and existing conditions and afterwards chose one of them. Or he can start moving right away towards something that he senses in an abstract manner but is not yet able to fully grasp. The little black fish chooses the second path. He tears the fabric of the logic and philosophy that dominate his environment and he disrupts traditions and customs. He cuts off his strong and numerous ties with the tribe of elder fishes and he departs for a different manner of living which he himself does not yet know concretely but which he knows he will discover gradually on the path's course.[18]

Nasim Khaksar's *Hamlet dar Mehvar-e Marg* expresses this same sentiment and line of thinking in a re-reading of Shakespeare's *Hamlet*:

> Hamlet is the language of mystery. The mystery of internal grappling with external issues. The fervors of within and without. The issue is not that of remaining. To remain is to fester. Festering is the start of decomposition and to decompose is to attain union with nothing. And nothing is not Hamlet's issue.[19]

And when Horatio says to his friends after seeing the ghost, 'by my advice/ Let us impart what we have seen to-night / Unto young Hamlet; for, upon my life/ This spirit, dumb to us, will speak to him', it raises this question for the audience: 'how is it that the ghost only speaks with the young Hamlet and simply passes all the others by?'[20]

In this text, Khaksar makes use of Hamlet's psychological space and social conditions to dig a tunnel directly to the existence of the guerrillas and the conditions of their struggle in those years. The writer takes a celebratory view towards the guerrilla struggle and affirms its refutation of *survival theory* because he believes that life has been degraded under the hegemonic shadows of Claudius-like figures and by the fear that dominates the society:

> Fear and dread rule over society's spirit. And the society is seething with profound contradictions. A bride and a mourner sleep side by side. Strangled and anguished, the people are surrounded by a concrete wall and if a bird takes flight to break the night's silence, it goes spiralling into the darkness. Life has been degraded and all that is settled is treachery.[21]

Part two: A look from within

The short story collection *Rowshanfekr-e Kuchak* (The Little Intellectual) by Nasim Khaksar was published in 1980. Before that, two of his short stories had been published in the periodical *Ketab-e Jom'eh* and one in the periodicals of the Iranian Writers' Association, *Daftar'ha-ye Andisheh-ye Azad* (Notebooks of Free Thought). Although he wrote the first story in this collection in 1973, the event that takes place in the story goes back to around six years earlier, to the year when he was imprisoned for the first time. Of all those political prisoners in Ahvaz in 1967, many have made a name for themselves through their poetry, fiction, translations and research. Some of them, too, lost their lives in street battles or in the criminal injustice systems of both regimes.

The character 'Adid in these stories was not based on any one individual; rather, the actions and demeanour of dozens of members of that generation that the author knew intimately all played a role in his construction of 'Adid. They belonged to a generation who had risen up to sacrifice their own lives for the establishment of a society emancipated from the fetters of any form of oppression. And towards this end, they had taken a new approach, an approach independent of its predecessors. Their ideal society emerged and took shape from their general readings or it emerged from within the dozens of political pamphlets that had been copied by hand, pamphlets that either they themselves had written or that had been written by other prominent figures from this same generation in other parts of the world.

The author's curious eyes in those years saw and register the countenances and conduct of those who had made up this generation's stock. 'Adid in the first story is a fictional figure who writes fiction himself, a twenty-year-old in 1965 who reads both Marx's *Capital* and the stories of J. D. Salinger, a modern American writer of the generation following Hemingway's. In another story, 'Adid is a nineteen-year-old youth who sets out to become a future guerrilla and to lose his life for his ideals. Of course, in the stories, these matters are referred to less often and it is more the characters' crawl towards the discovery of a new set of human value that receives emphasis. In the first story, 'Adid puts on all his theatrics so that his friend Yasin will not notice his mother's presence in front of the court. He knows that Yasin will be enraged to see his mother in such a helpless state among the soldiers. And this rage might make him lose control. A month earlier, during his interrogation in the military court, his mother was ejected from the building after she shoved some soldiers. These acrobatics on the high wire of feelings and passions on 'Adid's part create a new form of acrobatics in the arena of political struggle as well. At a later point in the book, the author tries, to the extent that the stories' structures allow, to talk about the books that the characters read. One of them is intensely interested in the works of Dostoyevsky, Kafka, Shamlou and William Faulkner. He also socializes with people whose literary circles discuss Fernando Arrabal and Samuel Becket, representatives of the Theatre of the Absurd in Europe and throughout the world in those years. In fact, the story wants to say that this same generation that later lit the fires of struggle at Siyahkal first arose from amidst these very literary circles. If travelling the circuit of emotions and passions forms half of the circle of their existence, then the quest for knowledge on how to further resist their enemy makes up the other half. In the story *Charm-e Kaf-e Pa-ye 'Adid* (The Leather for 'Adid's Heel), 'Adid works to develop the necessary leather to allow him to withstand the whip under torture. He has read a quote from Taqi Arani in Bozorg 'Alavi's book *Panjah va Seh Nafar* (The '53') about how an imprisoned political combatant should not lower his head and say yes when responding to his interrogator's demands. Rather, the prisoner must always raise his head when faced with the interrogator's questions and respond with a 'no', for in saying 'yes', an imaginary dagger under the prisoner's chin plunges into his throat. After prolonged torture, 'Adid discovers a new sense of value:

> He said: sometimes this Bozorg Alavi really drives a person to the end of his/her wits. Damn you, what sort of lesson is this?
>
> I didn't know what he was talking about. I waited for him to start talking again.
>
> He said: The Master writes that if you lower your head during interrogation, there is a dagger that will plunge into your throat and come straight out the other side of your head. And it's right, man, that you can't lower your head during interrogation. But you can turn your head from side to side. I was killing myself over this until I realized that there is another way. He said: If I get out, I want to write a pamphlet on turning your head from side to side.
>
> Then he put his finger under his chin and like a child imitating someone says: 'look!' Then he turned his head from side to side.
>
> He said: It doesn't even make a scratch. Then again, it wouldn't matter if it did. But it won't plunge into your throat. Do you get it, Yasin? I was killing myself over this until I found a way to form a bit of leather for my foot.[22]

In short, this story wants to say that this generation was in search of something and when it came to moving its head, it didn't want to limit itself to just the two directions of up and down and so it added side to side and looking at its surrounds to the field of possibilities. Najm is another figure in these stories, a young man around nineteen or twenty. When he finds out that a retired teacher has several useful books of Marxist literature in his library, he befriends him and one by one pilfers the books of Taqi Arani, Maurice Thorez and Maxim Gorky from his collection. Most of their conversations in cafes, bookstores or public gatherings revolve around debates, contemporary works of poetry and fiction, and articles in cultural publications like *Negin*, *Khusheh*, *Ferdowsi* and other literary magazines. It seemed that, once again, through these magazines and through translations of certain books, the world wanted to take up the task of creating a different sort of human beings. There was a wide market for translations of the works of Marcuse, Ernst Fischer, Carl Gustav Jung and Erich Fromm.

The references that the author's stories make to the titles of the above-mentioned books and to other banned and underground literature, which Najm's character must resort to stealing to obtain, show just how meager were the stockpiles available for reading and educating oneself in those days.

Hamid Enayat's translation of Hegel's *Lordship and Bondage* with Alexandre Kojéve's commentary was published in 1971 or 1972. At that time, I (Nasim Khaksar) was around twenty-eight years old. I remember how reading that work incited all sorts of heated debates amongst those of us who wanted to become familiar with philosophy. The book and the translator's introduction together do not comprise more than seventy or so pages. Our shared spirit of rebellion against the existing order caused us to have our own specific view and interpretation of the notions and concepts in the book. The main argument of the book centres on the processes of ascribing value to the human existence and of achieving self-consciousness through a battle for one's life.

Now that I look back to the discussions, critiques and views of that era, it occurs to me just how much Amir-Parviz Pouyan, who diligently read and translated philosophical works, formed his fundamental thinking on the refutation of the theory of survival based on the ideas set out in this book of Hegel.

A battle for one's life, the main point of discussion in this book, is also the fate that Najm, the hero of the final story of *Rowshanfekr-e Kouchak*, assigns himself. Najm is the fictive name for Majid Pirzadeh Jahromi, a member of the Fada'i guerrillas who was killed in 1975 after his safehouse in Tehran was betrayed and he fought against the enemy for his life. Those of us who were close in Abadan used to call him '*Rowshanfekr-e Kuchak*' on account of his youth, his small size, his Coke bottle glasses and his fiery nature that would come out in conversations and debates. I selected the fictitious name Najm for him because of the 'j' sound (the Persian letter *jim*) that is repeated in both his first and last names and because the name means 'star', which appears in his favourite poem, Ahmad Shamlou's 'Nazli'.[23] Najm loved books of philosophy and he had read Hegel's *Lordship and Bondage* several times.

Human self-consciousness, as Hegel defines it in the book, becomes realized through a battle for one's life:

> In other words, man's humanity 'comes to light' only if he risks his (animal) life for the sake of his human Desire. It is in and by this risk that the human reality is created and revealed as reality; it is in and by this risk that it 'comes to light', i.e., is shown, demonstrated, verified, and gives proofs of being essentially different from the animal, natural reality. And that is why to speak of the 'origin' of Self-Consciousness is necessarily to speak of the risk of life.[24]

Furthering this point of discussion, in regard to the battle that he establishes between lordship and bondage or lord and slave, a battle that serves for either side to make his value or, more precisely, his human value known to the other and in doing so establishes the grounds on which to realize an independent self-consciousness, Hegel writes:

> This Slave is the defeated adversary, who has not gone all the way in risking his life, who has not adopted the principle of the Masters: to conqueror or to die. He has accepted life granted him by another. Hence, he depends on the other. He has preferred slavery to death, and that is why, by remaining alive [in Pouyan's terms, read: choosing survival], he lives as a Slave.[25]

In his pamphlet *Zarurat-e Mobarezeh Mosalahaneh*, Pouyan further develops his argument on how some political groups claim the importance of their own survival by reasoning that they must wait for the requisite time and the apposite conditions for them to take action:

> The enemy has his own, entirely distinct set of criteria for his actions. He says: make a compromise with me so that you can survive. Submit to my dominance to preserve yourself from my death blows.[26]

Concepts in Pouyan's pamphlet such as 'taking risk' and 'venturing one's life' in order for the revolutionary vanguard's aspiration to become the aspiration of the working class, concepts expressed in a variety of forms, all rearticulate the terminology and concepts that Hegel employs extensively in *Lordship and Bondage*. In this regard, *The Refutation of the Theory of Survival* is a political-philosophical re-articulation of *Lordship and Bondage*, our favourite book in those years.

If Hegel, within the sphere of his own thought, refers to the dynamic essence of history and thought when he outlines the battle between lord and slave, Pouyan sees the dynamic and progressive nature of the working class when he uses the same outline in his refutation of survival theory. Indeed, his revolutionary intellectual becomes one stage in the existential evolutionary progression of a class that in Hegelian terms, proceeds from existing purely within the self towards existing for the sake of an independent self, a progression that requires one at this stage to wager his existence in a life-threatening combat.

In that period, when access to books about the history of political struggles in Iran was not feasible, either because the resources did not exist or because they had been censored, the intellectual did not pursue the model of his predecessors existing outside the self in order to realize his ideals; rather, as Hegel would have it, he pursued the pure self and the sphere of his own existence to a point where he had achieved knowledge of that self. Any time he departed from the self or the bases of his own existence, he was committing an error. For this reason, in order to preserve self-independence in his thought, from time to time and in critically dangerous situations where he was likely to stumble, he would retreat and take refuge in those same models from within his own existence and use those models, which had sprung from within his feelings, passions and conscience, as his signposts.

In 'Zahed', another story from *Roshanfekr-e Kuchak*, there is a character of the same name that, despite all his interest in political struggle, is excluded from his militant friends' political circle because he is paralyzed in the arms and legs. Their unspoken motivation for excluding him is their concern that his physical disability might impair them in their struggle. At the end of the story, when the group is arrested and imprisoned, Zahed grows anguished by the feeling that he leads a feeble existence and that he has nothing to offer to the political struggle. Before long, he commits suicide. When news of Zahed's death reaches Jabur, his closest friend from the group, in prison, he says to Yasin that he is afraid of becoming a motherfucker. When Yasin asks him what they could have done for him, Jabur responds,

'We should have informed on him.'[27]

His reasoning is that if Zahed had been with the rest of them, he would not have felt rejected.

> It would have been better if he had been here with us. We should have informed on him. If he had just been here with the rest of us it would have been fine.[28]

Another character says that they shouldn't have forgotten about him. And he believes that a person who forgets about certain things is a motherfucker.

This manner of regarding oneself, the world and human passions and of engaging with the self in such a language and tone all form an unorthodox method in the political realm. Mustafa Shoa'iyan writes just as candidly and uses expressions generally considered vulgar in his critiques and in letters to the guerrillas and to his comrades. The characters in *Roshanfekr-e Kuchak* have an anxiety for becoming motherfuckers. And one of the ways to prevent becoming a motherfucker is to resist against forgetting, an expression that, in the signification process, can take on a wider array of meanings, meanings such as rising up against the forgetting of others, against forgetting human covenants like love and friendship, against the forgetting of fidelity and the human existence, which carries with it a complex set of dimensions.

In the story *Charm-e Kaf-e Pa-ye 'Adid*, these are the same leathers that 'Adid seeks out so that, making him able to withstand torture and return from under the interrogator's whip unharmed.

Now, after all these years, when I take the images that remain in this fiction, drama and literature, and arrange them side by side, I arrive at this conclusion that our lives were devoted to the struggle: that even if the actions of guerrilla-intellectuals at that time were largely political actions, they formed, nonetheless, in their entirety, a movement towards knowledge of the self and towards proof of one's own existence as a human citizen possessing rights within society and the world. Or, in a manner of speaking, it was a philosophical revolt or rebellion in the discovery of the self more that it was an absolutely political movement. Wherever one departs from the self and from the effort to know himself/herself as a being who achieves such knowledge through action, one commits error. Indeed, Zahed's story in some sense predicts the political actions of this generation following the revolution.

The way that many militants of his generation not needed blindly followed ossified political doctrines, their acceptance of such doctrines as fixed values and their indifference towards independent thinking and towards that which had granted them existence as death-conscious beings, all prevented the survivors of this generation from accessing the proper paths of struggle and gaining new knowledge of their existence. Thus, this generation's youthful spirit aged before its time. The remnants of this generation still had much to learn when the Revolution and its demands imposed a sense of urgency upon them. Thus, they did not seek a newly fertile ground in a return to those same philosophical questions from their past that could have served as both a backward-looking critique and a framework for today's questions regarding their socio-political existence, which, in Hegelian terms, was still a pure existence. Instead, those remnants, with a certainty that lacked any basis in experience, turned to a set of beliefs that they themselves had not experienced, beliefs that held no future.

15

Looking back

Esfandiar Monfaredzadeh

I started school when I was six years old. The neighbourhood of Dardar Alley off Rey Street was a religious and traditional one. However, my father's artist friends, with an opposite sensibility, would gather in our home frequently to drink, sing and perform. And that is how early I grew accustomed to two contrasting life styles. As they say, a person's taste and social character are already formed by the age of nine.

At twelve, during my first year of high school, my classmates and I formed a band to perform at the Eghbal High School events. For rehearsals I used to hide my instrument – an Oud,[1] a Bass or a Tonbak[2] – without its case inside a sheet or a blanket so it wouldn't be recognized; and the instrument of taboo would remain concealed from the inquiring eye in the neighbourhood.

My father worked for the railroads, but to make ends meet, he opened a shop in Amirieh called Pakdaman where he tailored shirts. And in response to Prime Minister Mohammad Mossadeq's appeal to support the homeland's textile industry, he advertised that he would tailor Iranian fabric for free. And those who ordered shirts made from English poplin would also buy the Iranian kind to get their free shirts. His idea got a lot of attention, and his business took off so much so that he received a personal letter of thanks from Mossadeq himself.

Soon afterwards he opened a second shop in Lalehzar-e-now across the Metropole Cinema. The good times however did not last. His petty competitors set fire to both of his shops in one night.

My father became very depressed as a result. He decided to retire and stay home. Sometime later he started tailoring shirts again, with one sewing machine, out of one of four shop-fronts off our ancestral home in Dardar Alley.

He always had the radio on in his shop, listening to music and the news. And whenever Ayatollah Taqva Shirazi, congregation leader of Saheb-Zaman Mosque in Dardaar Alley, would pass by and hear the music, he would take his cane and strike the ground with anger and shout: 'Shut up that Satan's voice!' In response, my father decided to close up his shop and post a beautifully handwritten note on the window, singling out the Ayatollah's irreverent behaviour as the cause.

The news spread far, from our neighbourhood to other areas. My father's protest received such great support in the neighbourhood that it forced Ayatollah Taqva to come to our door for apology and reconciliation.

It is now 19 August 1953, and I have just turned thirteen. I can hear the sound of bullets in the distance and nearby. They are mostly volleys into the air to prevent the people from joining the demonstrations.

On Rey Street near the entrance to Dardar Alley a little down from the bus stop, we had our own piggy bank; and whenever we wanted to go to the movies and were short of cash, we paid it a visit. Rolling up the sleeves, we pushed aside the muck and mud from the drain and fished out the coins that had accidentally fallen from the hands of the bus conductor or passengers.

Fishing the drains was always a sweet affair until that very afternoon, where ten metres away, I saw a man's head blown apart by bullets. Blood gushed out and he fell. But not like I had seen in the movies. It was something completely different. Out of sheer terror I ran all the way home. The following days and nights were horrible. In that tender moment of youth, I had witnessed such violence that it remains unforgettable until this day, six decades later. I wish I had never seen it. Sometimes I think about the children who have been witness to public executions in the streets. I wonder what kind of future will they have and will build?

Every year close to Nowrouz, my father would buy us new clothes. But during my second year in high school, I pleaded with him to give me cash so I could buy my own fabric and have a suit made according to my taste. It took an intercession from my mother and a promise to buy only homegrown material for my father to concede. I bought an earthy red Iranian fabric and took it a tailor for a suit; and a few days before Nowrouz, it was ready.

On the first day of the new year, I put on my suit and went out into the street. I had taken only a few steps when I saw our neighbourhood street cleaner wearing his new clothes made of the same fabric and colour! That year the City Council had distributed uniforms made from the exact same material to all its street cleaners. Very annoyed, I returned home, and passed the 'Eid (new year festivities) wearing my old suit and putting up with my father's wisecracks.

I used to look down at street cleaners and wearing the same colour clothes as them was embarrassing to me. To say the words 'street-cleaner', 'worker' meant 'sweeper' or 'labourer'. The words were used as insult. It was much later that I realized, there was no shame in doing any kind of work, and that all professions were necessary and beneficial to society. And were any group to go on strike in society, it would disrupt it, with the exception of course of one faction: the clergy or as they like to call themselves, the Rouhaniun. In any country or religion were they to go on strike it would only be cause for great joy and celebration!

On 16 Azar 1332 (7 December 1953), the army attacked the Faculty of Engineering of Tehran University during a student protest there. That day three students representing different viewpoints, Bozorgnia, Qandchi and Shari'at-Razavi were shot dead by soldiers. To protest this atrocity, my generation launched a score of demonstration against the existing regime. It was through these demonstrations that I became politically conscious. It has now been almost seventy years, and to this day, the students of Iran's universities commemorate that day annually, so it would never repeat or be forgotten.

To support our family, my father opened a real estate office on Rey Street, near the Amin-Hozoor three-way junction. It is the winter of 1953, and my father is doodling on the picture of the Shah on the cover of a magazine; he gives him a full beard. The mechanic shop owner next door sees the cover and becomes agitated. He goes to the police station and returns with a police officer. In the interval my dad has taken off the cover and thrown it into the flowing drain ditch, running along the length of the street. The mechanic's assistant who has seen what my father has done, is ordered by the mechanic to run and grab the evidence from the drain and he recovers the discarded cover a long distance away. My father is then carried off with this evidence to the police station and later is imprisoned at the city jail.

The night he does not return home we become aware of his arrest. And later we discover that he has been charged under Article 5 of Martial Law, with the crime of 'Insulting the First Person of the Nation'.

My mother's efforts have now begun. Most days from morning to night she is at the city jail. And on Fridays she takes us, her four children, along with her. When her efforts appear fruitless, she appeals to a distant relative, Mr Izadi, the administrator of Princess Ashraf Pahlavi's Office. She appeals to him repeatedly until she manages to get a recommendation letter from him for my dad.

My father, after suffering one year of imprisonment and torture, and after signing a letter recanting all ties with 'the decadent Tudeh Party', and enduring the printing of the body of the letter in the newspaper by the order of Military Command, is released from prison. And all this knowing that he has never belonged nor has ever been a member of the Tudeh Party.

Seeing my father's silent tears was very hard for me. It tormented me. The many wounds of his incarceration were still fresh on his body and mind as he spoke of it to my mother.

In the absence of political freedom, and the people's constant historical struggle against the regime, two songs with opposite perspectives were placed side by side. One aligned with official taste 'the government-sanctioned art', and the other aligned with the aspirations of the people 'a nationalist/populist art'. One a welcome to the monarchy and its reinstatement after the people's uprising of 19 August (1953) with the beautiful poem by Roudaki:[3]

Shah the moon and Bukhara the sky
Behold the moon rise above!

And the other *Mara Bebous* (Kiss Me), a love song that became the people's elegy of choice, as protest against the execution of the officers who were members of the Tudeh Party.

The former was broadcast constantly on National Radio, with a beautiful orchestral arrangement to the peerless voice of maestro Gholam-Hossein Banan and the diva Marziyeh. And the latter was a simple rendition to the sound of one violin played by its composer Majid Vafadar and accompanied by two musicians. The people kept the story of the song's creation alive by word of mouth. And to quell the rumours, in retaliation, the government commissioned the artists at the National Radio to put a different lyric to the melody and, with a much better orchestration, broadcast it repeatedly over the airwaves. This battle of tastes between the government and the people was highly instructive for me.

Colonel Houshyar's wife always went about our neighbourhood without a veil. One day Ayatollah Taqva Shirazi saw her shopping at Shah-Gholams vegetable stand in the neighbourhood. He hollered 'don't sell vegetables to this unclean goat-head, it's a sin!' The woman burst into tears and ran. Soon afterwards a military jeep arrived with several armed soldiers. They grabbed the Ayatollah hand and foot without his cloak or turban, and carried him off over their heads, threw him into the jeep and left.

My friend and I related the incident to Mostafa 'Alameh, the haberdasher of Dardar Alley, who was also a member of the Fada'iyan-e Islam.[4] He said, 'Come along with me and bear witness to its telling before Navvab Safavi himself!' We agreed and the three of us headed to Mesgar-Abad on bicycles. Once there we entered a warehouse office that sold building materials. Navvab Safavi and Abdolhossein Vahedi were sitting on a large wooden platform. We related the event and bore witness to it. Vahedi dialled a number on the phone and said: 'This is Vahedi. I wish to speak with General Bakhtiar.' After a few moments' pause, he continued: 'His holiness Navvab Safavi speaks', and passed the phone over to him. Navvab Safavi in a few seconds, very soft-spoken but peremptory, said: 'Your people have violated the sanctity of Ayatollah Taqva Shirazi. You must seek his propitiation as soon as possible!' He then hung up and turned to us and said, 'Go, and if they have not returned the master within one hour notify us.' We returned home and watched with amazement as they returned Taqva Shirazi to his house. In those days General Bakhtiar was the Military Commander of Tehran, and of course Fada'iyan-e-Islam was officially an illegal organization.

I asked myself: who is behind Navvab Safavi and why does his word carry such weight?

Most of the neighbourhood kids were aware of the secret whereabouts of Navvab Safavi and Vahedi. Since we believed the Fada'iyan-e-Islam, accepted by Muslims, was fighting the tyranny of the Shah, we supported them, and kept their secret. For example, I together with Ahmad Mogharei (who later became an orthopaedic surgeon) knew that Hossein Ala was to be assassinated at Sepahsalar Mosque on the following day, 16 November 1955.

And according to an earlier arrangement, early that morning, one of two volunteers – Mozaffar and Mostafa 'Alameh (our very own haberdasher) – were to be chosen by Navvab Safavi to bring the prime minister to his reckoning. The previous night 'Alameh trusted us with the key to his shop and asked us for absolution. But in the end, it was Zolqadr who was chosen for the mission and went to Sepahsalar Mosque. However, he missed his opportunity.

It was then later decided that on the way to Khorramshahr Railroad Station, that was to be Hossein 'Ala's destination, Abdolhossein Vahedi would carry out the deed, but he also failed and was later arrested in Ahvaz on 21 November 1955.

The incident became a mandate for mass arrest of members of the Fada'iyan-e-Islam including Navvab Safavi and Khalil Tahmasebi[5] in December of that year, and their subsequent execution along with Mozaffar Zolghadr and Seyyed Mohammad Vahedi on 17 January 1955.

Nouri, athlete and math instructor, a friend of Gholam-Reza Takhti[6] was a generation older than us. He taught us chess so we would learn how to think. He brought Takhti to Dardar Alley to attend the wedding of a disabled man with the daughter of the caretaker of our neighbourhood's public refrigerator. We knew that Takhti had paid for the elaborate wedding ceremony and celebration that took place across the public refrigerator in the roundabout at the back of the alley. I was fourteen when Jahan-Pahlevan Takhti became my symbol of chivalry and love for humanity.

Cemeteries and shrines near Tehran, Bagh-e-Tooti (parrot garden), the shrines of Agha and Imamzadeh Abdullah, as well as Shahzadeh Abdul'azim in the city of Rey, on summer Fridays were places of outing for the middle to lower classes in Tehran. Bibi Shahrbanu's shrine whom many believed to be the daughter of Yazdegerd III[7] and married to Imam Hossein was also a favourite situated on a hill by the same name. People believed that if a man or a boy entered the sanctity of the grave he would turn to stone. That is why men and boys were not allowed there. However, one day I saw the caretaker, an old man, going in and out of that place. I asked the grownups, then why isn't he turning to stone? They said as all his ancestors were caretakers of the shrine, he is now privy to the sanctity of the place.

I was not convinced by that answer; and afterwards at fifteen, during summer nights lying out there in my bed on the roof I tried to figure it out. Till one Friday, accompanying my family to Bibi Shahrbanu, tempted by curiosity I threw caution to the wind. I put on my sister's veil, and trembling with fear I entered the shrine. And lo and behold I did not turn to stone! And walked out in one piece. And as a result of such experiences, I was able at sixteen to put religion and superstition behind me.

For the next two years I played music at the cafes and theatres of Lalehzar. And with a questioning eye and great curiosity studied the owners, workers and patrons that represented the full spectrum of society. And observed the relationships current among them. I learnt many things. Lalehzar was the laboratory that taught me a relative understanding of society that in turn became a great resource for my future life.

After taking one year off 'Elmiyyeh High School, I graduated in 1960, and was later admitted to the Youth Orchestra of Radio Iran (Iranian National Radio) as a bass player.

It is now 5 June 1953 and anti-government protests are organized by Khomeini. The army arrives to counter it. The people carry the many injured and fatally wounded to the hospitals. An acquaintance while having lunch with his family at a restaurant on the Shokoofeh Three-way Junction dies from a stray bullet. That day's incidents are passed around by word of mouth, but there is no reporting on the National Radio.

Khomeini is arrested at his house in Qom and imprisoned and is later deported first to Turkey and then to the city of Najaf in Iraq, A place not of exile, but of rest.

After that defeat, the culture and arts community as well as the intellectuals out of fear desisted from all political activity and focused their attention instead on literature and the arts. And although many writers and poets had turned to non-political work, very soon they were forced to express the social injustices that fuelled and inspired their creative efforts. This spread to other arenas as well such as the theatre and the cinema.

The winter of 1967 witnessed a mass effort by writers of varying and sometimes opposing views to form a union. A plan was proposed to create an organization with the name of *Kanoun-e Nevisandegan-e Iran* (the Writers' Association of Iran) to defend the freedom of thought and speech. And if this Association had been officially sanctioned and allowed to function, the intellectuals and activists could perform their historical function, and become a refuge for the establishment of 'political freedoms for all'. An ideal that could become the basis for the creation of a 'front to combat oppression and bring about the rule of the people'. Many of the intellectuals, poets and artists as well as teachers sought to remedy the absence of political parties through art and literature with writing and speaking in an indirect manner. Consequently a 'responsive art and literature' with subtle hints and innuendos broke the silence and became the guiding light for our generation.

All media was owned by the government, there was no independent media. Government exercised censorship and rationed out all cultural and artistic productions according to its own agenda. And having no choice the artist community complied. In those days, the radio was a closed off arena for me.

I did a lot of travelling. In the outskirts of the city of Ahvaz, I witnessed a family of four getting their sustenance and warmth from their one milk cow beneath a black tent. Can one ever forget such an image?

On Rey Street, in the neighbourhood of Abmangol, an honour-bound Muslim youth stabbed and murdered his sister's lover. He was arrested and imprisoned. A year later, at his trial, he was acquitted. Upon regaining his freedom, he returned proud and jubilant to the warm welcome of the people and hoodlums of his neighbourhood. They celebrated his return by sacrificing sheep.

Masoud Kimia'i made his movie *Qeysar* (1969) to the great approval of great many intellectuals, critics and with an unprecedented mass appeal. Houshang Kavousi, alongside several scholars who espoused the government perspective, criticized the film postulating that 'if someone were to rape your sister, you must go and file a police report'. However, many other respected critics including Ibrahim Golestan, Parviz Dava'i and Najaf Daryabandari defended the film for its artistic merits and cinematic qualities. The most intriguing aspect of all this, however, was that both camps failed to mention the tragedy of the girl's suicide. No one had found it objectionable!

Qeysar remains to this day a tragedy that is justified, sanctioned and repeated in a major part of our society. Does anyone ask why a girl who has been raped must then commit suicide out of shame, while the rapist and the killer proudly continue to live out their lives?

But the people interpreted *Qeysar* as 'justified reaction to injustice' and said: '*qeysar* means retaliation!'

Sometime later after the showing of *Qeysar*, a clergyman in the city of Qazvin, raped a girl under his pulpit. The girl's family took him out of town and threw him to the ground and drove over his body repeatedly until he was dead. The girl however stayed alive but became paralyzed for the rest of her life.

One could not openly criticize the government. And I could not, as I wished, create work that criticized the many injustices rampant in society. I left the Student Orchestra and Radio Iran. And together with Masoud Kimia'i took the path of the movies, the love of our youth.

In March 1969 after writing the score for *Qeysar*, and before its release into the theatres, I left for Munich, Germany.

Mohsen Pezeshkpour, the Pan-Iranist leader, had come to Karlsruhe with his followers to spread his message. In the protest that took place against them and the regime, I witnessed the ensuing clash that forced him to flee to a corner of the auditorium until the police came to his rescue. The police also recovered knives from the bags of his followers. The leaders of the Confederation of Iranian Students turned over photos of the bags' contents to the German press and they were published.

An essential and effective aspect of the Confederation of Iranian Students outside the country was its democratic structure that included many adherents of differing and sometimes opposing views. I became aware of the Confederation during my stay at Mansour Saharkhiz's home. I read Frantz Fanon's *The Wretched of the Earth* as well as other books that were supposedly banned in Iran. I became familiar with Che Guevara and guerrilla tactics. The Beatles moving beyond boundaries performed and broadcast their music from a radio station on the deck of a ship. Thinking of artists such as of John Lennon, and many sociopolitical movements of the sixties and the dominating artistic themes in Europe, I could no longer accept the notion of 'Art for art's sake' that many followed in order not to shoulder their social and humanitarian responsibilities. Henceforth art was no longer the goal for me, it instead became a tool. And to this day it remains an instrument for the expression of human ideals as well as my own experiences.

Promoting transparency as a desirable pursuit to remedy social ills is essentially the work of a free press and free political parties. In the absence of political freedoms, the creators of artistic and cultural works of protest in courting great danger could have a more negative outlook than a necessary one.

There were many lines those opposing the regime could not cross. Journalists, intellectuals, reformists and creators of works of art and literature did not have access to alternate means of communication with the people, to express their discontent with the autocracy.

The Islamic front however propagated its message via seminaries, mosques and pamphlets. Speaking of the 'Justice of 'Ali', the 'Martyrdom of Hossein the Wronged-One' and his efforts to seek retribution from the oppressors; and the many other fables they retold. And to assume the reins of power, some attracted a substantial number of the disenchanted youth to their message by presenting a deceitful modern facade. With constant repetition, talk of martyrdom and use of religious beliefs with both modern and traditional slant, and in the absence of a viable political alternative that was truly progressive, they gradually took over the universities.

In March 1970, I returned home to participate in the second Sepas Film Festival. And after receiving commendations for my score for the movie *Qeysar*, I decided to stay.

As Mehdi Bazargan had warned during his trial, the next generation that opposed autocracy would have no choice but to seek armed resistance as the sole means of liberation. They did choose it and took great risks and as a result lost their lives. And considering the mindset I had, in order to break the silence, I too became sympathetic to armed resistance. Henceforth I had no desire to make works of entertainment.

And in February 1970, artistic and literary works of protest that had lost much vigour since the Constitutional Revolution were revitalized by the Siyahkal Incident. An event that culminated in the loss of life for a group of lovers of mankind. It demonstrated to the people the defeat of 'absolutes' and the vulnerability of the regime; and it alerted the creators of works of art and literature to their social and humanitarian responsibilities. And I along with many others of the literati sympathized with the taboo-breaking Siyahkal Incident.

Initially I had considered composing a musical piece for Siyahkal. But there was no possibility to express openly my intentions regarding its creation, during the broadcast. And furthermore, as all musical compositions without words have always a purely cerebral expression, and can be interpreted in myriad ways that could be at times contradictory, I thought perhaps by writing music to a song I can give the movement some assistance. Lyrics to music, a song with the raspy and very unique voice of Farhad[8] could work and be effective. And it was.

One Friday afternoon Shahryar Qanbari[9] came over to my place to work on a song. I shared with him how I have always found Friday afternoons gloomy. He said he too has experienced its bitterness. And that is how he wrote his beautiful song *Friday* in one sitting as I fondly wrote the music. We used the song for the film *Khoda-hafez Rafiq* (Goodbye Comrade) and dedicated it to its director, our friend and fellow sufferer Amir Naderi. *Friday* was never broadcast on National Radio. However, after its distribution as a Single in the stores, when I heard that conscripted soldiers, leaving home for the barracks on Friday afternoons, would sing it in the bus, it made me exceedingly happy; for I had hit my target.

And as *Friday* was a song of protest and wasn't cut from the same material as all other 'government-sanctioned art', it became very popular especially among the youth. It was customary to print only the singer's photo on the cover of a Single. However, this was the first time that the photos of the creators of a song (Shahryar Qanbari, Farhad and me) were printed on a cover. (Later on, the idea was copied by a few. However, after the Islamic Revolution, the self-serving notions of the past were encouraged by the printing of a dozen photos of a singer on a cover.)

No production company was willing to touch the record, and I reluctantly sold the rights to the owner of a record store for the sum of 6,000 tomans.[10] And although we each had a different share in the proceeds of the sale, we divided it equally among us. It is noteworthy that after one year and *Friday*'s success, the rights of the song was re-sold to Stereo Disco for the sum of 50,000 tomans!

After the Siyahkal Incident, I along with my good friend, the talented filmmaker, Nasser Taqvai took the Chalous-Marzanabad Road past Lake Sama' to a village in the vicinity of Siyahkal. We had such a great time that we decided to spend the night there in a village by the lake and resume travelling the following day. In the village coffee house, we asked around for a place to stay the night. However, we became increasingly uncomfortable as villagers began eyeing us suspiciously while whispering among themselves. Finally, the village headman arrived and asked 'where are you from, who are you, and where are you heading?' They did not find our answers very convincing. The coffee house had by now become crowded with curious residents. The headman said: 'They have told us to beware of kidnappers who would show up to snatch our children to sell off their blood. We must report the arrival of suspicious strangers to the Police.'

There was no police station in that village. The villagers had started to follow us around. The village headman took us to his house. He put us in a room under guard; and asked for our identification papers so he could take it to a neighbouring village. There was a Sepah-e-Danesh[11] there who could examine our papers. Only I had my ID, the one from the Syndicate for Film Industry Artists. I gave it to him. He took my ID and left, as several frightened children watched us 'kidnappers' through the window.

The headman would not even allow us to enter the backyard to use the (outdoor) toilet. Angry villagers had gathered outside his house waiting. Time passed heavy and slow. Finally, the person they had sent over returned. To our good fortune the Sepah-e-Danesh had recognized me and confirmed my ID. Late into the night the headman dispersed the crowd with great difficulty and coldly asked us to leave as soon as possible. And we did. For we had not travelled there to inform or enlighten the people; our trip had been purely for pleasure.

As there was no review and assessment of songs for the movies in those years and the authorities were oblivious, I was able to write music that was quite different than my earlier work. These works were in contrast to the 'government-sanctioned art'. The manner of writing songs for National Iranian Radio and Television (NIRT) was such that first the composer would write the music and then the poet or songwriter would put lyrics to it.

Before my trip to Germany, I also worked in this manner. For example, I had written a piece that 'Abdollah Olfat according to his own taste had written lines in the spirit of 'Butterfly, the rose and the flame / A companion, the chalice and the wine …'; and it was performed by the famous and much-loved singer of the era Iraj.[12] The song was constantly broadcast on National Radio. The content of the songs was formed purely by the tastes of the lyricist, and the aesthetics of the composer had no say in it. All such songs expressed a lack of connection to the reality of our society. The artists and literati that play along with the government or stay clear of it, are always free to express themselves.

After this experience, upon my return to Iran, in order to make the lyrics conform to my taste I did the reverse. I chose poems and lyrics that resonated with my thinking and aspirations, and then composed the music for them. In this way the content of the songs were appropriate to the times. This gave me great satisfaction. Therefore, asking Shahryar Qanbari to write the lyrics for *Friday* was the onset of this new manner of working.

It was the '2,500-year Celebration of the Persian Empire' (1971). The Department of Theater of the Ministry of Art and Culture had asked Gholam-Hossein Sa'edi[13] to write a play for the occasion. He had evaded the answer. They consequently told him to write whatever he wished; he still did not respond. And every time I visited him at his clinic on Delgosha Street, he would show me a letter from the ministry. In the last letter they had threatened him that 'if within three months we do not receive your play at this office' such and such will happen. The deadline was now 48 hours away, and Sa'edi's response was total silence. Finally the ministry issued an edict that it will no longer collaborate with Sa'edi and that henceforth his physician's license will be revoked at all pharmacies. From then on, he worked without a license at the Akbar Clinic on Qazvin Circle; it belonged to his brother, also a physician.

The Research Centres within the Institute for Development of Children and Youth, The Ministry of Art and Culture, and the Office of Radio and Television were continually monitored by SAVAK. As far as I knew, the people who worked there had great integrity and laboured with great love. They went to the farthest corners of the country and carefully recorded the beliefs and customs of its people. They would then use this valuable knowledge to create programs that would benefit the society. SAVAK disposed of all this research in a single day by throwing them all into burlap sacks and sealed them and carried them off; nobody knew where?

For Shahryar Qanbari's tender and beautiful song *Namaz* (prayer) I lovingly wrote the music. It came out as a Single. The government pressured its singers Ramesh[14] and Fereydoun Foroughi to change the word *Namaz* to *Niyaz* (need) but failed. Both of them wanted to perform the song unchanged irrespective of the great pressure from the National Radio. I fought their censorship as well and did not turn over the music without the words, so they could recite the lyrics with its change to *Niyaz*. Finally, they had a sound engineer voice the word *Niyaz* over *Namaz*, so they could broadcast the song over the radio.

Remember, we are not talking about the censorship of the Islamic Republic, it was the radio of the Shah's government that would not broadcast the line '*Man namaz-am to ro har rooz didaneh*' (my prayer is to see you each day). SAVAK called me into one of their safe houses. They had also asked Shahryar Qanbari to attend to offer an explanation. I kept telling them 'this is poetic license; you can also find it in the works of our great poets such as Hafez'. But the interrogator would just repeat: 'You have insulted Islam and have caused havoc in Qom!'

I was the leader of the Youth Orchestra of the Iranian Radio, and later that of the University's Student Orchestra. With the creation of a Music Department in the Fine Arts Department of the University of Tehran in 1967, every year for the opening ceremony of the university before the Shah and the Queen, the ministers and the faculty, I would lead the University's Student Orchestra. At the reception after the program, the Shah would converse with Reza Narvand and I, asking questions and I would give answers to the ones pertaining to the arts.

Every year before September and the opening ceremony, during the summer nights lying in my bed on the roof, I would look at the stars and think of the star of resistance against tyranny that had been put out. And the dream of Shah's assassination and 'freedom' from his dictatorship would fill my mind.

Until the year 1971, when the time came for the University's opening ceremony attended by the Shah and Queen, they announced that all musicians must leave their instrument cases behind, and enter the main hall of Ferdowsi Auditorium for rehearsals, two hours ahead of time. Each musician and instrument were carefully inspected before entering the auditorium. Several violinists had forgotten to rosin their bows and asked if they could grab the rosin block from their cases. No matter how much they pleaded with the security, they were not allowed. Finally, Narvand begged 'Alinaqi 'Alikhani, the Chancellor of Tehran University, to intervene. The VP spent the next hour calling the authorities to get permission so that one person accompanied by two security guards could leave the auditorium and return with a single rosin block. They had the rosin tested and returned half an hour later.

The possibility of carrying a weapon into the auditorium where the Children and Youth Film Festival inaugurated by the prince was to be held was an inconceivable idea. However, several years later while at Evin Prison, I listened with amazement to the story of the prince taken hostage at the ceremony to free political prisoners.

Tehran, 100 kilometers was the name of a film that the late Arpik Baghdasarian had made for the Institute for Development of Children and Youth about the wretched conditions of the people living within 100 kilometres of Tehran, that remained banned till the revolution. One day along with Masoud Kimia'i and Nemat Haqiqi[15] we had gone to that very village for the shooting of the film *Khak* (Dust). That very night we had been invited to attend a dinner given by Amir-'Abbas Hoveyda, the prime minister, for several foreign guests. There were close to one hundred guests. But the banquet had been prepared for 500, with all manner of fruits, sweets, pastries and dishes. Seeing the well-fed guests ignore this elaborate feast was even more painful, especially for us who, only a few hours earlier, were witness to the poverty, hunger and the destitute conditions of the residents of that village. In truth the banquet displayed there was enough to feed the eighty families of that village for a whole year.

In 1973, I selected one of the *Shabaneh* (Nocturnal) poems of that 'great of poet of liberty' Ahmad Shamlou and turned it into song:

The alleyways are narrow
And the stores are shut
The homes are in darkness
And the roofs have caved in...

Farhad performed it beautifully. Masoud Masoumi, my good friend, prepared the photos for the cover. And to be conspicuous, we released it into the market priced at 5 tomans instead of the normal 3. A few days later, Khosrow Lavi, the producer, called to tell me that Sheikh Baha'i, the head of Chamber of Commerce, has complained 'because of its high price, the record must be pulled from the market!' We went to see him. He asked: 'The normal price for a Single is 3 toman, why is this one so expensive?' I replied, 'This is not really an everyday item to effect the people adversely.' And after arguing during two more visits, he regretfully said, 'Don't cause us trouble; SAVAK has told us to withdraw the record due to overpricing.' And that is how they stopped further production of the Single and the printing of its cover by Mr Taqizadeh's Lux Printers.

One Wednesday afternoon in early September 1973, I was arrested along with Hossein Samakar near the Institute (for Development of Children and Youth). They sat us between two guys with machine-guns into the back seat of a Paykan[16] and took us to Evin Prison. On the way there, I inquired for the reason. The heavily built driver, grinning, asked in reply: 'So this *"the alleyways are narrow... and there is no paraffin..."* and so on, is your doing?' I said, 'yes'. He laughed and said, 'I bought a whole bunch of them myself!' I asked myself: why does the re-issue of a poem, long published should cause so much consternation with the Intelligence service?

Of course, I had been a little devious with the design of the cover: I had placed an American flag in one corner of a jackpot machine, and with the coins showing the profile of the Shah with his head tilted towards the flag. I had not been arrested for writing the music for Shabaneh after all. (After the revolution it appears that someone who did not approve of the image has altered it in Photoshop and plastered a fake cover for the song all over the internet.)

I have mentioned I first heard of the hostage-taking of the Shah's son in those nine months I had been incarcerated at Evin.

For forty days I shared a cell with Keramat Daneshian.[17] He truly did believe in the words he had said that 'I would give my life to maim just one leg of Shah's regime'. I knew he would be killed. Would that he hadn't died and could have witnessed the total collapse of the full corpus of the monarchy. Yet he still lives among us for the gift of the verses *Baharan Khojasteh Baad!* (Blessed be the spring) that he left to us till the coming of the people's true sovereignty.

In early January 1978, in a meeting with Pedram Akbari and his friend Davoud, both close friends of Keramat, I welcomed their idea to perform it. I promised all my friends who hummed the verses to the different melodies of the day, to put it to music; I did and later recorded it.

It was much later that I learnt that the verses actually came from a poem by Abdollah Behzadi who had composed it in memory of Patrice Lumumba. And Keramat would sing the verses he loved as a chant for his comrades. I have said it many times and continue to say: this song truly belongs to Keramat! And it is because of his great sacrifice for mankind, and not my efforts or ours, that this song has been immortalized.

One of those who had been speaking of 'hostage-taking' had mentioned my name as a candidate to drive the car with the hostages quickly to the airport. It was my activist friends' misfortune they did not make me aware of this plan. With respect to the experience I have already related, if they had asked for my assistance, I would have dissuaded them from this impossible idea.

SAVAK had planned to use the 'hostage-taking' scenario to nullify the effect of the Siyahkal Incident, through the assistance of Amir-Hossein Fetanat who unfortunately was held in close confidence by Keramat Daneshian and managed to display its power to put down all opposition by televising live the trials for the populace at large. 'Political prisoners must be freed,' is but an incomplete chant if it is not combined with the words 'political prisons must be torn down.'

One night, Daryoush,[18] at the end of one his performances in a night club, had ignored the invitation of a customer to join him at their table and had left for home. He didn't know the individual was prominent in the establishment and his refusal had embarrassed the guy in front of his guests and had made him very angry. SAVAK decided to teach him a lesson. Very soon afterwards they printed a photo of Daryoush in the *Kayhan* newspaper showing him with some opium paraphernalia. Many of the people who were losing their trust in the establishment believed the photo had been faked, and Daryoush as a result become even more popular. When SAVAK realized the photo had not done its job to discredit him, it demanded that he should sing the song *Rasool-e-Rastakhiz*, (The Prophet of Resurrection) for the 6 Bahman (26 January) anniversary of the Shah's White Revolution.[19]

Considering that none of the song's creators had ever been arrested or imprisoned for the lyrics, music or performance of any song prior to the (Islamic) Revolution, it is important to note that in the spring of 1974 some other poets of progressive songs were arrested and kept in Evin Prison for several days after the creation of the Rastakhiz Party. After threats and signing of an agreement, Iraj Jannati-Atai under pressure of SAVAK had composed lyrics for two songs for the White Revolution that Daryoush would have to perform in praise of the Prophet (*Rasool*) of *Rastakhiz*. They also sought the help of Babak Bayat to put the lyrics to music. And on the 6th of Bahman of 1974, the performance was broadcast via the Iranian National Television.

Henceforth Daryoush and the poet became browbeaten and quietly minded their own business, with little resistance till after the (Islamic) Revolution and a new beginning.

Hormuz Ayrom, the Evin interrogator (with the alias, magistrate), had also asked Shahryar Qanbari to write lyrics to a song celebrating the White Revolution for Daryoush to perform, that Shahryar with the aide of his father's cunning was able to evade.

Finally, the interrogator asked me to put the lyrics that Jannati-'Atai had written for Daryoush to music. And I replied, 'Let him use the title music I have already composed for the film *Topoli*[20] [Chubby] for his lyrics.' With the excuse that 'I am currently busy finishing music for several films that need to be completed for the Festival of the Institute for Development of Children and Youth and have no time.' In answer to the interrogator's insistence, Hossein Samakar, the Institute's vice-president told him: 'The Festival will not happen if the music for the films is not completed.' Those very words were my salvation and I thanked Samakar for it. Had I not been able to evade that task, I believe after the Islamic Revolution I would have had to honestly express that I had done so under pressure from SAVAK.

'Ali Tajvidi, veteran composer, although not a poet himself had gone ahead and written some lyrics and music for Homeyra[21], and using the pretext went on to eulogize the Shah: 'O king of kings, may your crown and throne be eternal!' After the Revolution, out of fear and to escape punishment on account of those verses, he supported the Islamic Republic's efforts to ban the female voice from Iranian music. He volunteered to re-record the works he had composed and produced for the female voice, by using male vocalists and a more elaborate orchestration. And it is ironic that the alternate media that opposes the Islamic regime continues to broadcast these masculinized songs; and thus, unknowingly promotes the Islamic Republic's art policy.

In 1974 there were new censorship regulations for the songs being produced outside the National Radio and Television system. A creation of the new Rastakhiz Party that became in essence an edict to all recording studios. Henceforth, no one could record a song without first obtaining a license from the Ministry of Art and Culture.

'Abbas Khoshdel, flautist and composer, SAVAK's employee at the Ministry of Art and Culture, would visit one recording studio after another. He would listen to a recording by comparing it to the pre-approved text of the song. If there were any extraneous sounds, such as that of an owl or a rooster as I had done for *Shabaneh,* and they had not been used to convey any other meaning, he would give the go ahead to the recording.

In June 1974, the beginning of the shooting for the film *Gavazn-ha* (The Deer) coincided with my release from Evin. I went to the set, and Masoud Kimia'i told me the gist of the story. I was thrilled and amazed. Kimia'i worked too much out of love to be afraid or cautious. I believe *The Deer* was the zenith of dissident cinema at its time.

The innocent vulnerability of the characters in the film inspired me to take one of the folkloric children rhymes my mother used to whisper in my ear as a kid, melodic phrases that had not yet been put to music. I chose *Gonjeshkak-e Ashi-Mashi* (Teeny-tiny sparrow) and composed the music for it. And out of fear I censored myself by changing the phrase Hakem-bashi[22] to Hakim-bashi.[23] For certain had I kept the original intact, it would have given them cause to censor the film.

At the Tehran Film Festival at Roudaki Hall[24] and the Paramount movie theatre, *The Deer* was screened only twice. Esma'il Nouri-'Ala[25] had said: 'While watching the film I felt any minute now they are going to show up to arrest the audience!' The Ministry of Art and Culture as a consequence punished Bahram Reypour and several others who had authorized the script.

The audience's positive reaction brought down the weight of the establishment on Masoud Kimia'i and his film, it was no longer the Bureau for Affairs of Cinema, or the Ministry of Arts and Culture but SAVAK itself. Day after day SAVAK agents came to Mehdi Misaqiyeh's film studio. They would monitor the whole stretch of the alley outside the studio, until their assigned agent would show up and sit behind the editing desk and inspect the offensive segments minutely on the Moviola machine. It is hard to believe but he would say for example, 'A thief is not an intellectual, he should not be wearing glasses!'[26] I witnessed Misaqiyeh saying, 'Don't change any part of the film! Is it not my investment after all? Put it away and let it gather dust on a shelf. Leave it in storage!' But since the film had been shown at the film festival, its banning had caused lots of rumours among the population especially among the youth. SAVAK was adamant to have it shown in theatres as soon as possible. And finally with alterations that were feasible and Kimia'i unwillingly undertook, after nearly a year the film was released in the theatres. Dissident artistic efforts do not have the power of political parties and the media and cannot single-handedly affect change.

As two journalists, followers of the old regime, reminisced about their 'freedom of speech', one would say, 'I used to write whatever I wished.' And the other would add, 'Sometimes when I wrote an article at the printers, I could immediately send it to the printing press myself.' Indeed, they were both right. They were the Hossein Shari'atmadari's[27] of that era. And the Shari'atmadari's of today still continue to enjoy such freedoms.

After *The Deer*, Kimia'i reluctantly had to compensate by making a film to neutralize it. And the result was the film *Ghazal* (Sonnet). A year later, however, he returned to his own work and made *Safar-e-Sang* (The Stone's Journey) based on Behzad Farahani's[28] story *Sang-o-Sorna* (The Horn and the Stone).

For many long years now the people of Iran have been at loggerheads with those in power. Time has moved on, and they have become accustomed to the notion of 'the rule over the people' instead of 'the rule by the people'. Hezbollah knowingly set fire to Cinema Rex in Abadan, and made Shah's regime the culprit, and as a result provoked the oppressed masses to fill the streets in greater numbers against the Shah. The news or controversies such as Shahpour 'Alireza's[29] plane crash that caused his death, the so called suicide of Takhti, the death of General Khatam[30] in a kiting accident, the drowning of Samad Behrangi in Aras River and the death of Jalal Al-e Ahmad,[31] rightly or wrongly have always been used as leverage in the people's struggle against the government. The people have had no other recourse for protest. And until the government has been elected according to the will of the people, this mistrust will continue to persist. I have always viewed myself on the side of the people in my struggle against regime. The night that a fire inspector shared the result of his investigations into the Cinema Rex fire, I rejected everything offhand, although I knew in my mind, he was right, just to add one more atrocity to the dictatorship's criminal record.

In 1978, the Shah stated on National Television that he has heard the people's 'cry of revolution'. Although I must add a little too late! We in the opposition did not wish to acknowledge his retreat. There was no 'organized front' among us to take advantage of the moment and facilitate the transfer of power to the people. The moment thus passed.

A new opportunity presented itself, however, late in the hour. In December of 1978 along with friends and colleagues such as Nasser Zera'ati, Afshar Panah, 'Ali Rousta'i and several others, we proposed to form a cultural-political front called the *Anjoman-e Honarmandan-e-Khalq* or Artists' Association for the Masses, to enlist the participation of all dissidents; we were naively optimistic.

In Early March 1979, close to a thousand participants gathered at the Talar-e-Farhang (Hall of Culture), near Rudaki Hall. It was a promising response. We were determined to keep the organization independent of all political parties and ideologies. But 'Ali Rousta'i, a 'Maoist' became the moderator of the event, and abusing our trust, in an insulting manner and without reservation, began to discredit the Tudeh Party. By our next meeting the dissidents did not show up. And when the Association morphed into the Toilers' Party, it was shut down. All of us have been working for many years now towards creating a Democratic Front that is based on inclusion and not exclusion.

In conclusion: We have realized that in order to achieve 'rule by the people', the presence of dissident literature and art although necessary in not by itself sufficient.

Is it possible to reform a culture that accommodates totalitarianism, where its social traditions support and justify it?

It teaches us that with political, cultural, social and individual freedoms it is impossible to discredit and neutralize the effect of harmful values current in society. Governments together with most people are weary of changing their habits. They continue to defend the propagation of harmful traditions. In a nation, where its cultural and especially its religious traditions have cast a dark shadow into the lives of its people, is it at all possible to take a short cut to secular democratic governance?

Without political freedom, despots backed by many traditions, whether useful or harmful, always emerge victorious against modernity and civilization.

The path of achieving a modern society that is informed of its citizens' rights, and demands it, is through 'political freedom for everyone without exception'. That means the freedom of the media, the freedom of political parties, the freedom for peaceful protest and strike.

Was there ever another path we failed to take, to uproot tyranny?

What would you have done if you were in my place?

16

The impact of the guerrilla movement on contemporary Iranian theatre

Houman Azarkolah

I first met the actor Nasser Najafi in 1968. Our acquaintance had a profound effect on my life. Through him I became familiar with philosophy in general and with Marxism in particular. It was also through him that I entered art circles, and theatre became the centre of my life. In fact, since my adolescent days, I was interested in performing arts. I was involved in the school theatre program in high school. By the end of high school, I was also dubbing films for the Shahab Studio in Tehran. Of course, I also followed politics. My father supported the Prime Minister Mohammad Mossadeq, and, as far as I can remember, I was against dictatorship and an advocate of social justice. I remember attending the Jalaliyeh meeting on 18 May 1961, where a hundred thousand people came together. It was the first mass gathering of the Shah's opponents since the coup of 1953. I accompanied my father there. I also attended Gholam-Reza Takhti's memorial ceremonies which took place seven days and, again, forty days after his death in 1968. In addition, I also followed the tribunal of Bijan Jazani, whom I had personally met in the Tabli Film Studio,[1] as well as the detention of the Palestine Group and Shokrollah Paknezhad. However, I was not attracted to guerrilla struggle, but rather, as Nasser Najafi said, what I had in mind was along the lines of a cultural guerrilla and I therefore believed in 'committed art'.

The first piece I saw on stage was *Chub Bedastha-ye Varazil* (The Club-Wielders of Varazil, 1965) written by Gholam-Hossein Sa'edi and directed by Ja'far Vali. The same year I saw *Pahlavan Akbar Mimirad* (Pahlavan Akbar Dies) written by Bahram Beyza'i and directed by 'Abbas Javanmard.

The apex of Iranian theatre performances occurred between 1968 and 1970. Many plays, such as *Bolbol-e Sarghashteh* (The Wandering Nightingale, 1966) and *Looneh-e Shoghal* (The Jackal's Den, 1969) by 'Ali Nassirian, *Ay-e Ba-kolah, Ay-e Bi-kolah* (Short A, Long A, 1967) directed by Ja'far Vali, *Az Poshte Shisheha* (From Behind the Glasses, 1969) written by Akbar Radi and directed by Rokneddin Khosravi, and *Vay bar Maghlub* (1970) written by Gholam-Hossein Sa'edi and directed by Davoud Rashidi, and many more, were staged then.

Most of the plays of this period dealt with some level of social criticism and were presented with finesse and political discretion due to the repressive atmosphere.

Gholam-Hossein Sa'edi was one of the greatest dramatists of the time. Many of his themes dealt with the distressed lives of the lower classes, especially the peasants; either those who had remained in their villages or those who left the land and relocated in cities following the Shah's land reform programme.

Akbar Radi also wrote about the villagers' and peasants' tribulation vis-à-vis the landowners. And Nosratollah Navidi exposed the conflicts and difficulties of the villagers after the land reform (following the Shah's White Revolution) and the bankruptcy many farmers faced due to the massive obligations that the agricultural joint stock companies had imposed upon them. Bijan Mofid wrote about social corruption, and according to Nasser Rahmaninezhad, Mofid wrote about 'superstitions, traditions and arbitrary rules and regulations'.[2] And, there was Bahram Beyza'i whose criticism of dictatorship, suppression and its consequences was written in such a coded language that one figuratively required a key in order to decipher the hidden meaning.

An important event of this period was the founding of the Iran Theatre Association in 1968; pioneered by Nasser Rahmaninezhad. Young, passionate actors, most of whom had dissociated themselves from the Anahita[3] Theatre group, such as Sa'id Soltanpour, Mohsen Yalfani, Mehdi Fathi, Mahmoud Dowlatabadi, etc. were invited[4] to join.

Anahita was run by former Tudeh Party members who had run out of energy by the 1960s. The main characteristic of the Iran Theatre Association's work consisted of their militant protest. They shook the *status quo* as they attempted to challenge the boundaries of censorship which dominated the theatre back in those days. *Incident at Vichy* by Arthur Miller, the first work presented by this group, was warmly welcomed by students and even some intellectuals. In 1969, the second play, *An Enemy of the People* by Henrik Ibsen, was presented, but to avoid censorship, changed the name of the piece to *Dr. Stockmann*. The third work staged was *Amouzegaran* (The Teachers) written by Mohsen Yalfani[5] and directed by Sa'id Soltanpour. If my memory serves me correctly, it opened one month before the Siyahkal incident in January 1971. *Amouzegaran* played only a few nights. SAVAK shut down the performance and Soltanpour was arrested. I believe this was the first incarceration of theatre artists since the August 1953 coup.

One interesting fact is that the Theatre Workshop was founded at the same time as the Iran Theatre Association. Although the Workshop's manifest stated its intention 'to support all artists who have no place in official or established theatre',[6] in practice, they did not embrace the artists who believed in 'committed art'. The Theatre Workshop was the most important school of 'art for art's sake' in this period, and because of this, they were confronted with opposition and protests during some of their performances. The protestors were mostly young art students who disrupted the plays for a few minutes, and sometimes even stopped the performances altogether.

I recall that with the start of the guerrilla struggle, the political mood of the intellectuals changed. This transformation was so drastic that the intellectual community became polarized. One group preached 'art for art's sake' and another group advocated 'committed art'. In 1972, while preparing for the 2,500-year celebration of the Persian Empire, the Shah's regime started a widespread campaign against alleged 'saboteurs', which, ironically contributed to the appeal of the guerrillas. Meanwhile, the cultural organs of the regime started promoting 'art for art's sake'. I remember reading a statement in large character in the *Ettela'at* Newspaper from a French director who was visiting Shiraz Festival of Arts: 'I detest political performances.'[7] Many renowned artists like Jerome Savary, Peter Brook, and like-minded artists were invited to the Fifth Shiraz Festival of Arts, but, I believe, in those days, their work did not have much effect on our theatre.

In 1972, the City Theatre was inaugurated with Chekhov's *The Cherry Orchard*, directed by Arby Avanessian. I must point out that the state supported and facilitated the work of this group and groups similar to them. They were aided in every aspect of their productions. They participated in national festivals and won prices. *Nagehan Haza Habibollah*, written by ʿAbbas Nalbandian and directed by Arby Avanessian, was presented at the Sixth Shiraz Festival of Arts. This group was also allowed to participate in international festivals. In my opinion, the secret of their success was having nothing to do with social or political issues. Their work was more formalist and surrealist.

In contrast, independent groups who were for the most part, followers of 'committed art', had very few possibilities and many more difficulties in their pursuit of theatre. Most of these troupes consisted of youth who were against the existing conditions and were not aligned with the state. It was obvious that they were proponents of social political theatre; theatre for the people.[8]

From 1972 on, we witnessed another kind of theatre which also appeared in intellectual circles in Europe and the United States. This kind of theatre was known as the Theatre of the Absurd. It was introduced in Iran by young directors who had studied drama in Germany, England, France or the United States such as Hamid Samandarian, Davoud Rashidi, ʿAbbas Maghfourian, ʿAbdolhossein Fahim, ʿAli Rafiʿi and many more. These directors attempted to seek out both contemporary dramatists and the techniques of modern theatre. Thanks, mainly to art professors, plays such as *Waiting for Godot* by Samuel Beckett and Eugène Ionesco's *Rhinoceros and The Chairs* were presented in Ferdowsi Hall at Tehran University, while, *The Visit* by Friedrich Dürrenmatt was performed in Molavi Hall. Although this kind of theatre was generally welcomed by intellectuals and had a concrete effect on the form of theatrical performances, the content of these plays was not much liked by the leftist intellectuals in particular.

The year 1972 heralded the rise of armed struggle by the Fadaʾis and Mojahedin Organizations, and, the ensuing detentions and executions of militants who stood against the Shah's dictatorship. The play *Yek bar-e digar: Abuzar* (Once more: Abuzar) by Reza Daneshvar was performed this same year in Hosseiniyeh Ershad – the same place where ʿAli Shariʿati's fiery lectures had played an irrefutable role in the strengthening and growth of 'militant Islam' amongst the youth of the country. This bellicose drama – which I think was the first religious play in Iran (in the modern sense of the word) – was well received, as I, myself, witnessed it.[9] After all, it was a new work for inexperienced students back in those days.

The most belligerent producer of provocative and pugnacious theatre was Saʿid Soltanpour, who, needless to say, was arrested several times. The word was that he had been imprisoned just before he began *The Visions of Simone Machard*[10] in 1972 – a play by Bertolt Brecht. He started the work upon his release. I remember the play got great reviews,[11] and was lauded by dissident intellectuals and protesting students alike. It was in this fervent atmosphere when Bijan Mofid staged Brecht's *Fear and Misery of the Third Reich* in 1973.

I started my higher education in 1973 at the College of Dramatic Arts, University of Tehran. The atmosphere at the university was very politicized and subsequently watched by the police. Students, who, for the most part, were supporters of guerrilla warfare, who even showed solidarity with the militants of such organizations were arrested on specious charges. In general, our professors were intellectuals who were critical of the existing situation. Of course, fear of SAVAK hindered any explicit discourse, especially in the classroom. But the plays and the playwrights we studied and the plays we staged were all coloured with protest. Outside the university realm, the Bureau of Dramatic Arts put on plays with more explicit protest and confrontational content than before. *Ebrahim Toupchi and Agha Beyk* by Manouchehr Radin, which had already been performed in the past, was re-imagined on stage in Sangalaj Theatre in 1974. It was directed by Rokneddin Khosravi who was highly respected by the students. The new version was spectacular.

The detention of Khosrow Golesorkhi and his companions, their public trial in 1973, which was televised for reasons unknown to me, and the courageous self-defence of Golesorkhi and Keramat Daneshian proved to be a turning point in the political atmosphere of the country. From then onwards, not only university students, but also high school students showed solidarity with the opponents of the Shah and the guerrillas. The inclination towards 'revolutionary violence' grew stronger especially among art students. The fact that Daneshian, 'Abbas Samakar, Teyfour Batha'i and Reza 'Allamehzadeh were all students of the Academy of Film and Television also had an impact.

In 1974, the members of the Iran Theatre Association were arrested. I remember news of the detention of this group exploded like a bomb amongst students.[12] All the students I encountered were protesting the arrests.

Sa'id Soltanpour was an exceptional individual. He was fearless and intrepidly proceeded towards his goal. As soon as he was released from prison, he would continue on the same path. This made him very popular in certain circles. He had an amazing influence on the students in general, and, arts students in particular. Since he was perceived as a militant, maybe his activism was more revered than his artistic work. He believed that we should start the struggle from any ideological starting point.

Nasser Rahmaninezhad, a friend of Amir-Parviz Pouyan and known Fada'i sympathizer, was also well loved and respected by the students.[13] Nasser was sentenced to twelve years confinement and was brutally tortured in prison which resulted in severe heart problems. We were heavy-hearted when this news reached those of us who were involved in theatre. I had heard that he wrote plays and performed them with other political prisoners while incarcerated. This news reminded us of 'Abdolhossein Noushin who directed his plays from prison back in 1948.

At the height of the guerrilla struggle, in 1974–5, art students (from fine arts to theatre and cinema) were increasingly arrested and put in jail. The ones I remember are Akbar Afra, Cyrus Moshafeqi, Asghar Davari, Javad Zolfaqari.[14]

Under the threat of arrest and imprisonment, it is obvious which direction a young person would take. The number of dissertations submitted by theatre majors alone with socio-political subjects was a clear example of the increased interest in critical and protest theatre.[15] Most of the plays we put on had political themes. Many of these were stopped only a few days before opening night and all our work was, seemingly, for naught. In 1974, Mohammad Kowsar staged Brecht's *The Good Person of Szechwan* in Molavi Hall. His measured direction is unforgettable. This play was the beginning of a wave of translations of Brecht's plays which had been published since 1970.[16] Soon afterwards, Athol Fugard's *Hello and Goodbye* directed by Rokneddin Khosravi went on stage. In his works, Fugard never failed in the psychoanalysis of his characters. He confronts them in a manner which points out the general deficiency of mankind in all circumstances and shows that humans could achieve perfection and deliverance despite their weaknesses.

It was in the same year that Majid Mozafari worked on Jean-Paul Sartre's *The Wall* in which I had a role. Just as it was about to be performed, it was stopped for unknown reasons. The same happened to Albert Camus' *The Just Assassins*. They didn't permit these plays to be performed and, thus, antagonism increased. Hormoz Hedayat worked on Arnold Weker's *The Soldiers*. *The Soldiers* was translated by 'Ali Tolo' who had spent years in prison and was known to be Amir-Parviz Pouyan's and Masoud Ahmadzadeh's comrade. This book was published in 1973 and staged in 1975. That same year Bijan Jazani, alongside eight other political prisoners, was executed in the Evin Hills and the lie was promulgated that they were killed while trying to escape from prison. This unjustifiable execution greatly angered the intellectual circles, especially in universities. Student protests against this crime took place all over the country.

In 1976 *The Tower* by Peter Weiss was directed by Rajab Mohammadin. I performed in this play, which was about the younger generation's struggle to free themselves from the shackles of tradition. Rajab enhanced the play with torture scenes.[17]

In 1976, we simultaneously staged two playlets: Brecht's *The Beggar and the Dead Dog* directed by Mohammad Harati, and Anton Chekhov's *The Anniversary* directed by Tajbakhsh Fanaian. Both plays were banned after a few days, however, Brecht's *The Exception and the Rule*, directed by Cyrus Shamlou, was successfully staged in Molavi Hall.

In 1976, after Hamid Ashraf and all the leading cadres of the Fada'i Guerrillas were killed, a climate of fear and alarm took over the intellectuals. Pressure grew every day. It was the end of the year when Khosravi grabbed a hold of Brecht's *The Trial of Joan of Arc*, a piece with a large cast. The rehearsals took six months. Mohammad Harati did a beautiful job designing the set in the College of Dramatic Arts Theatre. Students from various universities filled the hall. Joan of Arc's torture scene and the inquisitorial court was very disturbing and ironically paralleled recent events. When the performance was over, the students left the hall shouting and chanting slogans. Security police streamed in and arrested a number of students and, needless to say, banned the play.

The Ministry of Art and Culture asked Khosravi to perform the play in the ministry for state officials so they could see for themselves what had caused such agitation. So we went to the ministry in Baharestan Square. We decorated the stage and performed the play in front of government officials and a few university professors. Afterwards, they told Khosravi that the play was officially banned and forbidden to be performed in Tehran or any other city. I remember we, the members of the theatre group, were sitting in a café, as Khosravi told us the story. The officials had summoned him to a meeting and asked: Do you think all Iranian girls are Joan of Arc? At least, that is what this play signifies! I can't remember what Khosravi's response was, but all of us who were sitting in the café responded: Of course, all Iranian girls are Joan of Arcs! I heard about Ghazal Ayati being killed, and, before that, I had heard about many more Joan of Arcs such as Nezhat Rouhi-Ahangaran, Nasrin Tavakkoli, Mahboubeh Motahedin, Sediqeh Reza'i, Mahvash Jasemi, Shokouh Tavafchiyan, just to name a few.

I think *The Trial of Joan of Arc* was Brecht's last play which was staged before the beginning of the people's movement that brought about the downfall of Pahlavi rule.

The primary reason Brecht was so successful in Iran during the 1970s was that the revolutionary and humanist spirit of his plays resonated with the social and political climate in Iran. They highlighted the necessity for resistance which was already taking place in Iran – overtly and covertly.

Here, I must say, some presentations of Brecht's plays were not good as not enough attention was being paid to the style and form of his plays, due to the lack of knowledge of fundamentals of Theater by directors who were attracted to this great artist. Because of this, some artists didn't value Brecht's work and refused to perform his plays. It is true that many of these theatre groups worked on Brecht in particular, and theatre in general – without necessarily knowing its techniques – because they saw the dramatic arts as a means to protest political autocracy and a government which did not care about the people. Let's not forget that we also had many great interpretations of Brecht by directors such as Samandarian, Khosravi, Kowsar, Soltanpour, Rahmaninezhad and the like.

In conclusion, the guerrilla movement and armed struggle shook artistic and intellectual circles. The message of the movement was simple and clear: 'the time for words is over, it is time for deeds and actions'. For some, action meant taking up arms and for others it meant protesting via art and culture. For theatre people, action meant taking it to the stage. Theatre provided a means to illuminate people's suffering and the existing social contradictions. Before the guerrilla movement, theatre pieces showed only social problems; after Siyahkal, we wanted to manifest protest and resistance. The message of most of the student productions, at least those who had the courage, was resistance against dictatorship and censorship. With their heroic struggles, the guerrillas won sympathy; even from people like me who did not believe in armed struggle but believed more in political and cultural struggle. My generation deeply believed in political and cultural struggle and we all hoped to become good cultural guerrillas. History will judge if we were successful or not. The strange thing is that after a one-year absence and only a month after the revolution which ended in the overthrow of the Shah, Brecht appeared on stage again, in February 1979, in the form of *The Exception and the Rule* directed by Rokneddin Khosravi. It was as if its message was that the 1979 Revolution was the exception to the rule for revolutions.

Notes

Preface

1. Amongst notable works published on guerrilla warfare in Iran within the English scholarly sphere are Maziar Behrooz, *Rebels with a Cause: The Failure of the Left in Iran* (London: I.B. Tauris, 1999), Peyman Vahabzadeh, *A Guerrilla Odyssey: Modernization, Secularism, Democracy, and Fada'i Period of National Liberation in Iran 1971–1979* (New York: Syracuse University Press, 2010) and ʿAli Rahnema, *Call to Arms. Iran's Marxist Revolutionaries* (London: OneWorld, 2021).

1 Formation of thoughts and foundation of the Iranian People's Fada'i Guerrillas

1. Bijan Jazani, 'Masaʾel-e Jonbesh-e Zed Esteʿmari va Azadikhahaneh-ye Khalq-ha-ye Iran', *19 Bahman Teʾorik* 4 (April 1976): 18.
2. Ibid., 48.
3. Ibid., 48–9.
4. Abolhassan Zia-Zarifi, *Zendeginameh-ye Hassan Ziya-Zarifi* (Tehran: Amindezh, 2004), 275–303.
5. Jazani, 'Masaʾel', 49.
6. Ibid., 2, 3.
7. Ibid., 17.
8. The precise translation of the speech delivered on 9 April 1961 is 'Cuba: Historical Exception or Vanguard in the Anticolonial Struggle'.
9. Jazani, 'Masaʾel', 48.
10. Ibid.
11. Ibid., 24.
12. Ibid., 22.
13. Ibid., 16.
14. Mohammad-Majid Kianzad, 'Yadmandehha', in *Be Zaban-e Qanun*, ed. Nasser Mohajer and Mehrdad Vahabi (Paris: Noghteh, 2017), 294.
15. For more information about the arrest, torture, resistance, imprisonment and the trial of the fourteen executed members, Nasser Mohajer and Mehrdad Vahabi, *Be Zaban-e Qanun* (Paris: Noghteh Books, 2017).
16. Jazani, 'Masaʾel', 28.
17. Ibid., 29.
18. Mehdi Sameʿ, 'Bijan Jazani, Marksist-e Khallaq', in *Jongi Darbareh Zendegi va Asar-e Bijan Jazani*, ed. Kanun-e Gerdavari va Nashr-e Asar-e Bijan Jazani (Paris: Khavaran, 1999), 134–5; Also see Mihan Jazani in the same book, 71.

19. Mihan Jazani in conversation with Nasser Mohajer pointed to regular letter correspondence between Hamid Ashraf and Bijan Jazani during 1969–70. Paris, 20 October 2008.
20. Bijan Jazani, 'Masa'el', 49.
21. Ibid., 1.
22. Ibid., 1–16.
23. Ibid., 18.
24. Ibid., 18–19.
25. Ibid., 18.
26. Ibid., 26.
27. Hamid Ashraf, *Jambandi Yek Sal Mobarezeh dar Shahr va Kuh* (n.p.: Entesharat-e Sazemanha-ye Jebheh-ye Melli-ye Iran Kharej az Keshvar (Bakhsh Khavarmiyaneh), 1973), 14.
28. Naqi Hamidian, *Safar ba Balha-ye Arezou* (Stockholm: Arash, 2004), 20.
29. Ibid., 20.
30. Ibid., 46–54.
31. Bijan Jazani, *19 Bahman Te'orik* 7 (1976), 3–5. Nasser Mohajer, *Zendegi va Andisheh-ha-ye Pouyan*. Forthcoming (Paris: Noghteh Publishers).
32. Nasser Mohajer, 'Amir-Parviz Pouyan az Cheshm-e Baqer Parham', *Iran Namag* 1, no. 4 (2017): 214–33.
33. Masoud Ahmadzadeh, *Mobarezeh Mosallahaneh, ham Estrateji, ham Taktik* (n.p.: Jebheh-ye Melli-ye Iran-Bakhsh Khavar-e Miyaneh, 1974), 32.
34. Bijan Jazani, 'Tashkil-e Guruh va Khosousiyat 'Omdeh-ye An', *19 Bahman Te'orik* 7 (June–July 1976): 5, 6.
35. Nasser Mohajer, 'Pouyan'.
36. Hamidian, *Safar*, 20.
37. Ahmadzadeh, *Mobarezeh*, 36–7.
38. Jazani, 'Tashkil', 90–1.
39. For example, see Younes Orang Khadivi, *Man Marg ra Surudi Kardam* (Tehran: Baztab, 2005), Behrouz Dehqani, *Majmueh-ye Maqalat: Maqaleh, Tarjomeh, Naqd va Barresi* (Aachen: Confederation of Iranian Students (National Union)), 1976.
40. Alireza Nabdel, *Chand Neveshteh va She'er* (n.p.: Entesharat-e Komunizm, 1977), 5.
41. Jazani, 'Tashkil', 91–2.
42. Jazani, 'Khususiyat', 12.
43. Ibid., 12–13.
44. Ashraf, *Seh Saleh*, 97.
45. Ibid., 10.
46. Ibid., 99.
47. Bijan Jazani, 'Rafiq Masoud Ahmadzadeh', *19 Bahman Te'orik* 4 (April–May 1976): 45.
48. Bijan Jazani, 'Tamas ba Guruh-ha va Jarian-ha-ye Makhfi Digar', *19 Bahman Te'orik* 7 (June–July 1976): 25.
49. Jazani, 'Ahmadzadeh', 43.
50. 'Daneshjouyan va Rowshanfekran-e Mobarez', *Nabard* 1, March 1971.
51. The Organization of the Iranian People's Fada'i Guerrillas is the title the Fada'i Guerrillas gave themselves in 1975. After the Siyahkal assault and the military operations in Tehran, these vanguards of armed struggle called themselves the People's Fada'i Guerrillas. With the growth and expansion of the guerrilla movement and formation of its Organizational structure in 1974, people's Fada'i Guerrillas transformed to the Organization of the Iranian People's Fada'i Guerrillas. Only after

expanding nationwide, did they call themselves an organization. This phase-to-phase naming is another aspect of the Fada'i Guerrillas, they always did their best to thoroughly reveal and express their understanding of things without any vanity.

52. Ahmadzadeh, *Mobarezeh,* foreword to third edition.
53. Ibid., 1-19.
54. Ibid., 10.
55. Ibid., 65.
56. Ibid., 9.
57. For an overview of Jazani's political and ideological thought, see Mehrdad Baba-'Ali's contribution in *Jongi*, 293-326.
58. Jazani, *Nabard*, 36.
59. Ahmadzadeh, *Mobarezeh*, 99.
60. Bijan Jazani, *Cheguneh Mobarezeh-ye Mosallahaneh Tudehi Mishavad* (n.p.: Entesharat Cherik-ha-ye Fada'i-ye Khalq, 1973), 28.
61. Jazani, *Nabard*, 30-1.
62. Nasser Mohajer, 'Jonbesh-e Cheriki, Andisheh-ha-ye Jazani va Chand va Chun yek Bohtan', in *Jongi*, 412.
63. Ibid.
64. Mostafa Sho'aiyan, *Enqelab* (Florence: Mazdak Publishing, 1974).
65. Mostafa Sho'aiyan, *Chand Khordehgiri-ye Nab* (Florence: Mazdak Publishing, 1974), 16.
66. Ibid., 16.
67. Hamid Momeni, *Molahezati Darbareh-ye Enqelab* (n.p.: 1973), 89.
68. Nabdel, *Azerbaijan*, 31-5.
69. Safa'i Farahani, *Enqelabi*, 1970, 37.
70. Bijan Jazani, *Tarh-e Jameshenasi va Mabani-ye Estratejik-e Jonbesh-e Enqelabi-ye Iran, Bakhsh-e Dovvom* (Tehran: Entesharat-e Maziar, 1978), 6-7.
71. Ibid., 9-35.
72. Jazani, *Nabard*, 91-5.
73. 'Andisheh-ye Mao Tse Dung va Enqelab-e Ma', *Nabard-e Khalq*, 2, 1974, 41.
74. Foreword, *Nabard-e Khalq*, 2, 1974, 1.
75. Foreword, *Nabard-e Khalq*, 3, 1974, 1.
76. "Amaliyat-e Tabligh-e Mosalahaneh va Mafahim-e An dar Marhaleh-yi Keh Gozasht', *Nabard-e Khalq*, 7, June 1976, 11-12.
77. Jazani, *Chegouneh*, 71-80.
78. '*Edam Enqelabi 'Abbas Shahriari* (n.p.: Entesharat-e Sazeman-e Cherik-ha-ye Fada'i-ye Khalq Iran, 1975), 6.
79. 'Jenayat-e Bozorg-e Shah 'Alayh-e Jonbesh Novin-e Khalq-e Enqelabi-ye Iran', *Nabard-e Khalq*, 6, 1975, 109.
80. Ibid., 109-10.
81. Ahmadzadeh, *Mobarezeh*, 159.
82. 'Shoa'r-ha-ye Vahdat', *Nabard-e Khalq*, 6, 1975, 2.
83. Ibid.
84. Bijan Jazani, 'Darbareh-ye Vahdat va Naqsh-e Estrateji-e Cherik-ha-ye Fada'i-ye Khalq', *Nabard-e Khalq*, 6, 1975, 12-122, 127.
85. Ibid., 118.
86. Ibid., 4-5.
87. Bijan Jazani, *Eslam-e Marxisti ya Marxism-e Eslami* (Paris: Rah-e Fada'i, 1984), 33.
88. Ibid., 6.

89. Ibid., 34.
90. Mohammad Taqi Shahram, *Bayaniyeh E'lam Mavaze' Ideolojik-e Sazeman-e Mojahedin-e Khalq-e Iran* (n.p.: Entesharat-e Sazeman-e Mojahedin-e Khalq-e Iran, 1976).
91. The PMOI first published its internal discussions with the OIPFG for the public through a pamphlet titled *Masa'el-e Had-e Jonbesh Ma* (The Critical Issues of our Movement). Consequently, the OIPFG published their first special bulletin which pointed to the internal discussions in the organization and stated in the foreword: 'considering the amount of confidential information which was mentioned in the PMOI publication, we believe that, for security reasons, even to publish it internally would be an unprincipled and irresponsible act. However, the PMOI did not take into consideration this very important matter, by changing the name of the bulletin from the *Nashriyeh Vijeh-ye Bahs-e Darun Do Sazeman* "Internal Exchanges between the OIPFG and the PMOI" to "The Critical Issues of our Movement" and then, by publicly publishing a second bulletin of the discussions between the OIPFG and the PMOI without consultation or agreement with our Organization', *Nashriyeh Vijeh-ye Bahs-e Darun Do Sazeman*, 1, March 1976, 6.
92. Questions about the 'Sho'ar-ha-ye Vahdat' (editorial of *Nabard-e Khalq*, 6) were posed by one of the PMOI's educational groups in *Masayel-e Had-e Jonbesh-e Ma*, 2, March 1977, 155, 162, 167, 180, 183, 189.
93. Ibid., 195–6.
94. Touraj Heydari Bigvand, *Te'ori-ye Tabligh-e Mosalahaneh: Enheraf az Markism-Leninism* (n.p.: Entesharat-e Jangal, 1977).
95. Ibid.
96. Ibid., 1.
97. Nureddin Kianuri, 'Baz ham Goftegoui Ba Cherik-ha-ye Fada'i Khalq', *Donya*, 3, June 1975, 7–16.
98. Nureddin Kianuri, 'Cherik-ha va Hezb-e Taraz-e Novin-e Tabaqeh-ye Kargar', *Donya*, 6, September 1975, 7–17.
99. 'Maoism Hamchenan Khatar-e 'Omdeh dar Jonbesh-e Enqelabi Ast', *Donya*, 9, December 1975, 34–8.
100. 'Nazari be Barkhi Javaneb-e Neveshte-ha-ye Cherik-ha-ye Fada'i-ye Khalq', *Donya*, 2, May 1976.
101. 'Sokhani Chand Darbareh-ye Natayej-e Shiveh-ye Mobarezeh-ye Mosalahaneh dar Shesh Sali ke Gozasht', *Donya*, 10, December 1976, 21–8.
102. Bijan Jazani, 'Chegouneh Mobarezeh Mosalahaneh Toudehi Mishavad' *19 Bahman Te'orik*, 2 and 'Nabard 'Alayh-e Diktatori Shah' *19 Bahman Te'orik*, 3.
103. Kianuri, 'Baz Ham', 7.
104. Nureddin Kianuri, 'Cherik-ha va Hezb Taraz-e Novin Tabaqeh Kargar', *Donya*, 6 September 1975, 11.
105. Ibid., 50.
106. The 16 Azar commemoration marks the occasion in December 1953 in which three students, two of whom supporters of the Tudeh Party, lost their lives after an attack by security forces against the Faculty of Engineering at the University of Tehran on the occasion of the official visit to Tehran of the US vice-president Richard Nixon.
107. *Payam-e Daneshjou*, 3, 1977, 24–7.
108. Ibid., 43.
109. Ibid., 60.
110. Ibid., 49–51.

111. Ibid., 54.
112. See Chapter 4 in this volume.
113. On this day, a peaceful gathering of civilians was shot upon by a contingent of troops who had been stationed in Jaleh Square after the imposition of martial law in the early morning. According to initial press reports, around sixty people were shot to death in cold blood by the troops. This event became a turning point in the revolutionary process of 1978–9.
114. *Dar in Qiyam-e Khunin keh Aghaz Shode Mardom ra Yari Konim*, OIPFG Flyer, 6 November 1978.
115. *Baz Ham Darbareh-ye Vazayef-e Asasi* (n.p.: Entesharat-e Sazeman-e Cherik-ha-ye Fada'i-ye Khalq-e Iran), 7–8.
116. Ibid., 10–11.
117. Ibid., 24.
118. *Nameh-ye Sargoshadeh Sazeman-e Cherik-ha-ye Fada'i-ye Khalq-e Iran beh Ayatollah Khomeini*, OIPFG Flyer, 2. See Chapter 12 in this volume on the Open Letter.
119. Ahmadzadeh, *Mobarezeh*, 6.
120. Ibid., 57.

2 The labour movement in the words and deeds of the Iranian People's Fada'i Guerrillas

1. For an overview of the Iranian Labour Movement in the aftermath of the Second World War, see Touraj Atabaki, 'L'Organization Syndicale Ouvrière en Iran', *Sou'al* 8 (1987): 35–54.
2. In support of the Central Council of Trade Unions of Iran, *Trud*, the press organ of the All-Union Central Council of Trade Unions of the Soviet Union referred to Yousef Eftekhari, as a 'provocateur and pseudo leftist', who 'practically provoked the workers to sabotage the military support of the Soviet Union'. Ibid., 48.
3. The Congress of Iranian Workers' Unions was formed in 1950 by merging of two syndicates of the Iranian Labourer's Union (SKI) and the Central Union of Labourers and Farmers of Iran (AMKA), both with the support of the government.
4. U.S.A. Government Records. Report about labour condition in Iran, 1960, 4 July 1963, quoted in Habib Lajevardi, *Labor Unions and Autocracy in Iran* (New York: Syracuse University Press, 1985), 205.
5. Ervand Abrahamian, *Iran Between Two Revolutions* (Princeton, NJ: Princeton University Press, 1982), 422.
6. For a historical review of the formation and practices of the developmental states, see Meredith Woo-Cumings (ed.), *The Developmental State, Cornell Studies in Political Economy* (Ithaca, NY: Cornell University Press, 1999) and David Ludden, 'Development Regimes in South Asia: History and the Governance Conundrum', *Economic and Political Weekly* 40 (2005): 4042–51.
7. The program of widespread economic reforms that the Shah promised was in fact the brainchild of Hassan Arsanjani. Arsanjani was a long-standing advocate for land reform and also a renowned expert in agriculture who had prepared this plan at the request of the prime minister, 'Ali Amini. See Gholam-Reza Afkhami (ed.), *Ideology, Process and Politics in Iran's Development Planning. An Interview with Manouchehr Goudarzi, Khodadad Farmanfarmain and Abdolmajid Majidi*

(Washington, DC: Foundation for Iranian Studies, 1999), 167–70. Iraj Amini, *Bar Bal-e Bohran: Zendegi Siyasi 'Ali Amini* (Tehran: Nashr-e Mahi, 2009), 171 and 385. Afkhami, *Ideology, Process and Politics*, 37.
8. National Iranian Oil Company (NIOC) Newsletter, 60, July 1963.
9. Planning and Budget Organization, *Gozaresh 'Amalkard Barnameh 'Omrani Sevvom 1941-1946* (Tehran: Planning and Budget Organization, 1968).
10. Ibid.
11. In order to refashion its relationship with the Soviet Union, in July 1962, the Iranian new government announced that Iran never let any country to install any military base for long-range missiles, a stand welcomed by the Soviet Union which opened a new chapter in diplomatic relation between two countries.
12. Bijan Jazani, *Masa'el Jonbesh zed Estemari va Azadibaksh-e Khalq Iran va 'Omdeh-tarin Vazayef-e Komunist-hay-ye Iran* (Paris: Sazeman-e Ettehad-e Fada'iyan-e Khalq-e Iran, 2003), 4–9.
13. Bijan Jazani, 'Jam'bandi-ye Mobarezat-e Si Saleh-ye Akhir dar Iran', *19 Bahman Te'orik*, 6 (December 1975–January 1976): 165–7.
14. Masoud Ahmadzadeh, *Mobarezeh-ye Mosallahaneh, ham Estrateji, ham Taktik* (Tehran: Sazeman-e Cherik-ha-ye Fada'i Khalq Iran, 1971), 2.
15. Ibid., 4.
16. Ibid., 7.
17. Ibid., 62.
18. Amir-Parviz Pouyan, *Zarourat-e Mobarezeh-ye Mosallahaneh va Rad-e Teoriy Baqa'* (Tehran: Sazeman-e Cherik-ha-ye Fada'i-ye Khalq Iran, 1971), 30–1.
19. Ibid., 23.
20. Jazani, 'Jam'bandi', 167–9.
21. Ibid., 164.
22. In the study of the labour movement and its history, two approaches can be identified. The first one, with a structuralist understanding of the class identity, focuses on the workers in the context of labour unions and investigates the history of the labour movement only in the framework of the history of the unions. It is based on an understanding of the labour struggle as a struggle connected only to the demands of the workers. But in challenging the dominant political structure it chooses a confrontational approach, the challenge in the trade struggles of the ruling political structure, a contradictory. The class identity of the working class also shapes the basis of the struggles of this class aiming to reach a class lower than itself. In contrast to this approach, there is another approach which is not structuralist and includes unorganized workers and adaptive (non-confrontational) struggles as being part of the workers' movement and the history of this movement. In this approach, the class identity of workers is not only limited to the context of their struggles but also concerns their representation and recognition. For further discussion, see Marcel Van der Linden, 'Labour History: The Old, the New and the Global', *African Studies* 66, nos. 2–3 (2007); Touraj Atabaki, 'From 'Amaleh (Labor) to Kargar (Worker): Recruitment, Work Discipline and Making of the Working Class in the Persian/Iranian Oil Industry', *International Labour and Working-Class History* 84 (2013): 159–75.
23. Habib Lajevardi, *Labor Unions and Autocracy in Iran* (New York: Syracuse University Press, 1985), 219.
24. Ibid.

25. Jazani, 'Jam'bandi', 165–7.
26. E. Robert Livernash and Kamal Argheyd, 'Iran', in *International Handbook of Industrial Relations*, ed. Albert A. Blumli (London: Aldwych Press, 1981), 267.
27. Asef Bayat, 'Workers' Control after the Revolution', *Merip Report* 113 (March–April 1983): 22.
28. Ladjevardi, *Labor Unions*, 240.
29. 'Elamiyeh-ye Sazeman-e Cherik-ha-ye Fada'i-ye Khalq Iran', *Nabard-e Khalq*, 4, August 1974, 15.
30. *Nabard-e Khalq*, 2, March 1974, 1–2.
31. Hamid Ashraf, *Jam'bandi-ye Seh Saleh* (Tehran: Negah, 1979), 9.
32. Ibid., 29.
33. Idid., 54.
34. Author's interview with Heydar Tabrizi, 23 December 2016.
35. Ibid.
36. Ibid.
37. 'Mokhtasari Darbareh-ye Asarat-e 'Edam-e Enqelabi Fateh', *Nabard-e Khalq*, 5, January 1975, 1–5, 67–88.
38. Bijan Jazani wrote this article in the summer of 1973 while in prison.
39. Bijan Jazani, 'Darbareh-e Vahdat va Naqsh-e Esteretajik-e Cherik-ha-ye Fada'i Khalq', *Nabard-e Khalq*, 6, May 1975, 122.
40. Author's interview with Heydar Tabrizi, 23 December 2016.
41. The Supreme Council of the OIPFG, which included the heads of departments, the central organ, and the heads of special categories and organs such as the editorial board was the highest body of the Organization, which was convened every six months. The meeting of the Supreme Council was not live for security reasons and to prevent a possible blow, it was held through council letters. The central organ or *markaziyat* (centrality) of the OIPFG (which consisted of the heads of the departments) was responsible for implementing the decisions of the Supreme Council. See Heydar Tabriz, 'Rafiq Bijan Jazani va Sazeman-e Cherik-ha-ye Fada'i Khalq-e Iran', *Jongi Darbareh Zendegi va Asar Bijan Jazani* (Paris: Khavaran, 1999), 265.
42. *Payam-e Daneshjou*, 1, November 1975, 30–1.
43. Ibid., 40, 62.
44. See Chapter 4 Qorbanali in this volume. One of the few workers who joined the OIPFG in this period was Behnam Amiri-Davan (1951–1976), who did so in 1974.
45. Author's interview with Heydar Tabrizi, 23 December 2016.
46. *Nabard-e Khalq*, 7, June 1976.
47. See the narrative of Marziyeh Shafi', Chapter 6 in this volume.
48. 'Abbas Hashemi, 'Safehhati az Biraheh-ha-ye Rah' *Akhbar-e Ruz*, 14 November 2016, http://www.iran-chabar.de/article.jsp?essayId=76627.
49. This is a reference to 'Third Congress of the Workers of Iran', which was inaugurated on May 1976 in Tehran. For a detailed report on the Congress, see *Ettela 'at*, 27 April 1976, 1 May 1976. See also *Rastakhiz-e Kargaran* 12 May 1976, 3.
50. *Nabard-e Khalq*, 7, June 1976, 160–1.
51. Ahmad Ashraf, 'Kalbod-shekafi Enqelab: Naqsh Kargaran San'ati dar Enqelab-e Iran', *Goftogou* 55 (2010): 59.
52. Ibid.
53. Declaration published by the OIPFG, dated October 1976.

54. Author's interview with Heydar Tabrizi, 23 December 2016.
55. Author's interview with Tahmaseb Vaziri, 25 December 2016.
56. International Labour Office, *Employment and Income Policies for Iran. Unpublished Report* (Geneva: ILO, 1972), appendix C, 6.
57. *Social Indicators of Iran 1978. Preliminary review* (Tehran: Plan and Budget Organization, 1978), 356.
58. *Preliminary Report of the General Census of Population and Housing* (Tehran: Statistics Centre of Iran, 1976).
59. Farhad Kazemi, *Power and Revolution in Iran. The Migrant Poor Urban Marginality and Politics* (New York: New York University Press, 1980), 3.
60. Ervand Abrahamian, *History of Modern Iran* (Cambridge: Cambridge University Press, 2008), 139.
61. Design and Architecture Consulting Engineers, *Empowerment Plan and Organization of Informal Settlements in Isfahan. First Stage Report. Identification of Informal Neighbourhoods* (Tehran: Urban Development and Improvement Organization, 2006). See also Azam Khatam, 'The Share of Government and Neighbourhood in Empowerment Projects: Ja'far -abad Neighbourhood of Kermanshah', *Haftshahr* 9–10 (2002): 33–4.
62. Author's interview with Tahmaseb Vaziri, 25 December 2016.
63. Bahman Nasseri, *Asnad-e Qiyam-e Tabriz: Gozareshha-ye Darun Tashkilati-ye A'za va Havadaran-e Sazeman-e Cherik-ha-ye Fada'i-ye Khalq Iran, Shakheh Tabriz* (Hanover: n.p., 1997), 45.
64. Ibid., 89–100.
65. Ibid., 101–238.
66. Declaration distributed by OIPFG, dated 7 November 1978: *Elamiyeh-ye Sazeman-e Cherik-ha-ye Fada'i Khalq Iran. Doroud Sazeman-e Cherik-ha-ye Fada'i Khalq Iran beh Kargaran-e Pishro-ye San'at-e Naft, Mashin-Sazi va Traktor-Sazi.*
67. The author's interview with Nasser Khaksar, 15 January 2013, and with Nasim Khaksar, 15 April 2014.
68. *Elamiyeh-ye Sazeman, Nabard-e Khalq*, 4, August 1974.
69. Author's interview with Tahmaseb Vaziri, 25 December 2016.
70. *Elamiyeh-ye Sazeman, Nabard-e Khalq*, 4, August 1974.
71. Ibid.
72. Author's interview with Nasser Khaksar, 15 January 2013, and with Nasim Khaksar, 15 April 2014. Author's interview with Tahmaseb Vaziri, 25 December 2016.
73. Declaration distributed by OIPFG, dated 25 January 1979, *Kargaran-e Iran Motahhed Shavid! Kargaran-e General Motorz-e Iran.*
74. In December 1977, the OIPFG laid bombs on buildings of the municipalities of Zanjan and Shahr-e Ray in support of the people living in the outskirts of these two cities.
75. Sazeman-e Cherik-ha-ye Fada'i Khalq Iran, *Gozareshati az Mobarezeh-ye Daliraneh Mardom Kharej az Mahdudeh!* (Tehran: OIPFG, 1978), 14.
76. One of the most comprehensive studies on the role of workers in the Islamic Revolution of 1979 has been conducted by Ahmad Ashraf. Ashraf's study, both quantitatively and qualitatively, is a noteworthy study that traces labour activism in relation to the political Organizations of Iran at that time. Ashraf, 'Kalbod-shekafi', 55–123.

3 The foreign relations of the Organization of Iranian People's Fada'i Guerrillas: From formation to the Revolution of 1979

1. In 1970 (1349) and 1971 (1350) comrades amongst the leadership of the Fada'i Guerrillas and also some of the comrades who had travelled abroad were captured alive and after subjecting them to torture SAVAK was able to obtain information about their activities outside Iran. However, from the winter of 1971–2 to January–February 1979, except for Hassanjan Farjudi who was captured alive in December–January 1976–7 in Mashhad and was a member of the Organization's central organ, none of the other members of the leadership or any other comrade who had information about foreign relations outside of Iran was captured alive. Farjoudi's information and the central organ members as a whole following the strikes of 29 June 1976 regarding foreign relations abroad was very limited. Moreover, in the talks I had at the beginning of the summer of 1978 with central organ members – Hadi (Ahmad Gholamian Langaroudi), Mansour (Mohammad Reza Ghebra'i) and Majid (Qorbanali 'Abdolrahimpour) and also Qasem Siyadati and Fati (Sheyda Nabavi) in a garden in Damavand – they all confirmed that although Farjudi was captured alive, he resisted and did not give SAVAK any information. Despite his considerable knowledge of operations and logistics, he did not reveal any of it and it all remained intact. None of the comrades who, during this period, were also active in the foreign operations section of the Organization or who travelled back and forth from abroad were captured alive and as a result little information fell into SAVAK's hands.
2. On 7 January 1976, Bahman Rouhi-Ahangaran, who was responsible for a group charged with propagating armed struggle, was arrested and died under brutal torture on 13 January. On 8 January three teams in Amol, Gorgan and Sari were hit by the security forces. Masrour Farhang, Fatemeh Hassanpour and Fatemeh Shams Nahani lost their lives in battle and Zahra Aqa-Nabi Qolhaki was arrested. After this strike against the Organization, several comrades were also arrested. On 12 February 1976, Hamid Momeni, who in theoretical terms was then the most influential comrade within the Organization, was killed in an armed confrontation with SAVAK agents following the arrest of Kamal Puladi and the revelation of his meeting. Zahra Aqa-Nabi Qolhaki was executed by firing squad in Chitgar Square on 10 January 1977.
3. From 16 May until 18 May 1976 during the planned attacks on SAVAK in pursuit of control of the Organization's telephone network, several bases in Tehran and other towns were hit and comrades – including Behrouz Armaghani, an OIPFG central organ member – were killed. For more information, see the Organization's statement in this regard. Heydar Tabrizi, *Ravabet-e Boroun Marzi-ye Sazeman-e Cherik-ha-ye Fada'i-ye Khalq Iran ta Bahman 1357* (Germany: Mortazavi, 2016), 90.
4. After the strike of 16 May and 18 May 1976, until 29 June 1976 several comrades including Nastaran Al-e Aqa from the supreme council of the Organization were killed in a series of assaults. On 29 June Hamid Ashraf with nine other individuals was killed in a fight with SAVAK agents at an OIPFG base in Mehrabad, south Tehran, and in this way the entirety of the organizational leadership and many of the experienced cadres and those in positions of responsibility were killed.
5. For the text of this forged letter, see Tabrizi, *Ravabet-e Boroun Marzi*, 90.
6. Ibid., 95.

7. When the two groups united, they chose the name 'People's Fada'i Guerrillas'. In 1974, with the spread and stabilization of its organizations, the name changed to the Organization of the People's Fada'i Guerrillas and indicated an evolutionary stage in the development of the Organization. In 1975 (middle of 1354), regarding the growth of activism inside and outside the country and the Middle East and the spread of relations with non-Iranian parties, organizations and movements the word 'Iran(ian)' (*Iran*) was added to the Organization's name, now known as the 'Organization of the Iranian People's Fada'i Guerrillas'.

    Until the winter of 1972 (end of 1350) there was no insignia for the Organization. This was until a fourth-year architecture student at Tehran University and talented painter, Faramarz Sharifi, designed one. This insignia slightly changed and was eventually completed when in 1975 (1354) in accord with its partisanship in favour of the workers, the hammer and sickle was added by the Organization's supreme council. See Tabrizi, *Ravabet-e Boroun Marzi*, 104–6.

8. For further research regarding the history of the Forest Group, see *19 Bahman Te'orik* 4 (April–May 1976) and Hamid Ashraf, *Jam'bandi-ye Seh Saleh* (Tehran: Negah, 1978).

9. For further research regarding the history of the Pouyan-Ahmadzadeh-Meftahi group, see *19 Bahman Te'orik* 7 (1976), and Ashraf, *Jam'bandi-ye Seh Saleh*.

10. Some of the internal letters and writings of the Pouyan-Ahmadzadeh-Meftahi group were hidden and one of the imprisoned comrades knew where they were located. After the revolution this comrade was freed and managed to get hold of these documents and sent them to the editorial board of the publication *Kar* (Labour). These internal writings were authored under pseudonyms, and we were therefore unable to identify the original authors. In these writings the issue of 'social imperialism' was one of the subjects of internal discussion of the group.

11. In the conversations I had with Manuchehr Kalantari prior to the revolution of 1979, he said that this pamphlet was primarily written by Hassan Zia-Zarifi.

12. 'Masa'el Jonbesh-e Zed-e Emperialisti va Azadibakhsh Khalqha-ye Iran va Vazayef-e Asasi-ye Komunistha dar Sharayet-e Kununi', *19 Bahman Te'orik* 4 (April–May 1976): 88–9.

13. *Ancheh Yek Enqelabi Bayad Bedanad* (n.p.: 19 Bahman Press, 1976). This pamphlet was printed abroad in February–March 1972 by the 19 Bahman Press. In the history of the Jazani-Zarifi group (published in *19 Bahman Te'orik* 4) which was compiled by Jazani in prison, it was said that the author of this pamphlet was 'Ali Akbar Safa'i Farahani, but there is the strong possibility that Jazani wrote it himself in Qom Prison and for a number of reasons attributed it to Safa'i Farahani.

14. Masoud Ahmadzadeh, *Mobarezeh-ye Mosalahaneh, Ham Estrateji, Ham Taktik* (n.p.: Hamaseh-ye Khalq Press, 1978).

15. Hamid Momeni, *Gerayesh beh Rast dar Siyasat Kharejeh Chin* (Germany: Committee in Support of the New Revolutionary Movement of Iran, 1977).

16. In the quoted version there is no date of publication or name of the distributor. Ibid., 83–5.

17. 'Ultimately Comrade A (Manuchehr Kalantari, whose name is not mentioned because of security considerations), went abroad for medical reasons and also to assess political and military possibilities. Given his inclination towards China he hoped this might be an option, but after a number of months these hopes turned into despair'. *Tahlili az Takvin va Takamol-e Guruh-e Pishtaz-e Jazani-Zarifi*, Bijan Jazani (An Analysis of the formation and Evolution of the Vanguard Group) (Jazani-Zarifi), *19 Bahman Te'orik* 4 (April–May 1976): 22.

Manuchehr Kalantari returned to Iran following the 1979 revolution and was a member of the editorial board of *Kar*. He sided with the Aqaliyat (Minority) faction in the OIPFG split and was then a member of the editorial board of the publication *Kar* Minority. He participated in the first congress of the Minority faction in 1981. In the spring of 1982 as he was leaving the country through Baluchistan, his location in Zahedan was exposed and was encircled and placed under siege by the Islamic Revolutionary Guard Corps. Kalantari ended his life so that he would not be captured alive.

18. 'Takvin', 29. For further information regarding the history of the Jazani-Zarifi group refer to the entire issue, *19 Bahman Te'orik* 4.
19. Ashraf, *Jam'bandi-ye Seh Saleh*, 7.
20. In the book, part of a memorandum of district office 1 of SAVAK to the main headquarters has been reprinted. In this memorandum, Saffari Ashtiyani's meeting with Jalal Talabani and the leadership of a group of armed Kurds is detailed. On the same page it is mentioned without any kind of reference that Safa'i Farahani and Saffari Ashtiyani were in an Iraqi prison for more than one month and afterwards the prison authorities stated that their request had been accepted and they were to be handed over to Syria. A little afterwards these two men were handed over to Syrian border guards and from there they were thrown into a Syrian prison. After a short interrogation and a couple of days in jail, they were sent to the border town of Dera'a and from there they entered Jordan. Finally at the Jordanian border they were taken by Palestinian commanders to one of the Palestinian military training centres. Regarding the accuracy or falseness of the book's claims, which were possibly extracted by means of interrogations, I have not had the opportunity to undertake more research. It is possible that the comrades who had been in prison for a time later joined Fatah.
21. These weapons and ammunition were very likely prepared in Palestine by Safa'i Farahani and Saffari Ashtiyani and afterwards were secretly brought to Iran at a point on the Iranian-Iraqi border near Basra-Khorramshahr. I could not obtain a source detailing further information. In the Naderi book, it is claimed on pages 380–6 without reference to any source that these weapons were prepared in Palestine and that they had been hidden away in a suitcase and in the course of an inspection had been uncovered at the Iraqi border. Safa'i Farahani, however, was able to retrieve these weapons and afterwards cross into Iran from Basra.
22. Ashraf, *Jam'bandi-ye Seh Saleh*, 7–8.
23. 'Takvin', 29. 'Ali Akbar Safa'i Farahani was a commander of the 'mountain group' and was arrested on 19 January 1971 (29 Dey 1349). After enduring brutal torture, he was executed by firing squad along with twelve other members of the Fada'i Guerrillas. The organ of Fatah published an article in commemoration of Safa'i Farahani (See appendix 6 of Tabrizi, *Ravabet-e Boroun Marzi*).
24. I asked Iraj Nayyeri regarding the trip and meeting with Panahian which Rowhani mentions, who recalled that Houshang Nayyeri prior to his arrest spoke with him about this meeting. He said that Houshang Nayyeri went with Saffari Ashtiyani to Iraq and they were arrested, imprisoned and tortured there. After two or three weeks the Iraqi authorities were assured that they were not spies and freed them. They had 70,000 tomans with them to purchase weapons and they said they had come to Iraq to secure weapons. The Iraqi authorities, which had confiscated the 70,000 tomans, returned it to them and gave them some arms and ammunition. The two comrades refused the weapons and said that their group does not accept any kind of foreign

dependency. The Iraqi authorities insisted and that the weapons were recompense for the harassment and imprisonment they had suffered. Finally, after much persistence, Saffari Ashtiyani and Houshang Nayyeri took the weapons and returned to Iran. They buried the weapons in an area near Ahvaz and later on Eskandar Sadeqinezhad went to recover the weapons and ammunition.
25. For a discussion of further international activities of the OIPFG, particularly the ties with the Turkish National Liberation Army, see ibid., 58.
26. For more on these radio activities, see ibid., 47–58.

4 A glance at the Organization of Iranian People's Fada'i Guerrillas (1976–9)

1. The Toufan Organization was formed in Western Europe in 1965 by ex-Tudeh Party activists who had embraced Maoism.
2. Unfortunately, I am unaware of Asghar's real name. He was amongst those who were killed by SAVAK on 17–18 May 1976. Others killed in these days were Mahmoud Khorramabadi, Mostafa Hassanpour, Farideh Gharavi, Touraj Ashtari Bigvand, Behrouz Armaghani, Esmail Abedini, Zahra Modir-Shanehchi, Hosseini Fatemi and Mitra Bolbolsefat. I have no information regarding Hossein Fatemi and Touraj Ashtari Bigvand; Asghar might have been one of them.
3. See Marziyeh Tohidast Shafi''s contribution (Chapter 6) in this volume for biographical details on Nastaran Al-e Agha.
4. See Siavush Randjbar-Daemi's chapter (Chapter 12) in this volume for a brief explanation of the Goethe Nights.
5. See Siavush Randjbar-Daemi's contribution in this volume for more on Mehdi Fatapour, 'Ali Keshtgar and their attempts to create this overt organization.
6. This should not be confused with the Rah-e Fada'i group which emerged shortly after the 1979 Revolution and produced a considerable amount of theoretical work.

5 Military actions in the Organization of Iranian People's Fada'i Guerrillas: Scales and modalities

1. This article could not be written without the help of my historian friend, Nasser Mohajer. I am sincerely thankful for his suggestions, contributions and the access he provided for me to the related archival materials. I must also thank Mehrdad Vahabi, who has read the draft of this essay and presented me with valuable comments and suggestions. It is evident that the author is solely responsible for any shortcomings in this work.
2. Bijan Jazani, *Nabard ba Diktatori-ye Shah* (n.p.: Entesharat-e Sazeman-e Cherik-ha-ye Fada'i-ye Khalq-e Iran, 1978), 38–9.
3. Nasser Mohajer, 'Amir-Parviz Pouyan az Cheshm-e Bagher Parham', *Iran Namag* 1, no. 4 (2017): 214–33.
4. Amir-Parviz Pouyan, *Zarurat-e Mobarezeh-ye Mosalahaneh va Rad-e Teori-ye Baqa* (n.p.: Entesharat-e Sazeman-e Cherik-ha-ye Fada'i-ye Khalq-e Iran, n.d.), 52, 70.
5. Jazani, *Nabard*, 43.

6. Masoud Ahmadzadeh, *Mobarezeh Mosallahaneh, Ham Estrateji, Ham Taktik* (n.p.: Jebheh-ye Melli-ye Iran, Bakhsh-e Khavar Miyaneh, 1974).
7. Hamid Ashraf, *Jam'bandi-ye Seh Saleh* (Tehran: Negah, 1979), 10.
8. Ibid., 27.
9. *Elamiyeh-ha va Bayaniyeh-hay Sazeman Cherik-ha-ye Fada'i-ye Khalq Iran* (Tehran: Entesharat-e Sazeman-e Cherik-ha-ye Fada'i-ye Khalq-e Iran, 1979).
10. *19 Bahman Te'orik* 4, Ordibehesht 1355 [May–June 1976], 43.
11. *Pareh-yi az Tajrobiyat-e Jang Cheriki-ye Shahri dar Iran* (n.p.: Jebheh-ye Melli-ye Iran dar Kharej az Keshvar), 102–7.
12. 'Elamiyeh-e Towzihi Cherik-ha-ye Fada'i-ye Khalq,' in *Pareh-yi*, 1.
13. *Bakhtar-e Emruz,* 28, Tir 1351 [June–July 1972], 3.
14. 'Elamiyeh Towzihi-ye Cherik-ha-ye Fada'i-ye Khalq,' 11 Khordad 1351 [1 June 1972].
15. Ibid., 2.
16. *Bakhtar-e Emruz,* 34, Esfand 1351 [February–March 1973], 4.
17. *Ettela'at*, 10 Mehr 1352 [2 October 1973], 1–4.
18. 'Ettelayieh Cherik-ha-ye Fada'i-ye Khalq', in *Pareh-yi*, 38.
19. 'Elamiyeh Cherik-ha-ye Fada'i-ye Khalq be Monasebat Hambastegi ba Mobarezeh-ye Khalq-e Zofar', in ibid., 33.
20. 'Elamiyeh-ye Cherik-ha-ye Fada'i-ye Khalq: E'dam Yeki az Doshmanan-e Jenayatkar-e Tabagheh-ye Kargar', *Nabard-e Khalq*, 4 Mordad 1353 [August–September 1974], 16.
21. Ibid., 35.
22. *Nabard-e Khalq*, 5, Dey 1353 [December 1974–January 1975], 12–13.
23. Ibid.
24. 'Elamiyeh-ye Towzihi-ye Cherik-ha-ye Fada'i-ye Khalq dar Rabeteh ba Enfejar-e Pasgah Zhandarmeri Soleymaniyeh Tehran,' in *Pareh-yi*, 103.
25. Ibid., 59.
26. Ibid., 74.
27. Ibid., 98.
28. 'Ettelayieh E'dam Enqelabi Sarvan Yadollah Nowruzi,' in *Pareh-yi*, 89.
29. *Nabard-e Khalq* (Supplement), Esfand 1353 [February–March 1975].
30. *Pareh-yi*, 130.
31. *Nabard-e Khalq*, 7, Khordad 1355 [June–July 1976], 103, 106–7.
32. Ibid., 63–71.
33. Ibid., 72–7.
34. Ibid., 78.
35. 'Ettelayieh-ye Sazeman-e Cherik-ha-ye Fada'i-ye Khalq,' 11 Azar 1356 [11 December 1977].
36. *Nabard-e Khalq*, 7, 180–8.
37. *Keyhan*, 8 Khordad 1355 [29 May 1976], and *Kar*, 18, 8 Tir 1358 [29 June 1978].
38. 'Elamiyeh-ye Sazeman-e Cherik-ha-ye Fada'i-ye Khalq dar Rabeteh ba Dargiriha-ye Akhir ba Mozduran-e Rejim', Aban 1355 [November 1976].
39. 'Elamiyeh Sazeman-e Cherik-ha-ye Fada'i-ye Khalq-e Iran dar Rabeteh ba Enfejar-e Shahrdari-ye Shahr Rey', Azar 1356 [December 1977].
40. Ibid.
41. 'Ettelahiyeh-ye Sazeman-e Cherik-ha-ye Fada'i-ye Khalq Iran dar Rabeteh ba Enfejar-e Anjoman-e Iran va Amrika', Dey 1356 [January 1978].
42. 'Ettelahiyeh-e Sazeman-e Cherik-ha-ye Fada'i-ye Khalq Iran, Hashtomin Salgard Aghaz-e Mobarezeh-ye Mosalahaneh beh Hemayat az Mardom Mobarez-e Qom va Tabaqat va Agshar Zahmatkesh-e Iran Shuru' Konim', Bahman 1356 [February 1978].

43. 'Gerami Bad Khatereh-ye Shohada-ye Tabriz', Esfand 1356 [February–March 1978].
44. 'Piruz Bad Mobarezeh-ye Haqtalabaneh-ye Khalq Zahmatkesh-e Iran, Enfejar-e Ye Vahed az Gashtiha-ye Polis-e Mashad be Poshtibani az Mobarezat-e Delavaraneh-ye Mardom', Farvardin 1357 [March–April 1978].
45. 'Elamiyeh-ye Sazeman-e Cherik-ha-ye Fada'i-ye Khalq: In Ast Pasokh-e Ma beh Koshtar-e Vahshiyaneh-ye Mardom-e Mobarez-e Iran,' 15 Shahrivar 1357 [6 September 1978].
46. ''E'dam Enqelabi-ye Sarhang Zamanipour, Mozdur Jenayatkar-e Rejim dar Mashad', 9 Mehr 1357 [1 October 1978].
47. *Elamiyeh-ha*, 69.
48. *Khabarnameh-ye Sazeman-e Cherik-ha-ye Fada'i-ye Khalq Iran*, 1, 20 Dey 1357 [10 January 1979] and 'Hamleh be Edare-ye Shahrbani va Maqar Gard-e Mozdur-e Rejim Shah-e Khaen dar Zanjan', 4 Azar 1357 [25 November 1977].
49. 'Gharargah-e Shomareh-ye Do Markaz-e Hedayat Gashtiha-ye Polis Tehran ba Mosalsal va Narenjak Mored Hamleh Gharar Gereft', 3 Azar 1357 [24 November 1977].
50. Cherik-ha-ye Fada'i-ye Khalq, *Elamiyeh-ha*, 89.
51. 'Nabud Baad Artesh Mozdur va Zed Khalqi-ye Shah', in ibid., 135.
52. *Khabarnameh-ye Sazeman-e Cherik-ha-ye Fada'i-ye Khalq Iran*, 1, 20 Dey 1357 [10 January 1979], 4.
53. Ibid.
54. Cherik-ha-ye Fada'i-ye Khalq, *Elamiyeh-ha*, 93; and *Khabarnameh-ye Sazeman-e Cherik-ha-ye Fada'i-ye Khalq-e Iran*, 2, 3 Bahman 1357 [23 January 1979].
55. Sazeman-e Cherik-ha-ye Fada'i-ye Khalq, 'Hamleh be Artesh-e Mozdur dar Meydan-e Shahr-e Sanandaj', in Cherik-ha-ye Fada'i-ye Khalq, *Elamiyeh-ha*, 169.
56. Sazeman-e Cherik-ha-ye Fada'i-ye Khalq, 'Havadaran Tabagheh-ye Kargar Dar Ejtema'at Va Tazahorat Che Khahand Kard?', in ibid., 179.
57. Sazeman-e Cherik-ha-ye Fada'i-ye Khalq, 'Hameh Mosalahaneh be Setad Jandarmeri-ye Kol Keshvar Dar Khiyaban-e Sih Metri', in ibid., 181.
58. 'Enfejar-e Yek Vahed az Gashtiha-ye Polis Mashad be Poshtibani az Mobarezat Delavarane Mardom', Farvardin 1357 [March 1978].

6 From school to safehouse: A woman Fada'i's account

1. Both Mahmoud E'temadzadeh (Behazin) and Bozorg 'Alavi were prominent leftist writers who had been active in the Tudeh Party of Iran prior to the August 1953 coup.
2. The 'Thousand Families' was a colloquial term for describing the upper, aristocratic elite of the second Pahlavi era.
3. Komsomol was the youth wing of the Communist Party of the Soviet Union.
4. In 1972, shortly after his release from prison and joining the Organization of Iranian People's Fada'i Guerrillas, comrade Yousef Zarkari completed his memoir describing one year of imprisonment under the Shah's regime. The book entitled *Khaterat Yek Cherik dar Zendan* (Memoirs of a Guerrilla in Prison) was published in early 1973 by the OIPFG. After Yousef's death on 2 February 1974, the life of this revolutionary worker was commemorated in *Nabard-e Khalq*, 3, June 1974, 61–2.
5. Maliheh Zehtab, 'Yadmandeha-yi az Zendegi-ye Cheriki', 2011, in https://www.bbc.com/persian/iran/2011/04/110411_siahkal_malihe_zahtab.

6. *Ettela'at*, 22 January 1974.
7. Zahra Aghanabi-Qolhaki was arrested on 8 January 1976 by SAVAK agents; she was tortured savagely and eventually executed on 20 December 1976.
8. *Nabard-e Khalq*, 7, June 1975, 109–11.
9. Marziyeh Tohidast Shafi', 'Beh Monasebat-e 8 Tir 1355, Ruz Shahadat Rofaqa Hamid Ashraf va Noh Tan az Yaran', 2013, https://www.kar-online.com/node/6549.
10. *Nabard-e Khalq*, 7, May 1976, 181–4.
11. *Kar*, 17, 28 June 1979.
12. 'Chegunegi Ta'ghib va Goriz Hamid Ashraf dar Goftegu ba Parviz Mo'tamed', https://www.pezhvakeiran.com/maghaleh-79200.html.
13. For more information, see 'Khaterati pas az Zarabat-e Sal 1355', https://www.bbc.com/persian/iran/2011/02/110206_l13_siahkal_masoomeh_shafee.
14. *Kar*, 47, 20 February 1980.

7 My beloved Organization

1. Hamid Momeni was a graduate of the School of Economics in Tehran University and worked at the Institute for the Intellectual Development of Children and Young Adults. Before joining the OIPFG, he had translated books by Soviet historians and authored research on villages and agricultural corporations in Fars Province which were published under his penname of M. Bidsorkhi (a reference to a village in Kurdistan). He had probably joined the Organization in 1972 along with Nezhat and Bahman Rouhi-Ahangaran. He was one of the theoreticians in the Organization and authored a book called *Shuresh Na, Gadam-ha-ye Sanjideh dar Rah-e Enqelab* in response to 'Rebellion' by Mustafa Sho'aiyan. He was killed in a clash after one of his meetings was disclosed to SAVAK.
2. Vida Goli Abkenari (1957–1982) born in Abkenar, a village in Gilan, north of Iran. In 1973, when she was sixteen years old and a high school student, she joined the Fada'i Guerrillas. After the Revolution of 1979, following the split in the Fada'is in 1980, she opted for the Aqaliyat (the Minority) branch of the Fada'is and defended the principle of the righteousness of armed resistance during the 1970s. In 1982, the house where she was living was raided by the Islamic Revolutionary Guards and Vida committed suicide with cyanide on the spot to avoid arrest.
3. Abdollah Panjehshahi (Heydar) was from Tehran and studied biology at the Teacher Training College. He probably joined the Organization in 1973.
4. Edna Sabet (1955–1982) was born in an upper-class Jewish family and was a mathematics student in the Aryamehr University who chose to leave her social extraction behind and probably joined the Fada'i Guerrillas in spring of 1974 and lived with an organic worker member of the Organization. She rejected the armed struggle in 1977 and left the Organization in the spring of 1978. She then joined the communist Sahand and later the Peykar Organizations. She was arrested in February 1982 and was executed on 12 February 1982 after undergoing severe torture in Tehran.
5. Mahmoud Naderi, *Cherik-ha-ye Fada'i Khalq. Az Nakhostin Koneshha ta Bahman 1357*, in two volumes (Tehran: Entesharat-e Moasseseh Motale'at va Pazhuhesh-ha-ye Siyasi, 2007). This book was published by one of the Islamic Republic's research institutes linked to its intelligence and security communities.

8 Female prison

1. Mastoureh Ahmadzadeh Heravi was born on 15 September 1945 in Mashhad. She was the first and the only girl in her family. Her brother, Masoud Ahmadzadeh Heravi was one of the first founders of the Iranian people's Fada'i guerrillas. The other brother, Majid Ahmadzadeh Heravi was also an active member of the Organization; the two brothers were both executed by firing squad in March 1971. A third member of the same family, Mojtaba Ahmadzadeh, was also executed on 29 October 1981 in Evin by the Islamic Republic authorities. Their father, Taher Ahmadzadeh Heravi was a well-known member of the pro-Mossadeq Iran National Front. The family's mother was an educated migrant from Baku-Azerbaijan. Mastoureh graduated from the Medical Faculty of University of Mashhad. She was arrested, tortured and detained four times by SAVAK's agents in both Mashhad and Tehran. After the revolution, she became a member of Fada'i guerrillas. When the Organization split in the period following the1979 Revolution, she joined the Minority Fada'i faction. In November 1979, she married her comrade Ahmad Gholamian Langaroudi (Hadi). He was killed in January 1982 in an armed clash with Islamic Republic's Revolutionary Guards in the Seyyed Khandan Neighbourhood in Tehran. Mastoureh, like many other Iranian political activists, was forced to leave Iran in the 1980s.
2. Sharon Laberking was a young (twenty-five to twenty-seven years of age) American woman who had a close relationship with Iranian student's confederation outside Iran. She was arrested in Mehrabad airport (Tehran's international airport) in July 1971. She was then recognized not guilty of espionage during her first court/trial and sentenced to three years. Later, in the court of appeals, she was sentenced to six months of imprisonment. She was the first political female prisoner who went on hunger strike twice in objection to her arrest, and once to her verdict.
3. Atefeh Ja'fari 's diary notes in Vida Hajebi-Tabrizi, *Dad-e Bidad*, vol. 1 (Tehran: Baztabnegar, 2004), 39.
4. Ashraf Dehqani was born in 1949 into a poor family in Tabriz. Her father was one of the active members of the Democratic Party of Azarbayjan in 1945–6 and her mother was one of the women who struggled against Pahlavi's dictatorship. She was the third child and had two brothers and two sisters. Her brother Behrooz Dehqani was a revolutionary activist in the 1970s. He was killed under SAVAK's severe torture in May 1971. Her sister Rouhangiz Dehqani was also executed by the Islamic Republic authorities in 1981. Ashraf Dehqani is now the leader of the Cherik-ha-ye Fada'i-ye Khalq.
5. *Az Salha-ye Khakestari*, ed. 'Ali Amiri (Rasht: Farhang Illia, 2013), 193.
6. Qasem Hassanpour, *Shakanjehgaran Sokhan Miguyand* (Tehran: Ebrat Museum, 1999), 299.
7. When Masoumeh Shademani (Kabiri) was imprisoned in 1975, she was a mother of six. She was sentenced to life in a military trial after her brave tenacity under torture. Her crime was supporting the PMOI. Masoumeh joined the group as soon as she was released from prison right before the victory of the Revolution of 1979. After the revolution, she was a PMOI candidate in the first post-revolutionary parliamentary elections. She was again imprisoned in 1981 and subject to severe torture. During the same year her son, Hassan Kabiri, and his wife were killed in a clash with security forces. There are two accounts regarding Masoumeh's death. The first narrates she

losing her life under torture, the second was a report by *Keyhan* newspaper reporting her execution on 27 December 1981 in Evin.
8. ʿAlireza Nabdel was born in 1944 in Tabriz. He was a law student at the University of Tehran when he joined the OIPFG. He was well-known among the revolutionary intellectuals. This group was later known as the Tabriz Revolutionary Group. Other members included Manaf Falaki-Tabrizi, Samad Behrangi, Behrouz Dehqani. He was executed by a firing squad in 1971 together with eight other Fadaʾi members in Tehran. Van Troy was a young Vietnamese partisan executed by firing squad during the Vietnam War in 1964 by the US military.
9. Farideh Lashaʾi was born in 1944 in Rasht. She studied language and translation in Munich and Art in Vienna. Later, she spent some time in Italy and benefited from Roberto Rossellini's classes. After her return to Iran, in 1973–4, she was arrested by SAVAK. The reason for her arrest was her contacts with her brother, the activist Kourosh Lashaʾi. Farideh was released after one and a half years of prison. She was a painter, writer and translator and held several exhibitions in Iran and European countries. Farideh passed away on 24 February 2013 due to cancer. Her heritage was a rich body of art, paintings and a story-like piece of work called '*Schal Bamoo*'.

9 The Organization of Iranian Peoples Fadaʾi Guerrillas' prison organization

1. The interview with Mohammad Reza Shalgouni was conducted by Nasser Mohajer on 3 June 2005.
2. This formation was named the Palestine Group because most of its members, mainly university students, were arrested while trying to leave Iran to get training in Palestinian camps.
3. Nasser Mohajer's interviews with Mohammad-Majid Kianzad throughout January 2017.
4. Nasser Mohajer interview with Mehdi Sameʿ in June 2005.
5. *Senf* means guild in Persian. The term has somehow entered the political lexicon of Iran's left movement in the 1960s and in this context refers to non-political daily issues of political prisoners.
6. Nasser Rahimkhani interview with Amir Mombini on 25 May 2013.
7. Nasser Rahimkhani interview with Naqi Hamidian on 25 May 2013.
8. Nasser Mohajer interview with Parviz Navidi, 27 April 2017.
9. *Nahj al-Balagheh* (The Path of Eloquence) is a collection of sermons, letters and sayings attributed to ʿAli ibn Abi Talib, the fourth Caliph after the Prophet Mohammad and the first Imam of the Shiʾa faith.
10. Nasser Mohajer interview with Jamshid Taheripour, 4 May 2017.
11. Nasser Mohajer interview with Mohammad Farsi, 5 May 2017.
12. Nasser Mohajer interview with Jamshid Taheripour, 4 May 2017.
13. Nasser Rahimkhani's interview with Asghar Izadi, 25 May 2013.
14. Shokrollah Paknezhad (1941–1981) was a prominent personality of the post-1953 coup opposition movement and one of the leaders of the Palestine group. He was killed by Islamic Republic prison officials soon after the all-out repression which swept the country following the dismissal of Abolhassan Bani-Sadr from presidency in June 1981.

15. Radio Mihan-Parastan (Radio Patriots) was an exile shortwave radio station based in Iraq.
16. *Epic of Resistance*, published by the OIPFG as *Torture & Resistance in* Iran was written by Ashraf Dehqani (1949–) in 1973. Ashraf Dehqani, one of the early members of the Fada'i guerrillas, managed to escape from prison in 1971. She lived underground for a short while and wrote her memoir before leaving Iran to join the Fada'i Branch abroad.
17. One of the most infamous prisons under the Pahlavi monarchs which was located in the Bushehr province in southern Iran.
18. Morteza Malek-Mohammadi's communication with Nasser Mohajer, April 2017.

10 The Organization of Iranian People's Fada'i Guerrillas and the University of Tabriz: A personal memoir

1. Dr 'Ali Akbar Torabi was a sociologist who taught at the University of Tabriz. He acquired a reputation for being a popular, dissident academic with leftist tendencies. See in this regard the remembrance published by Fariborz Sanjari, 'Be Yad-e Doktor Torabi', http://asre-nou.net/php/view.php?objnr=39106.

11 The Confederation of Iranian Students (National Union) and the Fada'i Guerrillas

1. The Star Group, a predecessor to the Communist Alliance Group (*Guruh-e Ettihad-e Komunisti*) and later the Organization of Communist Union (*Sazeman-e Vahdat-e Komunisti*), was the clandestine Marxist Organization behind the Organization of the National Front of Iran Abroad, Middle East Branch. While the ONFME held an outsized presence in CISNU, the Star Group attempted a merger with OIPFG between 1973 and 1976. See Eskandar Sadeghi-Boroujerdi 'The Origins of Communist Unity: Anti-Colonialism and Revolution in Iran's Tri-Continental Moment', *British Journal of Middle Eastern Studies* 45, no. 5 (2017): 14–15, 21–2.
2. *Ettela'at*, 18 January 1971.
3. Ibid.
4. *Peyman*, 'The Defense Arm of the International Confederation of Iranian Students, National Union', 31 March 1971, 1.
5. Afshin Matin-Asgari, *Iranian Student Opposition to the Shah* (Costa Mesa: Mazda, 2002), 124.
6. Hamid Shawkat, *Tarikh-e Bist Saleh-ye Konfederasion-e Jahani-ye Mohasselin va Daneshjuyan-e Irani (Ettehadiyeh-ye Melli* (Los Angeles: Ketab Corp, 2010), 102.
7. *Payman*, no. 25 (Bahman 1351 [January/February 1973]), 1.
8. Ibid., 1.
9. Afshin Matin-Asgari, *Konfedrasion: Tarikh-e Jonbesh-e Daneshjuyan-e Irani dar Kharij az Kishvar 1332–1357* (Tehran: Shirazeh, 2000), 356–7.
10. Matin-Asgari, *Konfedrasion*, 358–9.
11. Ibid., 422–3.
12. *Barresi-ye Sakht-e Eqtesadi-ye Rustaha-ye Fars* (n.p.: Entesharat-e Sazeman-e Cherik-ha-ye Fada'i-ye Khalq), 1974.

13. Message from the Organization of the People's Fada'i Guerrillas to the World Confederation of Iranian Students in *Nabard-e Khalq*, no. 6, April/May 1975, 161–3, 187.
14. Shawkat, *Konfedrasion*, vol. 2, 579–81.
15. *Nabard-e Khalq* 7, May/June 1976, 154–7.
16. *Pareh-yi az Asnad-e SAVAK* (Frankfurt: Confederation of Iranian Students (National Union), 1976), 1–2.

12 From Mehrabad-e Jonoubi to the technical faculty

1. Asghar Jilou, 'Ramzgeshayi az Ruydad-e 8 Tir', in *Bazkhani-ye Jonbesh-e Fada'i-ye Khalq*, ed. Masoud Fathi and Behrouz Khaliq (Köln: Furugh, 2010), 293.
2. Qorbanali Abdolrahimpour (Majid), 'Sazeman az 1353 Ta 1357: Gozareshi az Tahavol Fekri va Tashkilati'. https://www.bbc.com/persian/iran/2011/02/110206_l13_siahkal_ghorbanali_rahimpour.
3. *Payam-e Daneshjou*, 3, 1978, 26–8.
4. Ibid., 34–5.
5. The names in parenthesis throughout this chapter refer to the *nommes de guerre* through which the various Fada'is were known within the Organization.
6. *'Elamiyeh Sazeman-e Cherik-ha-ye Fada'i-ye Khalq-e Iran dar Rabeteh ba Dargiriha-ye Akhir ba Mozduran e Rejim-e Shah* (The Communiqué of the Organization of Iranian People's Fada'i with regards to the recent clashes with the agents of the Shah's regime), November 1976, 4.
7. Ibid.
8. *'Elamiyeh-ye Sazeman-e Cherik-ha-ye Fada'i-ye Khalq-e Iran Khatab beh Daneshjouyan* ('Fada'i Organization Flyer Directed to Students'), December 1976, 1.
9. Ibid.
10. This phenomenon became known as the *kharej az mahdudeh*, or 'beyond the [city] limits' struggle. For studies on the causes and consequences of these protests, see the insightful account overview in Nasser Pakdaman, *Dah Shab-e Sher (18-27 Mehr 1356): Barresi va Arzayabi yek Tajrobeh* (Paris: Kanoun Nevisandegan Iran dar Tabi'id, 1988), 25–8, as well as the more extended analysis in Mohammad Qaznavian, *Ta'amolati Darbareh Kharej Az Mahdudeh* (n.p.: Nashr-e Elektronik-e Praksis, 2016). and the field report produced by the Fada'i themselves, *Gozaresh Mobareze Dalirane Mardom, Kharej Az Mahdoude!* (Tehran: Sazeman-e Cherik-ha-ye Fada'i-ye Khalq-e Iran, 1978).
11. *Piruz bad Mobarezat-e Haqtalabaneh-ye Khalq-e Zahmatkesh-e Iran*, October 1977, 1–4.
12. *Payam-e Daneshjou*, 3, 1977, 2–3.
13. Ibid., 19.
14. For assessments of the Ten Nights, see Mandana Zandian, *Bazkhani Dah Shab* (Hamburg: Bonyad-e Daryoush Homayun, 2016); and Pakdaman, *Dah Shab-e Sher*.
15. P. J. Westmacott, 'The Internal Situation', 25 October 1977, in FCO 8/2980 Iran: Internal Political Affairs, 1977.
16. Author's interview with Mehdi Fatapour, 1 November 2016.
17. Author's interview with Mehdi Aslani, 1 December 2016.

18. Joint interview by the Author and Nasser Mohajer with Esfandiar Karimi, 30 June 2020.
19. Interview with Fatapour, 1 November 2016, and joint interview of the author and Nasser Mohajer with ʿAli Keshtgar, 15 November 2016.
20. *Haqiqat*, Dey 1356 [December 1977–January 1978].
21. *Setareh-ye Sorkh*, special issue, 67, Dey 1356 [December 1977–January 1978].
22. Author's interview with Fatapour. Following the Ten Nights at the Goethe Institute, the students of the Aryamehr Technical University attempted to hold their own series of poetry readings in December 1977 and invited the most prominent Tudeh-aligned intellectual inside the country, Mahmoud Eʿtemadzadeh (Beh Azin), to the same, but this initiative was met with the repression of the security forces and the arrest of Beh Azin.
23. *Piruz bad Mobarezat-e Porshukuh-ye Daneshjuyan-e Mobarez-e Iran*, December 1977, 1.
24. This figure is far in excess of the six seminary students who were effectively killed by the security forces on that day, as reported by official sources, but is still lower than other figures provided by the opposition, such as the one which appeared on the 21 January 1978 issue of the Tudeh central organ *Mardom*, which referred to unspecified 'foreign news agencies and press' to advance the claim that 100 people had been killed in Qom.
25. *Hashtomin Salgard-e Aghaz-e Mobarezeh-ye Mosallahaneh ra ba Hemayat az Mardom-e Mobarez-e Qom va Tabagheh va Aqshar-e Zahmatkesh-e Iran Shuruʿ Mikonim!*, February 1978, 1–12.
26. *Piruz Bad Mobarezeh Haq Talabaneh-ye Khalq-e Mobarez-e Iran*, March 1978, 1–3.
27. ʿAbdolrahimpour, 'Sazeman', BBC Persian.
28. Majid interview with *Kar* (Majority), Third Series, No. 201, 2000. Farrokh Negahdar has separately confirmed to this Author that the author was indeed Shandiz (Javad). In his separate reminiscences of Shandiz, Mehdi Fatapour notes that this was the first 'serious theoretical tract' that the OIPFG had produced since the Mehrabad Jonoubi incident and had the effect of ushering in a new era in the Organization's existence. Fatapour adds that the publication of this booklet had a galvanizing effect on the supporter base. Fatapour's memoirs on Shandiz in Roqiyeh Daneshgari (Faran), *Beh Yad An Parvaz*, second edition (Bochum: Aida, 2021), 48.
29. 'Vazayef-e Asasi-ye Marksist-Leninist-ha dar Marhaleh-ye Konouni-ye Roshd-e Jonbesh-e Komunisti-ye Iran', in *Tahlil-e Mowqiyat-e Niruha-ye Enqelabi dar Iran* (n.p.: Entesharat-e Sazeman-e Cherik-ha-ye Fadaʾi-ye Khalq-e Iran, 1979), 50.
30. Ibid., 53.
31. Ibid., 54.
32. 'Baz ham Darbareh Vazayef-e Asasi' in *Baz Ham Darbareh Vazayef-e Asasi Ma va Do Maqaleh-ye Digar* (n.p.: n.p., 1978), 83–4, 89.
33. *Jallad Nangat Bad!*, Fadaʾi Organization Communiqué, Shahrivar 1357 [August–September 1978].
34. The author of this communiqué was Farrokh Negahdar, who had recently joined clandestine life in safehouses. Negahdar later explained the reason for preparing such a text was that of convincing the Fadaʾis sheltering in safehouses and to join the protesting masses, thereby confirming the revolutionary nature of that moment. See in this regard Farrokh Negahdar, 'Sargozasht-e Qiyam ra Bavar Konim', *Kar* (Majority), Third Series, 201, 2001.
35. Fatapour, Interview with Author.

36. Author's interview with Mehdi Sameʿ.
37. 'Farar-e Shah', January 1979, as reproduced in *Elamiyeh-ha va Bayaniyeh-ha-ye Sazeman-e Cherik-ha-ye Fada'i-ye Khalq-e Iran* (Tehran: Sazeman-e Cherik-ha-ye Fada'i-ye Khalq-e Iran, 1979).
38. According to ʿAbdolrahimpour and Farrokh Negahdar, the latter was the author of this open letter. This open letter is one of the few Fada'i declarations of the revolutionary period which has been translated in full in English. See Behzad Touhidi (trans.), 'People's Fedayi Open Letter to Khomeini', in *MERIP Reports* 75/76 (1979): 31–3.
39. Touhidi, 'Open Letter', p. 31.
40. Ibid.
41. Author's interview with Mehdi Sameʿ.
42. A more extensive account of the rally and meeting of that day can be found in Mehdi Sameʿ, 'Gozareshi az Chand Mah-e Por Talatom', http://www.iran-chabar.de/article.jsp?essayId=32807 and Mehdi Fatapour, 'Tazahorat-e Ruz Bist va Yekom Bahman Mah', in *Bazkhani Jonbesh-e Fada'iyan-e Khalq*, 241–8.
43. Author's interview with Esfandiar Karimi, February 2019 and joint interview by author and Nasser Mohajer with Mehdi Sameʿ, 6 June 2020.
44. *Ayandegan*, 21 Bahman 1357 [10 February 1979].
45. Joint interview by the author and Nasser Mohajer with Jamshid Taheripour, 3 April 2017.
46. Joint interview of the author and Nasser Mohajer with ʿAbdolrahimpour.
47. See Touraj Atabaki and Nasser Mohajer (eds) *Rahi Digar*, vol. 2 (Paris: Noghteh, 2021), 367–70 for the full text of this resolution.
48. See *Ayandegan*, 24 Khordad 1358 [14 June 1979] and *Khabarnameh-ye Sazeman-e Cherik-ha-ye Fada'i-ye Khalq-e Iran*, 5, 30 Bahman 1357 [19 February 1979] for biographical details on Siadati.
49. Author's interview with Esfandiar Karimi, February 2019 and joint interview of the author and Nasser Mohajer with Mehdi Sameʿ, 6 June 2021.
50. ʿAbdolrahimpour, interview with *Kar* (Majority), 201, and Joint interview of the author and Nasser Mohajer with ʿAbdolrahimpour, 4 June 2020.
51. Text of the declaration in *Elamiyeh-ha va Bayanieh-ha*, 195.
52. This part of the Fada'i prescriptions share considerable similarity with those of Ayatollah Khomeini, who called for similar measures in a proclamation read out on Radio Tehran on 11 February.
53. This brief but historic announcement was produced by Mehdi Fatapour from inside the Technical Faculty. Maryam Satvat, Mohsen Modir-Shanehchi and Hamid Farkhondeh took it personally to the radio premises. Author and Nasser Mohajer interview with Mehdi Fatapour, and Mehdi Fatapour, 'Sazeman-e ʿAlani-ye Cherik-ha-ye Fada'i', http://www.iran-chabar.de/article.isp?essayld=86853.

13 Poetry praising passion

1. See a similar list that Faramarz Soleimani gives in his book *She'r Shahadat Ast* ['*Poetry is Martyrdom*'] (Tehran: Mowj, 1981), 9.
2. This is in line with the Soviet approach to art. In a broader sense, Rosa Luxemburg also says, 'Being unpolitical means being political without knowing it'. (Unpolitisch

sein heißt politisch sein, ohne es zu merken.) And the Polish Nobel laureate Wisława Szymborska says in a poem, 'We are children of the time/ the time is political' and the poem ends with the line 'unpolitical poems are also political'. (For my Persian translation via German, see *Gahnameh-ye Vizhe-ye She'r 3*, December 1996, 7.)

3. See, for instance, an article by Adnan Ghoreifi that I published in the aforementioned *Gahnameh*, 18–20. My own comments from a different point of view were also published in the same issue.
4. Literary criticism no more draws a dividing line between form and content. According to Bertolt Brecht, 'form is nothing other than the ultimate Organization of content'. 'Die Form eines Kunstwerks ist nichts als die vollkommene Organisierung seines Inhalts', in 'Über Formalismus und neue Formen,' chap. in *Über Realismus* (Frankfurt am Main: Suhrkamp Verlag, 1977), 156.
5. To use Esmail Khoi''s image in his poem 'Along the khaki street' (1967) from the collection *Bar Bam-e Gerd-bad* [On the Roof of Whirlwind] (Tehran: Raz Publications, 1973), 32.
6. All citations from *Piyadero-ha* [Sidewalks] (Tehran: Bamdad Publishers, 1968), 34, 99 and 12.
7. See a document published in *Zaman-e Now*, 6, 1984, 101.
8. Mohammad-Reza Shafiei-Kadkani, *Advar-e She'r-e Farsi* [Periods of Persian Poetry] (Tehran: Tus Publications, 1980), 88.
9. This occurred in a review of Shafiei's aforementioned book, which appeared in *Nameh-ye Showra-ye Honarmandan va Nevisandegan* published by writers who were members of (or were inclined to) the Tudeh Party.
10. These citations include a couple of lines by Khoi, some lines from Shamlou's 'Khatabe-ye tadfin,' and – interestingly – parts of the poem 'Delam baraye baghche misuzad' by Forugh Farrokhzad (who had died in early 1947) misinterpreted as a poem heralding armed struggle, while in fact – as Sa'id Soltanpour rightly mentioned – it is a poem against militarism and violence. And this regardless of the fact that, with what we know of Farrokhzad, she could have become an ardent supporter of armed struggle had she lived long enough to see the years of the Siyahkal movement.
11. *Now'i az Naqd bar Now'i az She'r* ['A Sort of Criticism of a Sort of Poetry'] (Saarbrücken: Nawid Publications, 1987). Roughly two-thirds of the book is about the poetry of Sa'id Soltanpour, and the title plays on the title of his book *Now'i az Honar, Now'i az Andisheh* ['A Sort of Art, a Sort of Thinking', 1351 = 1972]. In the first half of this article, I have cited heavily from that book, sometimes with modifications, and usually without mentioning my own book as a source.
12. As by Mohammad Shams Langaroodi in the fourth volume of his *Tarikh-e Tahlili-ye She'r-e Now*, ['*An Analytic History of Persian Modern Poetry*'] (Tehran: Nashr-e Markaz, 1998), 15–19 and 328–30.
13. The split of June 1980, which separated the 'Majority' (pro-Tudeh Party and supporting the Islamic Republic) from the more radical 'Minority'.
14. This week-long poetry festival was organized by Shamlou, who was the editor of *Khusheh* weekly at the time, from 15 to 19 September 1968 in Tehran's Municipality Club.
15. Shamlou is citing here – approvingly – a passage in his foreword from an article written by Baraheni in *Ferdowsi* (1/7/1347 = 23/9/1968); see *Yad-name-ye Nokhostin Hafte-ye She'r-e Khusheh* (Tehran: [Khusheh], 1347), 8. It is interesting that Shamlou not only does not mention Soltanpour's name, but also does not include in the

anthology any poem by the poet who was applauded most by the audience – and the anthology included hundreds of poems by 110 poets, some renowned and some quite unknown.

16. Mohammad Azimi, 'Yek payam-e now', *Jahan-e Now* 24, no. 1 (April–May 1969): 167.
17. Mostafa Rahimi, 'Fazai tohi dar she'r-e emruz-e farsi', *Jahan-e Now* 24, no. 2 (June–July 1969): 5.
18. M. Sereshk [pen name of Shafiei-Kadkani], 'Az bayan-e she'ri ta bayan-e manteqi', in ibid., 208.
19. *She'r Shahadat Ast*, 121.
20. This negative approach to 'formalism' came to Iran via the Soviet Union, where Formalists were under attack even before the full establishment of 'Socialist Realism' – as early as Leon Trotsky's 1924 *Literature and Revolution* – ignoring the fact that some major figures of the Formalists were Bolsheviks, and some Futurists like Mayakovsky were very close to Formalists. By the way, it is worth mentioning that even in the poems by this group (namely, the likes of Yadollah Ro'yai) sometimes you could see words like 'prison' and 'whip', which, when used in poems of that style, had the function of giving the poem a 'chic' appearance. See, for instance, the poem 'A Heart Beat between Us' by Ro'yai in Khusheh, no. 24 (August 1967): 25.
21. *Now'i az Naqd bar Now'i az She'r* [A Sort of Criticism of a Sort of Poetry], 27.
22. Esmail Nouri-'Ala, *Theory of Poetry – On Iranian Contemporary Poetics* (London: Qazal Publications, 1994), 168–9.
23. Shafiei-Kadkani, *Advar-e She'r-e Farsi*, 21–2.
24. Ehsan Tabari's preface to Shaban Bozorg-Omid [=Siyavash Kasrai], '... *Be Sorkhi-ye Atash, be Ta'm-e Dud*' [... *Red Like Fire, Tasting Like Smoke*] (first print, Tudeh Party Publications, 1976), 5.
25. Ibid., 5.
26. Ibid., 11.
27. Executions of the captured Siyahkal guerrillas were carried out in Esfand [= March] 1971, and March 21 is the Iranian New Year [= spring equinox] called Nowrouz.
28. From the poem '... *Be Sorkhi-ye Atash*' in ibid., 14–15.
29. Esmail Khoi, *Faratar az Shab-e Aknuniyan*, 2nd print (Tehran: Javidan, 1977), 21.
30. M.-R. Shafiei-Kadkani, *Az Budan va Sorudan*, 2nd print (Tehran: Tus Publications, 1978), 32–3.
31. Amir-Parviz Pouyan, one of the founders of the original Fada'i Organization, was killed in exchange of fire in Tehran (or probably committed suicide when he was running out of ammunition) when his hiding place was discovered and attacked by security forces on 24 May 1971.
32. [Kasrai], *Be Sorkhi-ye Atash...*, 16.
33. See Shamlou's special issue of his weekly *Ketab-e Jom'eh* (No. 27, 21 February 1980), 143.
34. A site of executions of political prisoners under the Shah.
35. Ahmad Shamlou, *Tarane-ha-ye Kuchek-e Ghorbat*, 1st print (Maziyar, 1980), 13. In a footnote, Shamlou says: 'Deylaman is a region in the north of Iran, one famous district of Deylaman being Siyahkal, and Siyahkal was where the armed struggle started in the last decade of the previous regime.' Shamlou's posthumously created 'official website' adds this information also about the creation of the poem: 'March 6, 1978, Princeton.'
36. Shafiei-Kadkani, *Advar-e She'r-e Farsi*, 90. By the way, all these words remind one primarily of the poems of Shafiei-Kadkani himself, who has not mentioned his own

essential role in the poetry of that period. 'Darya-wo mowj-o sakhreh', for instance, is the beginning of a line in one of his ghazals for Siyahkal (*Az Budan va Sorudan*, 10).

37. For the complete poem, see, among others: Safar Fadai-niya [= Saeed Yousef], *She'r-e Jonbesh-e Novin* [*Poetry of the New Movement*] (Tehran: Tus Publications, 1979), 18.
38. M.-R. Shafiei-Kadkani, 'Dar an-su-ye shab va ruz' [Beyond night and day], in *Dar Kuche-bagh-ha-ye Neshabur* [*In Nishapur's Garden Lanes*], 7th print (Tehran: Tus Publications, 1978), 75.
39. Ibid., from the poem 'Suk-nameh', 77.
40. Sa'id Soltanpour, 'Rud-khane-ye Pouyan' [Pouyan river, which can also mean flowing river], from the collection *Avaz-ha-ye Band* [*Prison Songs*].
41. From the same collection, the poem 'Agar az khab bar-ayad bimar' [If the patient wakes up].
42. Khosrow Golesorkhi, 'She'r-e bi-nam' ['Nameless poem'], from Golesorkhi's selected poems, ed. Majid Rowshangar (Tehran: Morvarid Publications, 1979), 86–7. (Also, in *She'r-e Jonbesh-e Novin*, 23–4.)
43. From the poem 'Siyahkal', I am citing here from *She'r-e Jonbesh-e Novin*, 36–7.
44. H. E. Sayeh, *Yadegar-e Khun-e Sarv* [*In Memory of the Blood of Cypress*] (Tehran: Tus Publications, 1981), 72.
45. The poem 'Nameh' was written in 1954 in Qasr Prison, published much later (with wrong date to elude censorship) in the collection *Shekoftan dar Meh* ('Blossoming in Fog'), 1970.
46. In the 1960s, Mehdi Akhavan Sales also wrote many 'prison poems', but his prison was a different story (and not political, unlike his brief prison time after the coup), and when he says in a poem, 'I am in prison for the crime of being a man,' he has a quite different kind of 'man' in mind.
47. Both poems from the collection *Parvaz dar Tufan* [Flight in Storm], reprinted in *Az Sanglakh va Sa'eqeh va Karevan* [From Rocky Paths and Thunderbolts and Caravans] (Sweden: Baran, 1993), 142 and 150.
48. I am citing here from *She'r-e Jonbesh-e Novin*, 101–2.
49. Shafiei-Kadkani, *Az Budan va Sorudan*, 67–8.
50. *Zaman-e Now*, I/1, Tehran, August–September 1981, 44–5. This *Zaman-e Now*, a single issue of which appeared in Tehran, differs from a periodical bearing the same name that later started to appear in Paris. Said Soltanpour was one of the first editors of this emerging periodical, but was executed before the first (and last) issue appeared – which led Shafiei-Kadkani to say that now this poem was more about Sa'id Soltanpour (referring to Soltanpour's *Seda-ye Mira* collection) than Amir.
51. Bijan Jazani (1938–1975) had been a member of the youth Organization of Tudeh Party in early 1950s, then became in mid-1960s a founding member of one of the two Marxist groups whose merging after Siyahkal formed the People's Fada'i Organization. Arrested in 1968, he was serving his fifteen-year sentence when SAVAK killed him and eight others on 19 April 1975, staged as an escape attempt during a transfer.
52. Written in 1967 and first published in local papers, later in: Saeed Yousef: *Zan Setarey Sukhtey Donbaleh-dar* ['*From the burnt comet*'] (West Germany: Hava-ye Tazeh Publications, 1984), 31.
53. See *Now'i az Naqd bar Now'i az She'r*, 172. See also: Saeed Yousef, *Poetics and Politics – East and West* (Canada: Javan Books, 2007), 10 and 152–3.
54. First published in *Jahan-e Now* (No. 2, June–July 1969), then in *She'r-e Jonbesh-e Novin* and *Zan Setarey Sukhte*....

55. First published in *Jahan-e Now* (No. 3, August–September 1969), together with, among others, a poem written by Mohammad Mokhtari for Palestine; later printed in the collection *Zan Setarey Sukhte*....
56. First published in *Muzik-e Iran* (No. 5, April 1971); the same issue printed a short story also ('The Big Cow') by Qolam-reza Galavi, a member of the 'Mashhad team' who was executed in February 1972.
57. Like Galavi, Bahman Azhang and Hamid Tavakkoli were Fada'i students of the Faculty of Letters of Mashhad University – and all three of them were executed in February 1972 along with others.
58. Published in *She'r-e Jonbesh-e Novin* and *Zan Setarey Sukhte*....
59. See: *Sorud va Taraneh* (Hamburg: Sonboleh, August 2001), 109; see also 265–66 (appendix I, a note written by me) to learn about the history of the creation and later evolution of this song. (The lyrics of twelve of the songs in this collection were written by me.)
60. The songs 'Kargar va sarmaye-dar' and '13 Aban' in the cassette *Bahman I*.
61. 'From a couple of drops to an ocean', autumn 1971 in Jamshidiyyeh prison (Tehran), published in *She'r-e Jonbesh-e Novin* and *Zan Setarey Sukhte*.... It was the Sassanid king Shapur II who pierced the shoulders of captive Arabs (c.325 CE) as punishment.
62. We later found out that this was one of SAVAK's tricks: he had been arrested and was being tortured as we were holding our ceremony. This trick allowed SAVAK to both track other guerrillas and torture him to death without anyone noticing it.
63. From the poem 'Che bayad bekonim?' ['What are we to do?', 1972], published in *She'r-e Jonbesh-e Novin*.
64. April 1972 in Qezel-Qal'eh Prison, printed in *She'r-e Jonbesh-e Novin* as well as *Zan Setarey Sukhte...* and *Ghobar-rubi* (Sweden: Baran, 1992).
65. Written in Qezel-Hesar Prison in 1973, published in *She'r-e Jonbesh-e Novin* and *Zan Setarey Sukhte*....
66. Written in Qezel-Hesar Prison in 1974, published in *She'r-e Jonbesh-e Novin* as well as *Zan Setarey Sukhte...* and *Ghobar-rubi*.
67. Akhavan uses this expression, among others, in his interview with Naser Hariri, published in the series *Darbare-ye Honar va Adabiyyat* (Ketab-sara-ye Babol, 1989), also in Akhavan's collected interviews (*Seda-ye Heyrat-e Bidar*, Zemestan, first print 1992, p. 425). Speaking of Akhavan, it must be said that if he mentions me approvingly a few times in his last interviews, it is based on his knowledge of some of my poems. Once, after hearing my poem 'Cherry Orchard' (mentioned above), he turned to Shafiei-Kadkani, who was present, and said, 'This is better than Shamlou's eulogies.' Of course, this could have been just another case of mocking Shamlou, whom he didn't like much, or maybe it was simply a 'ta'arof'.
68. Published in *Zan Setarey Sukhte...* and *Ta'ammoli dar Rah* (Tehran: Seda Publications, 1993).
69. I got to know Saeed Payan, a Fada'i who was a friend of Pouyan's, in prison; he was killed in winter 1976.
70. Another case was the pseudonym *F. Pashaki*: the poet and satirist Emran Salahi (1947–2006), who had known Farhad Seddiqi Pashaki before he was killed in summer 1976, told me once that he had been busy writing an article on Farhad's poems (which he had found impressive), until he had learned that I was the real poet. I told him that was okay, he could still write that article! But he apparently never did.
71. *She'r Shahadat Ast*, 16.
72. Published in *She'r-e Jonbesh-e Novin* and *Zan Setarey Sukhte*....

73. I was eighteen years something when Shamlou made this comment. See: *Khusheh* 12, no. 29 (10–17 September 1967): 4.
74. From the poem 'Payan?' ['The End?'] published in *Zan Setarey Sukhte...* and *Ghobar-rubi*.
75. From the poem 'Mi-shenasim hameh in gol ra' ['We all know this flower'] published in *Zan Setarey Sukhte...* and *Ghobar-rubi*.
76. Published in *She'r-e Jonbesh-e Novin* and *Zan Setarey Sukhte....* Reference to Rumi: see Mathnavi I/3001.
77. From the poem 'Dar tahlil-e nahaï' ['In the last analysis'], first published in *Cheshmandaz* (No. 3, Autumn 1987) and then in *Ghobar-rubi*.
78. Beh-Azin: *Az Har Dari... (Zendegi-name-ye siyasi-ejtemai)* [A socio-political autobiography], 3rd print (Tehran: Dustan Publications, 2008), Book II, 74–5.
79. Ibid., 76–7.

14 Reflections of the guerrilla struggle and the Siyahkal incident in literary prose and fiction

1. Samad Behrangi, *Mahi Siyah-e Kuchulu* (Tehran: Kanun-e Parvaresh-e Koudakan va Nowjavanan, 1968), 16.
2. Reza Daneshvar, *Mahboubeh va Al. Majmueh-ye Dastan* (Uppsala: Afsaneh, 1996), 117.
3. Houshang Golshiri, *Ayeneh-ha-ye Dardar* (Tehran: Niloufar, 1992), 78.
4. Ibid., 73.
5. Khosrow Davami, *Hotel Marcopolo* (Tehran: Niloufar, 2004), 33.
6. Shahrnoush Parsipour, *Majerah-ye Sadeh va Kouchak-e Rouh-e Derakht* (Stockholm: Baran, 1999), 194.
7. Ebrahim Golestan, *Khurus* (London: Rozan, 1974), 7.
8. Ibid., 30.
9. Golestan, *Khurus*, 89.
10. Ibid., 91.
11. Qodsi Qazi Nour, *Mehmani-ye Mahtab* (Tehran: Rouzbehan, 1978), 148.
12. Gholam-Hossein Saedi (Gowhar Morad), *Panj Nemayesh-nameh az Enqelab-e Mashrouteh* (Tehran: Amirkabir, 1972), 133.
13. Sa'id Soltanpour, *Hasanak* (n.p., n.p., n.d.), 24.
14. Ibid., 27.
15. Reza Daneshvar, *Khosrow-e Khuban* (Uppsala: Afsaneh, 1973), 9.
16. Ibid., 12.
17. Manouchehr Hezarkhani, 'Jahanbini-ye Mahi Siyah-e Kuchulu', *Arash* 1971, 18.
18. Ibid., 21.
19. Nasim Khaksar, 'Hamlet dar Mehvar-e Marg', *Seda* 1972, 62.
20. Ibid., 63.
21. Ibid., 67.
22. Nasim Khaksar, *Rowshanfekr-e Kuchak* (Tehran: Qoqnous, 1980), 21.
23. Translator's note: 'Nazli' refers to Shamlou's 'Death of Nazli' (*Marg-e Nazli*) a poem recited and celebrated by the author's generation of Leftist activists. The poem commemorates the death by torture of Vartan Salakhanian, one of the early victims of the 1953 Coup d'Etat. The poem reads:

Nazli! spring fell into laughter and the Judas-tree blossomed
At home, the old lilac beneath the window bloomed
Let go of illusion!
Don't raise your fist towards ominous death!
Better existence than becoming extinct, especially in the spring…
Nazli didn't say a word
Proud
He clenched his tired teeth upon his tongue and left…

****

Nazli! Talk!
The silent bird sits in her nest on the egg of the hatchling of a tragic death!
Nazli didn't say a word:
Like the sun
He rose from this darkness and lay in his blood and left

***

Nazli didn't say a word
Nazli was a star:
He shone in this darkness for a moment and flickered and left…
Nazli didn't say a word
Nazli was a violet:
He blossomed and delivered the good news: Winter has cracked!
and
He left…

(Translated by Samad ʿAlavi)

24. Translation of Hegel's *Lordship and Bondage* in Persian, Hamid Enayat (trans.), *Khodaygan va Bandeh* (Tehran: Khwrazmi, 1973), 33.
25. Ibid. 50.
26. Amir-Parviz Pouyan, *Zarourat-e Mobarezeh-ye Mosallahaneh va Rad-e Teoriy Baqaʿ* (Tehran: Sazeman-e Cherik-ha-ye Fada'i Khalq Iran, 1971), 17.
27. Nasim Khaksar, *Roshanfekr-e Kouchak*, 26.
28. Ibid.

15 Looking back

1. An Arabic instrument similar in construction to the European lute.
2. A Persian drum, also known as Zarb.
3. Rudaki (858–941): A poet regarded as the first literary genius of modern Persian, composing poems in the 'new Persian' alphabet.
4. Fada'iyan-e Islam [Devotees of Islam] was an Iranian Islamic fundamentalist group which was founded in 1946 by a twenty-one-year-old theology student named Navvab Safavi.
5. Khalil Tahmasebi: member of Fada'iyan-e Islam who assassinated Iranian prime minister ʿAli Razmara on 7 March 1951.

6. Qolam-Reza Takhti (1930–1968): Iran's wrestling champion and Olympic gold medalist, nicknamed *Jahan-Pahlevan* [World champion] was found dead in his hotel room on 7 January 1968. The Iranian government officially proclaimed his death a suicide, however it is widely believed that he was murdered by SAVAK due to his anti-Shah sentiments.
7. Yazdegerd III (590–651): The last king of Sassanid Dynasty in Iran before the Moslem conquest.
8. Farhad Mehrad (1944–2002): Musician, songwriter and singer of protest songs. He became an icon for generations of Iranian youth and activists.
9. Shahryar Qanbari (1950–): Poet, writer, lyricist, songwriter, singer, director, TV and Radio producer.
10. 6,000 tomans equals 60,000 rial; prior to Islamic Revolution of 1979, 7 tomans were approximately equivalent to 1 dollar.
11. Literacy Corps: An educational program implemented by the Shah within framework of his White Revolution (1963–79).
12. The stage name for Hossein Khajeh Amiri.
13. Qolam-Hossein Sa'edi was the screenwriter of Daryoush Mehrjui's film *Gav* [The Cow], which ushered in the New Wave of Iranian Cinema.
14. The stage name of female pop singer Azar Mohebbi (1946–).
15. Nemat Haqighi: Cinematographer and actor.
16. An Automobile manufactured in Iran based on the 1967 design of the British Rootes Group's Hillman Hunter.
17. Keramat Daneshian was a poet and political activist who along with Khosrow Golesorkhi was arrested for allegedly plotting the hostage-taking of the Shah's son and crown prince. They were both executed after a famously televised trial on 18 February 1974.
18. Daryoush Eghbali (1951–) is a prominent pop-singer and songwriter of ballads and socio-political songs.
19. Commemoration of the Shah's White Revolution plan, which was put to referendum on 26 January 1963.
20. A 1972 film by Reza Mirlohi, loosely based on John Steinbeck's *Of Mice and Men*.
21. The stage name of Parvaneh Amir-Afshari (1945–) who is a singer and veteran of Iran's Golden Years of music. Her voice has been measured to span three octaves.
22. Sovereign lord, ruler.
23. A maester: physician and scholar.
24. Has since been renamed Vahdat Hall.
25. Esma'il Nouri-'Ala (1943–): Writer, critic, editor and film director.
26. A character portrayed by Faramarz Gharibian.
27. Hossein Shari'atmadari: Current managing editor of *Keyhan*, an extreme right-wing Iranian newspaper, and reputed interrogator of political prisoners in the 1980s.
28. Behzad Farahani (1945–): Writer, screenwriter and actor.
29. 'Ali Reza Pahlavi (1922–1954): Shah's younger brother, killed in a plane crash in Alborz Mountains.
30. Mohammad Amir Khatam (1920–1975): Brother-in-law of the Shah and his advisor, Commander of the Air Force.
31. Jalal Al-e Ahmad (1923–1969): Prominent writer, thinker, political and social critic.

16 The impact of the guerrilla movement on contemporary Iranian theatre

1. Jazani's company Tabli Film developed TV advertising in Iran.
2. 'Theater va Dastan', *Shahr-e Qesseh*, 73.
3. Anahita Theatre was founded in 1958 in the former Goldis Cinema in Yousef Abad through the efforts and private capital of Mostafa and Mahin Oskou'i. Mostafa Oskou'i (1923–2005) and Mahin Oskou'i (1930–2006) were both 'Abdolhossein Nushin's students and, by his recommendation, married each other while they were active in the Ferdowsi Theatre. In 1948, they left for France to study, and from there, continued to the Moscow State Institute of Performing Arts. After residing in the Soviet Union for several years, they moved to Switzerland and the Federal Republic of Germany and finally returned to Iran in 1958. Anahita Actor's Academy had three departments: acting, printing and publishing and theater according to the Stanislawski's method. Anahita Theatre was inaugurated on 18 March 1959 with 'Othello', directed by Mostafa Oskou'i, and played for ninety-one nights. Performances continued for a few years. But, by 1964, Anahita Theatre was insolvent, closed its doors and the property was confiscated. Mostafa and Mahin Oskou'i divorced in 1971. Oskou'i has written about the Anahita Theatre and its closure in his book *Pazhueshi dar Tarikh-e Teatr-e Iran* (Tehran: Nashr-e Anahita, 1999).
4. On 6 March 2017, Nasser Rahmaninezhad told the author of this article: The Iran Theatre Association was, in fact the coalesced, expanded and evolved reconstruction of the Mehr Theatre which was founded by me in 1966. After two years of stage and TV work, considering the new political circumstances, I thought it necessary to strengthen and transform the group so that it could withstand and resist the state theatre which had been renamed, 'The Iranian Centre for Dramatic Arts' after the White Revolution. We invited many of our former theatre colleagues such as Mehdi Fathi, Mahmoud Dowlatabadi, Said Soltanpour, Hadi Vahdani, Habib Aeli, Yadollah and Vali Shirandami, and many others. We also reinforced the group with friends who used to work with the Mehr Theatre in the past such as Iraj Rad, Behzad Farahani, Said Amirsoltani, Iraj Emami and others. With this new collaboration, and after many discussions and meetings, we decided to change the name of our group, and, thereby, chose the Iran Theatre Association. Mohsen Yalfani was not in the group at the beginning. Yalfani joined the Iran Theatre Association in 1970 with the play *Amouzegaran* (The Teachers). Of all the friends who joined the group, the only one who stayed and continued with us was Sa'id Soltanpour.
5. The play *Amouzegaran* [The Teachers] was supposed to run from 4–18 January 1971 at the theatre of the Iran-America Cultural Society. After eleven nights, it was halted due to SAVAK's interference. Soltanpour and Yalfani were both arrested and spent three months in prison. From then on, Yalfani was prohibited to publish and stage his plays. For instance, the play *Davandeh Tanha* [The Lone Runner] which was written in 1974 was never published. Nasser Rahmaninezhad, 'Theatre in Prison', 29 April 2014, http://asre-nou.net/php/view.php?objnr=30792.
6. Arbi Avenessian's words in the 'Iran, Seday-e Taze' [Iran, New Voice] programme at the Barbican in London, with the support of the Iran Heritage Foundation, 29 November 2008.
7. Interview with Jerome Savary, *Ettela'at*, 1 September 1971.

8. If I recall correctly, in 1968 the Theatre Zendeh [Living Theatre] group, supervised by the late Farhad Majdabadi performed Bertolt Brecht's educational plays, such as *The Decision* and *He Said Yes / He Said No*. Another theatre group, Theatre Piyadeh [Theatre Afoot, 1968] supervised by Daryoush Farhang, performed *The House of Bernard Alba* and *Blood Wedding* by Federico Garcia Lorca.

9. The play *Bar-e Digar: Abouzar* was performed at the Hosseiniyeh Ershad and, like its first performance in Mashhad, was much welcomed by the spectators. Reza Daneshvar was born in 1948 in Mashhad. From the beginning, he was attracted to theatre and, along with Davud Kianian, Darius Arjmand, Anoshirvan Arjmand, Reza Saberi and Reza Kianian, played an important role in the formation of theatre in Mashhad. He studied Persian literature at Mashhad University and Tehran University. During his university years, he wrote *Abu Zarr*, a play derived from the book *Abu Zarr Ghafari: The God-Worshipping Socialist*; translated and edited by ʿAli Shariʿati. This monodrama was presented in Mashhad during the winter of 1970 and was warmly received.

10. Brecht fever in Iran: 'In the restless and volatile atmosphere of the 70s, Bertold Brecht's unique work with a revolutionary message became popular. His playlets *Fear and Misery of the Third Reich* translated by Sharif Lankarani and the 'educational plays' (*Lehrstücke*) translated by Faramarz Behzad were performed many times in Tehran and other cities. And Brecht's other plays with political interpretations and provocative messages were performed again and again. Plays such as *A Man's a Man*, *Señora Carrar's Rifles*, *The Mother* (based on Maxim Gorky's famous novel), *The Exception and the Rule* and many more. Some other well-known directors presented interesting pieces from Brecht such as *The Visions of Simone Machard* directed by Said Soltanpour, *Round Heads and Pointed Heads* directed by Nasser Rahmaninezhad, *The Trial of Joan of Arc* directed by Rokneddin Khosravi...' ʿAli Amini, 'A Look at the History of German Plays', *Deutsche Welle*, 11.04.2012, https://www.dw.com/fa-ir/a-15435992.

11. Asghar Ahahanin wrote the following in *Honar va Andisheh-ye Emruz* 1, 51: 'The *Visions of Simone Machard* by the great German playwright, poet and theatre director Bertold Brecht. Through the efforts of the Free Theatre Group of Iran – who is the real face of 'committed art' in this country – and directed by Said Soltanpour, was first performed at the Tehran University theatre. The great welcome by the audience manifests the need to present serious topics in theatre.' *Tehran Mosavvar*, 1535, March 1973, 44.

12. *The Petty Bourgeois* by Maxim Gorky was performed over only five nights in Rasht. In 1974, before it was to be performed in Tehran, all the members of the Theatre Association were arrested and imprisoned. Nasser Rahmaninezhad was sentenced to twelve years in prison.

13. 'One of the plays was an adaptation of Saltykov-Shchedrin's *The Liberal*. Another one was the adaptation of Branislav Nušić's *The Deceased*, *Hakem-e Varamin* an adaptation of Saltykov-Shchedrin's *Unfinished Talks* and *A Chameleon* based on Anton Chekhov's play with the same name....' Nasser Rahmaninezhad, 'Theatre in Prison'.

14. Javad Zolfaghari was a member of Tehran Theatre Association and was arrested along with fifty-three other members in November 1974.

15. *Federico Garcia Lorca* by Cymin Davoudi Abarghoi in 1971, *Albert Camus* by Mariam Hakimi in 1972, *A review of the socio-political situation of Germany in Brecht's oeuvres*, by Hassan Shadab, 1972, *Seán O'Casey* by Manouchehr Azar, 1972, *Ben Jonson* by Keyvan Shemirani 1973, *Bertolt Brecht's Theatre* by Reza Keshani 1973, *Maxim*

Gorky's Thoughts by ʿAlireza Madadi 1975, *Analysis of the People's Enemy* by Hayedeh Abdollahi 1975.

List of the dissertations of the graduates of the College of Dramatic Arts, *Theatre Magazine*, 1989, 4 and 5, 269–86.

16. Examples of such translations include Mostafa Rahimi (trans.), *An Keh Goft Ari va An Keh Goft Na* (Tehran: Ketab-e Hafteh 1963); Fereydoun Ilbeygi (trans.), *Tofangha-ye Naneh Karara* (Tehran: Ketab-e Hafteh 1963); Sharif Lankarani (trans.), *Adam Adam Ast* (Tehran: Kharazmi Publishing House 1968); Mahmoud Eʿtemadzadeh (trans.), *Estesna va Qaedeh* (Tehran: Entesharat-e Agah 1969); Khashayar Qaemmaghami (trans.), *Baal* (Tehran: Amir Kabir, 1972); Siavash Kasrai (trans.) *Madar* (Tehran: Amir Kabir, 1972); Mostafa Rahimi (trans.), *Madar Shojaʿat* (Tehran: Ketab Publishing, 1966).
17. ʿAli Amini writes: 'Rajab Mohammadin presented an interesting performance of The Tower with university facilities.' *Deutsche Welle*, ibid., https://p.dw.com/p/12lbc.

Select Bibliography

Abrahamian, Ervand, 'The Guerrilla Movement in Iran, 1963–1977', *MERIP Reports* 86, 1980.
Abrahamian, Ervand, *Iran between Two Revolutions* (Princeton, NJ: Princeton University Press, 1982).
Ashraf, Hamid, *Jambandi Yek Sal Mobarezeh dar Shahr va Kuh* (n.p.: Jebheh-ye Melli-ye Iran-Bakhsh-e Khavar Miyaneh, 1973).
Ahmadzadeh, Masoud, *Mobarezeh Mosallahaneh, ham Estrateji, ham Taktik* (n.p.: Jebheh-ye Melli-ye Iran-Bakhsh Khavar-e Miyaneh, 1974).
Behrooz, Maziar, *Rebels with a Cause: The Failure of the Left in Iran* (London: I.B. Tauris, 1999).
Behrooz, Maziar, 'Iran's Fadaiyan 1971–1988: A Case Study in Iranian Marxism', *JUSUR, UCLA Journal of Middle Eastern Studies*, 6, 1990, 1–39.
Hamidian, Naqi, *Safar ba Balha-ye Arezou* (Stockholm: Arash, 2004).
Jazani, Bijan, *Cheguneh Mobarezeh-ye Mosallahaneh Tudeh'i Mishavad* (n.p.: Cherik-ha-ye Fada'i-ye Khalq, 1973).
Jazani, Bijan, *Tarh-e Jameshenasi va Mabani-ye Estratejik-e Jonbesh-e Enqelabi-ye Iran, Bakhsh-e Dovvom* (Tehran: Maziar, 1978).
Jazani, Bijan, *Islam-e Marxisti ya Marxism-e Islami* (Paris: Rah-e Fada'i, 1984).
Kanun-e Gerdavari va Nashr-e Asar-e Bijan Jazani (ed.), *Jongi Darbareh Zendegi va Asar-e Bijan Jazani* (Paris: Khavaran, 1999).
Matin-Asgari, Afshin, *Iranian Student Opposition to the Shah* (Costa Mesa: Mazda, 2002).
Naderi, Mahmoud, *Cherik-ha-ye Fada'i-e Khalq. Az Nakhostin Konesh-ha ta Bahman 1357* (Tehran: Moasseseh-e Motale'at va Pazhouhesh-ha-ye Siyasi, 2007).
Pakdaman, Nasser (ed.), *Darbareh-ye Rowshanfekri: Yek Bahs-e Qalami* (Köln: Furough, 2007).
Pouyan, Amir-Parviz, *Zarourat-e Mobarezeh-ye Mosallahaneh va Rad-e Teori-ye Baqa'* (Tehran: Sazeman-e Cherik-ha-ye Fada'i-ye Khalq Iran, 1971).
Rahnema, 'Ali, *Call to Arms. Iran's Marxist Revolutionaries* (London: Oneworld Academic, 2021).
Salehi, Anoush, *Mostafa Sho'aiyan va Romantism-e Enqelabi* (Spanga: Baran, 2010).
Shahram, Mohammad Taqi, *Bayaniyeh E'lam Mavaze' Ideolojik-e Sazeman-e Mojahedin-e Khalq-e Iran* (n.p.: Sazeman-e Mojahedin-e Khalq-e Iran, 1976).
Sho'aiyan, Mostafa, *Enqelab* (Florence: Mazdak, 1974).
Vahabzadeh, Peyman, *A Guerrilla Odyssey: Modernization, Secularism, Democracy, and Fadai Period of National Liberation in Iran 1971-1979* (Syracuse: Syracuse University Press, 2010).
Vahabzadeh, Peyman, *A Rebel's Journey: Mustafa Sho'aiyan and Revolutionary Theory in Iran* (London: Oneworld Academic, 2019).
Zabih, Sepehr, *The Left in Contemporary Iran: Ideology, Organization and the Soviet Connection* (New York: Hover Institute Press, 1986).
Ziya-Zarifi, Abolhassan, *Zendeginameh-ye Hassan Ziya-Zarifi* (Tehran: Amindezh, 2004).

Index of Names

Abad-shahi, Qasem 116
Abdolrahimpour, Qorbanali (Majid) 31, 51, 69–76, 78–82, 118–19, 217–19, 221, 225, 227, 234–5
Abedini, Esma'il 73–4
Aghanabi-Qolhaki, Zahra 101–4, 112, 149, 154
Ahmadi Oskou'i, Marzieh 130, 139
Ahmadzadeh, Majid 90
Ahmadzadeh, Masoud 10, 12, 15–18, 20, 22–3, 25, 27, 30–1, 33–4, 41–5, 47, 61–3, 70, 79, 84, 86, 90, 100, 102, 126, 145, 157, 176, 177–9, 184, 186, 260, 295
Ahmadzadeh, Mastoureh 151
Akbari Shandiz, 'Alireza (Javad) 78–9, 81, 227
Akbari, Pedram 286
Akhavan Sales, Mehdi 189, 241, 253, 255
'Allamehzadeh, Reza 88, 230, 294
Al-e Agha, Nastaran 75, 105–9, 111, 114–17
Amini, Fatemeh 154
Amiri-Davan, Behnam 144–5
Amiri-Davan, Behzad 112–15, 144–5
Arab Herisi, Asghar 13
Arabzadeh, Hassan 233
Armaghani, Behrouz 24, 70–1, 74–5, 182, 227
Aryan, Sa'id 90, 152
Asadian, Siamak (Eskandar) 117, 119
Asadollahi, Rahim ('Ali) 78, 227
Ashraf, Hamid (Mahmud) 6, 15–16, 24, 29, 47, 49, 58, 61, 63–4, 66–8, 73, 76, 84, 93, 110–11, 113–17, 123–4, 126, 130, 136, 144, 158, 174, 182, 196, 217–20, 252, 295
Ashrafzadeh Kermani, Manijeh 154
Ayati, Ghazal 144, 146, 296
Ayrom, Hormuz 287
Ayyazi, Nader 80
Azhang, Bahman 250, 251, 253
Azhari, Gholamreza 229

Baraheni, Reza 240, 256
Batha'i, Teyfour 294
Bazargan, Mehdi 10, 233, 281
Behazin, Mahmoud E'temadzadeh 101, 225, 256–7
Behrangi, Samad 11, 13–14, 101, 103, 122, 189, 191, 195, 227, 232, 260, 262, 267, 289
Behzadi, Abdollah 286
Bigvand Heydari, Touraj 24, 28–9, 218, 223
Bijanzadeh, Saba (Hajar) 119, 125, 135–6, 138–9, 144–5, 219, 221

Choupanzadeh, Mohammad 6, 65, 169, 185

Dabirifard, 'Ali 112
Daneshgari, Roqiyeh (Faran) 69, 151–2, 154–5, 160, 162, 164
Daneshian, Keramat 88, 191, 209, 230, 286, 294
Daneshvar, Reza 260, 266, 293
Daneshvar, Simin 262
Darvishiyan, 'Ali-Ashraf 238
Daryabandari, Najaf 280
Davari, Asghar 294
Debray, Régis 4, 14, 22, 157
Dehqani, Ashraf 59, 130, 151–3, 158–9, 161, 183, 208
Dehqani, Behrouz 13, 61, 89, 191, 227, 232, 238
Dehqani, Mohammad 152
Doustdar-Sanayeh, Akbar 78, 227
Doustdar-Sanayeh, Iradj (Bahram) 119

Ebtehaj, Houshang (Sayeh) 246
Ettehadieh, Maryam 88

Fahim, Abdolhossein 293
Falaki Tabrizi, Manaf 69, 159
Farahani, Behzad 288
Farhoudi, Ahmad 15, 122, 179

Farrokhzad, Forough 189
Farsi, Mohammad 168, 177, 179, 183, 186
Fatapour, Mehdi (Khosrow) 78, 81–2, 223–5, 227, 229–30
Fathi, Mehdi 292
Fazeli, Hadi 7
Fazilatkalam (Mo'azed), Shirin 104, 130, 211–12
Foghani, Mohammad Mehdi 93

Ghane' Khoshkbijari, Yousef 93
Gharavi, Ezat 116
Ghebra'i, Hossein 73, 75
Ghebra'i, Kazem (Kuchek Khan) 118–19, 135, 139, 145
Ghebra'i, Mohammad Reza (Mansour) 76, 78, 80–1, 118–19, 135, 137–8, 141–2, 144–9, 179, 183, 219, 221
Gholami, Mohammad 198
Gholamian Langaroudi, Ahmad (Hadi) 78, 80, 125, 135, 138–41, 145, 147–9, 221
Golesorkhi, Khosrow 88, 159, 191, 209, 239, 241, 244, 246, 254, 294
Golestan, Ebrahim 262–3, 280
Goli Abkenari, Vida (Leyla) 125, 135, 138–40
Golshiri, Houshang 209, 260–3, 266
Guevara, Che 4, 5, 103, 170, 238–9, 249, 281

Habibian, Mohammad-Reza 136–8
Haddad-Khiyabani, Mohammad 71
Hajebi-Tabrizi, Vida 158
Hamidian, Naqi 11, 122–3, 143, 168, 171, 178, 183, 186
Haqnavaz Mohammad Hosseini (Mansour) 75–6, 93, 125–8, 134–6, 138–9
Hashemi, 'Abbas (Hashem) 51, 76, 140
Hassani, Hassan 79
Hassani, Vahid 79
Hassanpour, Ghafour 7, 61, 91
Hassanpour, Mostafa 123, 128
Hedayat, Hormoz 295
Hedayat, Sadeq 189
Hezarkhani, Manouchehr 267
Hojjati Kermani, Mohammad Javad 169
Hormatipour, Mohammad 59, 208
Hosseini Abardeh, Asghar 73, 75, 93

Hosseini, Mir-'Ali 201
Houshmand, 'Abbas (Parviz) 144–6, 252

Izadi, Asghar 168, 177–8, 253
Izadi, Kiumars 6

Ja'fari, Atefeh 151, 161
Ja'fari, 'Ali Akbar (Khosrow) 71, 123, 127–8
Jalalzadeh, Nahid 161
Jalil-Afshar, Ahmad 6, 185
Jamshidi-Roudbari, 'Abbas 63, 253
Jasemi, Mahvash 154, 296
Javan Khoshdel, Mostafa 185
Javanmard, 'Abbas 291
Jazani, Bijan 2, 6–7, 10, 16–20, 22–32, 34, 39, 43, 45–7, 49–50, 52, 58, 60–1, 63–4, 66–8, 70–1, 78–9, 83–4, 91, 99–100, 119, 126, 137, 144–5, 157–8, 167, 169, 172–4, 176, 183–6, 189, 193–4, 198, 218–19, 223, 248, 291, 295
Jazani, Mihan 137–8, 173
Jilou, Asghar 218

Kalantari, Manuchehr 17, 65
Kalantari, Mash'ouf (Sa'id) 6, 65, 185
Karimi, Behzad 17, 69–71
Karimi, Esfandiar 224, 233, 235
Karimian, Rahim 121–3, 148, 178–9, 183
Kasrai, Siyavash 239, 241–2, 244–5, 249, 256
Khalili Moghaddam, Ibrahim 87
Khaliq, Behrouz 70, 81, 119, 234
Khaliqi, 'Ali 80
Kharratpour, Qolamali 93
Khatam, Mohammad 'Ali 288
Kheyri-Abriz, Ebrahim 123
Khodadadi, Rahim 71
Khoi, Esma'il 238–9, 244, 248
Khomeini, Ruhollah 2, 32–3, 59, 67, 153, 163, 198, 219, 225–6, 229, 231–5, 279
Khorram, Tahereh 93
Khorramabadi, Ahmad 198
Khoshdel, 'Abbas 287
Khosravi, Rokneddin 291, 294–6
Kianouri, Noureddin 28–9
Kianzad, Mohammad Majid 6, 65, 168, 169
Kimia'i, Masoud 189, 193, 197, 264, 280, 285, 287–8

Index of Names

Kordlou, Moharramali 221
Kowsar, Mohammad 295–6

Lenin, Vladimir Ilych 10, 18, 28–9, 34, 74, 104, 119, 126, 131, 157–8, 176, 182–3, 186

Maghfourian, ʿAbbas 293
Mahmoud, Ahmad 158, 162
Malek-Mohammadi, Morteza 168, 177, 187
Marighella, Carlos 14, 103, 157
Marx, Karl 10, 22, 74, 119, 126, 131, 157–8, 179, 187, 268
Masoumi, Masoud 285
Meftahi, Asadollah 122
Meftahi, ʿAbbas 10, 11, 15, 59, 61, 122
Memar-Hosseini, Mehri 71
Memaran-Benam, Rafʿat (Ashraf) 80, 141–2
Mirzazadeh, Neʾmat 205, 209, 238–9, 241, 247
Moʾini-Araqi, Esmaʿil 7
Modir-Shanehchi, Mohsen 224, 230, 233
Modir-Shanehchi, Zahra (Zohreh) 101, 103
Moghadam Salimi, Manuchehr 88
Mokhtari, Mohammad 241, 251, 254
Mombini, Amir 168, 170
Momeni, Bagher 157
Momeni, Hamid 17, 21, 23–4, 49–50, 63, 102, 111, 125–6, 129, 135, 145
Montaseri, Houshang 152
Moshafeqi, Cyrus 294
Mossadeq, Mohammad 4, 10, 21, 122, 189, 196, 203, 222, 230–1, 275, 291
Motahedin, Mahboubeh 296

Nabdel, ʿAlireza (Okhtay) 13, 22, 62, 159, 191, 227, 238–9
Nahani, Shamsi (Fatemeh) 123
Nahani, Shamsi 123
Najafi, Nasser 291
Navabi, Sheyda (Fati) 137–8
Navidi, Nosratollah 292
Navidi, Parviz 168, 173–5, 182, 185
Nayyeri, Houshang 59, 67–8
Nayyeri, Iraj 67–8
Negahdar, Farrokh 6, 31, 33, 81, 234
Noshirvanpour, Ebrahim 91
Nouri-ʿAla, Esmaʿil 242, 288

Nowrouzi, Hassan (Tariverdi) 47, 105, 107, 109–10
Nowzari, Nasser (Rasouli) 154

Olfat, ʿAbdollah 283

Paknezhad, Shokrollah 179, 291
Panjehshahi, Abdollah 77, 109–10, 144–9
Panjehshahi, Jaʿfar 119
Panjehshahi, Nasrin 144
Panjehshahi, Simin 144
Parsipour, Shahrnoush 262
Peyvasteh, Soleiman 80
Pouyan, Amir-Parviz 10, 11, 13, 15, 22–3, 42–5, 47, 61, 63, 70, 84, 86, 90, 126, 157, 177, 179, 184, 193, 238, 244, 248, 260, 270–1, 294–5

Qajar, Nahid (Mehrnoush) 76, 121–30, 132–45, 234
Qandchi, Ahmad 276
Qeysari, Farhad 88

Radi, Akbar 291–2
Radin, Manouchehr 294
Rafiʾi, ʿAli 293
Rajavi, Masoud 174, 177
Rezaʾi, Sediqeh 161, 296
Riyahi, Hormoz 238
Riyazi, Ahmad 69
Rouhi Ahangaran, Azam 102–3, 154
Rouhi Ahangaran, Bahman 102, 123
Rouhi Ahangaran, Nehzat 101–2, 112–13, 296
Ruzpeykar, Hassan 69

Saʿidi, Fatemeh 139, 154
Saʿadati, Kazem 13
Sabet, Edna (Pari) 77, 145–9
Sadeqinezhad, Eskandar 7, 16, 47, 61
Safaʾi Farahani, ʿAli Akbar (Abu al-ʿAbbas) 6, 9, 10, 15–16, 59, 61, 65–8
Safavi, Navvab 278
Saffari Ashtiyani, Mohammad 6, 61, 65–8
Saharkhiz, Mansour 281
Salehi, Parviz 191
Salehi, Simin 211–12
Salsabili, Yadollah 80
Samakar, Hossein 285, 287

Samakar, ʿAbbas 88, 230, 294
Samandarian, Hamid 293, 296
Sameʿ, Mehdi 168–9, 172, 176, 217, 230, 233–5
Sanjari, Khashayar 109–10
Sanjari, Kioumars 115–16, 118, 125, 129, 135, 145, 148
Saqebfar, Morteza 267
Sarmadi, Aziz 6, 185
Sartre, Jean-Paul 103, 206, 295
Sedighi-Pashaki, Farhad 111, 254
Sepehri, Farhad 101
Sepehri, Farrokh 101
Sepehri, Iraj 58, 101
Sepehri, Parvin 101
Sepehri, Sirous 101
Seyyed-Baqeri, Qasem 224, 233
Shademani, Masoumeh (Kabiri) 154
Shafiʿ Tohidast, Shamsi (Marziyeh) 51, 101–20, 205
Shafiei-Kadkani, Mohammad Reza 205, 238–42, 244, 246–8, 254
Shahram, Mohammad Taqi 27
Shahriari, ʿAbbas (also: ʿAbbasali) Eslami 24, 63, 90–1, 185, 193
Shahrzad, Heshmatollah 6
Shalgouni, Mohammad Reza 168, 170, 175, 183–5
Shali, Khodabakhsh 117–18
Shamlou, Ahmad 190, 195, 198, 205, 230, 239–40, 245, 247–50, 255–6, 269–70, 285
Shariʿat-Razavi, Mehdi 276
Shariʿati, Ali 153, 189, 209, 293
Shayegan Shamasbi, Abolhassan 125, 127
Shayegan Shamasbi, Nader 211
Sheybani, Hemad (Mahmoud Akhavan-Bitaraf) 59
Shoʿaiyan, Mustafa 17, 20–1, 23, 238
Shokri, Farhad (Fereidoun) 73
Siadati, Qasem 98, 133, 137–8, 141–2, 144–9, 201, 235
Siahpoosh, Morteza 88
Soleimani, Behrouz 80

Soleimani, Faramarz 241, 254–5
Soltanpour, Saʿid 197, 224, 230, 238–42, 246–52, 254–7, 265, 267, 292–4, 296
Souraki, ʿAbbas 6, 185
Stalin, Joseph 21–3, 74, 126, 131, 158

Tabari, Ehsan 242, 256
Tabrizi, Heydar 48–51, 57, 59–60, 67
Taheripour, Jamshid 81, 168, 173–4, 177, 234
Takhti, Gholam-Reza 10, 278–9, 288, 291
Talebzadeh-Shoushtari, Mina 147
Tavafchiyan, Masoumeh (Shokouh) 154, 296
Tavakkoli, Hamid 90, 152, 250–1
Tavakkoli, Nasrin 296
Tavakkoli, Shahin 151–2, 159, 161, 171
Tavakkoli, Simin 117
Torabi, ʿAli Akbar 191
Toufani, Bahram 80
Toufani, Mohyedin 80
Tse Tung, Mao 10, 22–3, 27, 74, 101, 126, 131, 159, 161, 179, 183

Vafadar, Majid 277
Vahedi, Abdolhossein 278
Vahedi, Seyyed Mohammad 278
Vaziri, Tahmaseb 53, 80, 119, 148

Yasrebi, Mohammad Reza 75, 93, 110
Yousef, Saʿid (known as Saʿid Payan) 47, 254–5

Zahedian, Zarar 6, 189, 191
Zarkari, Jaʾfar 114
Zarkari, Qolam-ʿAbbas 115
Zarkari, Yousef 47, 106, 109, 176
Zehtab, Maliheh 108–9, 119
Zia-Zarifi, Hassan 2–3, 6, 60–1, 63, 185
Zolanvar, Kazem 185
Zolfaqari, Javad 294
Zolqadr, Mozaffar 278

www.ingramcontent.com/pod-product-compliance
Lightning Source LLC
Chambersburg PA
CBHW071759300426
44116CB00009B/1140